# ART
## is an
# ENDANGERED SPECIES

*A History of Western Art: Paleolithic—Romanesque*

Revised Printing

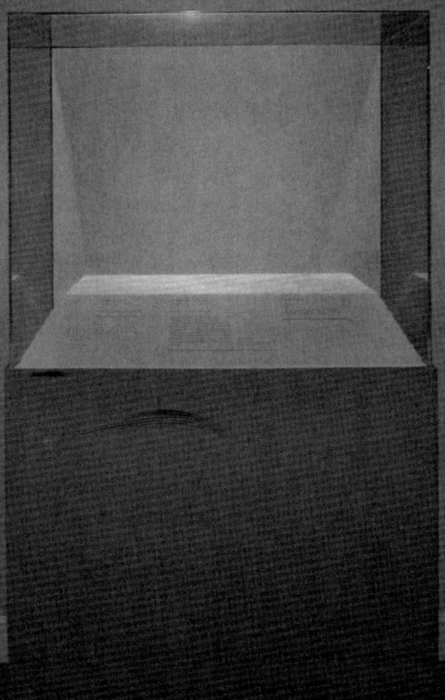

Margaret Ann Zaho

Kendall Hunt publishing company

Cover images and design by Geoff Castillo.

Kendall Hunt
publishing company

www.kendallhunt.com
*Send all inquiries to:*
4050 Westmark Drive
Dubuque, IA 52004-1840



Revised Printing: 2014

ISBN 978-1-4652-4981-4



Printed in the United States of America
10 9 8 7 6 5 4 3 2

*for* Edmond

*per sempre*

# Contents

# Introduction

The history of art is fundamentally the study of the cultural and artistic heritage of humanity. It is a remarkable discipline that draws inference and information from a variety of subjects including history, archaeology, anthropology, religion, literature, philosophy, and more. The study of the history of art allows for an exploration of the past and present through the artistic creations of cultures and people that in many cases, seem removed from modern life.

An understanding of the history of art is crucial because we live in a world saturated by images. As a society we are bombarded with images every day, all day long; on television, in books, on billboards, in magazines, through videogames, smart phones, the Internet, webcasts and other developing media. Therefore, people who have the ability to speak intelligently about images and are comfortable interpreting them have a great advantage. The ability to speak about and understand the history, function, and power of images is called "visual literacy."

One of the single most important lessons to gain from the study of the history of art is an understanding that art is a reflection of the culture that made it. All art, Ancient, Medieval, Western or Non-Western, Pop or Modern, is a reflection or expression of its culture, maker, time, and place. That means that every single art object or artistic production is immensely complex and can best and perhaps only be well understood when studied in conjunction with the circumstances and events in which it was created.

Art historians look at art as a cultural signifier, a repository of cultural and societal taste, a propagandistic tool, and for clues about an artist, patron, time period, city, or culture. This investigation of all aspects of a work of art, in order to understand its place in time, is the foundation of art historical study. Art history, however, goes far beyond the ability to answer basic questions such as who, what, where, and when. Indeed, art historians pose much farther reaching queries such as why, for whom, for what purpose, and in what way does an object reflect the culture/person that made it. Some of the basic questions to consider in relationship to any image or artistic production should include, but not be limited to, what is the purpose, function, date, location, style, medium, and subject of the work. Other important questions to ask when investigating a work of art might include the following. Is the work religious, political, historical, mythological, private, or public? Does it attempt to explain, instruct, convince, incite, or appease? Is it tiny, small, life size or colossal? How do scale and medium affect its impact? Is it colorful or subdued, is it simple or complex, is it abstract, is it a portrait, is it expressive, mysterious, sensual, or hierarchical?

What is the subject of the work? Is it figural? Is it a landscape? Is it, tribal, or familial? Does it tell a story, commemorate, memorialize, aggrandize, or document a real or imaginary event?

As an art historian, I believe it is important to stress that one should approach all art with an open mind and a willingness to understand it, regardless of whether or not one likes it, agrees with it, or appreciates its form, content, or point of view.

One way to achieve a compassion for art is to recognize that art is an endangered species and that in many cases much of it survives only due to luck or chance.

All over the world, in all its various forms, art is constantly in danger and at risk. It is in danger from natural disasters such as fires, floods, tsunamis, volcanoes, typhoons, earthquakes, hurricanes, and tornadoes. Art is also in danger from destructive forces such as war, religious intolerance, social upheaval, and terrorism. It is in grave danger from theft, vandalism, misunderstanding, and misappropriation. Art is also threatened by time itself, erosion, pollution, and acid rain. It is threatened by societies changing taste and fashion. Surprisingly, it is often even in danger from restoration and conservation.

The discipline of the history of art is, therefore, not just the study of objects but in many cases is a crucial factor in the preservation of art for the future.

# Acknowledgements

I am indebted to many of my colleagues at the University of Central Florida for their unfailing encouragement and support; particularly my Art History cohorts Dr. Francis Martin and Dr. Ilenia Colón Mendoza.

Many thanks are due to Professors Robert Rivers, Robert Reedy, Carla Poindexter, and the roving Scotsman George Donald, for their generosity, invaluable advice, and captivating discussions about art, teaching, travel, and life.

I am also grateful to Professor Charlie Abraham for his patience and thoughtful guidance and to Dr. José Maunez-Cuadra for his counsel and support.

I am extremely grateful for generous grants from LIFE@UCF and the Office of Research and Commercialization at the University of Central Florida.

Thanks are due to Theresa Hilton and Michelle Bahr at Kendall Hunt for their support and direction throughout the publication process.

Special thanks to Geoff Castillo for his cover design and to Gabriel Ribeiro and Eric Robbins for generously providing line drawings.

My family and friends deserve thanks for their love, praise, and gentle yet persistent nudging to get this manuscript to print.

Finally, I must thank all of the students who continually motivate, challenge, and inspire me.

# Chapter 1 STONE AGE ART

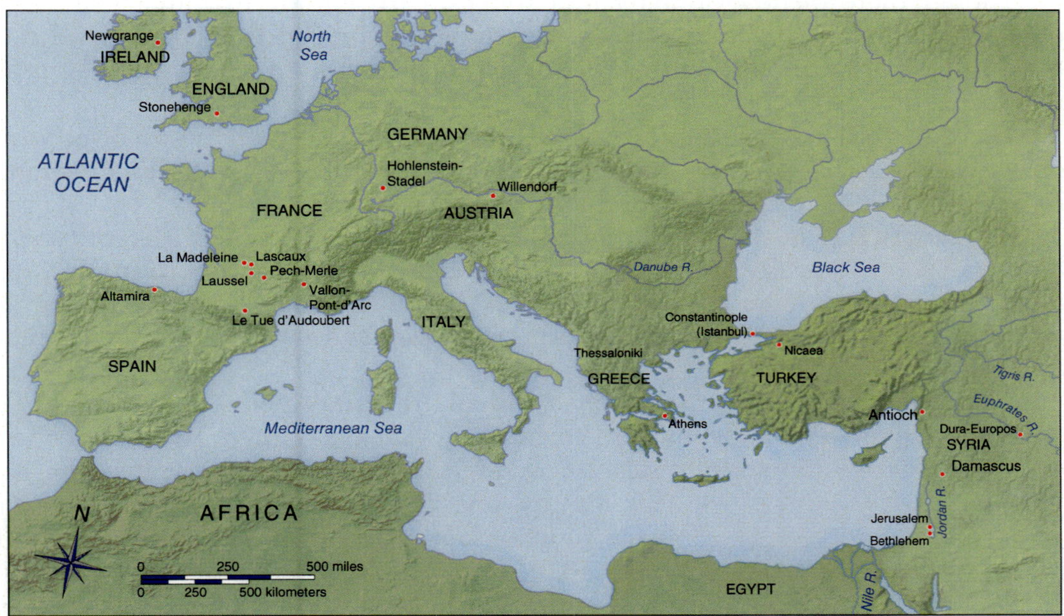


Prehistoric sites in Europe and the Eastern Mediterranean.

The words *primitive* and *primeval* are often used to describe the early phases in the artistic production of humanity, but both adjectives can be misleading. The words suggest that art production in the Prehistoric period was crude and/or without skill. That is not the case, much of it is remarkably sensitive and skilled in its production and refined in its representation. The terms *primitive* and *primeval* also imply that prehistoric cultures in general lacked a sense of time or interest or acknowledgement of the past and that is also not the case. Prehistoric, the best term used to describe the earliest periods in human civilization, simply means ƀ efore written record."

The Prehistoric period, or Stone Age, is generally further divided into three stages or periods: Paleolithic (c. 2 million–10,000 BCE), Mesolithic (c. 10,000–8000 BCE), and Neolithic (c. 8000–2000 BCE). The word *Paleolithic* comes from the Greek words *paleo* (old) and *lithos* (stone), therefore the Old Stone Age, as follows the Mesolithic period is the Middle Stone Age and the Neolithic means the New Stone Age.

The approximate, and not wholly agreed upon, time span for the Stone Age is roughly 2 million–2000 BCE. The dating of objects from these very early periods is generally established through a technique called radio carbon dating (RCD). RCD is a system of determining age according to the rate of disintegration of the radioactive isotope carbon 14 in organic material.

Though there are no written records from the early periods in human evolution it does seem apparent that there was already a long standing tradition that included the transmission of information from the past to be used and considered in the present and the future.

The generally undisputed beginning of art production, or the point at which objects were clearly made for interests or reasons other than a utilitarian function, is dated to c. 38,000 BCE or the Paleolithic period.

Art production in the Paleolithic period includes a variety of different types of artifacts such as jewelry, art making tools, and the representation of humans and animals in various materials like stone, ivory, bone, and clay. It is in this period that we also find the creation of small and large wall paintings as well as engraving, relief, and three-dimensional sculpture.

What we cannot and should not say about all Stone Age art is that the objects are related to or were made in direct connection with a magical or ritualistic concept or belief. There is no specific scientific evidence that supports that hypothesis. It is simply one of a number of ideas concerning the function and purpose of image-making in the period.

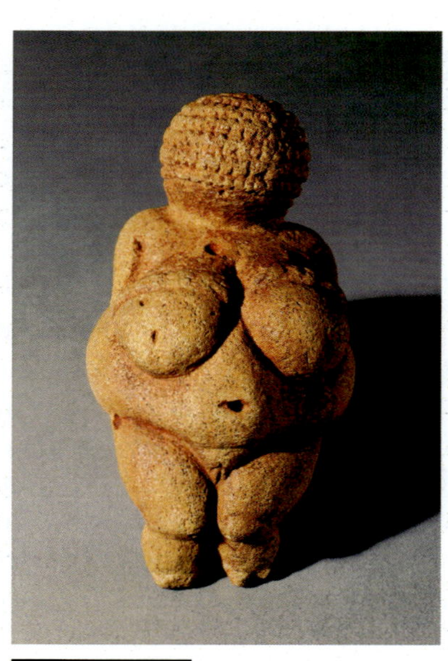

**1-1:** Nude Woman, c. 28,000–25,000 BCE, Limestone, Willendorf, Austria, 4 ¼″ high. Naturhistoriches Museum, Vienna.

Animals, including bison, horses, and mammoths are the most common subjects of Stone Age art. When these animals are represented they are almost always represented in profile. This is perhaps, in part, because the profile view offers the artist and the viewer the most information about an object and is simply easier to produce than a frontal view which would require some foreshortening.

Interestingly, when the human figure is represented it is almost always female (images of men are actually quite rare from this period) and almost always depicted in a frontal view.

One of the oldest extant sculptures from the Paleolithic period is a small three-dimensional sculpture nicknamed the Venus of Willendorf.

She is usually affectionately called the Venus of Willendorf because she was found in Willendorf, Austria. The name Venus, however, is misleading because there is no evidence that the object represents a goddess or deity nor does it impart any information regarding concepts of beauty or love, attributes most closely associated with the Roman goddess Venus. This small sculpture is most likely not intended to represent a goddess or any specific person. The anatomically exaggerated figure is faceless with her head encircled by what appears to be neat rows of curly hair.

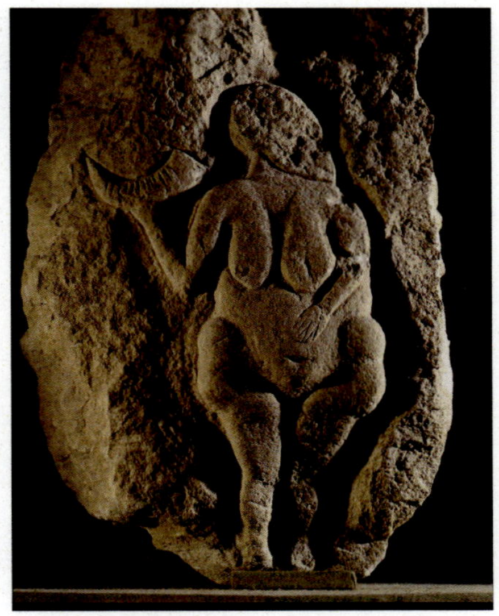

**1-2:** Woman Holding a Bison Horn, c. 25,000–20,000 BCE, painted limestone, Laussel, France, 18″ high. Musée d'Aquitaine, Bordeaux, France.

The exaggeration of her female parts, particularly her large breasts, belly, buttocks and pubic area has led to the suggestion that she was a fertility figure. The fact that she is plump however could simply mean that she was healthy, lazy, or of a higher social rank than other members of her hunter gatherer group. It is possible that she was intended to serve as a personification of femaleness or even in a more general sense, life itself. She is powerful, large, plump, full, or swollen, and therefore regenerative like the earth itself.

We do not know what purpose or function the figurine served. The fact that her feet, though broken off, taper and do not seem as if they would have supported her standing upright gives us some clues. Since she could not stand, she was meant to be carried, which would further suggest that she is a more private image than a public one. The private nature of the object would then also be related to the fact that she would have been revealed as opposed to displayed.

Further complicating an understanding of the figurine is that the stone from which it is carved is not stone local to where it was found, and it appears that it was once tinted with red ochre.

Another example of the female form from the Paleolithic period is a relief carving in France.

This is one of the earliest known examples of relief sculpture. The term *relief* refers to objects or designs that project from a background of which they are a part. Relief sculpture is generally divided into three categories: high relief, low or bas relief, and sunken relief. High relief projects substantially from the surface, bas relief projects a little, and sunken does not project at all, rather it is sunken into the surface.

The image of the woman holding a bison horn was originally carved into a huge rock at the entrance to a rock shelter and was in essence an open air sculpture. This suggests that she was not a private or sequestered image but

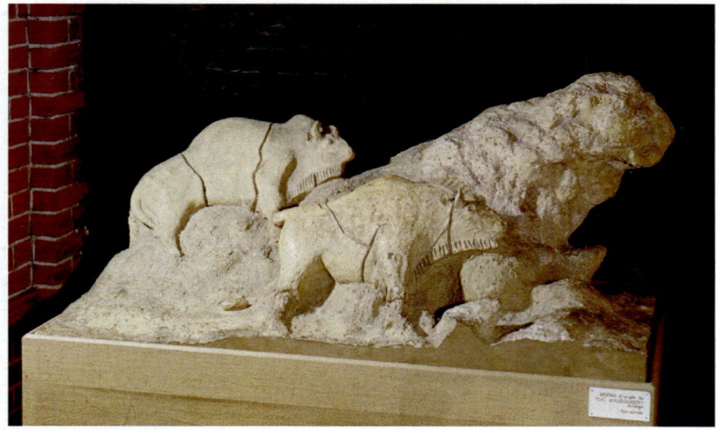

**1-3:** Two Bison, c. 15000–9,000 BCE, clay, Le Tuc d'Audoubert, France, 2′ length each.

a fairly public one. Like the Venus of Willendorf she is faceless and has large exaggerated breasts, wide hips, and a defined pubic area. Unlike the Venus of Willendorf, however, she places her hand on her belly, perhaps drawing attention to it, and she holds up a bison horn. Traces of a red ochre pigment have also been found on her suggesting that she was painted at one time or at least adorned with color for some purpose.

These two Bison were created in clay that was deftly modeled onto a natural rock formation inside a cave. The natural geological feature of the rock is used to enhance

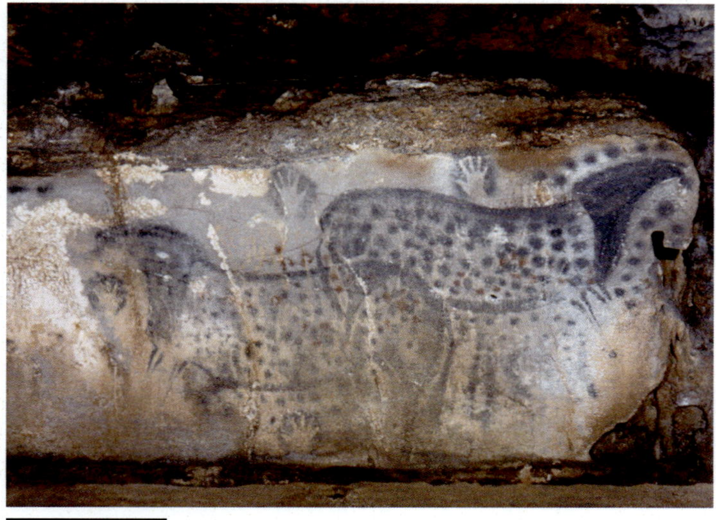

**1-4:** Spotted Horses and Handprints, wall–painting, Peche–Merle, France, c. 25,000–22,000 BCE, 11′2″ long.

the subject providing both a support for the sculpture but also a depth and sense of volume.

These bison, at about two feet in length each, are considered some of the largest Paleolithic sculptures known. The work shows the sophisticated choices made by the artist such as the particular location of the work as well as the variety of methods used to create them. These Bison were formed by building up the surface and modeling the clay by hand, and using sharp edged tools for the hair. It seems the artist or artists made a real effort to give them a three-dimensional quality and to present them not as an outline or shape of an animal but as living, breathing, dynamic creatures.

The inclusion of handprints in Paleolithic art is not particularly uncommon. The prints were produced in one of two methods; the first method, seen here, and the most common, is the negative handprint. A negative handprint is created when a hand is placed on a surface and then pigment is blown, sprayed, or painted around it. The positive handprints are created by simply pressing the hand in pigment and then applying it to a surface.

We cannot be sure of the function or meaning of these prints, but they certainly could serve as a type of signature.

The horses, depicted back to back, are painted on a section of cave wall that terminates at the far end in what looks like the shape of a horse's head. The integration of this shape into the design once again points to the sophisticated choices made by the artist/artists to integrate and utilize a geological feature to his artistic advantage. The horses are surrounded by several negative handprints as well as a number of large dots or circles.

Perhaps the best known examples of Paleolithic art come from a large cave complex in Lascaux, France.

In 1940 four teenagers in southwest France accidentally discovered a large cave decorated with tremendous wall paintings.

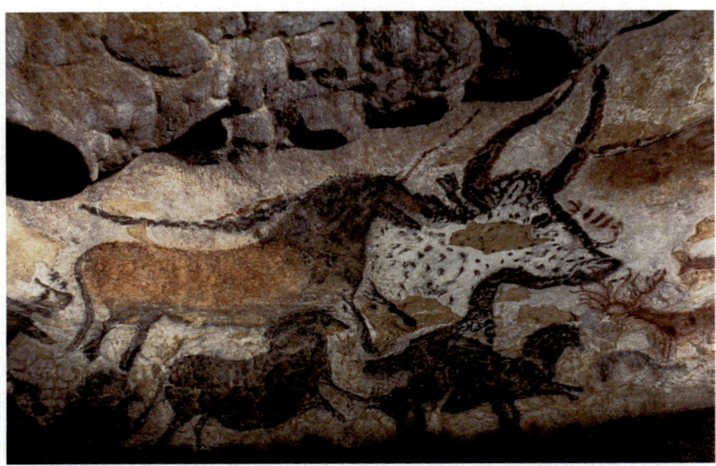

**1-5:** Hall of the Bulls, wall painting, Lascaux, France, 15,000–13,000 BCE, 11′16″.

## Art is an Endangered Species

The cave was initially opened to the public in 1948, but by 1955 the paintings were beginning to form a black mold on the surface because of the introduction of hundreds of viewers a day into the cave. The damage was due to the release of carbon dioxide and by 1963 the cave was mostly closed to the public. In 2000 the French Government decided, without conservation consultations, to add an air conditioning unit to the cave. The addition of the ill advised machine and the inexperienced installers, the system caused further damage at the site including water damage and the introduction of new molds. Further damage was done when the unit failed resulting in the growth of a new fungus. In 2007 a new round of black mold was found to be growing in the cave. Sadly the caves and the art that survived so beautifully intact for over 17,000 years have been greatly and irreversibly compromised.

Lascaux II, a digitally designed scale replica of two of the cave halls, the Great Hall of the Bulls and the Painted Gallery, was opened in 1983. It is located just 200 meters from the original cave. Unfortunately, the location of the parking lot for Lascaux II appears to sit directly on top of the original cave, and there is now a great deal of concern about the weight of the cars, the vibrations they cause, and their emissions.

Fairly deep inside the entrance area of the cave is a sort of large circular gallery, roughly 60 feet long and 22 feet wide, that gets almost no natural light at all. On the walls and overhang in this space, several species of animals, not just bulls, are depicted. There are some 36 animals depicted here including horses, cows, bulls, and deer. One of the bulls measures 16 feet in length and is considered the largest image of any animal in Paleolithic cave art. The images of animals overlap each other which suggests that they were not all painted at the same time but instead accumulated over time.

Artists here would have employed the use of stone lamps filled with fat and an organic material as a wick to provide light. For the images artists used primarily raw yellow and red ochre and charcoal. They mixed ground mineral and organic materials with water in order to apply color to the wall surface. Evidence of a variety of artists' tools such as palettes, brushes made from reeds and twigs, as well as hollowed out pieces of bone or reed used to blow pigment has been found at many of the adorned caves sites in prehistoric Europe. At Lascaux it also appears that scaffolding was constructed in order to reach some of the areas that hold decoration.

The animals, all shown in profile, are depicted in either silhouette (shadow) or outline form, two of the most basic approaches in prehistoric art.

Most of the animals are also depicted in a manner so that both horns of the animal are visible, as if seen from the front, though the body remains in profile, a technique called twisted perspective. Since the artist is not providing an image of the animal from a single viewpoint, which would be called an optical approach, but instead attempts to give more information by turning or twisting a portion of the animal's body, it is called a descriptive approach.

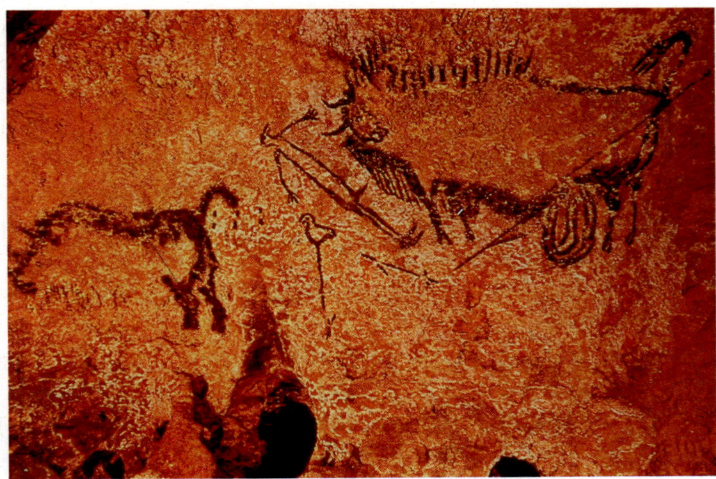

**1-6:** Rhinoceros, wounded man, and Bison, wall paining, Lascaux, France, 15,000–13,000 BCE, 3′8″.

Without written records, the function and purpose of these images is unclear. They could be magical, religious, decorative, documentary, narrative, or more simply just the artist attempting to convey the world around him.

Also from Lascaux, from another part of the cave and from deep inside a well shaft, is an image that may represent one of the first images of man in Paleolithic art and may also be one of the earliest examples of narrative art in the history of image making.

This rather enigmatic image presents some interesting problems in an attempt to decipher meaning. Most scholars agree that the rhinoceros, at the right, and appearing to move in a direction that leads away from the image of the man and the bison may not be part of the narrative. The dark outline and rounded contours of the animal have led many to suggest that it was not created by the same hand as the image of the bison and man. Just beneath the tail of the rhinoceros are six small dots arranged in pairs. The meaning or significance of the dots is unknown.

The other figures, the man and the bison, as well as the objects near them, may be related to each other. The man, whose penis is exaggerated perhaps to stress his manliness, seems to lie on the ground, his legs together his arms stretched out to his side. His face appears oddly beaked, suggesting that he may wear some sort of mask. His position, perhaps on the ground, might be explained by the clearly agitated bison that stands in front of him. The bison, with its head lowered and hair bristling seems angered, in part because it appears to have been struck by a long spear which has wounded and partially disemboweled it. At the feet of the man is an atlatl, or spear throwing apparatus, and next to that a kind of stick or staff with a small bird at one end. It is impossible to know how one is intended to 'read' such an image, if in fact that is what was intended at all. If the figures are somehow related then this scene exhibits a remarkable advancement in image making and represents a much more complex artistic endeavor that the mere representation of figures and animals.

Around 10,000 BCE there was a significant climate change as much of the earth's ice began to melt, and glaciers receded to expose larger land masses. The shift in climate, vegetation, and animal populations thereby necessitated adaptation by the human population. By 8000 BCE with the dawn of the Neolithic age, humans began to live a more sedentary existence as opposed to a hunter gather lifestyle. The New Stone Age is marked by the domestication of animals, and the development of agriculture and livestock as the primary food sources. Humans in this period began to build fixed homes often clustered together in clans or groups. In the Neolithic age there were significant advances made in farming, weaving, pottery production, metal working, and even simplified accounting.

The oldest known settlements or settled communities have been found in the area at the eastern end of the Mediterranean, generally called the fertile crescent. The fertile crescent is an arc shaped area of land that extends from the Nile delta in Egypt to ancient Anatolia (modern Turkey) and includes ancient Mesopotamia. The area was rich in agricultural grains like wheat and barley, animals were plentiful, and the area had sufficient rainfall; all critical requirements to sustain a more settled existence.

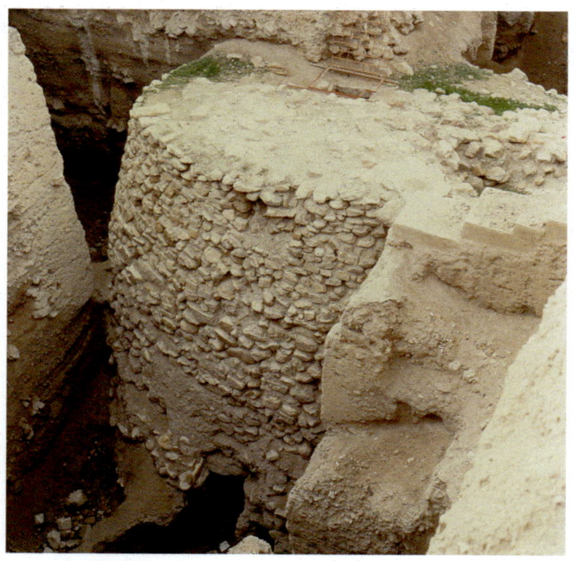

**1-7:** Great Stone Tower, settlement wall, Jericho, 8000–7000 BCE.

One of the earliest settled communities, dating to c. 8000 BCE, is located on the West side of the Jordan river at Jericho. The inhabitants of this community built mud brick houses on stone foundations, and by c. 7500 BCE, with an approximate population of about 2,500, built a wide ditch and a solid stone wall encircling their town.

The walls at Jericho measured some 5′ thick and in some places 13′ tall. Integrated into the wall was a large circular stone tower, 33′ in diameter and 28′ tall with an internal staircase.

These walls and tower are the first known permanent stone fortifications.

The walls suggest a collective community in order to plan, design, and construct such a wall. This walls and tower are a tremendous achievement that show a complex idea of township, town planning, design, and function, and an industrious effort of a group of people for the betterment and security of the group. Perhaps most important is that the settlement walls and tower at Jericho mark the beginning of the history of monumental architecture!

This is the same Jericho that is described in the Old Testament and whose walls were blown down by Joshua and his armies.

## Çatal Hoyuk

Another Neolithic community is located at a town called Çatal Hoyuk in southern Anatolia. The settlement dates to c. 6150 BCE and like Jericho is one of the earliest examples of suburban living. It is also considered the largest of all Neolithic communities.

The location for the town of Çatal Hoyuk was probably based on its plentiful natural resource, obsidian. Obsidian is a glass-like volcanic stone used by Neolithic toolmakers and weapons makers because it could be worked into a sharp chiseled edge. This is important because it seems that the town was established and built based on its access and control of a valuable material that it could trade or sell.

Çat al Hoyuk is particularly interesting because, unlike other towns, it has no streets separating the houses. The mud-brick houses adjoined to one another by the rooftops with access to the interior provided through openings in the roofs. This design provided some distinct advantages such as making the small living structures more stable and easier to defend.

The basic plans of the houses were very similar, showing only variation in size, and the walls and floors were both plastered and painted. The interiors were furnished with benches along the walls that served for sitting and sleeping. Some larger rooms, called shrines, were more elaborately decorated than others with bucrania (bulls skulls), bull horns, and plaster reliefs. The dead, often coated with red ochre and deposited with grave goods such as jewelry and weapons, were buried beneath the floors of the living spaces.

The types of painted decoration at Çatal Hoyuk range from hunting scenes to landscapes.

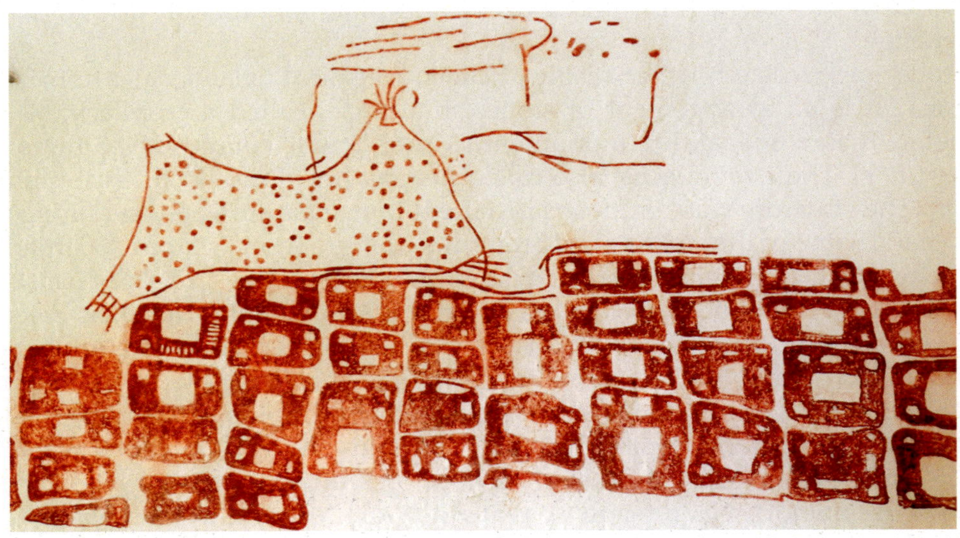

**1-8:** Landscape with volcanic eruption, mural painting, Çatal Hoyuk, Turkey, c. 6100 BCE.

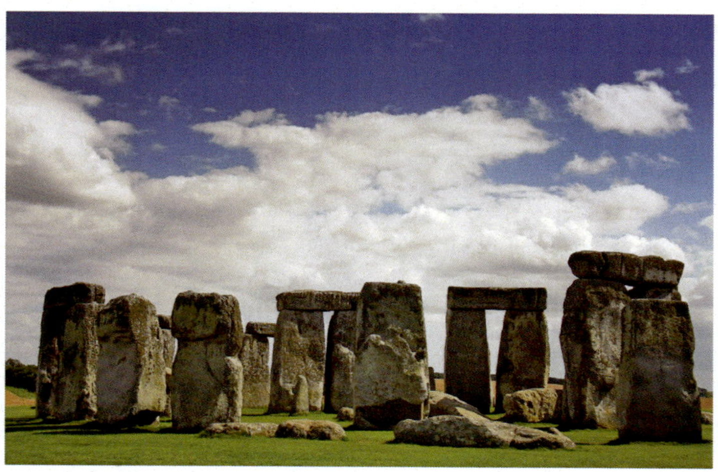

**1-9:** Stonehenge, Wiltshire, England, c. 2600–1600 BCE, 97′diameter, 24′ tall.

In one of the larger rooms at Çatal Hoyuk a painting was discovered that is generally considered the world's first landscape.

The painting depicts a town with rows of rectangular houses located side by side in the foreground. Behind the schematized town a twin peaked mountain appears to spew lines and dots from one peak. Most scholars agree that this is not simply a landscape painting but one that actually depicts a volcanic eruption. The volcano, Hasan Dag, is a 10,000 foot twin peaked volcano that sits some eight miles to the east of the village.

Perhaps the single best recognized Neolithic monument in the world is Stonehenge.

Stonehenge, located on the Salisbury Plain in Wiltshire England, dates from 2600 BCE–1600 BCE. It is an arrangement of stones in a circle, called a cromlech, 97 feet in diameter. It is a megalithic monument, a monument composed of huge (*mega*) stones (*liths*). These cromlechs, also called henges, are almost exclusively limited to Britain. The structure was composed in at least four separate stages spanning at least 1500 years. Some of the stones were brought to the site from as far as 200 miles away.

A circular ditch roughly 350 feet in diameter was the earliest phase of construction here. Then a series of 56 pits or holes, called the Aubrey holes (for their discoverer) were added just inside the ditch. They may have marked where timbers were originally placed and they may also have originally held cremated human remains.

The outer most ring of stones is comprised of thirty (originally) standing monolithic sarsen (sandstone) stones capped by lintels. Each post, roughly 13′ tall, was then fitted with a large, slightly curved lintel at the top. The lintels were attached to the posts with the use of mortise and tenon, so that when all the lintels were in place it created a complete circle.

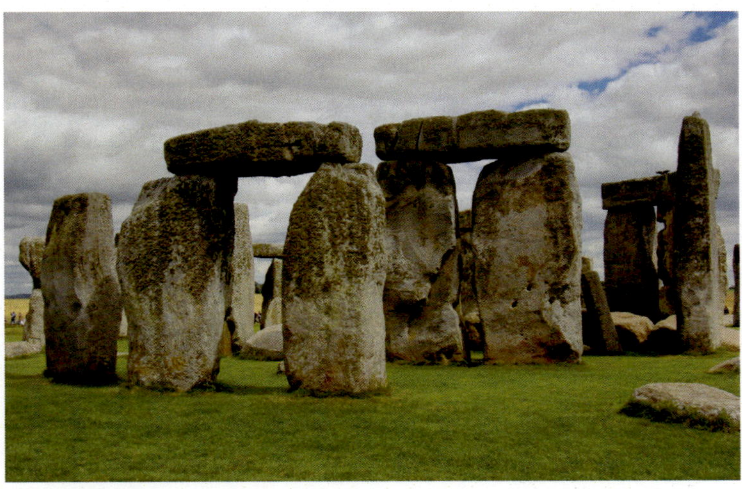

**1-10:** Stonehenge detail: Trilithons.

Just inside the outer ring is a much smaller ring of 60 bluestones that stand upright. The bluestones encircle a horseshoe arrangement of five trilithons (three stone post and lintel constructions) that open out toward the east. Each stone in one of these trilithons weighs approximately 45 tons, while the largest of the trilithons measures 24 feet tall. Just inside the trilithons is another set of bluestones also arranged in the same horseshoe shape. The inner horseshoe-arranged stones open to the east and are aligned with a separate single standing stone called the heel stone. A person standing in the center of the complex could look eastward toward the heel stone which marks precisely the point where the sun rises every year at the summer solstice. The summer solstice is the longest day of the year, or the day with the longest daylight and hence the shortest night; it falls on June 21 or June 22.

Stonehenge, though we still do not completely understand its function, is at minimum an astronomical observatory and a very accurate solar calendar.

The monument stands as a testament to the very sophisticated observations, mathematical and astronomical knowledge, and engineering skills of a culture that is often described as "primitive."

The variety in terms of subject, medium, and style of art produced in the Stone Age reflects the importance of image-making to societies that had no written language. The Paleolithic period saw the production of small scale figurines as well as complex and perhaps even narrative wall paintings. In the Neolithic period we see the development of communal living, the decoration of homes, as well as the establishment of monumental architecture. In the later Neolithic period there is evidence of tremendous engineering skills and impressive and complex astronomical knowledge.

Name ______________________________________ Date ________________

## Chapter 1

# Stone Age Art Questions

1. Which Neolithic site contains the earliest stone fortifications?

2. What seems to have been the purpose of Stonehenge?

3. What is the term or terms for a circular stone arrangement?

4. What is the significance of the heel stone and at which site is it found?

5. Describe the difference between optical and descriptive approaches.

6. Compare the representation of the female form in the *Venus of Willendorf* to *Woman Holding a Bison Horn*.

7. Describe the images and style of the wall paintings of Lascaux?

8. When did sedentary societies develop? How did that change art?

9. What is the significance of Catal Hoyuk?

10. What is the function or purpose of handprints in mural painting? What types are found?

# THE ART OF THE ANCIENT NEAR EAST

## Chapter 2

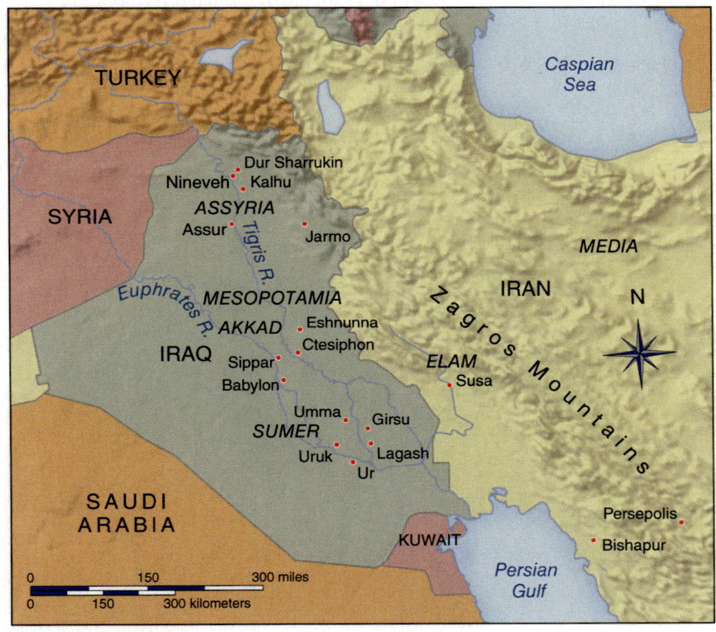


The ancient Near East.

The art of the ancient Near East comprises essentially the art of ancient civilizations in and around Mesopotamia. *Mesopotamia* is a word that comes from the Greek (*potam* = river) and means "the land between the rivers." The two rivers are the Tigres and the Euphrates, to the east and west respectively.

Ancient Mesopotamia, part of what is often called the Fertile Crescent, is where civilization truly began. The Fertile Crescent is a geographical area that comprises a crescent shaped area of land that includes all of Mesopotamia, Phoenicia and the Levant, the whole of the eastern end of the Mediterranean Sea, and lower Egypt. From this region comes the first evidence of stone settlements, the invention of the wheel, the first evidence of writing, the first system of recorded law, and the first literary epic.

Discoveries in the early 20th century made by archaeologists, particularly a British man named Leonard Wooley, helped to raise attention and awareness of the riches that lie in the area. In the 1920s he found the Royal Cemeteries at Ur in Southern Mesopotamia, and the Near East was soon seen as a rival or at least on equal footing with Egypt as a source for material and archaeological discovery.

Sumer (what is now southern Iraq) is one of the earliest of the Mesopotamian city states to flourish around 3800 BCE. It was the Sumerians who transformed the dry area into a fertile one with the use of plows and the ability to harness and control river flooding.

Cities in Mesopotamia, like almost all in this region, were constructed of mud brick. The city itself was composed of a central temple complex raised above the surrounding town. It was the focal point of ancient life and both a religious center and a political and administrative one. The most prominent feature of the city center was the temple located on a tall stepped platform or ziggurat. Ziggurats, the earliest examples of which measured around 50 feet in height, were intended to symbolize a stairway to heaven; or a kind of tangible link between heaven and earth.

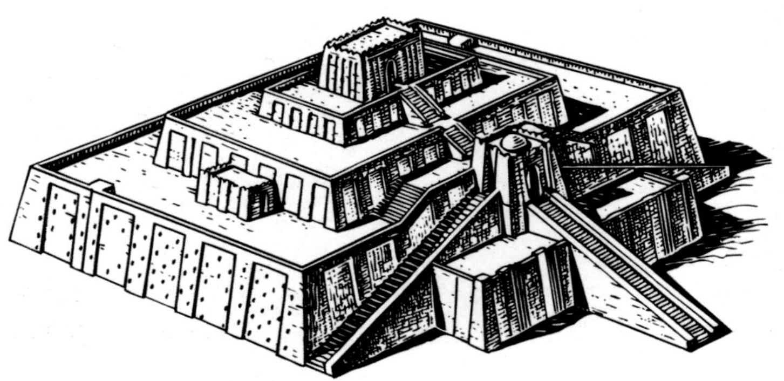

**2-1:** White Temple and Ziggurat, mudbrick, Uruk, Iraq, c. 3400–3000 BCE.

Some of the most impressive remains of an early Sumerian temple are those of the White Temple at Uruk. It was called the White Temple due to its once whitewashed mud brick surface. The small temple stood on top of a ziggurat that raised it about 40 feet above street level. A stairway led counter clockwise around the ziggurat terminating at the temple's entrance on the north side. This winding or indirect approach is called a bent-axis approach, as opposed to a direct or axial approach like those used for Egyptian pyramids.

The temple, probably dedicated to Anu the sky god, was small and measured only about 61 × 16 feet. The temple's size indicates that it was not built for the masses but instead was used primarily by the temple priests and other select few. Inside the temple there were several small rooms or chambers situated around a central hall or cella. At the center of the cella was a stepped altar that housed a statue of the divinity.

The temple was referred to by the Sumerians as a "waiting room" perhaps because it was here that the priests waited for the gods to descend from the heavens.

A remarkable find from Uruk is a carved white marble female head. The use of marble clearly establishes this head as an important object since it was created from an expensive and imported material. The function of the object is unknown but it may have served as the face of a cult statue, perhaps of the goddess Inanna. It is interesting that the face is flat on the back and appears to have holes as if the face was meant to have been anchored or attached to a body, presumably made from wood or other perishable material. The face is often identified as Inanna because the head was found in a temple precinct once devoted to the goddess. Inanna is one of the oldest and most revered of the Sumerian gods and is the goddess of love and war.

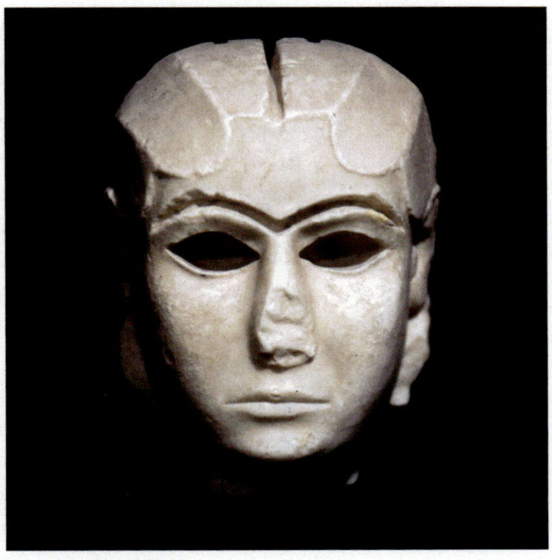

**2-2:** Female head: Inanna? Marble, Uruk, Iraq, c. 3200 BCE, 8″ height, Iraq Museum, Baghdad.

In its original condition the face would have been striking. It would have included the use of precious materials to enliven it. The large brow and the almond shaped eyes would have been filled or inlaid with shell and colored stones and the groove at the top would have anchored a wig, perhaps of gold or copper.

### Art is an Endangered Species

The female head was one of many objects looted from the National Museum of Iraq in Baghdad in April of 2003. Fortunately, it was recovered five months later and returned to the museum.

## Writing in the Ancient Near East

It is from c. 3400 BCE that we find the oldest surviving examples of written documents. The Sumerians developed an early form of writing called pictographs. Pictographs are simplified pictures used to stand for words. These pictographs were then incised with a sharp tool or stylus into soft clay tablets and left to harden and dry. They were read from the top down and from right to left. The earliest examples of clay tablets with pictographs appear to be simple accounting records.

By c. 3000 BCE pictographs evolved and were simplified into a system of wedge-shaped signs, called cuneiform. This marks the development of writing and shortly thereafter the development of literature.

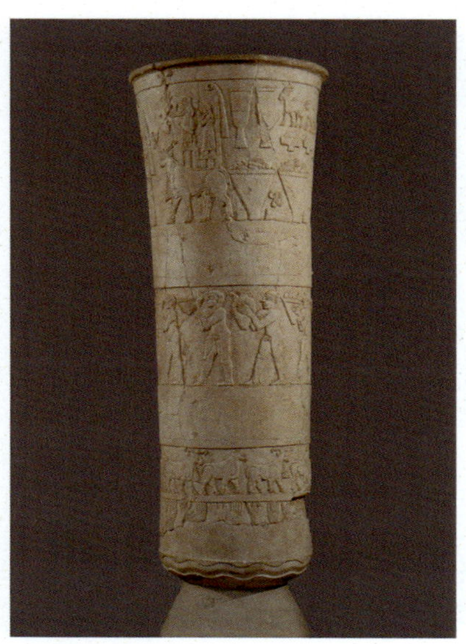

**2-3:** Warka Vase, Alabaster, Uruk, Iraq, c. 3200–3000 BCE, 3′1/4″, Iraq Museum, Baghdad.

The earliest extant example of literature, which survives on cuneiform tablets dating to about 2100 BCE, is an epic saga entitled Gilgamesh. The epic poem, probably first composed c. 3000 BCE, tells the story of a legendary King of Uruk and is a mixture of history, legend, and myth.

The hero, Gilgamesh, who was one-third mortal and two-thirds god, was blessed with beauty and courage. In the epic he spurns the advances of the goddess of love, loses his best friend, and goes on an arduous and ultimately unsuccessful quest for eternal life.

It is important to note that this epic saga of a hero and his quest was written some fifteen hundred years before Homer's epic poems the *Iliad* and the *Odyssey*!

Another luxurious object from ancient Uruk is the so-called Warka vase. This large alabaster vessel is considered to be the first great work of narrative relief sculpture known. It is one of the first works of art that attempts to tell a coherent narrative or story. The decoration on the vessel appears to depict a festival or procession in honor of the goddess Inanna.

The vase is divided into decorated horizontal bands (also called registers or friezes) of low relief. Two bands with no decoration are located above and below the central band.

The lowest register, at the very bottom of the vessel, depicts abundant vegetation that appears to emerge from a marsh or river. In the next register alternating ewes and rams, depicted in profile, amble around the vase from left to right.

In the next figural register is a procession of naked men, also in profile, moving from right to left. The men carry different types of baskets and jars that overflow with offerings. These offerings may be votive offerings (gifts made to a deity out of gratitude or in hope for reply).

Notice that none of the images of the animals or of the men overlap in any way, probably to ensure clarity in the design. Also the animals and men are shown in a composite view; both are depicted with profile legs, frontal shoulders, profile heads, and a frontal eye.

In the uppermost figural register, a goddess wearing a tall horned headdress receives one of the men carrying a basket. Her large size, she is considerably taller than the other figures, is a way to indicate her importance. This method of indicating importance through relative size is called hierarchy of scale. Just behind the goddess is a collection of various offerings.

The vase is exceptional as one of the real examples of relief narrative sculpture, and it is unfortunately an example of Art Is an Endangered Species:

## Art Is an Endangered Species

On April 10–13, 2003 the Museum in Baghdad was sacked and looted. Some 17,000 artifacts were either lost or destroyed in the senseless violence. The Warka vase was smashed off its mount on a podium and stolen. When it was finally returned, after several months (in June 2003), it was badly damaged and broken into fourteen separate pieces. There were plans in place to begin to restore the vessel but it has yet to be completed.

The destruction of a remarkable object like the Warka vessel should not be viewed as a loss just for the museum, or for Iraq, but instead should be understood in a wider context as a loss for the whole of humanity.

Another glimpse into Sumerian religion and religious practices or beliefs is provided by a cache of sculptures found buried beneath the floor of a temple at Eshnunna (modern Tell Asmar). The statuettes, carved out of gypsum and limestone, were inlaid with shells and black limestone. The statuettes range in size from about one foot to just under three feet tall. The statues are of both males and females and occasionally even children.

The figures share a similar pose with their arms folded together in front of their chest, often holding a small cup or occasionally a flower or branch. The objects they hold are most likely votive offerings.

In most cases the men are bare-chested and wear belted and fringed skirts. They also sport a typically Mesopotamian-style squared plated beard and hairstyle. The women wear longer robes with a long shawl covering their left shoulder and exposing their right breast.

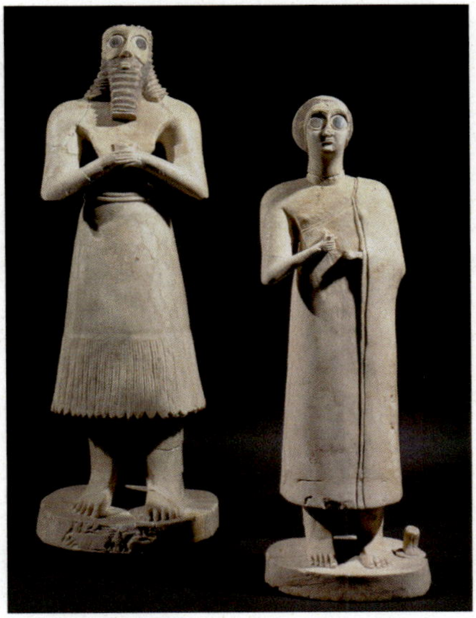

**2-4:** Statuettes of Worshippers, Limestone, Alabaster, and Gypsum, Eshnunna, Iraq, c. 2700–2500 BCE, 2′6″ male figure, Iraq Museum, Baghdad.

The statuettes are fairly cylindrical in shape and often stand on small bases that include inscriptions on them giving the name of the donor, the name of the person to whom the offering is presented, and sometimes even little prayers.

These statuettes are not intended as portraits of any specific individual but rather representative of man, woman, or child as worshiper. All share the attribute of very large wide-open eyes. The large eyes represent them in the act of worshipping. Their wide-eyed stares represent a kind of attentive, and eternal aspect of unfaltering prayer and devotion.

Some of the most interesting Sumerian finds come from a series of subterranean tombs in the Royal Cemetery at Ur (the biblical home city of Abraham).

These tombs, dated to 3000 BCE–2600 BCE, make up a series of vaulted chambers beneath the ground in which a variety of costly materials were discovered including sculptures, gold helmets, daggers, gold beakers, jewelry, musical instruments, and chariots.

Some of the tombs were also discovered to contain dozens of bodies, not all of whom were dead when they were buried. These attendants, which included musicians, servants, charioteers, and soldiers were most likely ritually killed in order to accompany the tomb owner, clearly of high social status perhaps royalty, into the afterlife.

An impressive and enigmatic find from one of the largest tombs is the so-called Royal Standard of Ur.

The object is trapezoidal in shape and wider at the bottom than at the top. It is composed of panels of wood inlaid with shell, limestone, and lapis that were once set

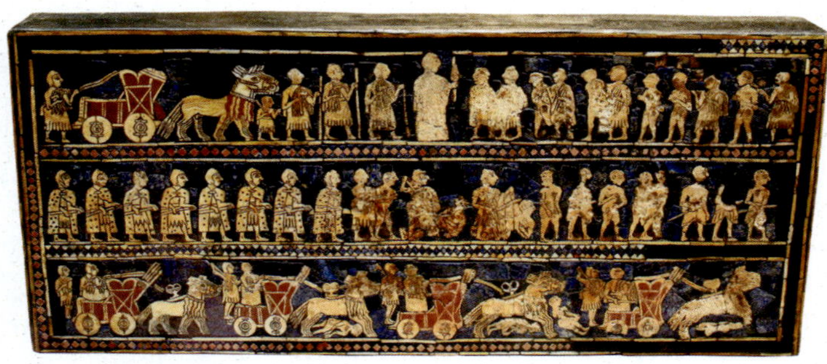

**2-5:** Standard of Ur, Wood inlaid with shell, limestone and lapis, Royal Cemetery Ur, Iraq, 2600 BCE, 8.5″ × 1′7″, British Museum, London.

into a wooden framework. The two long, sloping sides are decorated with narrative images in three superimposed horizontal registers. The two short ends, also divided into registers, are very damaged but were also decorated.

The decoration is a mixture of military images, banquet scenes, and on the short ends, animals and human figures.

The images on the long sides are generally read from left to right and from bottom to top. They seem to represent, on one side, called the war side, images relating to a military campaign including the battle, the taking of prisoners, and a review of prisoners. The other side, often called the peace side, appears to depict preparations for a banquet, the herding of sacrificial animals, and a banquet in the presence of a King or royal person.

## On the war side

In the lowest register, beginning at the left are four four-wheeled chariots drawn by horses mowing down enemies. The battered fallen enemies are shown on the ground beneath the horses. A sense of motion and movement is implied as the chariots and horses seem to pick up speed as they move from left to right.

In the next register are armored hooded soldiers pushing or herding prisoners from the left to the right. Notice how the soldiers are depicted in matching uniforms with short swords on their sides while the enemy is shown semi-naked, tattered. and disheveled. The contrast in the way the two groups of people appear is one way of showing the dominance and superiority of the Sumerian army.

In the uppermost register the soldiers are depicted presenting the tied and bound prisoners to a large figure in the center. He is clearly the most important figure, perhaps royalty, evidenced by the fact that he is depicted so much larger than all the other figures. This indication of importance as depicted through relative scale is a method of representation called hierarchy of scale.

Not only is the figure larger than the rest but behind him is a retinue of men which include a large chariot with a driver.

## On the peace side

In the lowest register are men carrying provisions in sacks tied onto their backs and accompanied by animals. In the next register the movement is still read from the left to the right and the carrying of provisions has evolved into the leading of what appear to be sacrificial animals, including two bulls, two rams and a ewe. In the uppermost register, the direction shifts as this section appears to be better understood when read from right to left. Here six figures are seated on chairs with carved legs facing a larger man seated in an even bigger chair. Each of the figures appears to hold a small cup or vessel of some sort in their right hand. Standing behind the seated men are two figures, probably musicians or entertainers, since one holds a bull-headed lyre while the other seems to gesture as if to indicate he is singing.

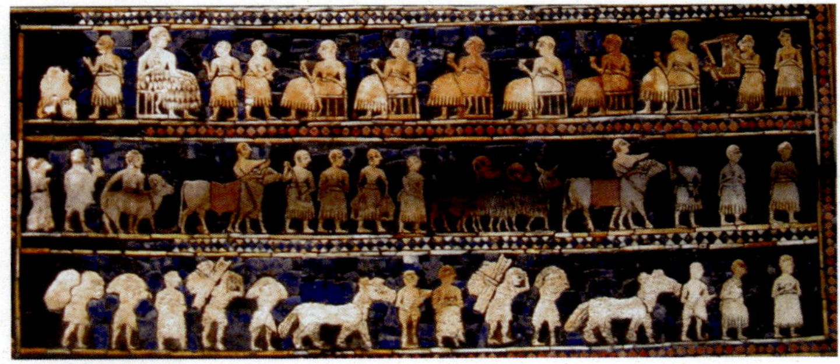

**2-6:** Standard of Ur, Wood inlaid with shell, limestone and lapis, Royal Cemetery Ur, Iraq, 2600 BCE, 8.5″ × 1′7″, British Museum, London.

The function and meaning of the object are unclear, particularly because it has no accompanying inscriptions. The banquet could be read as either preparation for the war or a celebration of victory, or perhaps both.

The archaeologist that discovered it in 1922, Leonard Wooley, found it lying next to a soldier and thought that the object may have originally been carried on a large pole, making it a type of military or parade standard.

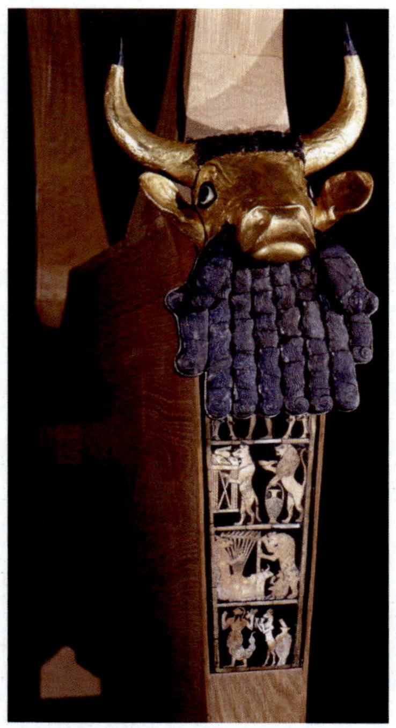

**2-7:** Bull Headed Lyre from Royal Cemetery at Ur, 2600 BCE, wood with inlaid gold, lapis, and shell, 5′5″ University of Pennsylvania Museum, Philadelphia.

Also from the royal cemetery at Ur comes a lyre (like a small harp though strummed when played not plucked). The instrument, just like the one depicted on the Standard of Ur, is decorated with a bull's head and has a front panel of inlaid decoration.

The bull's head is wood gilt with gold and has inlaid lapis eyes and a lapis beard. This may represent the sun god Shamash who is described in ancient texts as a golden bull with a lapis beard.

On the front of the sound-box, divided into four registers, is a series of interesting and rather enigmatic images.

The scenes contain odd composite creatures many of which perform human tasks. Note that all the animals are shown in profile while the hybrid-human figures are shown in a composite view.

The top scene depicts a male figure, shown in composite view, with two symmetrical figures of human-faced bulls on either side him. This compositional arrangement with a central vertical image flanked by symmetrical images is called a heraldic composition.

In the next panel a hyena depicted with a knife tucked into his belt carries an offering table piled with food while a lion walks behind carrying a large amphora and a drinking vessel.

In the third panel, an ass plays a bull-headed lyre, while another creature, perhaps a bear, dances or adjusts the lyre while a small companion animal, seems to play another small instrument. In the bottom register a hybrid man-scorpion carries aloft two objects while a gazelle follows behind holding two drinking goblets.

The scenes most likely have some funerary context or meaning, and they might serve some apotropaic

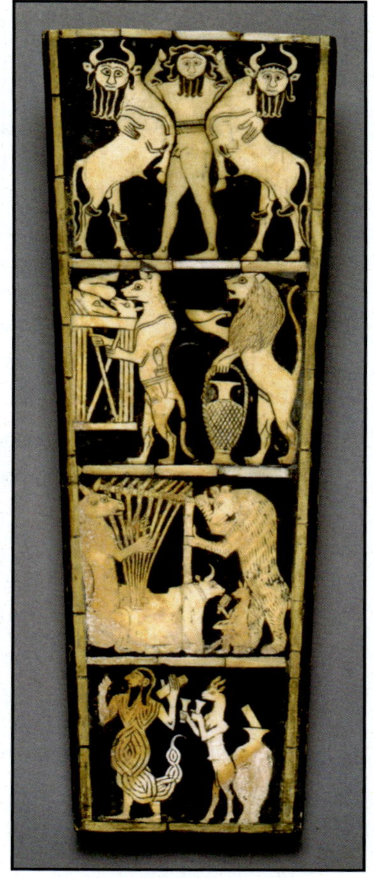

**2-8:** Bull Headed Lyre, detail from Royal Cemetery at Ur, 2600 BCE, wood with inlaid gold, lapis, and shell, 5′5″ University of Pennsylvania Museum, Philadelphia.

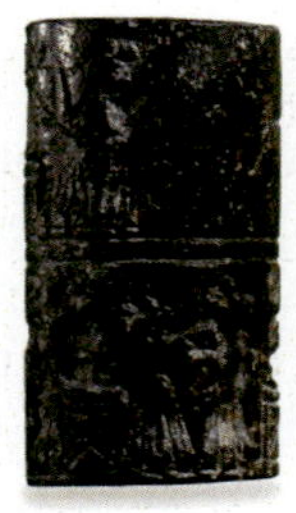
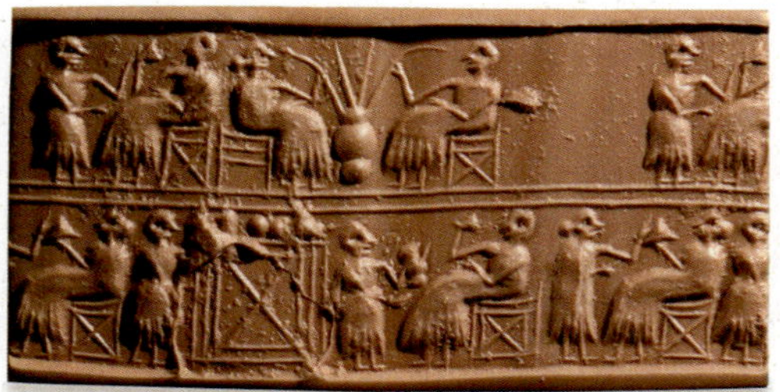

**2-9:** Cylinder Seal and Impression, Royal Cemetery at Ur, Iraq, c. 2600 BCE, Lapis lazuli, 2″, British Museum, London.

(capable of warding off evil) function. While the full meaning is unclear, it is perhaps the first time in Western art that we find human actions and behaviors attributed to animals.

Seals, both stamp and cylinder, are carved objects often made of stone used to impress pictures and or inscriptions into soft clay thereby leaving a raised impression. The stamp seal, probably first invented c. 4000 BCE even before the development of writing, is generally small in size and reveals a more simplified image engraved on its flat surface.

The cylinder seal, which developed c. 3500 BCE, is a stone cylinder that is engraved with pictures and/or inscriptions encircling the whole stone. The seal is then rolled, for as long as is desired, over soft clay leaving a raised impression in a strip. The cylinder was used for a variety of purposes including as signature of ownership, as confirmation of receipt, or to mark clay tablets and building blocks, to secure doors, and even to seal objects for export. Often they were worn by their owners on a string that passed through a hole drilled through the vertical length of the cylinder.

This cylinder seal leaves an impression that is divided into two registers with a banquet scene on both the upper and lower half. In the upper register a woman, whom we recognize by her hairstyle and the shawl over her right arm, and a man face each other and appear to toast with drinking beakers in their raised hands. The lower register depicts a similar scene further suggesting banqueting.

The seal is inscribed on the left behind the image of the seated woman, with the name "Lady" or perhaps "Queen" Pu-abi. Since the seal was found not only in her tomb, but actually next to her body, it is possible that she is the one depicted in the banquet scene.

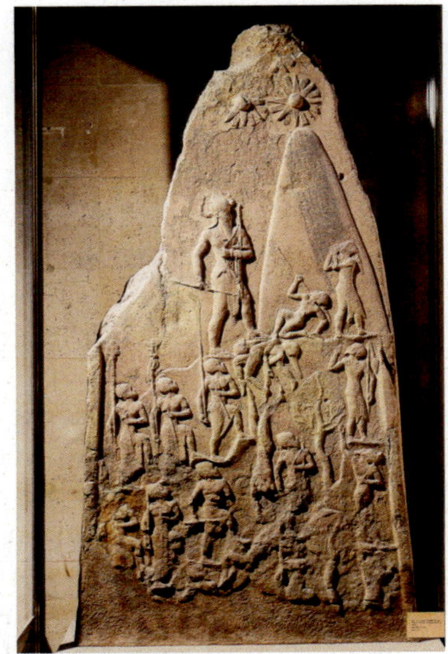

**2-10:** Stele of Naram-Sin, originally erected in Sippar, c. 2254–2218 BCE, pink sandstone, 6′6″, Louvre, Paris.

## Akkadian Art

In 2334 BCE Sargon (means "true King") of Akkad and his armies conquered Sumer as well as neighboring Syria and Elam. The Akkadians were a people of Semitic origin, different from the Sumerians, and they spoke a language more similar to Hebrew and Arabic. Akkadian became the new language of power in Mesopotamia and the gods of ancient Sumer and Akkad became fused creating a new pantheon.

The Akkadians also brought with them a new concept of kingship or ruler-ship, based on the idea of loyalty to a king as opposed to the Sumerian concept of loyalty to the city-state. The Akkadian kings saw themselves as better or more than just mortal and instead believed themselves to be a kind of god on earth. The king also served as the primary priest since it was he who had the closest connection to the gods.

Sargon's grandson Naram-Sin, who ruled from c. 2254–2218 BCE, expanded the borders of his empire in every direction.

The god-like qualities and supreme power attributed to the Akkadians kings is often evident in their art.

This stele, a carved stone slab used to mark a grave or to commemorate historical events, was made to commemorate the Akkadian defeat of the Lullabi, a mountain people. In this relief-sculpted narrative, Naram Sin, depicted larger than everyone else, leads his soldiers up the slopes of a wooded mountain. The enemy are depicted falling, begging, or crushed at their feet. Notice too that the images are not designed in registers but are placed in such a way that they appear to wind and ascend toward the top. This aspect of climbing or ascending seems to parallel the action of rising and winding upward on a ziggurat.

Figures are shown in composite view, with Naram-Sin, isolated against a blank background. His proximity to the stars and the fact that he wears the horned helmet of divinity, usually reserved exclusively for the gods, suggest he is deified.

This stele marks the first time in Mesopotamian art that a ruler or king appears as a god.

Akkadian power did not last long, and once again the various city-states in Mesopotamia began vying for power. The struggle for control of the region did not significantly subside until the rule of the Babylonians in the 18th century BCE.

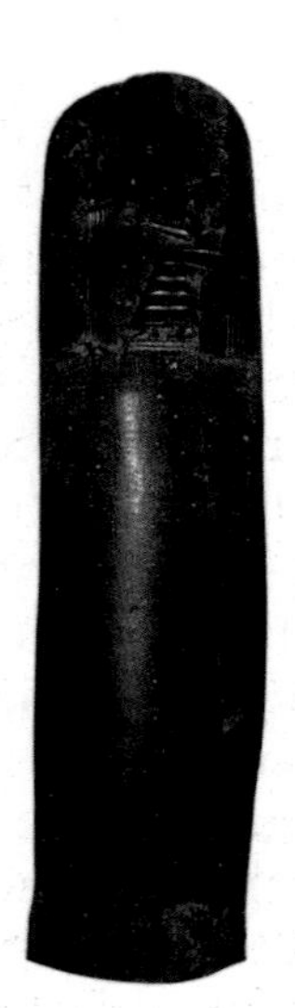
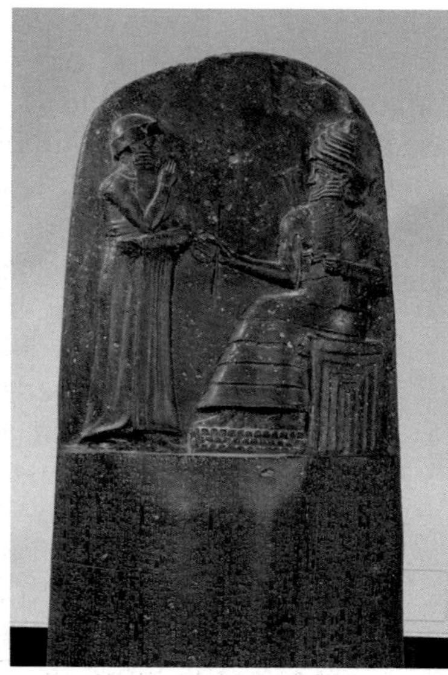

**2-11:** Stele with law code of Hammurabi: Susa, Iran, c. 1760 BCE, 7′4″, basalt, Louvre.

The most successful and recognized of the Babylonian kings was Hammurabi, who ruled from c. 1792–1750 BCE.

Hammurabi is famous not only for his military conquests but for the creation and establishment of a law code. Though there is evidence that some forms of earlier law codes had been recorded in Mesopotamia none were nearly as detailed or specific.

His code survives, in a text of 3,500 lines, engraved on a tall, black basalt stele.

The stele is not only a significant piece of art but is perhaps more importantly a significant historical document. The text on the stele gives a glimpse into the organization of this society and also serves as a basis for Roman law, which is ultimately the basis of the Western legal system.

The code, inscribed in Akkadian cuneiform (wedge-shaped script) on the lower three quarters of the stele, is topped with an image depicting King Hammurabi standing in front of the seated sun-god Shamash.

Shamash wears a long pleated skirt and huge horned headdress and has flames shooting from the tops of his shoulders. Shamash, sporting a long plaited beard, offers Hammurabi a rod and a ring. These instruments, a measuring rod and coiled rope, probably derive from builders' tools and symbolically suggest the ruler or King as builder and creator or constructor of society.

Hammurabi, here depicted much smaller than the god, stands with one arm raised perhaps in a gesture of respect or acknowledgement.

The placement of the image, above the inscribed text of the law, implies that the laws were not written at the whim of the King but that they were sanctioned and god given. It further suggests that the laws, because of their divine origin, are eternal and irrefutable.

The law, inscribed in 44 columns and 28 paragraphs, contains 282 laws and corresponding punishments. The legal articles address various aspects of daily life including contract dispute, divorce, property rights, adoption, murder, inheritance, and even treatment of children and of slaves. Also important is that not only is the infraction of law described but the punishment is also indicated.

Some infractions and penalties include:

If one over-floods his neighbor's crops, then he shall pay for the damages.
If a man breaks into a house in an attempt to rob it and is caught he will be sealed up in the wall as a patch.
If a son strikes his mother, his hands shall be cut off.
If a slave strikes his owner, his ear will be cut off.
If a husband runs away from home, and his wife goes to another home, and then the husband returns, the wife does not have to go back.
If a man put another man's eye out, then his eye will be put out also.

What is clear from the laws, however, is that punishment and its severity is administered in direct relationship to the social status of the offender.

The Babylonian empire fell to the Hittites (from Anatolia) in 1595 BCE, and then several other groups fought for control of the region until the Assyrians took control by the early 13th century BCE. The Assyrian Empire achieved its greatest geographical extent and power in the 7th century BCE.

The Assyrians, who take their name from their capital city of Ashur, were perhaps the most successful and most violent of all of the preceding peoples. They ultimately ruled a territory that included all of Mesopotamia and reached as far as the Nile River and Asia Minor.

As a civilization the Assyrians are recognized for building enormous fortified city complexes with large palaces adorned with massive sculptures and extensive sculptural relief panels depicting royal power and control.

The citadel (a fortress or strongly fortified building or city) of Sargon II at Dur Sharrukin (present-day Khorsabad, Iraq) is an example of the strong fortifications and defensive measures employed in the building of Assyrian cities. At the back of the complex, across a large open courtyard, and protected by another tall turreted wall, stood the palace. The palace complex was elevated above the other buildings about 50 feet and contained some 30 courtyards and over 250 rooms.

Standing guard at the gates to Sargon's palace (and most Assyrian places) were colossal limestone beasts called lamassus.

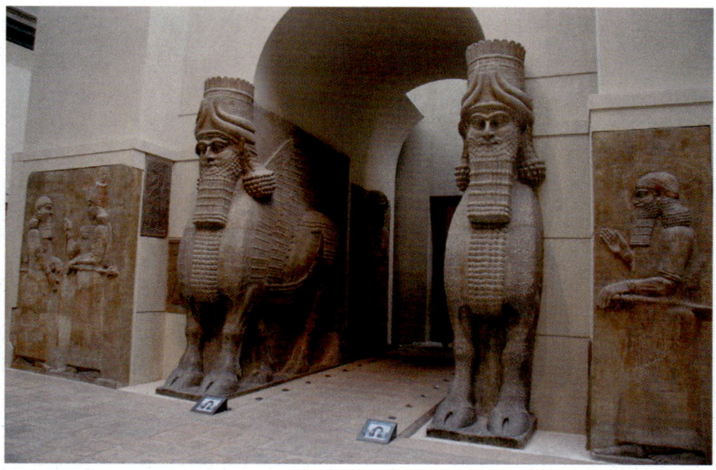

**2-12:** Lamassu, limestone, from the Citadel of Sargon II, Dur Sharrukin, Iraq, c. 720–705 BCE, 13'10", Louvre, Paris.

A lamassu is protective deity depicted in the form of a winged bull or winged lion with a human head. These composite creatures were often carved in pairs since they were frequently found flanking doorways. The function of the lamassu was apotropaic; capable of warding off evil. Their composite form is most likely intended to represent the qualities of the Assyrian king. His strength is represented in the

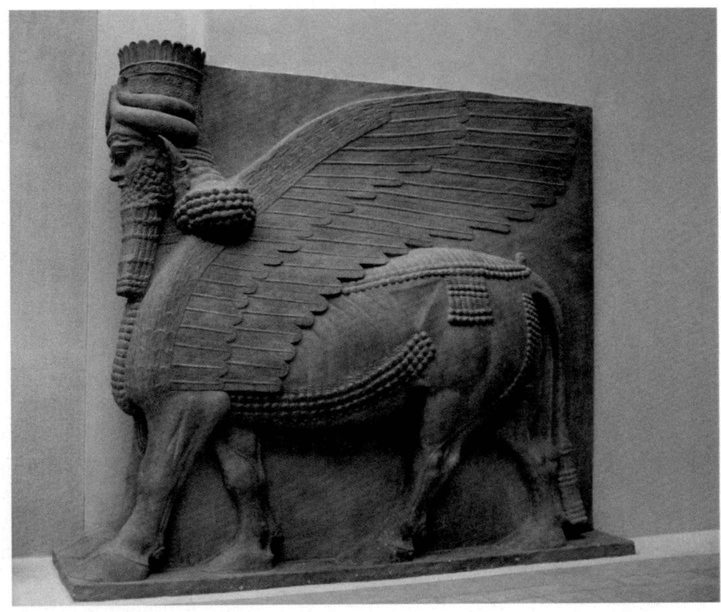

**2-13:** Lamassu, limestone, frontal view, from the Citadel of Sargon II, Dur Sharrukin, Iraq, c. 720–705 BCE, 13′10″, Louvre, Paris.

body of the bull or lion; his swiftness by the large eagle wings, and his intelligence and wisdom represented by the human head.

The lamassus were usually carved in high relief (there is documentary evidence some were cast in bronze but none survive) that in some cases approaches carving in the round.

They also are conceived from two distinct vantage points. In profile, the beast appears to be ambling forward, therefore all four legs are visible. However, when viewed from the front, the beast appears to have two firmly planted legs. From a three-quarter view it is apparent that the animal has been depicted with five legs. This convention, called a double-aspect, was done so that the viewer has a complete sense of the creature whether viewed from the front or the side.

The face of the lamassu has typical Near Eastern features with almond shaped eyes, a single arched brow, and squared hair and beard. The lamassu also wears the tiered horned helmet of divinity that both Shamash and Naram-Sin were depicted wearing.

Assyrian palace walls were often decorated with extensive low-relief sculpture intended to display royal power and authority. Color was often added for emphasis.

One of the earliest and most extensive cycles of Assyrian narrative relief sculpture was discovered in Nineveh at the palace King Ashurbanipal (r. 668–627 BCE).

The lion hunt was both an actual event in the ancient Near East and Egypt as well as a metaphorical one representing a King's power and military skill. The events were often staged using caged lions released within an enclosed area for the purpose of killing.

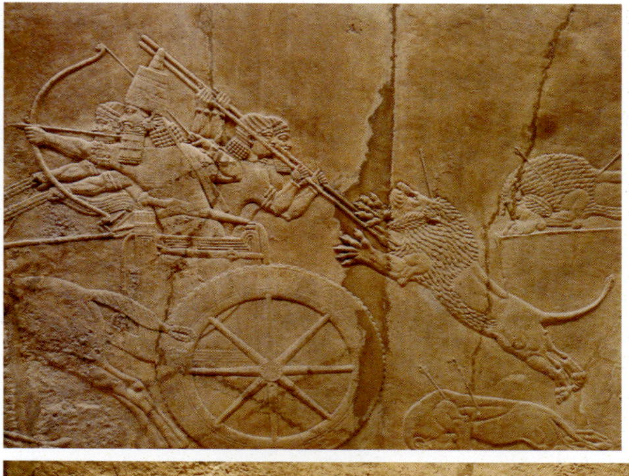

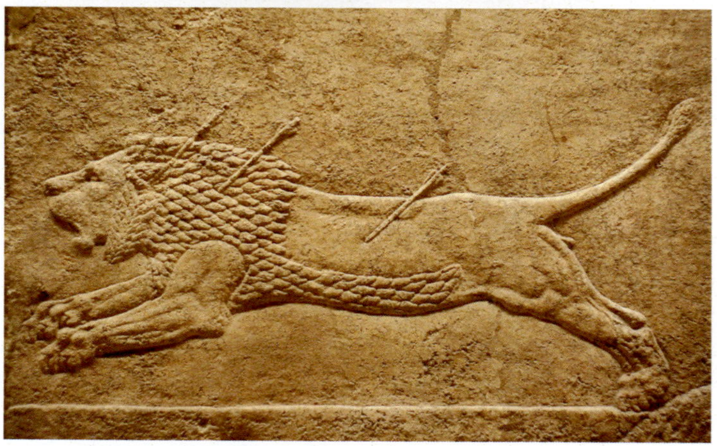

**2-14 a and b:** Lion Hunt, Gypsum, Nineveh, Iraq, c. 645 BCE, 5′4″ high, British Museum, London.

In this section, selected from a much larger series of panels, the King is depicted riding in a chariot wielding a large bow. He shoots at lions in front of him while those he has killed and injured litter the ground behind him. Servants finish off one large male lion who leaps toward the back of the chariot.

The sensitivity with which some of the animals are depicted may seem incongruous with the purpose of the images. The scenes of the suffering and violent deaths of the beasts, which today are heart wrenching, were not meant to be met with empathy or distress by the viewer. Instead, the images of the brave lions who roar and struggle to fight even after they are terribly wounded is a way to further glorify and exalt their executioner. This depiction of an adversary as strong and valiant ennobles the enemy and is used as a way to underscore the exceptional skill of the victor.

For all his rather violent tendencies it is important to note that King Ashurbanipal also collected an amazing library at his palace in Nineveh. The library included thousands (the British Museum counts over 30,000) of clay tablets including royal inscriptions, mythological texts, religious texts, contracts, administrative documents, and even an Epic of Gilgamesh.

Like the other ruling empires in this region the Assyrian empire also collapsed, first to the Medes from the East, and then finally to a resurgence of the Babylonians in 612 BCE. These "Neo-" Babylonians controlled the area until the conquest of the Persians in the 4th century BCE.

The most powerful Neo-Babylonian King was Nebuchadnezzar II (r. c. 604–562 BCE) who is named in the Old Testament as a conqueror of Judah and Jerusalem.

Nebuchadnezzar II rebuilt the city of Babylon and embellished it with a massive fortified palace, incredible gates, an enormous ziggurat (the legendary Tower of Babel), and the hanging gardens.

The city itself was comprised mostly of mud brick buildings to which he had added a series of exceptional and exquisite bright blue fire-glazed brick entrance gates.

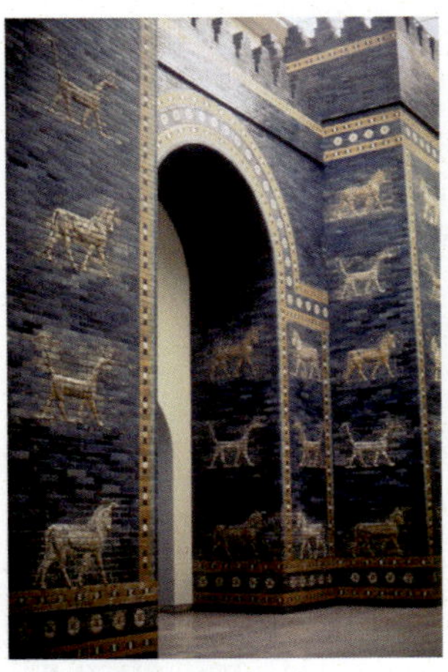

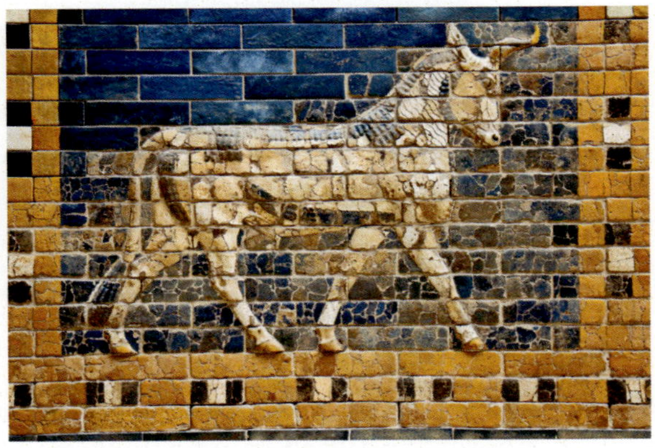

**2-15 a and b:** Ishtar Gate, glazed brick, Babylon, Iraq, c. 575 BCE, height c. 47′, partial reconstruction in Staaliche Museum, Berlin.

This gate, one of several leading to the palace proper, was dedicated to the goddess Ishtar, the Babylonian goddess of sex, love, and war. The double-gate was a huge structure with a large central arch flanked by large crenellated towers. The facade is covered with bright glossy blue baked glazed bricks. The bricks were molded into specific shapes creating raised figural designs such as ambling bulls, lions, griffins, dragons, and other animals. Bright orange colored bricks establish a framework around the gate creating a decorative border.

The splendid bright blue battlemented gate would have been an amazing and impressive site in the harsh sunlight and contrasted with the mostly mud-brick city.

Nebuchadnezzar II is, however, best remembered for the creation of a lush terraced garden often mistakenly described as the hanging gardens of Babylon. The gardens were considered for centuries one of the seven wonders of the ancient world. Ancient accounts, particularly one from the 1st century BC written by the Roman historian Quintus Curtius Rufus, make clear that the gardens did not actually hang but instead that they appeared to hang above the city. The gardens were built on a series of terraces on which the garden grew so that from a distance it would have seemed to hang above the city.

In 538 BCE, under the rule of King Cyrus the Great (r. 559–529 BCE) of Parsa, the Babylonian empire collapsed. Cyrus the Great (also known as Cyrus II of Persia) was the founder of the Achaemenid dynasty and traced his lineage back to an 8th century mythical king named Achaemenes.

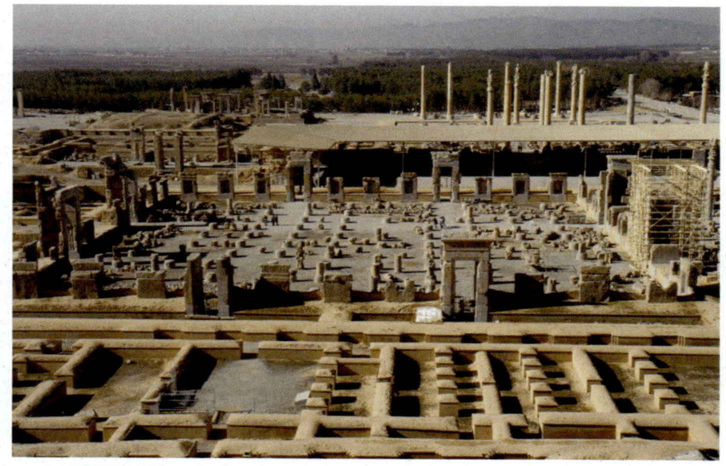

**2-16:** Royal Audience hall, Persepolis, Iran, 518–465 BCE.

This new powerful Persian dynasty conquered not only Mesopotamia but also Egypt, in 525 BCE, and then fought the Greeks in and around Athens, even sacking the Acropolis, in 480 BCE.

The best examples of Persian art come from the now mostly destroyed administrative palace complex at Persepolis in modern Iran. No monumental temples remain from the Achaemenid dynasty since religious festivals, following the Zoroastrian tradition, were held outdoors.

The approach to the palace complex was down a long avenue and through a series of impressive gates guarded by lamassu type beasts. The palace, begun by Darius I in 518 BCE, was constructed on a platform 40 feet high which was accessed by a double stairway. According to ancient accounts about the palace, it was designed on a grid plan, and displayed a blend of materials and stylistic influences from across the empire; including cedar from Lebanon, bricks from Babylon, gold from Bactria, and silver from Egypt.

The most important room in the palace was the raised royal audience hall, or **apadana.** The hall measured 217 feet square and was constructed using 36 columns

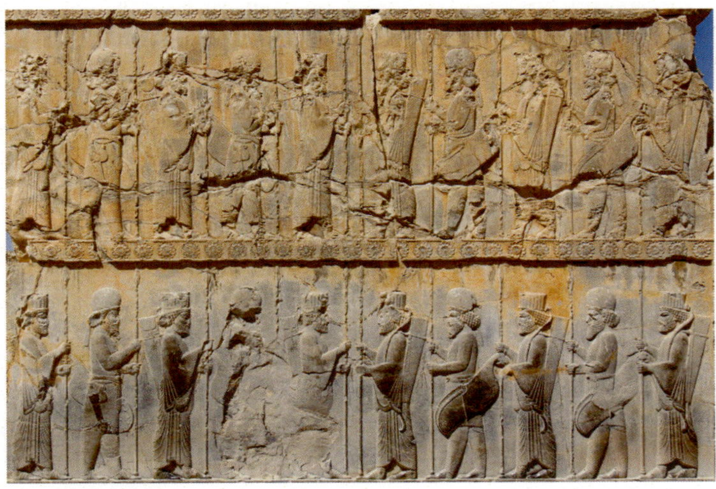

**2-17:** Processional Frieze, Terrace of the Apadana, at Persepolis, Iran, 518–465 BCE.

40 feet tall supporting a wooden roof. The apadana was reached by a broad ceremonial double staircase that was decorated with low relief sculptures of royal processions.

The reliefs on the walls of the terrace and staircases depict processions of nobles and dignitaries from the 23 subject nations under Persian rule. The individual figures are shown in native costumes and carry a variety of appropriate and traditional gifts as offerings. The finely chiseled details reflect influence from Egyptian, Assyrian, and even archaic Greek artistic styles. This synthesis of style is evidence of the substantial interchange of art and ideas across the whole of the Mediterranean and Near East. Interestingly, traces of pigment on the stone relief suggest that some or most of the reliefs would have been brightly painted.

The palace complex at Persepolis was ultimately destroyed by Alexander the Great in 330 BCE in a gesture that suggested he was not only destroying the palace but also, metaphorically, the past imperial power of the Persians.

Name ______________________________ Date ____________

## Chapter 2

# The Ancient Near East Questions

1. The development of what written language marked the beginning of writing?

2. What is the term for a high temple platform utilized in Sumerian architecture?

3. What work contains the first known example of narrative relief sculpture?

4. What is the term that correlates the size of a figure to his/her importance? Describe one work that shows this.

5. Define votive offering and give an example from this chapter where this term applies.

6. The Warka Vase and Standard of Ur are both organized utilizing what design element?

7. A composition that is symmetrical on either side of a central figure is called what? Which work from the Royal Cemetery at Ur depicts this type of composition?

8. What was the primary purpose of cylinder seals within Sumerian society?

9. What purpose did the lamassus serve? Describe their unique design.

10. Which ruler successfully ended the period of Persian imperial dominance and razed the site of Persepolis to the ground?

# THE ART OF ANCIENT EGYPT

## Chapter 3

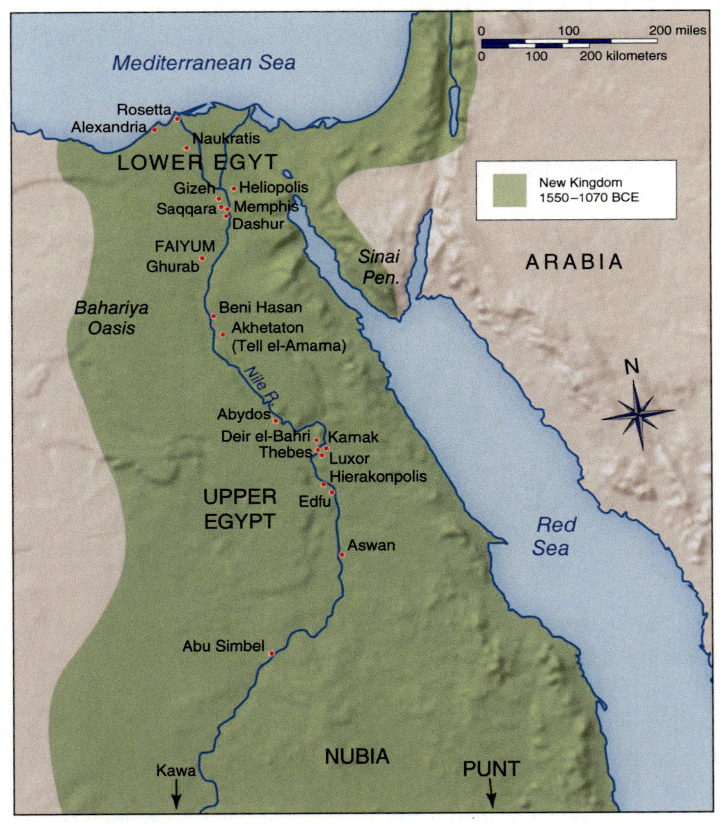


Ancient Egypt.

The cultures of Ancient Egypt and Ancient Mesopotamia were advancing at roughly the same time. However, different from Ancient Mesopotamia, in Egypt there was continuity; continuity in terms of rulership, culture, language, and religion.

Ancient Egyptian culture was shaped, in many ways, by its geography. Egyptian civilization grew up along the Nile River, which served literally as its lifeline. It provided water, food, shelter, nutrients for the soil, as well as a means of travel and trade. The yearly Nile floods also provided a kind of rhythm and cyclical quality to daily life.

The Nile River valley is an intensely green and lush oasis in an otherwise brutal desert. The vast barren stretches of desert that flank the river on either side served as natural borders, both isolating and protecting Egypt.

The Nile, the longest river in the world at approximately 4000 miles long, flows from the high mountains in the middle of Africa (in the south) toward the Nile Delta (in the north). That means that it flows from south to north, because, like all rivers, it flows downhill.

In terms of geography, and the manner in which one describes the territory that is Egypt, the northern part of the Nile valley is called *Lower Egypt* and the southern part of the Nile valley is called *Upper Egypt*.

Historians tend to divide Egypt's long history into periods based on dates, dynasties, and the succession of rulers. Scholars often do not agree on these subdivisions and therefore there are periods called 1st, 2nd, and 3rd Intermediate (dynasties 7–10, 14–17, 21–25 respectively), as well as the Late period (26–31), and then the Greco-Roman period or Hellenistic period which includes the Ptolemaic dynasty.

For the purposes of this chapter, in the context of art, the major periods are:

| | | |
|---|---|---|
| Early Dynastic: | c. 3100–2685 BCE | (Dynasties 1–2) |
| Old Kingdom: | c. 2685–2180 BCE | (Dynasties 3–6) |
| Middle Kingdom: | c. 2130–1700 BCE | (Dynasties 11–14) |
| New Kingdom: | c. 1550–1070 BCE | (Dynasties 18–20) |

Egyptian culture embraced polytheism (belief in many gods), and its religious beliefs and practices were extremely complex, though they remained remarkably consistent over a period of about 3000 years. The major deity was the sun-god Amon (also called Re or Ra or Aten). Other major deities included: Hathor, the sky goddess who was the mother, wife, and daughter of Ra; Osiris, the god of the underworld; Osiris' wife Isis, a fertility goddess and mother of their son Horus; Maat, the goddess of truth and order; and Anubis, the god of cemeteries and embalming.

The Egyptian gods were often depicted in composite form as both man and animal. Therefore, Horus was often depicted as a hawk or a hawk-headed man; Hathor as a cow, Amon as a falcon, Anubis as a jackal, and Maat as a feather.

The Egyptian belief in an eternal life after physical death was paramount and explains not only the fascination with the preservation of the body after death, through mummification, but also the desire to create tombs that could hold offerings to be used by the deceased in the afterlife.

The Egyptians did not have an unnatural or morbid fascination with death, rather they planned for happiness and abundance in their eternal afterlife, a period that would last considerably longer than their relatively short earthly one.

Our earliest evidence of what is often called pre-dynastic art, or art that predates the beginning of the Early Dynastic period, includes pottery, painted tomb decoration, and other artifacts, dating to at least as early as c. 3500 BCE.

In the pre-dynastic centuries Upper and Lower Egypt were separate rival kingdoms. The unification of these separate kingdoms, c. 3100 BCE, is often attributed to the Pharaoh Narmer.

The palette of King Narmer is an object that seems to refer to that Unification.

A palette is a utilitarian object used for mixing kohl, the Egyptian black cosmetic that was worn by both men and women. Kohl was used around the eyes to shield the sun, as an antiseptic, and perhaps for apotropaic or dramatic effect.

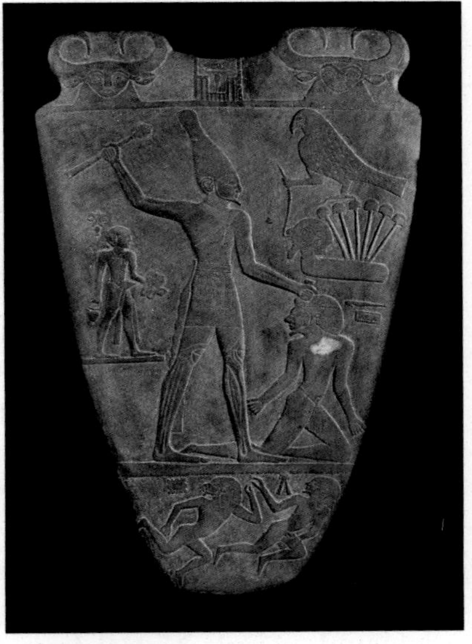

**3-1:** Palette of King Narmer, Slate, Hierakonpolis, c. 3100 BCE, 2′1″, Egyptian Museum, Cairo.

The Palette of Narmer is a formalized and enlarged version of the common household kohl-grinding palette; it may have served some ritual function, since it was found in a temple precinct with other objects dedicated to the god Horus.

The Palette is carved in low relief on both sides. On one side King Narmer wears the **White Crown of Upper Egypt** (the "bowling pin" crown) and on the other he wears the **Red Crown of Lower Egypt** (the "curlicue" crown). That he is depicted wearing both crowns on the same object would seem to indicate that he is ruler of both kingdoms. Not only is this artifact one of the earliest historical artworks preserved from ancient Egypt, but it appears to record an historical event: the actual unification of the two kingdoms.

At the top, on both sides, are heads of the goddess Hathor, represented as a cow with a woman's face. She is appropriate here since she is the goddess of the heavens and a divine protector of the pharaoh.

Between the heads is a hieroglyph for Narmer's name and title.

## On the back

The back side (the one without the depression for mixing the kohl), is divided into figural registers or friezes.

In the large central register is the pharaoh, wearing his crown of Upper Egypt, holding an enemy by the hair. The much larger figure of the king raises his hand to smite the enemy with a large club. The captive man is not meant to represent a single individual but instead stands for an army or whole race of people.

This posture of the king, arm raised to smite a kneeling enemy, becomes the standard representation or formula for portraying an Egyptian pharaoh's victory over his enemy. Behind the king is his sandal bearer.

In front of the king is the god Horus, in the form of a hawk with human arms. The god holds a captive enemy by a nose rope. The captive enemy, actually incorporated into a hieroglyph, is shown with a papyrus plant growing out of it. This is intended to symbolize the land of Lower Egypt because papyrus grows well in the marshy land of the Egypt delta (the plant symbol for Upper Egypt is the lotus).

In the lowest register are two more defeated enemies. Notice they have the same hairstyle and beard as the enemy depicted above.

## On the front

In the central register are two feline creatures with impossibly long necks (serpopards) that entwine to form the circular depression that, in a normal utilitarian palette, would have held the ground kohl. On either side, and significantly smaller, two men try to control the exotic beasts. This intertwining is perhaps intended to symbolize the idea of unification, or more precisely of the two separate kingdoms coming together and uniting.

In the register above is Narmer, again barefoot, this time wearing the red curlicue Crown of Lower Egypt. Narmer walks in a procession that leads him to inspect the defeated enemy. Notice how they have all been decapitated and their severed heads placed neatly between their feet. In the bottom register there is another symbolic representation of Narmer, this time in the form of a large bull. The bull (Narmer) is shown trampling his enemy underfoot and breaking down the walls surrounding a citadel.

On the palette, as in other representations, the pharaoh is depicted as performing his functions and achieving his victories isolated and separated from others. He alone is responsible for the triumphs over the enemy; he alone is invincible and divine.

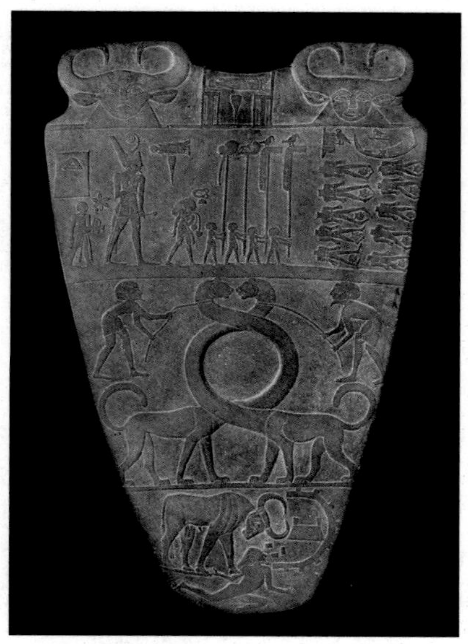

**3-2:** Palette of King Narmer, "front side" Slate, Hierakonpolis, ca. 3100 BCE, 2'1" Egyptian Museum, Cairo.

The palette is important not only as a historical record but also as an example of the Egyptian formula for figural representation that would last for some 3000 years. The Egyptians developed a highly formalized and static system for the depiction of the human figure. The human figure is almost always shown with a profile head, legs, and arms, but with a frontal view of the torso and eyes.

The palette was discovered in almost perfect condition in Hierakonpolis, the ancient capital of Upper Egypt, in the late 19th century.

The remarkable consistency in Egyptian art and culture may be attributed in part to the ever-present and unwavering belief in several basic concepts:

- The pharaoh (king) is divine.
- The preparation in this life, for the safety and happiness in the afterlife, is of extreme importance.

- The soul, or *ka,* lives on after the death of the body.
- A person's tomb must supply all that the owner would need in the eternal afterlife.

## Egyptian Monumental Architecture

One of the earliest examples of monumental architecture in Egypt is the mastaba (from the Arabic word for "bench"). The mastaba was the standard tomb type for the rich in early Egypt. It should be noted that stone was generally reserved for tomb architecture and the king's palace; almost all other structures were made from mud bricks.

The mastaba was a rectangular brick or stone structure with sloping sides erected over an underground burial chamber. A shaft connected the burial chamber with the outside so that the ka, or soul, could have access into and out of the tomb.

The burial chamber was surrounded by storage rooms and compartments which held the goods needed for the afterlife. Often these rooms and goods exceeded the space of the actual burial chamber and spilled out onto corridors and hallways.

The interior walls of the mastaba were often decorated with frescoes and relief carvings depicting daily life scenes. These scenes were intended to magically comfort, nourish, and amuse the deceased.

Built into the mastaba, or sometimes attached to it, was a small room or chapel that was used for housing a statue of the deceased. This small concealed chamber is called a serdab. The serdab, often designed with two holes or slits at the eye level of the statue, was the place from which the deceased could "view" the rituals of his cult. The ancient Egyptians believed that the statue in the serdab would serve as a "back up" vessel for the *ka* should the original mummified body be destroyed.

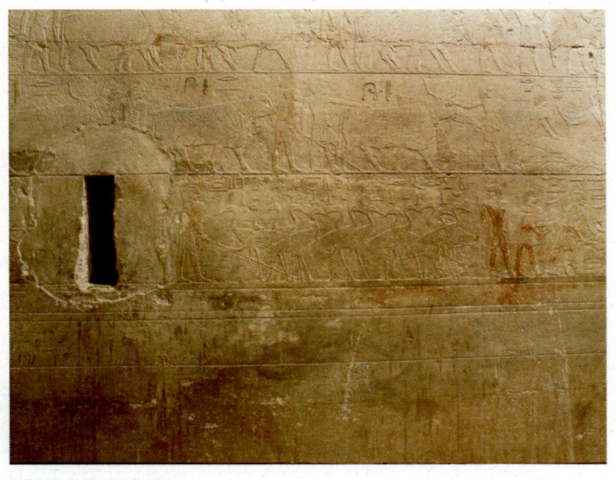

**3-3:** Slit in relief decorated wall of sealed serdab, tomb of Ty, Old Kingdom, 5th cen BCE, Saqqara.

## The First Pyramid

The first pyramid in Egypt was a stepped pyramid. It was built by a man named Imhotep, who was the royal builder/architect for the third dynasty pharaoh Djoser (r.c. 2660–2630 BCE).

Imhotep, who served as the king's chancellor and the high priest of the sun-god, is also the first known and recorded name of an artist in history.

The tomb is one of the oldest stone structures in Egypt and is the first truly grand royal tomb. It is located on the west side of the Nile River in Saqqara in Lower Egypt.

Saqqara was the necropolis (from the Greek meaning "city of the dead": necro = dead and polis = city) for the capital city of Memphis.

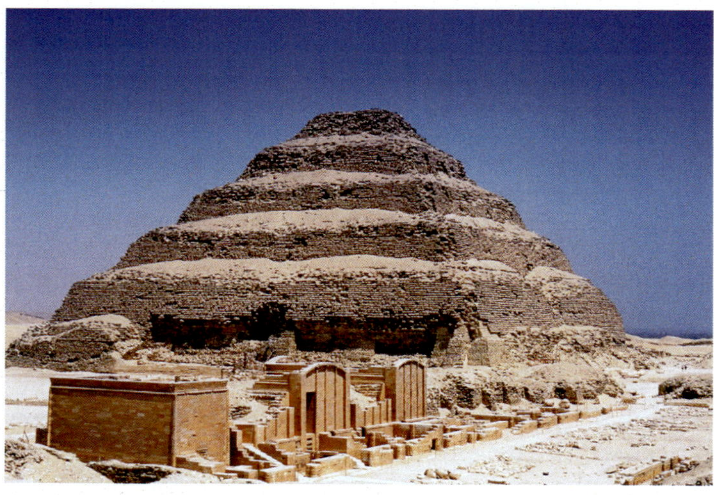

**3-4:** Imhotep, Stepped Pyramid of Djoser, Saqqara, c. 2681–2662 BCE, 204′ tall.

The stepped pyramid began as a large mastaba that was then stacked with progressively smaller mastasbas on top. The burial chamber, which usually included the mummified body (contained within a sarcophagus), was located underground, beneath the structure.

The function of Djoser's stepped pyramid was not only to protect his mummified body and his possessions, but also to symbolize, by its great size, c. 200 feet tall, the pharaoh's god-like and absolute power.

The stepped pyramid stands at the center of a great mortuary precinct that is bounded by a rectangular enclosure wall some 34 feet high and over a mile long. The complex included several buildings including a large funerary temple, smaller shrines, chapels, several courtyards, and over a dozen gateways.

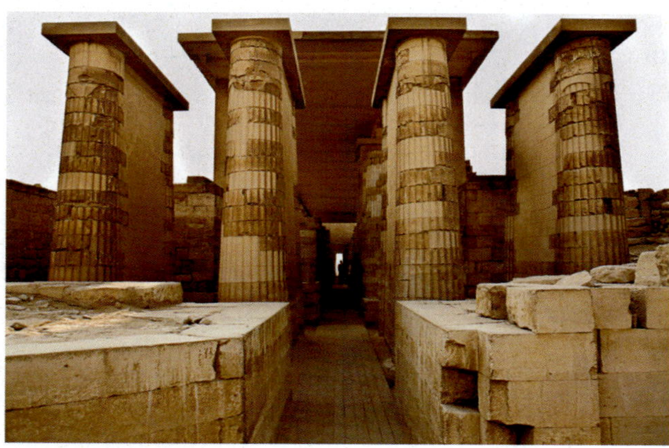

**3-5:** Engaged columns, Southeast entrance, Stepped Pyramid of Djoser, Saqqara, ca. 2681–2662 BCE.

Only the southeast gateway provides entrance to the complex. At that location is an impressive entrance corridor lined with engaged columns (*engaged* means the columns are attached to or inset into the walls). The columns' design imitates bundles of reeds or papyrus stalks. The stone columns at the Saqqara complex, which certainly inspired the Greeks later, are often considered the first stone columns in the history of architecture.

# The Old Kingdom

## The Great Pyramids at Gizeh

On the West bank of the Nile River in Lower Egypt, just across from the modern city of Cairo, are the three Great Pyramids. All three were built during the Old Kingdom, and all three were built under pharaohs during the Fourth Dynasty. They are identified with the pharaohs Khufu (r. 2551–2528 BCE), Khafre (r. 2520–2494 BCE), and Menkaure (r. 2490–2472 BCE).

Though there is debate as to the origin of the design for the smooth-sided pyramid, most scholars agree that the pyramids are symbols of the sun's rays. Their form symbolizes the rays that shine down from the sun and that the Pharaoh would use to ascend to the heavens. When completed each pyramid would have been dressed with smooth gleaming white limestone and the tip would have been covered with a thin layer of gold.

All three of the pyramids are aligned to the four cardinal points with the entrance to each one on the north face. Each pyramid was also originally circled by a large enclosure wall.

The three pyramids at the Gizeh pyramid complex are:

| | | |
|---|---|---|
| **Khufu (Cheops):** | c. 2551–2528 BCE | (oldest and the largest) |
| **Khafre (Kephren):** | c. 2520–2494 BCE | (associated with the Sphinx) |
| **Menkaure (Mykerinus):** | c. 2490–2472 BCE | (smallest) |

Khufu's pyramid is the largest and oldest of the pyramids. Except for the galleries and burial chamber this pyramid is almost solid stone. Surrounding this huge pyramid are a royal cemetery with fifteen mastabas on the west, boat pits on the south, and three small queens' pyramids on the east. The three small pyramids on the east side, called queen's pyramids, are for his daughter (the mother of Khafre), his wife/sister, and another queen.

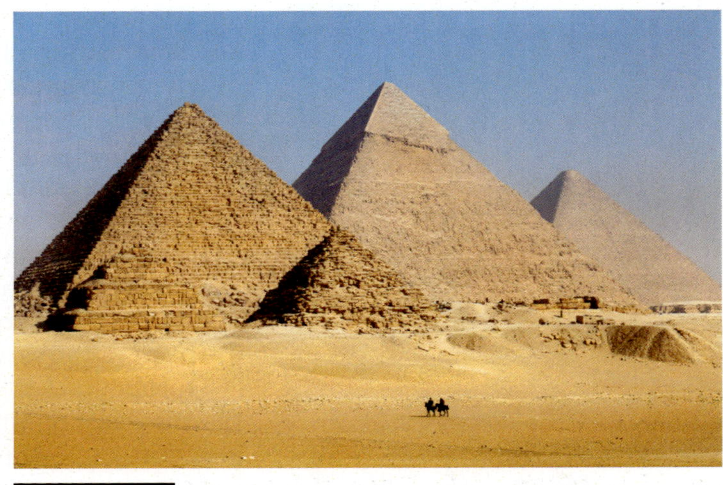

**3-6:** Great Pyramids, Limestone, Gizeh, Egypt, 2551–2472 BCE.

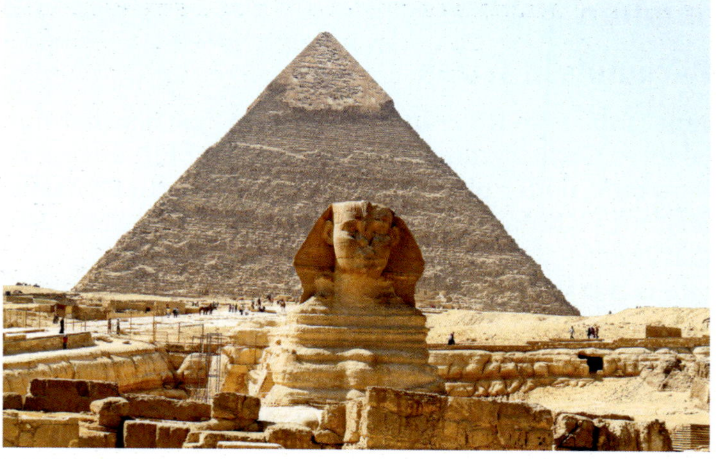

**3-7:** Pyramid of Khafre with Great Sphinx in foreground, sandstone, Gizeh, Egypt, 2520–2494 BCE.

Khufu's size is staggering. At the base, the length of one side is 775 feet, and originally it stood over 480 feet tall. It contains approximately 2.3 million blocks of stone, each weighing an average of 2.5 tons. Unlike the mastaba and step pyramid where the burial chambers lie beneath the structure, here the actual burial place of the Pharaoh is at the center of the pyramid.

Khafre was Khufu's son and his tomb is slightly smaller than that of his father, though it tends to look bigger because it is built on higher ground. It is 448 feet tall and one side of its base is 706 feet long.

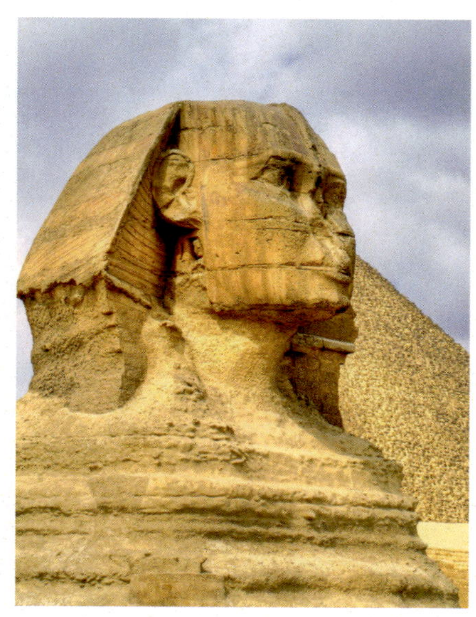

**3-8:** Great Sphinx, sandstone, Gizeh, Egypt, c. 2520–2494 BCE, approx. 65′ tall.

It is also the only one of the three pyramids with any of its limestone casing intact, just at the top. We have a much better sense of the function and significance of the buildings associated with the pyramid since much of the original funerary complex has been reconstructed.

The complex included not just the pyramid but also smaller mortuary temples and the remains of a covered walkway or causeway that led from the river to the pyramid. This causeway was decorated on the interior with painted reliefs. Also preserved is a small valley temple at the head of the causeway.

Just beyond Khafre's valley temple causeway sits the giant Sphinx. The Sphinx, with the body of a lion and a human head, serves as a protector or guardian to Khafre's pyramidal tomb. The face of the Sphinx is believed to be the face of the Pharaoh Khafre himself. The Sphinx was often used by the pharaohs as symbols of royal power and strength. The composite form suggests that the pharaoh possessed the strength and courage of the lion combined with human and divine intelligence. That it is the face of a pharaoh is clear because it wears the royal headdress, or nemes, and had another royal symbol, the sacred cobra, or uraeus, at the forehead.

The colossal figure of the Sphinx is 260 feet long, 20 feet wide, 65 feet tall, and faces east. It is actually carved from the living rock, which is sandstone, making it one of the largest single-stone statues on earth. Since it is solid stone it has no interior space. In the 18th Dynasty the Pharaoh Thutmose IV (r. 1397–1388 BCE) restored and removed the sand around the Sphinx and installed a large carved stone stele between its front paws.

A legend states that it was Napoleon who blew the Sphinx's nose off. He did not. There are drawings from the year 1737, made well before his arrival in 1798, that show that the nose was already gone. There is, however, some evidence from the 15th century that says a radical Muslim in the 14th century was opposed to the face because it was against Islamic religion to show the human form, so he sawed the nose off and destroyed it.

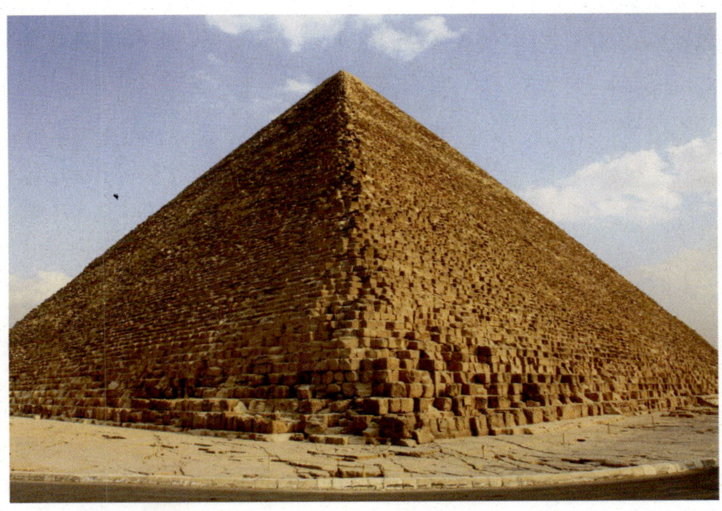

**3-9:** Pyramid of Menkaure, Limestone and Granite, Gizeh, Egypt, 2490–2472 BCE.

The smallest pyramid is that of Menkaure, son of Kafre and grandson of Kufu. This pyramid is only 215 feet tall and the length of one side is 339 feet. It is only about one-tenth the mass of Khufu's pyramid, though its builders did attempt to encase the lower courses of stone in granite.

On the south side of the pyramid are three smaller pyramids, none of which were completed.

## Egyptian Sculpture

Statues were important in Egyptian culture, particularly for a tomb. They served in some cases as literal stand ins for the mummified body of the deceased, so that if the body was destroyed, the ka had a place to reside. The statue was literally meant to take the place of the person it represented and was intended to last forever. The statues of the pharaohs were not intended to be portrait likenesses of the individual but instead were idealized and perfected and intended as symbols of the pharaoh's divinity and power.

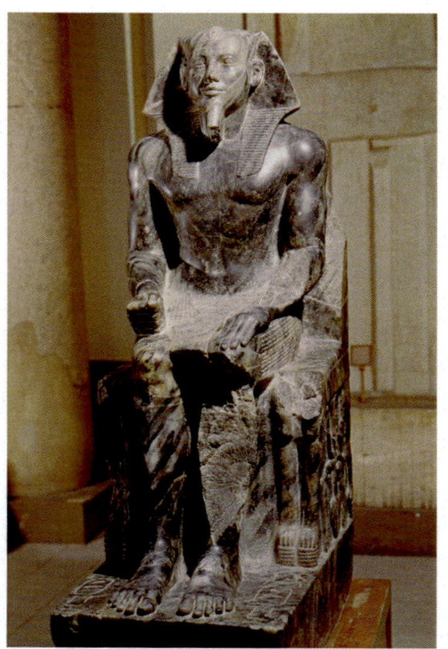

**3-10:** Seated Statue of Khafre, Diorite, Gizeh, Egypt, 2520–2494 BCE, 5′6″ high, Egyptian Museum, Cairo.

This seated portrait statue is carved in diorite, an incredibly hard dark stone that was imported from the south. It was carved, along with at least 23 others, for Khafre's mortuary temple near the Sphinx.

Khafre is depicted seated on a throne, wearing a short pleated kilt. He wears the false beard and on his head he wears the nemes, or royal headdress, that falls in pleated folds over his shoulders. Behind his head sits the god Horus who protects the pharaohs. The throne is composed of stylized lions at the front with images of the lotus (Upper Egypt) and papyrus (Lower Egypt) plants depicted on the sides.

The portrait is an idealized one. He has a perfectly muscled firm body and a smooth, perfect face. It therefore seems timeless and is an appropriate image for a pharaoh, who is revered like a god. It is intended as an image of power, serenity, and control. Adding to this sense of control is the work's symmetry, and block like quality.

The composition, with the firmly seated figure with his arms close to his sides, his feet securely planted, staring straight ahead, made from hard, compact stone, seems impenetrable and unbreakable. It reflects in all its parts its purpose: to survive for eternity.

The seated statue is, however, only one type of formal portrait, part of a fairly limited range of the types of images that were produced in the Old Kingdom. Another type is the standing portrait. These standing portraits can represent a single person, a couple, or rarely, a group.

An example of a royal double portrait, found in Menkaure's valley temple, is that of Menkaure and his Queen Khamerernebty II.

This portrait of Menkaure and his wife is, like the one of Khafre, idealized. The figures are stiff, solid, symmetrical, and still attached to the stone block from which they are carved. There is a conventional pose here as well. The standing pose is one that shows the figure fully frontal, arms straight down, hands clenched, and with the typical left foot forward stride. Menkaure wears the typical accoutrement of the pharaoh, the false beard, nemes, and short kilt. His wife is depicted in the same pose, except her right arm encircles her husband at the waist, a gesture that signifies their marital status.

There are traces of paint found on the sculpture, so this one, like most of Egyptian sculpture, would have been painted.

Notice that Menkaure holds something in both of his closed hands. Many images of pharaohs and officials, both in sculpture and in paint, from the 4th Dynasty forward share this attribute. Though there is a great deal of debate about what is held, it is most commonly believed that these are small rolled or folded pieces of cloth. Some scholars have also suggested that they might be stone cylinder seals, and others, including the Director of UFO research in Russia, have labeled them, rather mysteriously, the "wands of Horus."

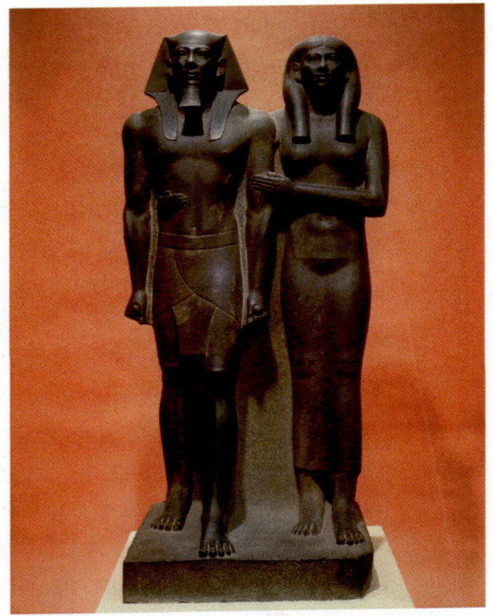

**3-11:** Menkaure and Khamerernebty II (?), Graywacke, Gizeh, c. 2490–2472 BCE, 4′6″ high, Museum of Fine Arts, Boston.

In addition to the very formal stone portraiture of pharaohs there was another trend in Old Kingdom portraiture that reveals a very different attitude. This is a type of painted statuary, some carved from stone and others from wood, that are much more realistic or naturalistic in their representation.

This sculpture comes from a mastaba in Saqqara, and most likely depicts the tomb's owner, identified as Kay. Kay was a scribe at court, and is depicted seated on the ground, with a papyrus scroll in his hand and a pen or stylus (now lost) in the other. Since Kay is not a divine pharaoh he can be represented in a more human and natural manner. Instead of ageless and perfected, the artist depicts Kay as he may have really been, with big ears, thin lips, and a paunch belly. These attributes, in this case, may represent Kay as wealthy and experienced with age. Notice how natural his hands appear compared to those of the pharaohs that have flat hands or clenched fists. His highly-prized position in the court, as scribe, still makes him a member of a higher social class.

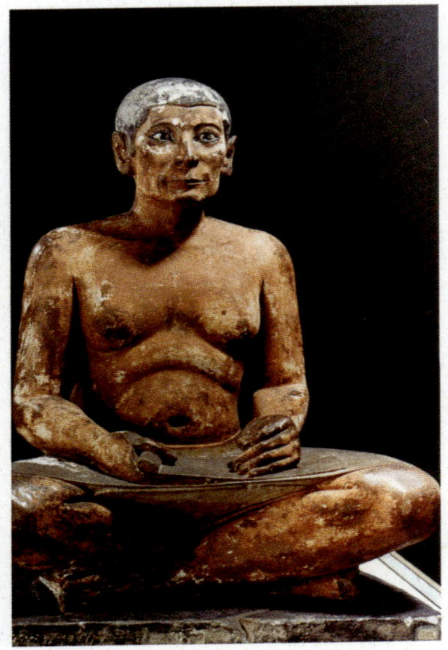

**3-12:** Seated Scribe, painted limestone, Saqqara, c. 2400 BCE, height 1′9″, Louvre, Paris.

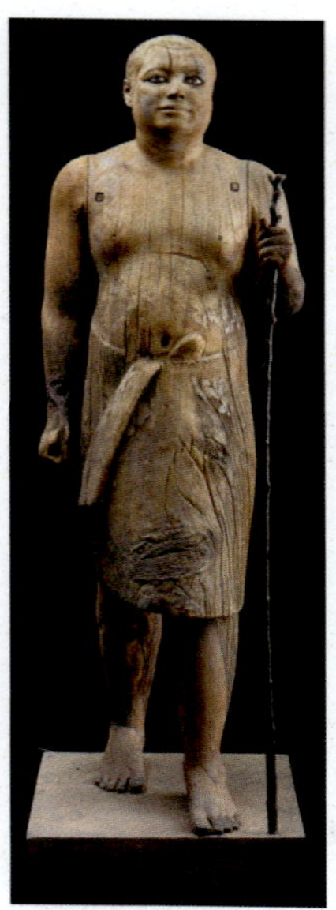

**3-13:** Ka-Aper, painted wood, Saqqara, c. 2450–2350, height 3′7″ Egyptian Museum, Cairo.

Similar naturalism and sensitivity are evident in another portrait statue, this time carved of wood.

This well-preserved painted wood sculpture was also found in the owner's mastaba at Saqqara.

Ka-Aper was an official at court, the walking stick in his left hand signifies his rank as an official. Although the pose is fairly stiff and arranged in the left foot advanced pose, it does show a new freedom of movement. This freedom is due in part to the fact that he is free-standing and not a part of any larger block of stone or wood. His physical features, such as the round head, full cheeks, paunch belly, thick legs, and eyes inlaid with rock crystal, give the statue a strikingly life-like appearance.

It is interesting to note that in general, in the history of art in western culture, that as the importance or social rank of an individual decreases, the level of realism depicted often increases.

The dead were also depicted in their tombs, not only in sculptural form, but also in relief carvings and mural paintings.

Ti was an official of the 5th Dynasty and his titles included royal hairdresser and overseer of cattle and poultry. His tomb, perhaps the most famous of all non-royal tombs in Egypt, was completely covered with painted low relief carvings depicting agricultural scenes, banquets, and hunting scenes. These types of scenes are intended to represent bounty, wealth, leisure,

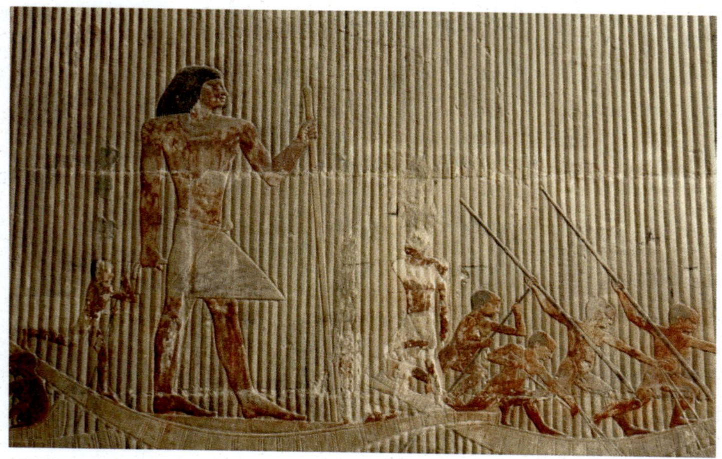

**3-14:** Ti Watching a Hippopotamus hunt, painted limestone relief, Saqqara, c. 2450–2350 BCE, height approx. 4′, Saqqara, Egypt.

and therefore, success. The image of the successful hunt was used as a metaphor for success in the eternal life.

Ti, depicted much larger than the other figures, is shown standing in a boat, as his servants use their long poles to push their way through thick plants.

The plants tower above the figures in their boats and terminate in thick flowers and foliage that are populated with small animals, birds, and even a little fox. Notice too that Ti stands in the traditional composite view (left leg advanced pose) but that his servants are depicted in much more active and varied poses. Ti is not an active participant in the hunt but in this case is a rather passive one, much like his ka would be.

## The Middle Kingdom

From c. 2130 BCE–1700 BCE Egypt was enveloped in a series of civil and invader wars. After this, until c. 1560 BCE, Egypt was ruled for a time by the Hyksos pharaohs; or "foreign rulers".

There were several major artistic and architectural innovations during the Middle Kingdom. One of the most striking innovations was the integration or depiction of emotion and age in the depiction of the pharaohs; another was the development of the rock-cut tomb. In sculpture, the Middle Kingdom was responsible for a new statuary type, called a block sculpture.

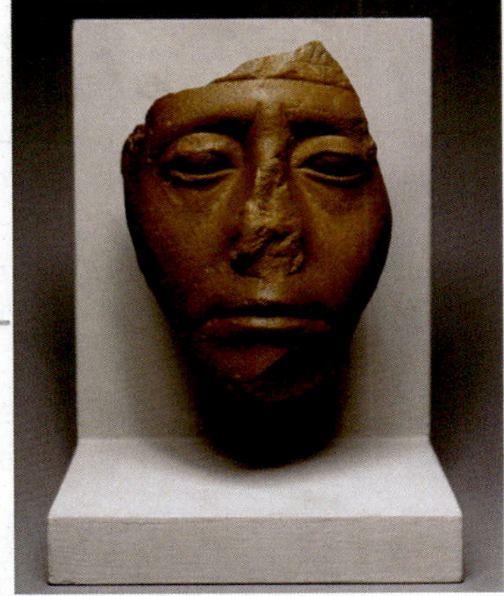

**3-15:** Portrait of Senusret III, Quartzite, c. 1860 BCE, 6 1/2", The Metropolitan Museum of Art, New York.

The fragmentary portrait of the Pharaoh Sesostris (also Senusret or Sesostris) reveals a new interest in expression and age. Unlike the portraits of the pharaohs before him, who were generally represented as idealized and ageless, this portrait shows the face of a mature man. The face also seems to reflect a kind of wise, experienced, and even concerned ruler, evidenced by his furrowed brow and deep heavy-lidded eyes. Perhaps the image was intended to reflect the hardship of the years of civil unrest in Egypt prior to his rule, and the burden of his role as military commander. Nonetheless, his military campaigns and reign of prosperity led to acknowledgement of him as the greatest ruler in Egypt during the whole of the Middle Kingdom.

Another innovation during the Middle Kingdom was the use of rock-cut tombs. While mastabas continued to be the most popular burial type, there was a marked increase in the use of rock-cut tombs during the period. These rock-cut tombs,

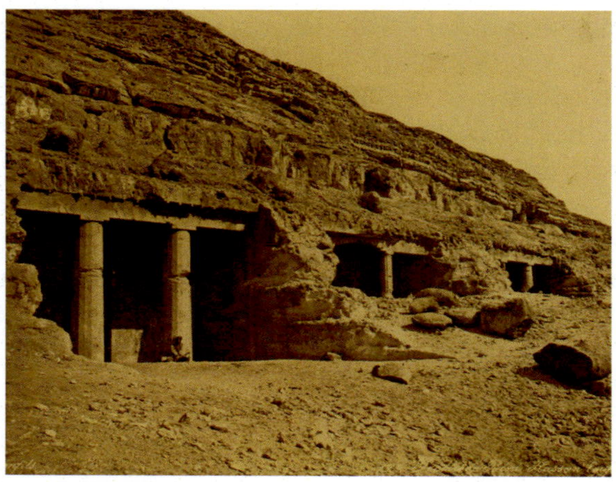

**3-16:** Rock-Cut Tombs, Beni Hasan, 1950–1900 BCE (19th cen photo).

which continued to be built into the New Kingdom, were cut into the cliffs to create artificial cave chambers, and became the most popular type for aristocrats and court officials. Later, Thutmose I (ruled c. 1504–1492 BCE) was the first pharaoh to be buried in a rock-cut tomb.

Beni Hasan, located halfway between Memphis and Thebes, is where the best surviving examples of Middle Kingdom rock cut-tombs remain. The tombs are located high on the cliff side on the east side of the Nile. The tombs are reached via a long, steep flight of stone steps that lead up from the river below. There are about 39 tombs here of which only 12 of have interior decoration.

The tombs were permanent monumental resting places that were decorated and elaborated with painted relief carvings, textual inscriptions, and sculptures. The tombs were hollowed out of the rock and often preceded by a columned porch that led to a burial chamber.

The interior decoration of the tomb consisted of painted reliefs that showed typical scenes from daily life and, interestingly, a new focus on military scenes and images of foreigners.

Amenemhet was the regional governor and commander-in-chief to the Pharaoh Senusret I, and his tomb is a little more elaborate than many of the earlier tombs located here.

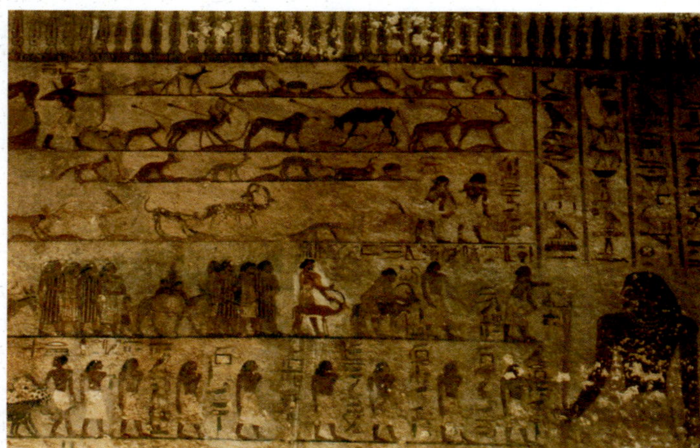

**3-17:** Tomb of Amenemhet (BH2), rock-cut tomb, Beni Hasan, Egypt, c. 1950–1900 BCE.

The tomb has a small courtyard and a double-columned portico at the entrance to the tomb chapel. The chapel itself is a large rectangular space with four polygonal columns that then open into the burial chamber. The main axis leads to a large statue niche that once contained a seated statue of the owner.

The wall murals depict scenes similar to earlier tombs, with agriculture and industries, hunting in the desert, military activities and funeral rites. Amenemhet is depicted seated with his wife in front of a table containing various produce from the lands that he oversees.

Another innovation of the Middle Kingdom period is the introduction of a type of statuary called a block statue, a type that would remain popular for almost 2000 years.

Block statues were mostly used as funerary monuments of non-royals. They generally consist of a man seated with his knees drawn up to his chest and his arms folded on top his knees. Often, these figures are depicted wearing a garment that conceals the entire body. There were two main types of these statues: one with feet that protrude from under the garment and one without protruding feet. In some cases the 'body' of the sculpture encompasses another smaller figure, sometimes a wife, child, or even the façade of a small temple. These statues are frequently covered in hieroglyphic inscriptions.

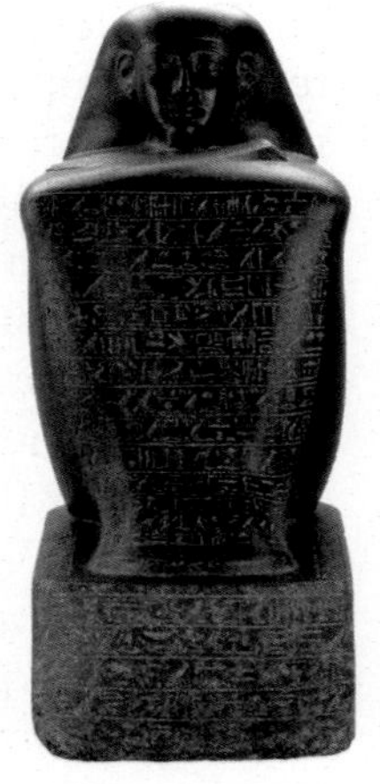

**3-18:** Block statue of Sennefer, Thebes, Egypt, c. 1450 BCE, 2'9", British Museum.

In this later example of a block sculpture , we see Sennefer, a royal and court official for the Pharaoh Thutmose III. The sculpture is of extremely high quality evidenced by the serene expression of the figure as well as the smooth finish and lustrous polish of the stone. Three major inscriptions on the block statue include prayers for Sennefer, a speech by him to the gods asking that he be well provided for in his afterlife, and one that records the names of his parents.

## New Kingdom

The New Kingdom in Egypt is generally dated from c. 1550–1070 BCE, and includes the 18th, 19th, and 20th Dynasties. It was a period of expansion and extended contact and trade with Asia and the Aegean, and the development of a new capital city in Upper Egypt. The capital of Egypt was moved from its Old Kingdom home at Memphis in Lower Egypt, to the new capital at Thebes in Upper Egypt. Thebes was built up on both sides of the Nile with grand palaces, temples, and tombs. The first pharaoh of this new period in Egyptian history was Ahmose I (1550–1525), the first king of the 18th Dynasty.

One dramatic difference between the Old Kingdom and the New Kingdom is evident in burial practices and the location of royal tombs. In the New Kingdom, the building of royal pyramids was essentially abandoned in favor of rock-cut tombs. These tombs were located in the Valley of the Kings on the west bank of the Nile across from the capital, Thebes. The entrances to the tombs were hidden for security in an attempt to preserve their riches and the mummified kings inside. As of 2009, 63 tombs have been located and/or excavated in the Valley of the Kings, although unfortunately almost all had been discovered and robbed in antiquity.

The New Kingdom is also recognized for the building of vast royal mortuary temple complexes, sometimes called memorial complexes. These mortuary temples were often constructed adjacent to or near a royal tomb (though they were not the actual burial site). They were designed to commemorate the reign of the pharaoh and serve as a permanent site for worship during his reign and after his death.

These mortuary temple complexes were often impressive buildings that were lavishly decorated with painted reliefs, inscriptions, and sculptures.

One of the earliest and most impressive of the New Kingdom mortuary temples was built for the Pharaoh Hatshepsut. Hatshepsut is the first great female ruler about whom we have any written record. She ruled Egypt from c. 1479–1458 BCE.

Hatshepsut was the daughter of the Pharaoh Thutmose I and her reign is marked by a peaceful period which also saw the reestablishment of trade routes. Hatshepsut was a great patron of the arts and during her reign she commissioned hundreds of buildings, temples, and sculptures. Images of Hatshepsut vary considerably; some clearly showed her as female, others did not. Either way she was always depicted as a pharaoh, wearing the costume of the pharaoh, including the nemes, short kilt, and false beard. In most written inscriptions she is referred to as *his* majesty.

Unfortunately, after her death, her jealous stepson Thutmose III (Hatshepsut married her half brother Thutmose II, though they had no heirs), the son of her husband with a minor wife, tried to erase her image and memory by destroying all she had made, her name, and images of her. Luckily some survived.

Her most impressive commission was for the construction of her mortuary temple complex. This complex, located at Deir el-Bahri on the west bank of the Nile, was designed by her architect (and possibly lover) Senenmut.

Hatshepsut's immense temple is built into a large cliff face. It consists mainly of three ascending colonnaded terraces connected by a series of ramps. Each of the terraces is 97 feet in height and each has a double colonnade of square chamfered (beveled) piers. The temple would have been preceded by a long avenue lined by portrait sphinxes of the Pharaoh.

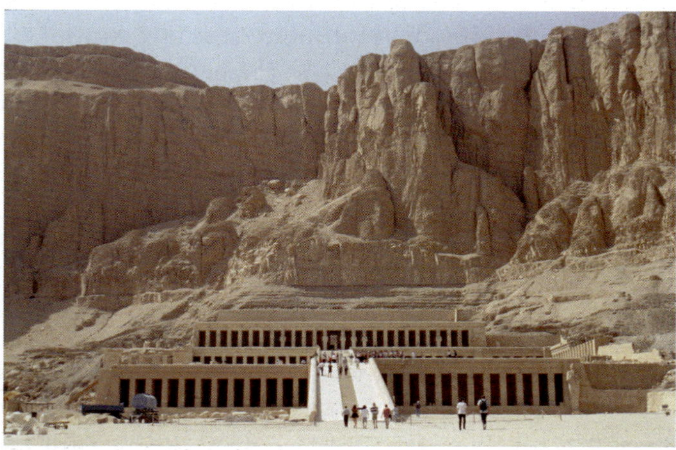

**3-19:** Mortuary Temple of Hatshepsut, Senenmut, Deir el-Bahri, c. 1473–1458 BCE.

The temple was originally lavishly decorated with sculpture, relief sculpture, and frescoes depicting the pharaoh. The painted images showed her as a king being crowned by her father Thutmose I, and many also showed her divine birth as a daughter of the sun-god Amen-Re. She was also shown in over 200 sculptural examples as a sphinx, and depicted in various poses standing, seated and kneeling, in various places around the temple.

In Hatshepsut's time the temple complex would not have appeared as blank and stark as it appears today. Instead, it would have been planted with gardens, plants, and trees. There also would have been water features making the whole complex appear lush and colorful, like an oasis.

Several examples of her statues survive though many have had to be heavily reconstructed after they were discovered smashed to pieces and discarded.

This statue is one of eight colossal statues that decorated the mortuary temple at Deir el-Bahri. Hatshepsut is depicted wearing the clothes of a male pharaoh, including the short kilt, nemes, and false beard. She is shown kneeling, holding two round offering jars, called *nw* jars, that she is in the act of presenting to the god Amen-Re. It is important to note that she is kneeling because she, the pharaoh, would only have ever kneeled in the presence of a god.

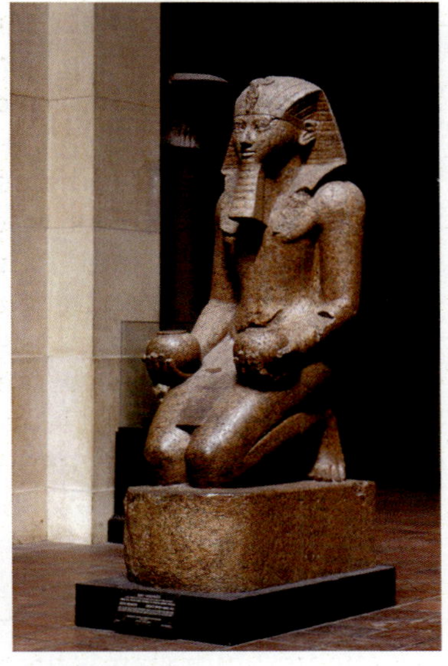

**3-20:** Hatshepsut with offering jars, Red granite, c. 1473–458 BCE, 8′6″, Metropolitan Museum of Art, New York.

Another image associated with the Pharoah Hatshepsut actually depicts her daughter and her architect, Senenmut.

Senenmut was Hatshepsut's chancellor and was her most trusted official. Senenmut held numerous (over 80) titles and positions, some of which included Overseer of the Works, Overseer of the Fields, Overseer of the Gardens of Amen, Conductor of Festivals, Steward of the King's Daughter Neferura, and Chief of the King.

This block statue depicts Senenmut and the princess Nefrura. Senenmut is shown seated with his robe wrapped around his knees, the typical pose of a block statue. Here the daughter of the Pharaoh is enfolded in the robe and just her tiny head is shown peeking through, as if she were seated on his lap and protected by him.

The whole of the block is covered with hieroglyphic inscriptions that refer to Senenmut, his role at court, and his adoration of Hatshepsut. One of the inscriptions reads:

"Companion greatly beloved, Keeper of the Palace, Keeper of the Heart of the King, making content the Lady of Both Lands, making all things come to pass for the Spirit of Her Majesty."

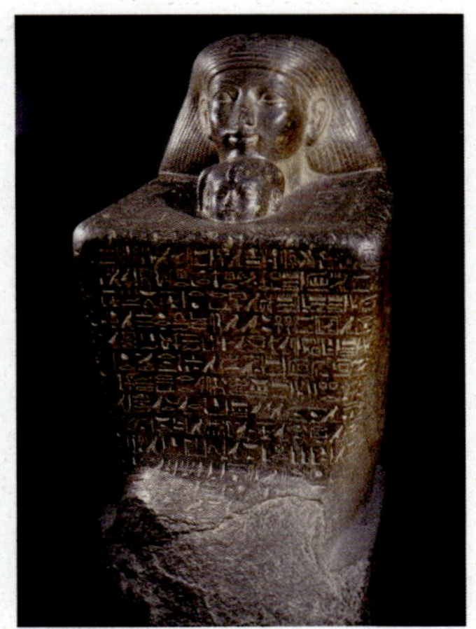

**3-21:** Senenmut with Princess Nefrura, Granite, c. 1460 BCE, 3′ ½″, Egyptian Museum, Berlin, Germany.

Another spectacular example of New Kingdon art is found in the mural paintings that decorate many tomb walls.

Mural paintings decorate almost every tomb in Egypt and were often low relief sculpture and painted. The stone surfaces would have been prepared using a whitewash layer and then pigments, mixed with a binder would have been painted onto the dry plaster. A thick coating of resin, or varnish, would have been applied over the top as a protective and glossy finish.

In some cases these frescoes have survived in very good condition, in part because of the dry climate and their isolated locations.

Nebamun was a Theban nobleman whose official titles included Scribe and Counter of Grain. From his tomb near Luxor come a series of painted fragments that reveal how vividly decorated his tomb once was.

One scene shows Nebamun standing in a small boat flushing birds from the papyrus swamp. He does this by threshing or beating the bushes with the stick he holds just behind his head. In front of him a cat, with gold gilt on the eye, has done well and caught birds in his front paws, back paws, and in his mouth. Nebamun too holds several birds in one hand. In front of him fly an assortment of brightly feathered birds and even a large butterfly.

Behind him stands his wife, who is wearing an elaborate dress, and beneath him, between his legs, sits his young daughter. Mother and daughter both carry lotus flowers. Notice the cone-like objects on the tops of the women's heads; they are scented fat cones, or unguent cones. The cones were intended to gloss and perfume the thick wigs worn by women, so that in the heat and with time the cones would melt and add luster and shine to the wigs while perfuming them.

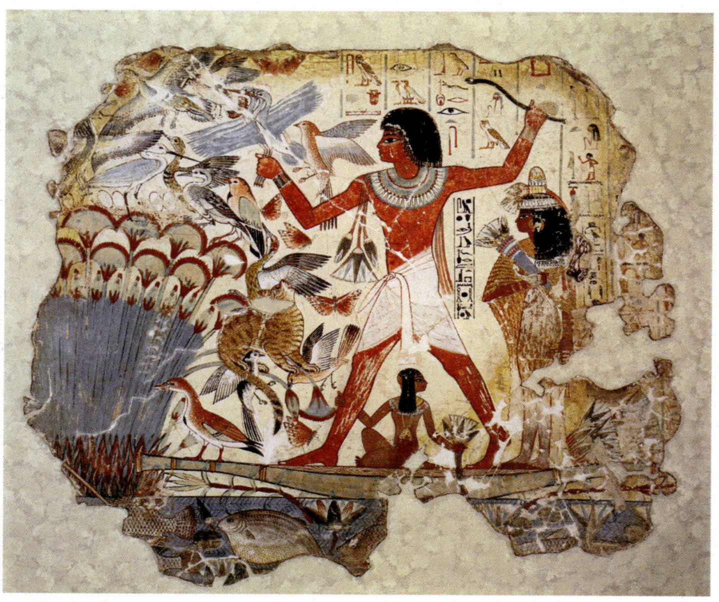

**3-22:** Fowling scene, Tomb of Nebamun, Thebes, 1400–1350, fresco on dry plaster, 2'8", British Museum, London.

The hieroglyphic inscription beneath his raised arms tells the viewer that Nebamun is enjoying recreation in his eternal afterlife.

Unlike Ti's tomb painting depicting the hippo hunt, here Nebamun does not just watch the activities but participates in them. While he does not flail about he does show action and some suggestion of movement. Notice even his back foot is slightly raised! Like in Ti's tomb there is attention to detail and the animals are rendered with great care and sensitivity.

Also from the tomb of Nebamun is a fragment that depicts musicians and dancers. This scene shows four female musicians who play instruments and clap while two young female dancers perform. The scene represents the type of funerary banquet and festivities that would have accompanied Nebamun's burial. Notice on the right the large wine amphoras.

The funerary banquet would have re-occurred once every year to commemorate the death and original banquet. By decorating the tomb with this scene, it is implied that this festive banquet occurs perpetually.

The composition shows that artists in the New Kingdom were experimenting with different views of the human body, as well as the depiction of motion. Remember the lower class or less important the person the more freedom the artist used in their depiction.

The frescoes also depict the luxurious life of a nobleman and the kinds of activities that would have been a part of his life; hunting, fishing, good food, wine, drink, parties and banquets. The scenes though, it should be remembered are less about his life than they are about what is hoped for in his afterlife.

## Akhenaton

During the 14th century BCE the New Kingdom was enveloped in revolution.

It begins with the reign of Amenhotep III (r. 1390–1352 BCE) and his Nubian wife Tiye. At their court a new cult arose dedicated to the sun-god Aton, and their son, Amenhotep IV, was greatly influenced by this new cult.

When Amenhotep IV became pharaoh he changed is name to Akhenaton and abandoned the worship of all the Egyptian gods in favor of the worship of the one god, Aton, who was identified as a solar or sun disc.

Akhenaton declared that Aton was the universal and only god. He then set out to destroy, remove, damage and erase all memory of the Theban god Amen, in favor of the new sun-god Aton. He then moved his capital north toward Lower Egypt, away from the capital at Thebes, to a new city he built and named Akhetaton.

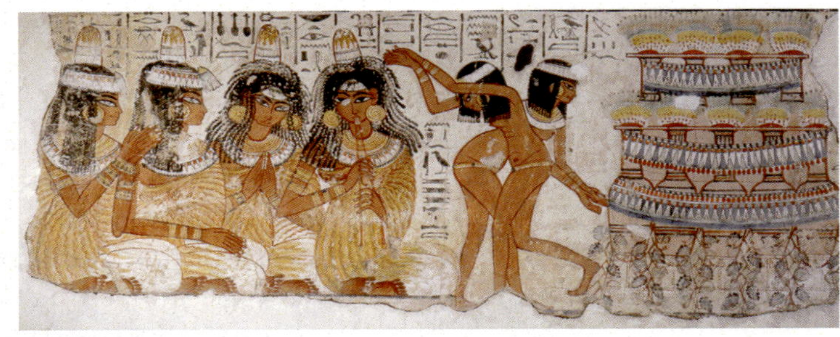

**3-23:** Musicians and Dancers, from the Tomb of Nebamun, Thebes, c. 1400–1350 BCE, fresco on dry plaster, 1′ × 2′5″, British Museum, London.

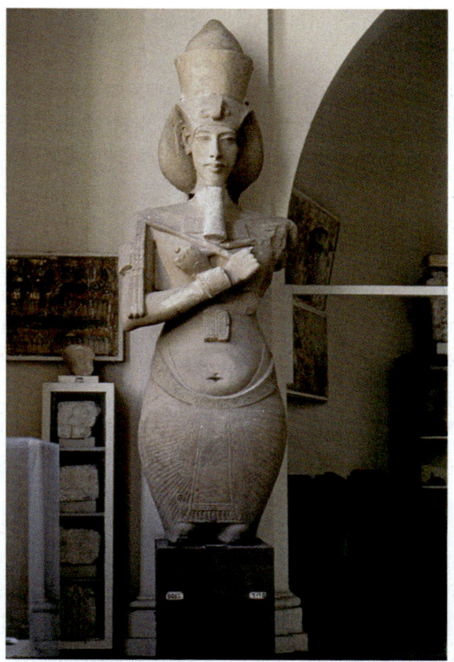

**3-24:** Akhenaton, sandstone, from the Temple of Aton, Karnak, 1353–1335 BCE, 13′, Egyptian Museum, Cairo.

The site of Akhetaton is also called el-Amarna, and the period of the artistic and religious revolution that marks Ahkhenaton's rule is often refered to as the Amarna period.

The pharaoh Ahkenaton claimed to be both the son and the sole prophet of the god Aton, and the only person to whom the god would make any revelations. This decidedly upset the class of priests of the others gods who over time had become the ruling social class in Egypt. Ahkenaton had virtually declared himself the sole political and religious ruler of all of Egypt, and its only prophet and priest.

The new god Aton was also not to be depicted in any animal or human form but instead only in the form of a solar disc emitting life-giving rays.

During this influential yet brief religious revolution, profound change in art occurred. That change is clearly evident in the monumental portrait sculpture of Akhenaton from Karnak.

This statue of Akhenaton looks radically different from all earlier depictions of the pharaohs. This work shows the Pharaoh with a rather effeminate body that is soft and curvy, with narrow shoulders, and facial features that are elongated. His eyes are pronouncedly almond in shape and his lips are full. It seems the entire canon of proportions has changed to one that is decidedly elongated and curvaceous.

He is shown wearing the combined crown of Upper and Lower Egypt and he holds the crook and flail, attributes of Osiris and royalty. Cartouches, which frame the names and royal titles of the King, appear on his body, on either side of his beard and on his belly, as well as on his wrist bracelet and the border of his garment.

The reasons for the Pharaoh's usual appearance are often debated. Many scholars have argued that the shape reflects some actual physical deformities of the Pharaoh, perhaps caused by disease or as the result of inbreeding. Other scholars suggest instead that the radical departure from the sculptural styles of the past is another instance of the Pharoah departing with established norms and that this new style may reflect his conscious desire to create and establish an entirely new canon of proportion, reflective perhaps of his reign. The most compelling argument for the shift in the representation of the pharaoh from the ageless stoic images of the past is that the new sun-god Aton was a sexless god.

So that by taking this form the Pharaoh, like his god, is neither distinctly male nor female.

Not only images of the King but other images from the period of his reign reflect this new canon of proportion and change in style.

This portrait bust depicts the Pharoah's wife Nefertiti. This painted bust of the Queen, whose name means "the beautiful one is here," is exceptional for its naturalism and gracefulness. She is depicted wearing a type of crown that is particular to her, called a Nefertiti cap crown, that seems to accentuate her elongated features.

The sculpture was discovered in 1912 at Amarna in the artist Thutmose's workshop. The piece is unfinished with the left eye socket lacking the inlaid quartz found in the right.

A truly revolutionary work of art from this period is a limestone sunken relief stele showing Akhenaton with his wife and children.

This sunken-relief stele provides an intimate and rare glimpse into the private family life of the Pharaoh. The stele, which may have come from a private shrine in the palace, shows the Pharaoh enthroned,

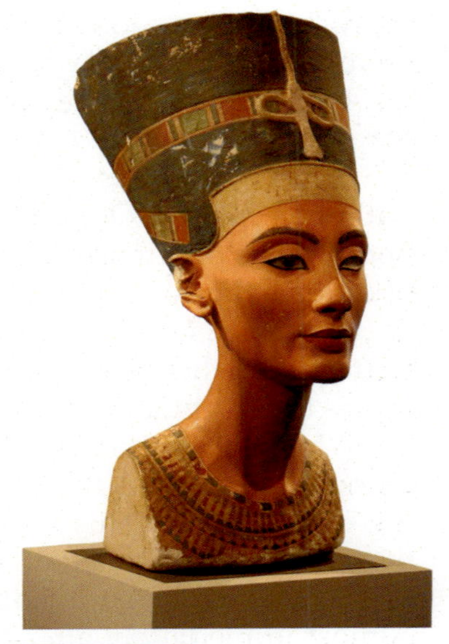

**3-25:** Bust of Nefertiti, Thutmose, painted limestone, Amarna, 1353–1335 BCE, 19", Egyptian Museum, Berlin.

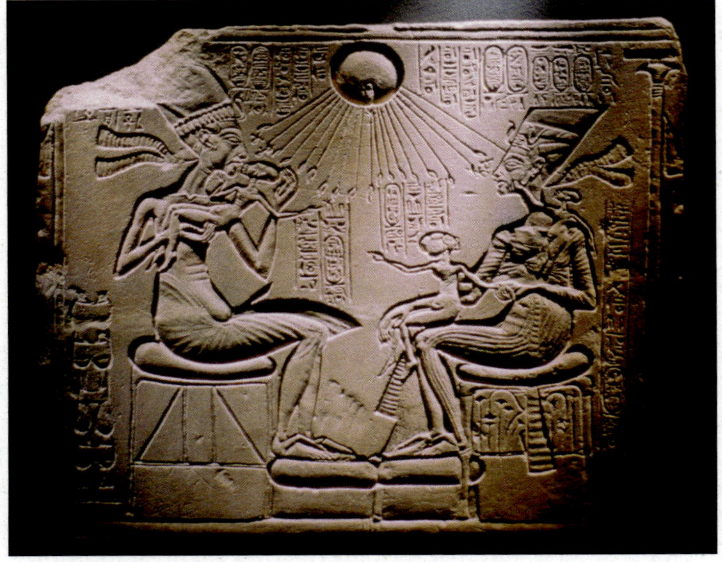

**3-26:** Akhenaton, Nefertiti, and three Daughters, Limestone, Amarna, 1353–1335 BCE, 13" × 15" , Egyptian Museum, Berlin.

facing his enthroned wife Nefertiti, who we recognize from the bust portrait, as they seem to cuddle and play with their daughters.

The figures have the same elongated proportions and curviness seen in their earlier portraits.

Akhenaton raises one tiny child up to give it a kiss while two others are seated with their mother. One child sits on her mother's shoulder and the other is seated in her lap. The differences in their sizes may be meant to indicate that the children are of different ages.

The entire family sits beneath the radiant solar disc of the god Aton whose rays terminate in the form of little ankhs. An ankh, a cross with a single oval loop at the top, is the Egyptian symbol for life.

What is so striking about this family portrait is how different it is from earlier works that stressed the pharaohs as emotionless, regal, everlasting and unchanging divine rulers. This intimate family portrait instead depicts the gentleness and humanness of Akhenaton.

The radical revolution initiated by Akhenaton did not last much beyond his rule. Almost immediately after his death his successors began to reinstate the old gods and the old ways and to wipe out all the buildings and sculptures and temples that he had built. Akhenaton's new capital city at Amarna was destroyed and the old capital at Thebes reestablished.

No one is really sure what happened to Nefertiti after her husband's death, though her tomb may recently have been discovered.

## Tutankhamen

The young Pharaoh Tutankhamen (r. 1333–1323 BCE), the son of Akhenaton by a minor wife, returned Egypt back to its traditional polytheism and moved the court back to Thebes.

Tutankhamen came to power at the age of nine or ten and ruled very briefly before his death at age 19. He is, however, perhaps the best recognized of all Egyptian pharaohs because of the fortuitous discovery of his tomb.

In 1922, Howard Carter, a British archaeologist, discovered Tut's tomb in the Valley of the Kings not far from Deir el-Bahri. The discovery was exceptional in the history of Egyptian archaeology because the inner chamber of the tomb was still sealed and it therefore had never been plundered; unlike all other tombs discovered thus far had been. The undisturbed contents of tomb were staggering and the boy King lay still wrapped in his royal linens inside three nestling coffins.

Howard Carter recorded the event of the opening of the tomb in his journals; the day he opened the tomb was Sunday, November 26, 1922. When Carter finally made a small breech in the sealed outer wall of the tomb he was asked what he could see and he replied "it is wonderful." He later described his first impression of the exotic treasures in the tomb and likened the contents to "the property-room of an opera of a vanished civilization."

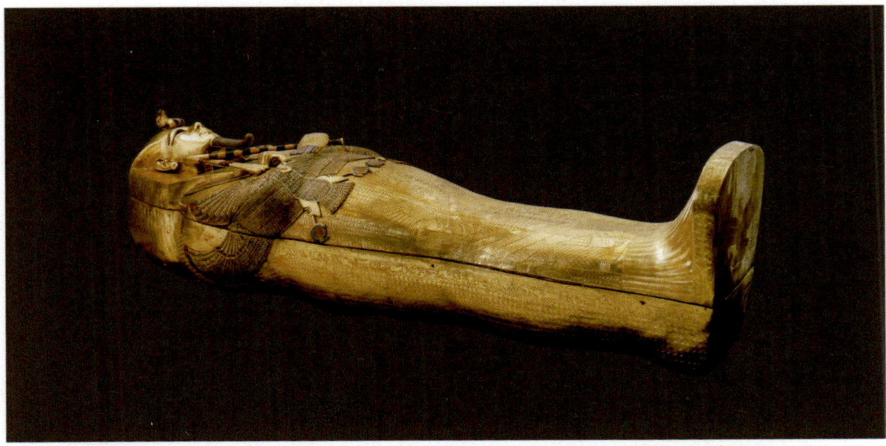

**3-27:** Inner Coffin, Tutankhamen's Sarcophagus, Gold inlaid with glass and semiprecious stones, 1332–1323 BCE, 6′1″, Egyptian Museum, Cairo.

The tomb contained gilded couches, alabaster vases, a carved chair, a golden throne, stools, sculptures, parts of a chariot, and much, much more.

The King's three mummiform coffins were placed one inside the other and then set inside a carved quartzite sarcophagus, whose cracked lid was made of granite.

The gold innermost coffin, which weighs some 243 pounds, depicts Tut posed in the guise of Osiris, the Egyptian god of the dead and king of the underworld, holding the crook and flail with his arms crossed over chest. Inside this gold coffin lay the mummified remains of the boy king and over his face and chest was a gold mask.

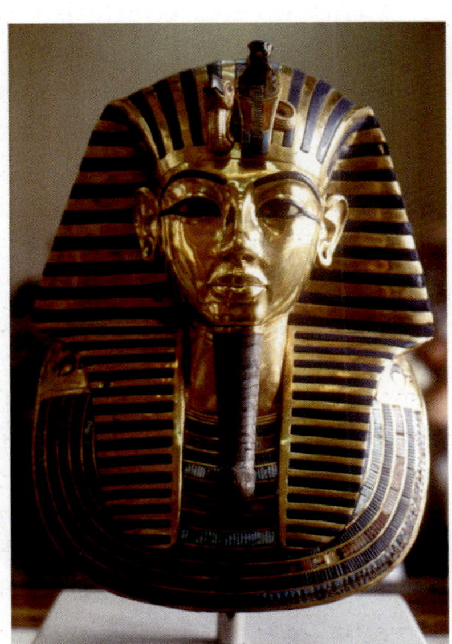

**3-28:** Death Mask of Tutankhamen, gold inlaid with glass and semiprecious stones, 1332–1323 BCE, 1′9″, Egyptian Museum, Cairo.

The death mask of the boy king is one of the single most recognizable images of ancient Egypt. The mask is made of solid gold, and is an idealized portrait mask of the young boy. The boy's face is round and youthful in appearance, his eyes are large and he has thick full lips. He wears the royal nemes headdress, the crown of Upper (vulture head) and Lower Egypt (cobra), and the false beard. The mask is inlaid with glass paste, lapis lazuli and other semiprecious stones.

Although it is difficult to judge how closely the face represents a true likeness of the King, it is at least a close approximation. The rather narrow eyes, the shape of the nose, the fleshy lips, and the chin are all in agreement with the features visible in his

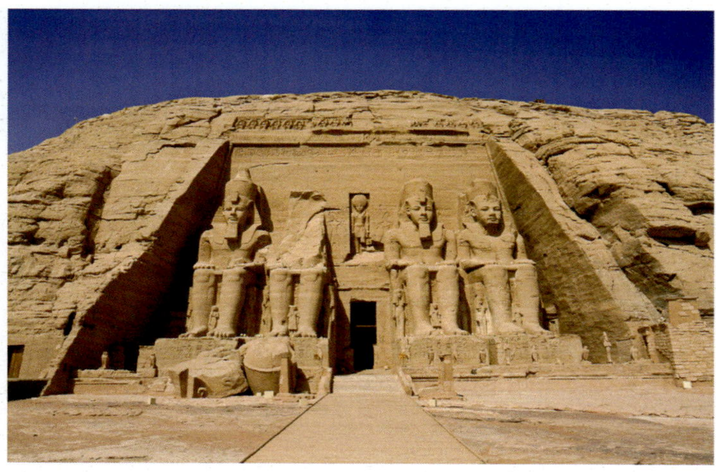

**3-29:** Temple of Ramses II, Abu Simbel, Egypt, 1290–1224 BCE, sandstone, 65′ feet high.

mummy, and the whole countenance is unmistakably youthful. Perhaps it is slightly idealized, but essentially it seems to be a faithful portrait. On the back of the mask is an engraved text from the Book of the Dead, which relates parts of the mask with various Egyptian gods.

Though the young boy King left a magnificent tomb, another New Kingdom pharaoh would leave some of Egypt's most impressive and massive monuments. Ramses II, also called Ramses the Great, ruled for 67 years (c. 1290–1224 BCE) and was one of ancient Egypt's greatest rulers. His commissions for buildings rivaled the scale of the Old Kingdom. One of his most impressive monuments is his immense and impressive mortuary temple built at Abu Simbel.

The temple, carved into the sandstone cliffs of the Nile bank, is located in the south in Upper Egypt on the ancient border with Nubia (ancient Kush). The location was significant since it reinforced Ramses II political and military control rule over the region.

Abu Simbel was built in honor of Ramses the Great to demonstrate his power and his divine nature. Four colossal 65-feet-tall statues of him sit in pairs flanking the entrance to the temple; in each he wears the royal nemes, crown, and short loincloth. At his feet are his wife (his principal wife was Nefertari), children, and his mother.

The head and torso of the statue to the left of the entrance fell during ancient times, as the result of an earthquake.

Just above the entrance to the temple, in a niche, is a statue of the falcon-headed sun-god Re-Harakhty, who is clearly recognizable by the solar disc on his head.

The temple faces east and has a solar alignment so that twice a year (roughly on October 21 and February 21) the sun's rays would reach into the innermost sanctuary to illuminate seated statues of the Pharaoh and several gods located on the back wall.

The entrance to the temple leads into an enormous pillared hall where eight giant 32-foot-tall figures of the King as Osiris face each other across a narrow space. The pillars are not true columns as they do not support any structural weight but instead are carved from the rock itself. A pillar or support or column in the shape of a man is called an atlantid (atlantes); in female form they are called caryatids.

## Art is an Endangered Species

Progress and the building of the Aswan High Dam in Egypt threatened to submerge the entire temple at Abu Simbel. In 1959 an international campaign was launched to raise awareness and funds to help save the monument. Between 1964 and 1968 a team of archaeologists, engineers, art historians, heavy equipment machinists and operators, under the direction and supervision of UNESCO and the Egyptian government, undertook the task of cutting the temple into massive blocks. The blocks were lifted and moved and then reassembled 213 feet higher and 690 feet back from their original position. The efforts cost over 40 million dollars and over 4 years to achieve, but were successful, even retaining the temple's solar alignment.

Death and the afterlife were of great concern for all Egyptians, whether they were workmen or pharaohs. From as early as the Old Kingdom a number of different spells, incantations, and recitations were written on funerary objects and then, later, painted on walls in tombs and on papyrus scrolls. These spells and magical incantations were intended to assist the dead on their journey into the afterlife. The modern term for the collection of these texts is the Book of the Dead, though in ancient Egypt they were referred to as the Texts of the Coming Forth by Day.

There is no one single "book" that contains all the spells but instead there are various selections made from them and then found in various order in tombs and on papyrus scrolls. In some cases these spells are accompanied by illustrations; one of the most popular texts and one of the most illustrated is a scene often referred to as the Last Judgment.

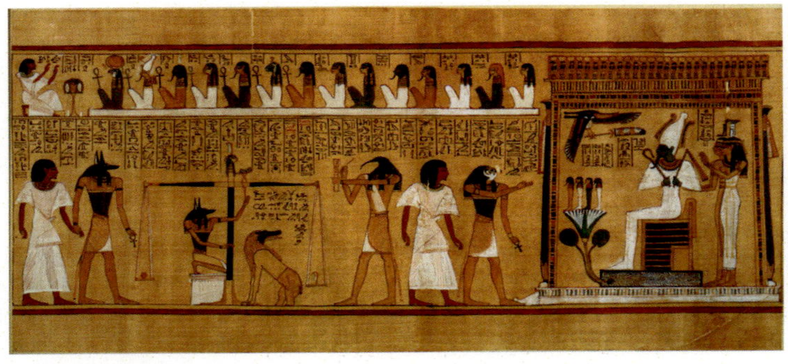

**3-30:** Last Judgement of Hu-Nefer, painted papyrus, c. 1290–1280 BCE, 15 5/8" high, British Museum, London.

Hu-Nefer was Overseer of Royal Cattle, Royal Scribe, and Steward of the Pharaoh Set I. These titles indicate that he was a prominent figure at the court of the Pharaoh and therefore a wealthy and privileged member of society. The exceptional quality of his Book of the Dead papyrus is also evidence of his high social status.

The scene of Hu-Nefer's Last Judgment is preserved in remarkably good condition and depicts, in continuous narrative, the weighing of his heart and the result, on his journey to the afterlife.

At the far left Anubis, the jackal-headed dog and god of embalming, leads the deceased (Hu-Nefer dressed in white) to the hall of judgment. The god than adjusts a large scale in order to weigh the dead man's heart against a feather of the goddess Maat.

To be successful the heart must be lighter than the feather; if it is not, the hybrid monster Ammit (half hippo and half lion) will devour it. In front of the scales, the Ibis-headed god Thot records the proceedings. Hu-Nefer has passed the test and we see him led by the falcon-headed god Horus into the presence of the green-faced god Osiris and his sisters Isis and Nephyts to receive eternal life. Above the scene Hu-Nefer kneels in front of a long line up of Egyptian gods and gives them thanks.

The text, inscribed all around the illustration, is intended to educate the deceased and provide him with the correct verses to be said along the journey. The recitations declare what the deceased had not done in his life and include sayings such as: I have not scorned the gods, I have not stolen from the temples, I have not polluted myself, and I have not committed any evil upon men.

The goal for the Egyptian, in order to enter his long-anticipated eternal afterlife is ultimately to be "light" hearted and not to have committed any sins that would have offended the gods.

Name ______________________________ Date ______________

Chapter 3

# Ancient Egypt Questions

1. What political event does the Palette of Narmer depict?

2. What is the standard tomb type in early Egypt?

3. What is the significance of the "ka" and a serdab?

4. What is the best explanation for the depiction of Akhenaton's unique body type in art?

5. During which period did Egypt extend its borders east beyond the Euphrates and south to Nubia?

6. What painting technique was employed in the production of early Egyptian tombs?

7. Who did Akhenaton declare the universal and only god? How did the artistic depiction of his new god differ from those of earlier gods?

8. During which period were the great pyramids constructed?

9. At which site did stone columns first appear?

10. What is the significance of Hatshepsut's reign?

# THE ART OF THE ANCIENT AEGEAN

## Chapter 4

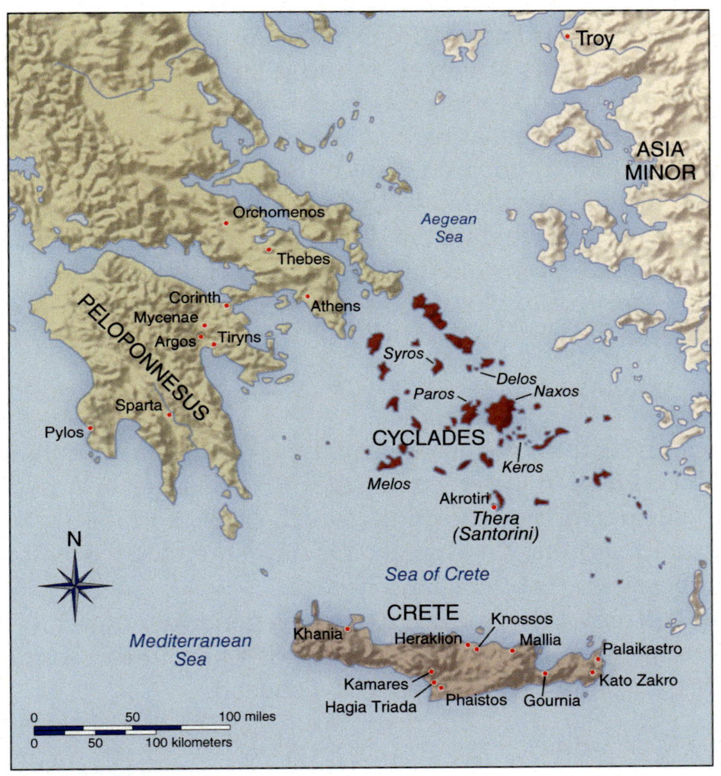


Ancient Aegean.

Until the late 19th century the stories, names, places, treasures, and accounts of terrific battles described in Homer's epic poems the *Iliad* and the *Odyssey* were thought to be mostly fictional.

The *Iliad*, written, or compiled in about 750 BCE (though existing for much longer in oral tradition) by Homer, the blind poet, tells the story of the beautiful Spartan Princess Helen, wife of King Menelaus of Sparta, and her Trojan lover and abductor Paris, and the fierce battle that ensued to return her home.

The *Odyssey*, compiled around the same time as the *Iliad*, tells the story of the Greek warrior Odysseus, one of Agamemnon's generals at the Trojan war, and his ten-year journey home to Ithaca, after the fall of Troy.

One man, a wealthy German businessman named Heinrich Schliemann, who had read the great epics of Homer as a child, decided that they could not be just fiction; he believed that that the names and places were too specific and too precise to be fiction. So in 1870, using his own money, he began work at a site in Turkey called Hissarlik, believing that it was the site of ancient Troy.

A British archaeologist, Frank Calvert, was already digging near there but had found nothing. Schliemann however, found a great deal. The site yielded many treasures including the foundations of a great walled city destroyed by fire in the 13th century BCE. Scholars now agree that this was the site of ancient Troy.

Schliemann not only discovered Troy but went on to discover or identify other major sites and cities described by Homer, including Mycenae, the city of King Agamemnon (brother of Menelaus), a city with a massive fortress, huge walls, and elaborate and luxurious tombs filled with vast amounts of gold.

It was in this spirit of exploration and discovery that many of the sites of the ancient Aegean were brought to light.

## The Aegean World

Unlike the ancient Near East and ancient Egypt, the sea dominates almost every aspect of life and culture in the ancient Aegean. The sea, as opposed to inland, trade was the source of prosperity, protection, travel, trade, and food. Living surrounded by the sea required serious naval skills and it also created isolation by separating groups within their own distinct island or area.

The art and culture of the ancient Aegean is generally dated to roughly c. 3000–1200 BCE. This period is also then generally divided into three geographically distinct areas or cultures: Cycladic, Minoan, and Mycenaean.

Cycladic art and culture, centered on the area in the southern Aegean Sea comprised of the Cycladic Islands, is roughly dated to c. 3000–2000 BCE.

Minoan art and culture, distinct to the large island of Crete, is generally dated to c. 1900–1400 BCE.

Mycenaean art and culture, centered in mainland Greece on the Peloponnese, is generally dated to c. 1600–1100 BCE.

The Cyclades are a group of islands in the southern Aegean between Asia Minor and mainland Greece. They serve like little stepping stones from Asia Minor in the east to the Peloponnesus and the rest of mainland of Greece. They were in essence the access point for eastern cultures to enter the Greek world. These islands, especially Naxos and Paros, had exceptional supplies of fine white marble.

Perhaps the most common sculpture produced in the Aegean during the Cycladic period were small nude figurines.

These unusual figurines rarely exceed 12 inches in length, although some have been found that are life-size.

The figurines are found in three major types or themes: *female figures*, *male figures*, and *musicians*.

Artists carved these figurines from marble and worked them with carving and shaping tools made from bone, copper, bronze, and emery (a highly abrasive stone).

The figures are strikingly simplified, and often even appear shockingly 'modern' The figurines' abstracted and stylized forms and sleek shapes look a great deal like some 20th century art and sculpture.

By far the most commonly-found type is the female figurine. The figurines are frequently depicted fully frontal, nude, with their arms folded across their middles. In profile, the figurines are also quite flat.

The features and shapes are angular often with an inverted triangular-shaped head and tapered body. The legs, some with articulated thighs, are short and taper to feet that have lines to indicate toes. The feet, however, are not flat at the bottom and therefore these figurines were never intended to stand upright. The breast and the pubic areas are both emphasized leading some scholars to believe that these are intended to serve perhaps as fertility figures, though there is little evidence to support that.

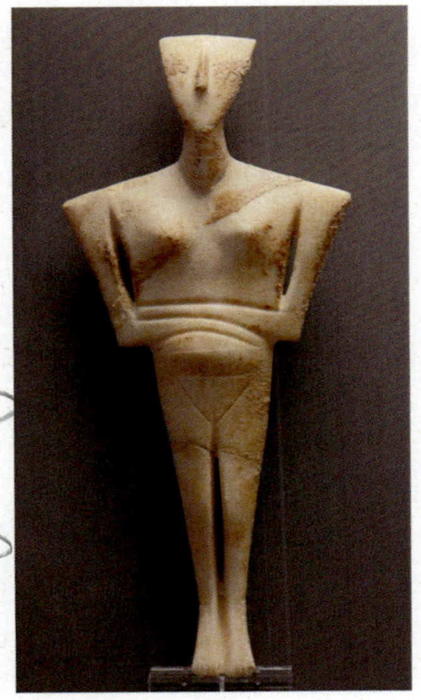

**4-1:** Female Figurine, marble, from the Island of Syros, c. 2500–2300 BCE, 18″, National Archaeological Museum, Athens.

However, since most of these figurines are found in graves, they seem to serve primarily as funerary offerings. It is easy to imagine that the figures are simply reflective of the dead person, male or female, with whom they are found. The figures seem to echo the same pose that bodies are often buried in, with their arms crossed over their chests and their legs out straight, feet together.

Traces of paint are often found on the figurines indicating that they were occasionally painted. The addition of paint would have added a great deal of animation and life to these figures, which now look blank without eyes and mouths. Some also seem to have been painted wearing jewelry.

The figurines of male musicians are the most elaborate types of the Cycladic figurines. This musician is seated on a high-back chair with decorative legs that arch and echo the shape of the instrument he holds. The musician holds in his lap an instrument like a harp or a lyre that appears to be decorated or embellished, perhaps with a duck-head. A similar type of musical instrument, the bull headed lyre, was found in Mesopotamia and this may reflect some cultural transmission between the two cultures.

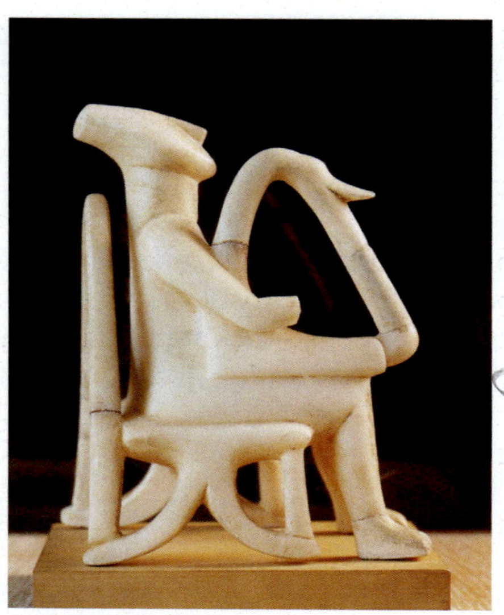

**4-2:** Male Lyre Player, marble, from the Island of Keros, c. 2700–2500 BCE, 9″, Museum of Cycladic Art, Athens.

Although we still do not know the function of the small figurine, it does imply a great deal about Aegean society. It might suggest that Aegean society had a clear appreciation for music, or that there were skilled musicians in this society, and it seems that instruments may have been made or imported from elsewhere.

Since these figurines are most commonly found in graves, then one can speculate about funerary practices: for example, did funerals include music? Was there some association between music and the afterlife? Was there a desire to make those who have died comfortable, soothed, or happy in death?

It should be noted that the figurines do not appear to be gender specific; so that female figurines have been found in both male and female gravesites and vice versa.

Interestingly, the production of the Cycladic figurines begins to decline at about the same time that the Minoan civilization on Crete begins its rise to power.

## KNOSSOS

The island of Crete, the largest in the Aegean, was a wealthy sea power and traded with the Near East, Egypt, and mainland Greece. It was also home to a distinct Bronze Age culture that flourished, at its height between 1900 and 1450 BCE.

This peaceful culture is identified with the building of large-scale open palace complexes. The most impressive of which, and the one mentioned in Homer's *Iliad*, is the Palace at Knossos, dated to c. 1700–1400 BCE. The site today is about 5 kilometers from the main city of Heraklion.

The site was discovered by the British archaeologist Sir Arthur Evans in 1900. In 1921 Evans published his excavation reports in a six-volume work he entitled *The Palace of King Minos at Knossos*. Evans made the association of the site with the mythical King Minos, and therefore called the culture Minoan."

According to Greek myth, Minos was the son of the god Zeus and a mortal woman named Europa. Europa was seduced by Zeus in the form of a white bull, who swept her away (from Phoenicia) to the island of Crete on his back.

On Crete, Europa had Zeus' son whom she named Minos. Later, Europa married the King of Crete, Asterius, who made Minos heir to the throne.

When the young Minos grew up and became King he married a woman named Pasiphae, with whom he had four sons and four daughters (one of whom is Ariadne).

One day Poseidon gave King Minos the gift of a beautiful white bull that Minos was supposed to have sacrificed in the god's honor. But Minos did not sacrifice the animal and thereby angered the god Poseidon. In order to punish Minos, Poseidon instilled a wild lustful desire for the bull in the heart of Minos' wife Pasiphae. Under this spell Pasiphae ordered the court craftsman Daedalus to construct a beautiful large wooden sculpture of a cow that was hollow so that the Queen could hide inside and mate with the bull. From this unusual union was born a creature that was half man and half bull, a creature called the Minotaur. The Minotaur, an embarrassment to King Minos, was then imprisoned in a labyrinth in the palace. King Minos exacted an obligation from the Athenians to send seven young girls and boys to Crete every ninth year to be devoured by the Minotaur. One year a youth named Theseus offered to go to Crete to be sacrificed. Once on Crete, Theseus fell in love with Minos' daughter Ariadne and she promised to save him. She then gives Theseus a ball of string to bring into the labyrinth with him so that he could find his way out after killing the Minotaur; he succeeds and the two escape from the island of Crete.

What led Evans to make the association of the site and the myth of Minos was what he found there, which included a labyrinth-like arrangement of rooms, sacrificial axes, and perhaps most intriguing, an array of bull-related imagery.

The site at Knossos is complicated and reveals that there were actually several layers of building and occupation on the site. The palace is dated c. 1700–1400 BCE. It was by far the largest and most elaborate of any previous structures built on this site or any other on the island.

The palace, located on a low hill, was the administrative, commercial, and religious center of Minoan life.

The palace at Knossos, which covers an area of about 3 acres, was carefully planned and organized around a large central courtyard. It included spaces for bedrooms, bathrooms, shrines, storerooms, gathering halls, and even entertainment in the forum of a small theater. The complex also had a long series of magazines, or store rooms, which stored many things including large earthenware jugs of grain, oil, wine, and honey.

Perhaps what is most unusual about the palace complex is that there is no evidence of any substantial fortifications, towers, or defensive walls around the city or even around the palace itself. This suggests that the Minoans had no real enemies, or at least none they perceived as any great threat.

The palace, like others on the island, was constructed with thick walls composed of rough stones embedded in clay. The interior walls were plastered smooth and painted with

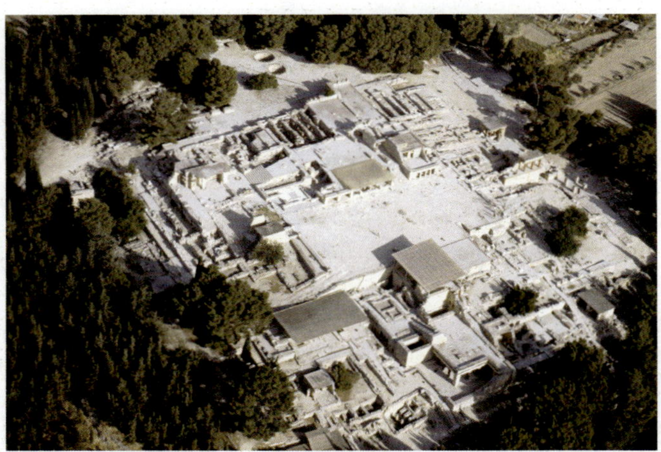

**4-3:** Aerial view of Palace at Knossos, Crete, Greece, 1700–1400 BC.

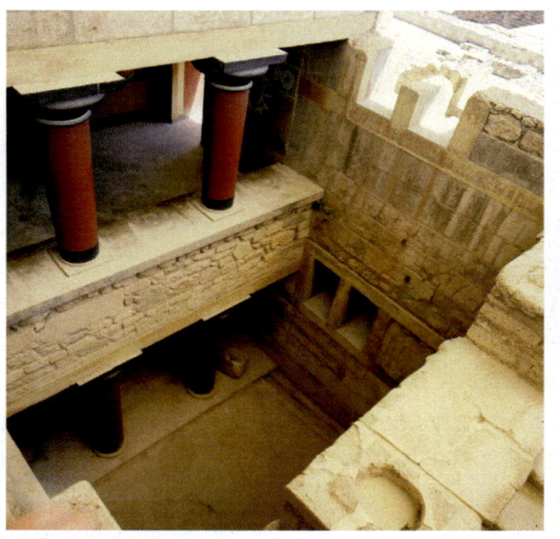

**4-4:** Stairwell at Knossos, plastered and painted wood, Knossos, Crete, c. 1700–1400 BCE.

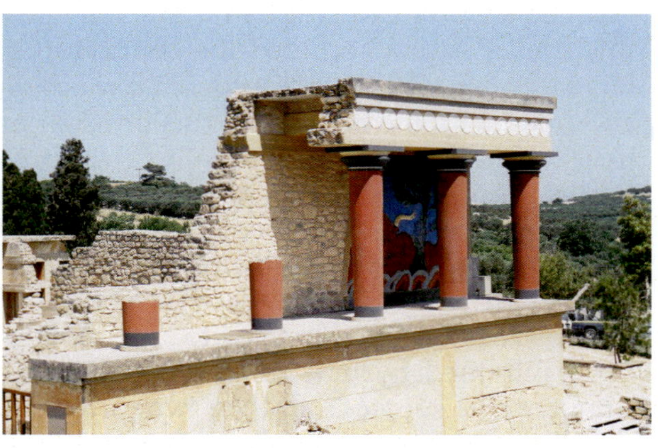

**4-5:** Reconstructed balcony, palace of Knossos, Crete, Greece, 1700–1400 BCE.

frescoes, and even the columns, made of wood, appear to have been plastered and painted. The palace even had a very efficient system of underground terracotta pipes that provided fresh water and drainage.

The columns used in the Cretan palace were often made from wood and had a unique design. They tapered from smaller in diameter at the bottom to larger in diameter at the top. These tapered columns then terminated in a bulbous cushion like a capital.

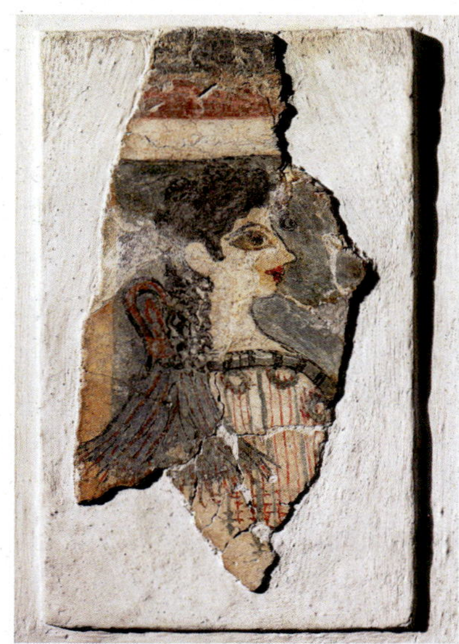

**4-6:** Minoan Woman, La Parisienne, fresco, palace at Knossos, c. 1700–1400 BCE.

Often the wooden columns were plastered and then painted red and black.

These interior staircases were built to include air-wells that provided ample light and air flow through the different levels of the palace.

The palace at Knossos was lavishly decorated with numerous frescoes of a wide variety of sizes and subject matter; including landscapes, geometric borders, and figural works, including mundane scenes like fishing, as well as more enigmatic scenes. The Minoans used both types of fresco techniques: true fresco or buon fresco and dry or fresco secco.

One fresco fragment, clearly part of a larger composition, depicts the profile portrait of an elegant woman with long dark hair, large eyes, and ruby lips. The young woman also wears an elaborate dress with a striped pattern and large fabric

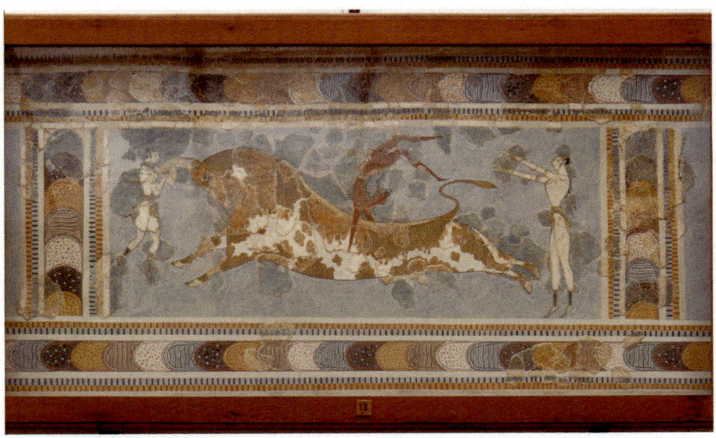

**4-7:** "Bull Leaping," fresco, Palace at Knossos, Crete, 1450–1400 BCE. 2′8″ high with border, Archaeological Museum, Iraklion.

loop or knot at the back. Her hair is actually piled up on the top of her head and then worked into long ringlets that fall down the back. When she was discovered by Evans he was so impressed with her beauty and apparent glamour that she was nicknamed La Parisienne' or the Parisian lady. It is unclear who she was or what she might have been doing.

Perhaps the best- recognized, if not the most enigmatic, fresco from the palace is the one that depicts bull-leaping.

The central scene is surrounded by a brightly multi-colored border of oval shapes and hatch pattern lines. The use of a border clearly defines the image and isolates the scene at the center.

In the center is a lively scene that depicts three figures and a bull. An elongated figure of a bull is flanked at the front and back by two female figures, both who wear similar hairstyles to the Parisienne lady fresco. The female in the front holds the bull's horns while the other seems to direct the action from behind. At the center a young male is depicted above the bull with his arms on its back and his feet over his head. It appears that the young man has leapt into the air and is upside down holding the back of the bull with both arms and flipping his legs over his head. If successful it would seem that the young male would land on his feet behind the bull facing the female with the outstretched arms.

The bull is depicted in motion, evidenced by the fact that none of its feet seem to be touching the ground and its tail seems to whip into an S-curve.

All the figures are highly stylized with elongated features, long legs, and pinched waists. The faces are shown in strict profile but with a frontal eye.

It is unclear as to the meaning of the event taking place but it has been rendered with great care and brilliant color. The event might depict some sort of entertainment, or it could be a religious ceremony, or festival, or even perhaps a sporting event.

The large open courtyard with surrounding balconies at the center of the palace would surely have provided space enough for such an activity.

The site, it should be said, has been rather romantically restored by Arthur Evans and much of what is seen is conjecture. But, the 'Palace of Minos' is unquestionably the most impressive palatial site in the whole of the ancient Aegean world.

While there is no extant literature from this period in Aegean history, there are a great number of texts that survive. Most of these, like early Near-Eastern writing, are in the form of pictographs that then developed into a more linear script. The two major scripts discovered in this area are called Linear A and Linear B. Unfortunately Linear A has not yet been completely deciphered.

## Thera/Santorini

The reason for the collapse of the Minoan civilization c. 1500 BCE is still rather mysterious, but at least one of its causes may have been the huge volcanic eruption that took place on the nearby island of Thera.

Sometime around 1600 BCE, the small island of Thera (modern Santorini) in the Cyclades was torn apart by an enormous volcanic eruption. The entire center of the island was blown out and was then filled in with seawater. The preceding earthquakes and following climate shift may have greatly contributed to the eventual downfall of Minoan civilization, though not all scholars agree with that hypothesis.

In 1967 the remains of the small town of Akrotiri were discovered; the town had been completely buried beneath tons of ash and rock. Preserved from the city are exquisite fresco decorations that reveal a glimpse into society and life in the ancient Aegean. The frescoes, striking similar to some of those found on Crete, showed city views and seascapes, daily life activities, and impressive landscapes.

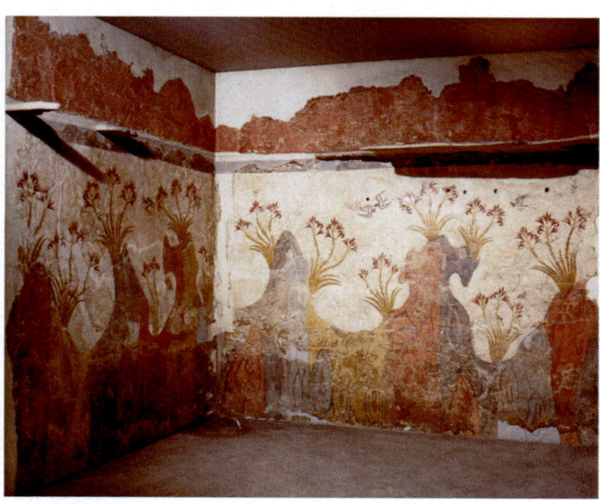

**4-8:** Landscape with Swallows, fresco, Akrotiri, c. 1650 BCE , 7′6″, National Archaeological Museum, Athens.

The landscape frescoes preserved from a room in a house at Akrotiri are some of the earliest examples of pure landscape painting known. The frescoes, sometimes referred to by the title *Spring*, depict a fantastical rocky landscape. The undulating line that defines the rocks suggests a rhythmic movement as the images wrap around the walls. The peaks and valleys are then exaggerated by the use of cool blue and warm ochers. Sprouting from the rocks are wild lilies that seem to bend in an imaginary breeze.

The desire to paint and decorate the surfaces of the walls, and to celebrate nature, carries over to pottery decoration of the same period. There was, in the ancient Aegean, clearly a desire to make beautiful even the everyday utilitarian objects.

Here the curvy circular pattern made by the tentacles of the octopus actually echo and follow the round shape of the pot and accentuate its form. In the negative spaces around the octopus are pieces of coral. The decoration enlivens the whole surface of the vessel and reveals a sophisticated and harmonious marrying of function, form, and decoration. Typical of this period is the use of a dark-colored design on a lighter background, a style often referred to as the Marine style.

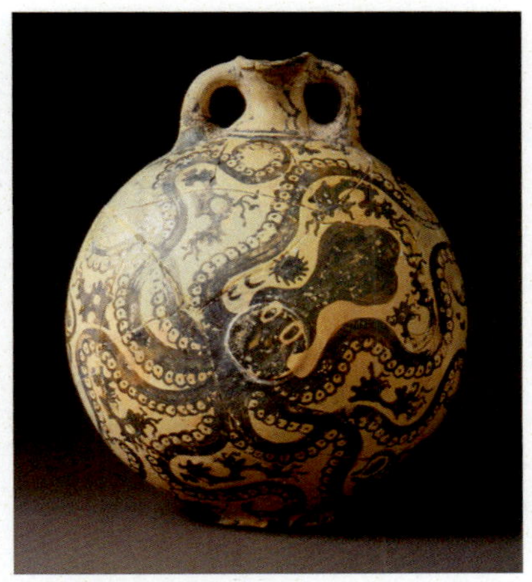

**4-9:** Octopus Jar, pottery, Crete, c. 1500 BCE, 11″ Archaeological Museum, Heraklion.

## Hagia Triadha

From another important site on the island of Crete comes an intriguing painted limestone sarcophagus.

This sarcophagus is an important example not only of Minoan painting, but also as a clue to some Minoan religious beliefs and customs.

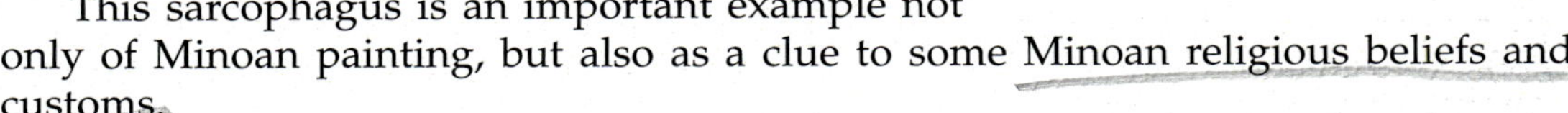

Haghia Triada (which means “Holy Trinity” in Greek) is another Minoan palace site on the island of Crete, not far from Knossos. It has yielded some of the most beautiful and expensive luxury objects that have been found in that area. The most significant is a painted stone sarcophagus covered in decoration on all four sides.

On one of the long sides a woman is shown pouring a libation into a large vessel in front of her, set between two double axes with birds perched on top. Another woman approaches her carrying more vessels and a man behind her plays a lyre. At the other end of the scene, and moving in the opposite direction, three men are depicted carrying animals and a small boat (it may be a real boat or perhaps a model) toward a dark-skinned figure who stands next to a tree in front of a set of stairs and what appears to be a tomb. Notice that the tomb in the scene matches the decoration on the actual sarcophagus.

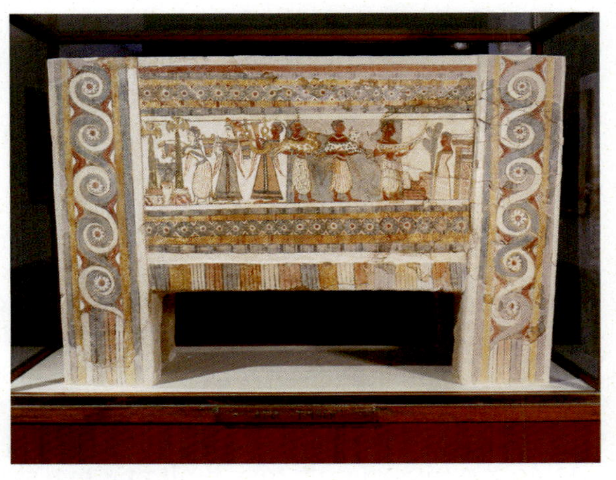

**4-10:** Sarcophagus, painted limestone, from Hagia Triada, Crete, c. 1450–1400 BCE, 4′6″, Archaeological Museum, Heraklion.

The figure at the tomb may represent the deceased who stands in front of his own tomb and receives gifts or homage.

The other side shows a procession of women, led by a flute-playing male

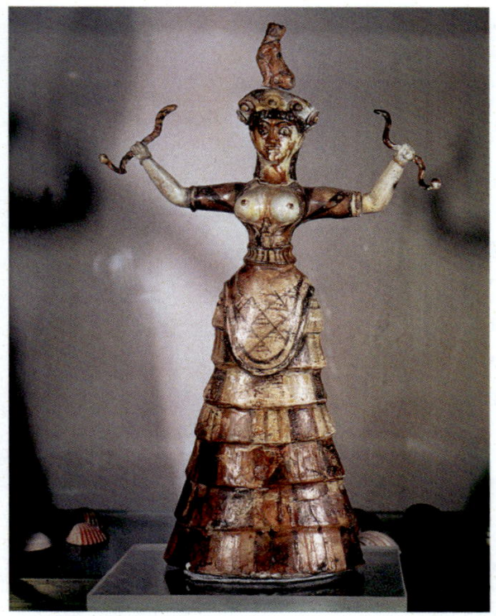

**4-11:** Snake Goddess, faience, from palace at Knossos, Crete, c. 1600 BCE, 13″, Archaeological Museum, Heraklion.

figure, heading toward a table on which lies a sacrificed ox or cow. In front of the table a female figure stands with her eyes looking upward at an altar near a tree. In the background are fruit baskets and decorated earthenware pots.

The scenes on the sarcophagus, while lively and descriptive, do not yield any concrete answers about Minoan funerary customs or practices.

Other mysterious Minoan objects are the so-called "snake goddess figurines."

Many of these figurines are made from a glossy, glazed earthenware called faience.

Although these small figurines may hold some religious significance, they cannot be associated with a specific temple or specific god. This figurine was actually found in a pit in the floor of a room on the west side of the central courtyard at the palace of Knossos. To date, no monumental temples or statues of gods have been found on Minoan Crete.

Many of these small statuettes have been found at several palace sites on the island and they are all quite similar. Most of the figurines share many of the same attributes: they are female and wear long, bell-shaped skirts, often tiered or pleated, with a short decorated apron over it. The figures are small-waisted and wear a tight bodice that is open at the front exposing full, round, breasts. The figures often have snakes in each hand, or occasionally the snakes wind around their arms. The figurines also wear elaborate headdresses, often topped with an animal. This small figurine seems to have a small cat or leopard perched on her head.

The fact that the figures are female, and have accentuated breasts as well as some unnatural power over the animals, might indicate that they may be religious deities or fertility figures.

## Decline

Around 1400 BCE the Minoan civilization experienced a decline, and by 1200 BCE the palace complex at Knossos had been completely destroyed.

The decline may be the result of the rise of a different culture, the Mycenaeans, based not in Crete or in the islands, but on the mainland of Greece.

The Mycenaeans were a distinctive and powerful culture quite different from the Minoans; for example they built massive stone structures with heavy defenses, unlike their Minoan neighbors.

Mycenae was described by Homer as the legendary home of the great ruler Agamemnon, brother of Menelaus, whose wife Helen was abducted by a Trojan prince. Homer also described the cities as rich with treasure. In fact, the ancient sites of Mycenae have yielded exceptional gold and artifacts that support those claims.

The Mycenaean city of Tiryns is one of the best preserved of all the Mycenaean sites; Homer even called it "Tiryns of the Great Walls."

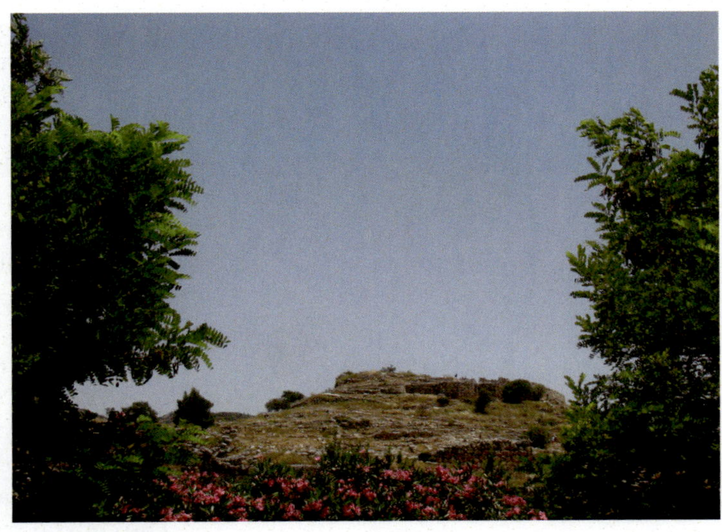

**4-12:** View of the citadel at Tiryns, Greece, c. 1400–1200 BCE.

Tiryns is a fortified citadel with impressive protective fortification wall stone. The walls, built from massive limestone blocks, are some 20-feet thick, and follow the contours of the land to completely surround all of the central buildings.

The massive fortification walls at Tiryns were so impressive that the ancient Greeks believed no mortal could have built them and the legendary giant Cyclops must have constructed them. Historians continue to use the term Cyc lopean masonry" to describe the type of huge roughly-cut stone blocks that form the walls here and at other Mycenaean sites.

One section of the walls at Tiryns is composed of a long gallery covered by a orbeled vault.

One of the vaulted galleries within the walls at Tiryns was created using a corbel technique. A corbeled arch or vault is created when horizontal rows of stones are piled in a cantilevered arrangement, setting each successive row of stones slightly more inward, little by little, until the side walls final meet at a pointed irregular arch.

Perhaps more remarkable is that there was no mortar used in the construction.

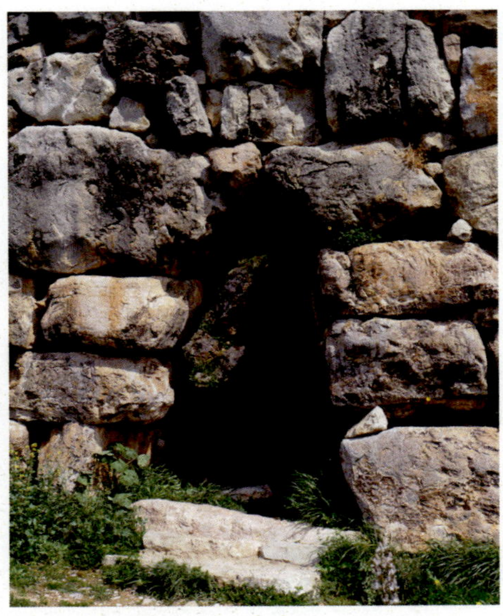

**4-13:** Corbeled Gallery, limestone blocks, Tiryns, Greece, c. 1400–1200 BCE.

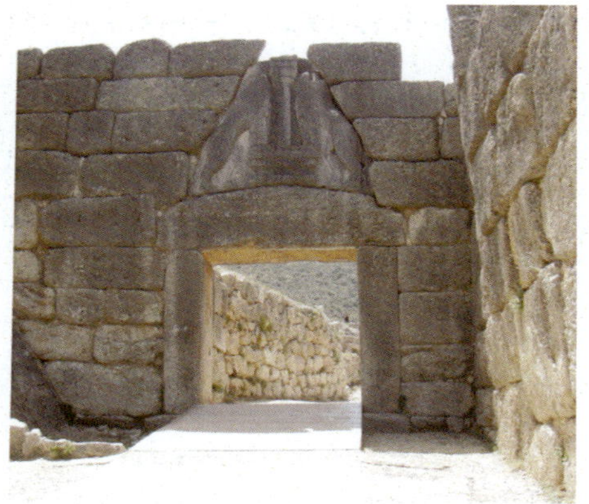

**4-14:** Lion Gate, limestone, Mycenae, Greece, c. 1300–1250 BCE, central relief panel 9′6.

At the citadel of Mycenae, the visitor, or invader, was greeted by a massive entrance called the Lion Gate.

The entrance to the city is located at the end of a 20-foot-wide stone channel that anyone approaching the site would be forced to pass through. This provided an excellent defensive feature, as the soldiers of the city could line the top of the Cyclopean walls and loom over anyone approaching.

At the end of the stone channel was an impressive and awe-inspiring stone gateway created by two large monoliths, topped with a large 20-ton lintel. Above the lintel the stones form a corbeled arch.

The central triangular section formed by the corbelled arch, called a relieving triangle, was then filled with a stone triangular relief depicting two heraldic lions flanking a Minoan style column. This motif, symmetrical on either side of a central figure, is called a heraldic composition. The large lion relief sculpture is often considered one of the earliest large-scale sculptures known on the Greek mainland.

New kinds of tombs and burial practices are also evident at Mycenae.

Some wealthy citizens of Mycenae were buried outside the city walls in beehive-shaped tombs built of stone and then covered by mounds of dirt. There are nine such tombs at Mycenae. The best preserved type of this tomb, called a tholos tomb, is the one often referred to as the "Treasury of Atreus," though it is neither a treasury nor did it belong to Atreus (Atreus is the legendary father of Agamemnon and Menelaus).

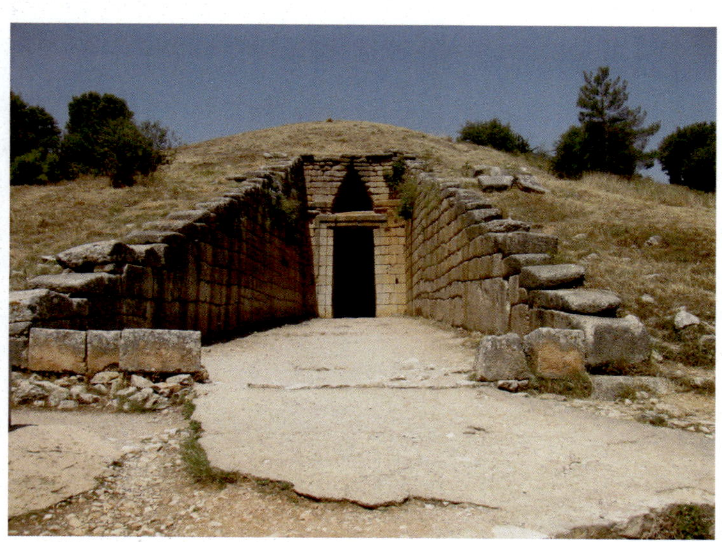

**4-15:** Treasury of Atreus, Mycenae, Greece c. 1300–1250 BCE.

The tomb was empty when it was discovered.

The tomb, which is approached by a long passageway called a dromos, has an entrance that is a similar to that at the Lion Gate, with a corbelled arch and a relieving triangle at the top. The tomb consisted of a large central circular chamber, and a small passage that led to a small, square chamber used for the burial.

The tholos was constructed by the use of horizontal strings or bands of stone that are laid on a circular base, and finally end in a large vault or dome. The rough stones were then finished and smoothed, once in place. The diameter of the structure is 48 feet and the height of the dome is 43 feet; it is the largest vaulted space that had ever been built and it was not until the Romans some 1500 years later that a dome of this size was ever built again.

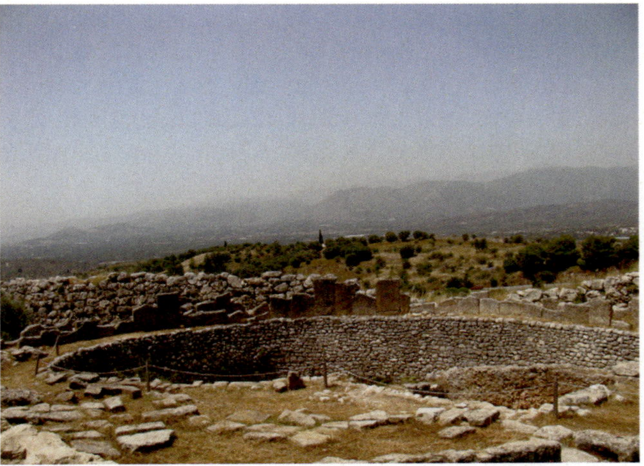

**4-16:** Grave Circle A, Mycenae, Greece, c. 1600–1500 BCE.

The evidence of the riches and splendor of the wealth at Mycenae comes from the astounding assortment of grave goods discovered there. Although the so-called treasury was empty, other graves at Mycenae have yielded impressive finds.

Inside the walls of the city, near the Lion Gate, Heinrich Schliemann discovered, in 1867, is a gravesite he called Grave Circle A (there is a smaller circle grave called Grave Circle B). The grave is older than both the walls of the city and the Lion Gate and seems to have come from a period when the city must have been at its height in terms of power and wealth. It was then encircled within the walls, perhaps for safety.

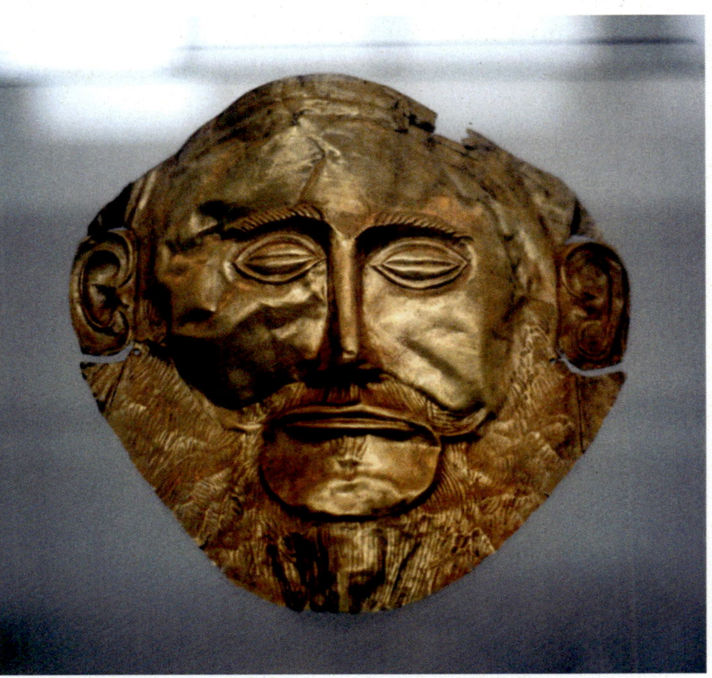

**4-17:** Funerary Mask, gold repoussee, Grave Circle A, Mycenae, Greece, 1600–1500 BCE, National Archaeological Museum, Athens.

Grave Circle A enclosed 6 shaft graves with at least 19 people buried in them: eight men, nine woman and two children. Each of the six graves had a decorated stone stele erected over it. These appear to be the graves of an elite family;pe rhaps a ruler and his family.

The Mycenaeans generally buried their dead in stone-lined shafts in the ground and then placed a variety of grave goods in the tomb. Some of the most remarkable objects discovered at Grave Circle A are hammered gold funerary masks that covered the faces of five of the male dead.

The masks were created using a technique called repousse, which means to beat or push out from the back, and then chased or worked from the front to add detail. Each of the masks display a distinct physiognomy, some have round or thin faces while some have beards and others do not. The individuality in the faces of the masks seems an attempt at portraiture.

This mask, which Schliemann called the "Mask of Agamemnon", depicts a mature man with a thin face and thin lips, almond-shaped eyes, and a handlebar moustache.

Though not nearly as technically advanced as the death mask of King Tut (dated c. 1300 BCE), these are impressive and represent the earliest known attempt at life- size portraiture in Greece.

Among the objects discovered in the circle graves at Mycenae, including earrings, rings, diadems, pendants, bracelets, cups, and various other luxuries, were several exquisitely made and decorated dagger blades.

The daggers blades were made of bronze and then inlaid with gold, silver, and niello; a black metallic alloy. The blades were decorated with various battle and hunting scenes. This example depicts shows 5 warriors on a lion hunt. Notice the forward-most man has fallen as the lion attacks. Two other lions turn and run, but one even looks back over its shoulder. These, like the other lion hunt images we have seen, are clearly images of power.

This kind of wealtht— he gold, jewelry, and inlaid daggers, particularly as it is associated with an individuali— s beyond anything ever discovered in the Cyclades or even at the palace of Knossos.

By 1100 BCE, like those earlier civilizations, wealthy or not, the Mycenaeans civilization also fell into decline.

After the decline of the Mycenaean civilization Greece entered into what has often been described as a Dark Age: a time when almost all artistic and cultural achievement seem to have ceased. This Dark Age lasted almost 200 years, before the rise of a new Greek peoples, the Dorian or Doric Greeks, who will bring Greece back to the forefront of Western Civilization.

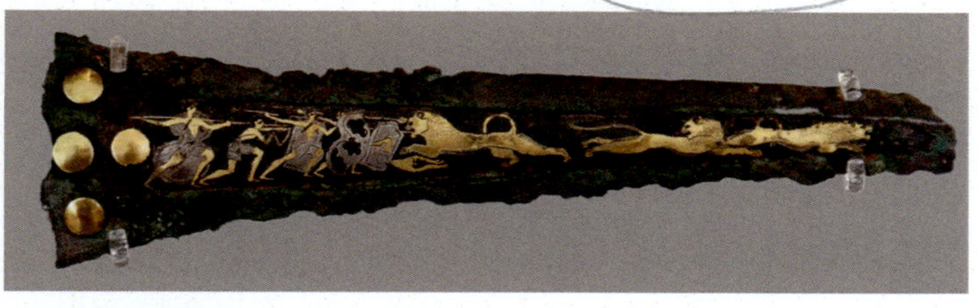

**4-17:** Dagger blade, Bronze inlaid with gold, silver, and niello, Grave Circle A, Mycenae, Greece, c. 1600–1500 BCE, 9″ long, National Archaeological Museum, Athens.

Name ______________________________ Date ____________

## Chapter 4

# Art of the Ancient Aegean Questions

1. Describe Minoan architecture?

2. What is significant about the design of Minoan columns?

3. The Minoans utilized which method in works such as *La Parisienne*?

4. What term is used to describe the massive masonry utilized at Tiryns and other Mycenaean cities?

5. What technique was utilized in the production of Mycenaean funerary gold masks?

7. Who discovered the site at Mycenae? Who was believed to be buried there?

8. What is the subject matter on the dagger from the tomb at Grave Circle A?

9. What myth features prominently into the interpretation of the Palace at Knossos?

10. How were males and females depicted differently in Minoan fresco painting?

11. What work motivated Heinrich Schliemann to uncover Troy?

# THE ART AND ARCHITECTURE OF ANCIENT GREECE

# Chapter 5

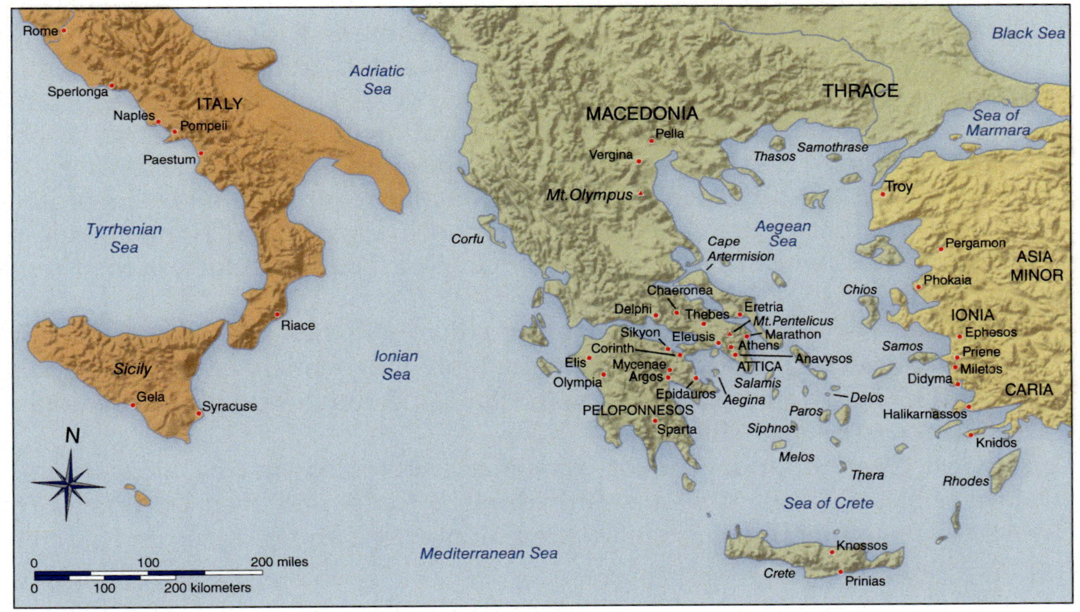


Ancient Greece and the Mediterranean.

In the 5th century BCE the Athenian statesman Pericles described the Greeks as "lovers of the beautiful." In general, the culture of the Greeks was one that valued physical strength, beauty, and intelligence.

The gods of the ancient Greeks assumed human form and shared human emotions and frailties; they were jealous, lustful, angry, spiteful, and shared the same passions as men. Unlike the early gods of Egypt and the Near East, the Greek gods were very human, except that they were immortal. They also had little else to do than meddle in the affairs of mortal men.

Fate was a concept that ruled much of everyday life and thought. Fate is the inevitable course of events and it is a dominant theme in many Greek myths. The Greeks believed three women (the Moirai) were in charge of a person's fate: Klotho, who spun the thread of life; Lakhesis, who measured the thread of life; and Atropos, who cut the thread of life. Both mortals and gods were subject to fate.

As early as the 8th century BCE, in the epics of Homer, we find the names and stories of the gods and their interactions with men. In c. 700 BCE, the poet Hesiod wrote the 'Theogony' in which he describes the major deities and their complex genealogies.

There were twelve main gods, called Olympian gods; they are: Zeus, Hera, Poseidon, Hestia, Demeter, Ares, Athena, Hephaestus, Apollo, Artemis, Aphrodite, and Hermes. They are all ultimately the offspring of two main elements in the universe: Gaia, the earth, and Uranus, the heavens. Gaia and Uranus mated and produced 12 Titans, including Oceanus and the youngest Kronos. Kronos usurped his father by castrating him and then marrying his sister. Kronos was as bad a father as he had been a son. He was so afraid that one of his children would usurp him that as soon as each one was born he would swallow them. When Zeus was born his mother protected him by feeding Kronos a rock instead of the child. When Zeus grew up he attacked his father and then made him regurgitate all of his brothers and sisters. The group then overthrew him and the rest of the Titans to rule the world from Mt. Olympus (highest peak in Greece). Zeus, therefore, is the King of the Olympian gods.

The Greeks, who call themselves Hellenes did not in their early years form a single unified nation but instead were separated into independent city-states or poleis (polis = city). There were the Dorians on the mainland and Peloponnesus and Ionians on the west coast of Asia Minor.

In most cases the independent city-states were ruled first by kings, then by wealthy nobles who controlled wealth through trade, and then by tyrants (not always evil as implied). The tyrants were first overthrown in Athens and a democracy was born.

In 776 BCE the separate Greek-speaking city-states held their first ceremonial athletic and religious games at Olympia. The event was the Olympiad and it was open only to Greek-speaking men. One result of these games was that it helped form a unique Greek sense of identity and camaraderie that had not previously existed.

The Greeks, and Athenians in particular, aimed at a balance in all things. They sought a perfectly harmonious way of life aimed at physical and intellectual strength, beauty, discipline in action and behavior, and rational thought and action. The Greeks fostered art, philosophy, literacy, science, and politics. From boyhood, Greek men were trained in physical strength and intellectual thinking with a focus on military strategy.

Though Greeks spoke of democracy they did own slaves and they believed that some men were born free and others were born slaves.

In their view women were in no sense equal to men. Women were mostly secluded and sheltered and allowed to participate in very few activities except for events such as religious ceremonies, weddings and funerals. Most women were only identified by the male familial relationships.

Greek art and culture is generally divided into seven major periods:

| Greek Periods: | |
|---|---|
| Geometric | c. 900–700 BCE (emergence, discovery, Homer) **Discovery** |
| Orientalizing | c. 700–600 BCE (Eastern influences) **Influences** |
| Archaic | c. 600–480 BCE (origins, architecture, grin) **Origins** |
| Early Classical | c. 480–450 BCE (Athens defeats Persians) **Rise** |
| High Classical | c. 450–400 BCE (Pericles and the Acropolis) **Apogee** |
| Late Classical | c. 400–323 BCE (Peloponnesian war, Athens defeated) **Defeat** |
| Hellenistic | c. 323–31 BCE (death of Alexander to Roman rule) **Drama** |

## Geometric Period: 900–700 BCE

The Geometric period followed the several hundred years of Dark Ages in Greece that followed the collapse of the Mycenaean civilization. During this period there was the development of the independent city-states and the Greek alphabet, as well as a huge population growth. Trade was resumed and the great epic poems and myths, which had been sung or narrated, were finally recorded in written form, and the Olympic Games were established.

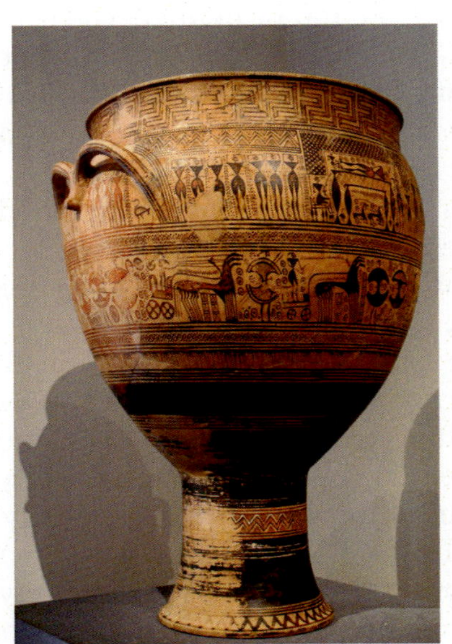

**5-1:** Geometri Krater, terracotta, Dipylon Cemetery, Athens, 740 BCE, 3′4″, Metropolitan Museum of Art, New York.

In art the Geometric period was marked by a mastery of varying materials and crafts including weaving, wheel–made pottery, painting, metal working and casting, gem engraving, and gold work. Often the decorative elements included geometric patterning and motifs such as zigzags, chevrons, squares, circles, triangles, and meanders.

A krater is a large-mouth bowl on a foot that was used for mixing wine and water. This very large example, over 3-feet high, was ceremonial and was used to mark the grave of an Athenian man.

The bottom of the vessel is open so that libations could be poured into it and then run through the vessel into the grave to serve as a libation for the dead.

The surface is almost completely covered with decorations situated in horizontal bands, registers, or friezes that wrap around the vessel. The two largest bands, located on the body of the vessel, have figural decorations, while the rest is covered in geometricly patterned designs of meanders, lines, and zigzags.

The figural decoration in the upper figural register depicts a funeral, or *prothesis*. The *prothesis* is a funerary practice in which the dead body is laid out on a raised bier and then mourned by family and friends.

Mourners stand on either side of the bier and tear at their hair or beat their heads in a gesture of despair.

In the frieze below is the funerary procession, or *ekphora*. After the *prothesis* the deceased was brought to the cemetery in a procession that included family and friends. The *ekphora* depicted on this vessel includes soldiers (their bodies are blocked by their shields) who walk or ride in horse-drawn chariots. Soldiers only appear on those vessels that depict a male deceased.

The figures (men, women, and animals) depicted on the vessel are reduced to their most basic geometric shapes with no real attempt at naturalism. The figures are shown in silhouette in odd composite views.

The size, decoration, and function of the object certainly attests to the wealth and status of the individual buried.

Note that the type of vessel, a krater, is associated with men; it was an object used in the symposia; a gathering or meeting of men to share intellectual conversation. The krater was therefore reserved as a grave marker for men. For women, the type of vessel used for a grave marker was the amphora. The more slender and shapely amphora was a domestic object and therefore more commonly associated with women.

This solid-cast bronze statuette depicts a man and a centaur, perhaps engaged in battle. The man is nude except for a belt and an unusual hat or helmet. The centaur, a mythological creature that is half-man and half-horse, is depicted with the chest of a man and the back half of a horse. His tail reaches the ground behind him.

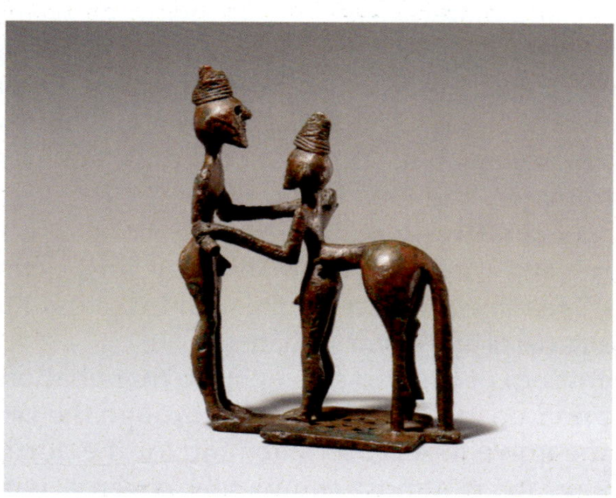

**5-2:** Man and Centaur, bronze, from Olympia, Greece, c. 750–730 BCE, 4″, Metropolitan Museum of Art, New York.

It is possible that this is intended to represent the semi-divine hero Hercules and his nemesis, the centaur Nessos.

The statuette reveals the Greek interest not only in mythological subject matter, at a very early date, but also with the nude male figure. Male nudity was fairly common in Greek society, especially since Greek men exercised and competed in the nude. This nudity is in contrast to the societies of the Near East and Egypt which almost never displayed nudity.

## Orientalizing Period: 700–600 BCE

During the Orientalizing period there was a marked increase in trade with other eastern nations, and an increase in artistic production. The artistic productions of the period clearly reflect the contact with the neighboring East, including Mesopotamia and Egypt. During the Orientalizing period numerous small-scale figurines were crafted that incorporated eastern-looking styles and motifs.

This little votive offering of a nude male figure reveals a rather simplified silhouette but also shows the Greek interest in the human form, and the desire to create three-dimensional statues.

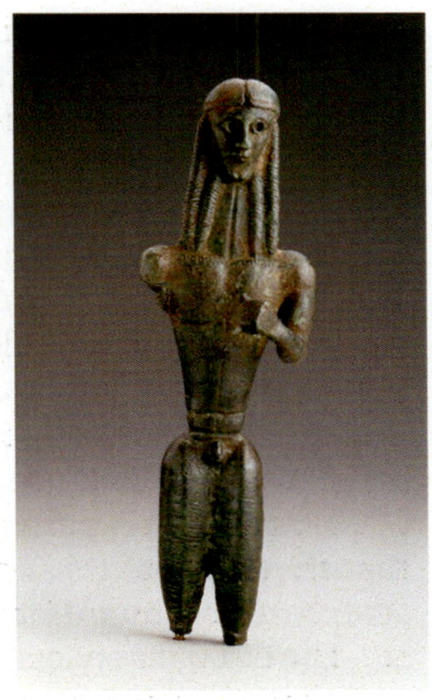

**5-3:** Mantiklos, Apollo?, bronze, Thebes, Greece, c. 700–680 BCE, 8″, Boston Museum of Fine Arts, Boston.

This statuette has a long inscription across the front of both thighs that reads "Mantiklos dedicated me as a tithe (offering) to the far shooting lord of the silver bowl; that you Phoebus (Apollo) give some pleasing favor in return." The boustrophedon (written from right-to-left and left-to-right) inscription makes it clear that this was a gift to Apollo from Mantiklos. What is not clear is whether the figurine represents the donor or the god. The figure once held something in the left hand, perhaps a shield or a bow.

The figure is nude, except perhaps for a wide belt. The eyes are hollow and would have been inlaid, while a hole at the top of the head and on the forehead seems to have anchored something, perhaps a helmet.

While the forms are still stylized and geometric in shape they do reflect a heightened interest in the human body. The shoulders are round and the clavicle is clearly articulated. The elongated neck, narrow, rather pointed shape of the head, and ropes of braided or plaited hair, visibly reflect its Eastern influences.

Another Orientalizing sculpture that reflects eastern influence is the Lady of Auxerre.

This *kore* (maiden) statue is nicknamed for the French town where she was discovered in a storage vault.

The small statuette, likely a votive offering, wears a long skirt, wide belt, and shawl or cape over her shoulders. She has no headdress of any kind and has her right hand on her breast in a rather ambiguous gesture.

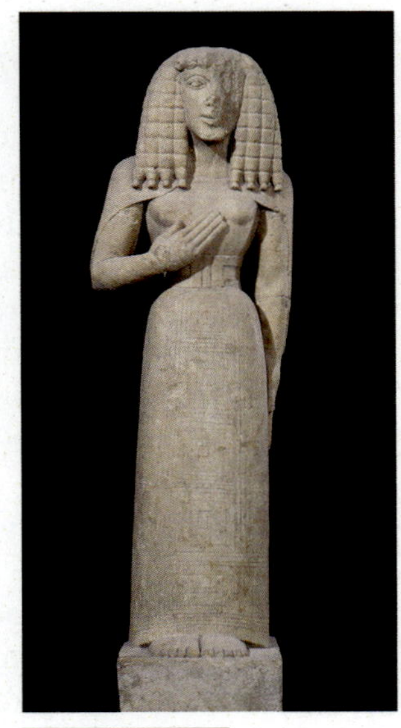

**5-4:** Lady of Auxerre, limestone, Crete?, c. 650–625 BCE, 2′ high, Louvre, Paris.

She would have originally been brightly painted, and the shell pattern and concentric square pattern that decorates her skirt would have been clearly visible.

Almost all Greek stone statues, as well as architectural decoration, would have been brightly painted.

The technique used most often in painting these works is *encaustic:* a method in which pigments were mixed with warm wax and then applied to the object while still warm.

The Lady of Auxerre represents an example of a style that is called *Daedalic*, named after the legendary skilled craftsman Daedalus. Daedalus was supposed to have built the labyrinth on Crete, as well as traveled to ancient Egypt where he was influenced greatly by the art and architecture. He then imported those ideas and translated them into Greek architecture and sculpture.

This legend is perhaps one way in which the Greeks acknowledge the artistic debt that they owe to the Egyptians, particularly in the development of large-scale stone sculpture and monumental stone architecture.

The Daedalic style reflects the strict frontality, stiff pose, and block-like quality of much of Egyptian sculpture.

This influential statuette also represents the beginning of a tradition of free-standing three-dimensional stone sculptures of young female and male figures. Female figures, or maidens, are called *kore* (plural *korai*) and youthful male figures are called *kouros* (plural *kouroi*). Note that kore figures are always clothed.

The Lady of Auxerre is ultimately best described as an Orientalizing, Daedalic, kore.

## The Archaic Period: 600–480 BCE

The development of kouros and kore figures dominates the sculpture of the archaic period. A feature of many sculpted figures created during the archaic period is a facial expression that suggests a grin; the grin is not intended to represent happiness but instead was a way for the sculptor to animate the face.

This life-size *kouros* is a perfect example of the Daedalic style. The figure emulates the Egyptian style left foot forward stance, is rigidly frontal, and the arms are held straight down at the sides with the hands clenched.

In the Archaic period kouros and kore figures replaced the earlier large-scale geometric vases as the preferred choice for grave markers. This one stood at the head of a grave in the countryside near Athens.

This same kind or type of kouros was also used for votive offerings at temples. These types of sculpture, because they were rather generic and mass-produced, could be easily appropriated for different purposes.

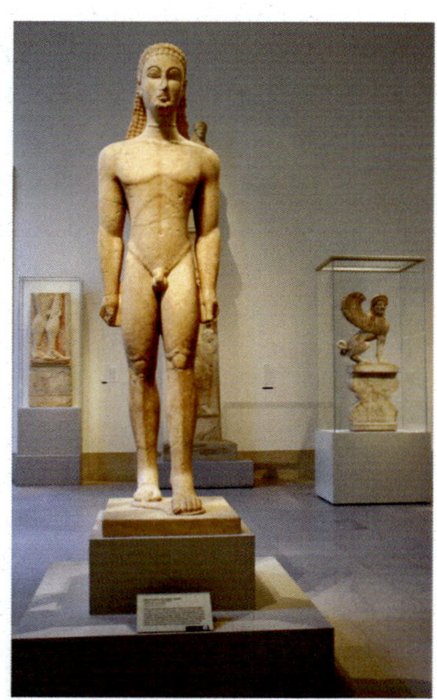

**5-5:** Kouros, marble, c. 600 BCE, 6′½″ Metropolitan Museum of Art, New York.

Another early kouros figure is the Calf-Bearer, or Moschophoros.

This figure, found in pieces on the Athenian acropolis, has a partial inscription on the base that states that Rhonbos dedicated it.

The statue is likely meant to represent the donor actually in the act of bringing a calf as an offering to the goddess Athena. While this work still reflects a general Egyptian influence, particularly with the left foot forward stance, it is not so rigidly frontal or block-like. The calf-bearer has a beard and wears a thin cloak, unusual for an Athenian, suggesting that this figure may represent a citizen from another city in Greece.

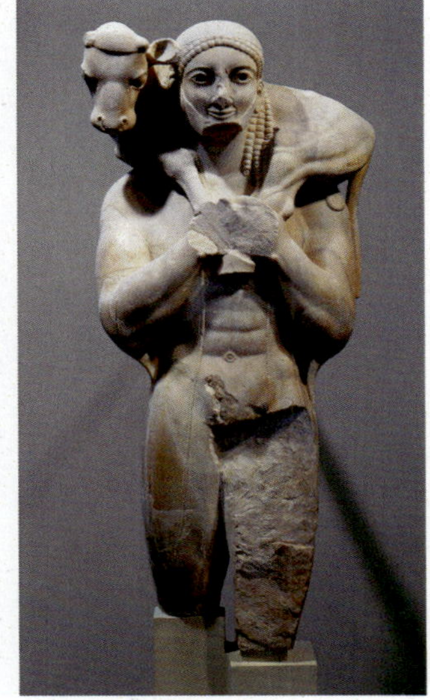

**5-6:** Calf bearer, Moschophoros, marble, Acropolis, Athens, c. 560 BCE, 5′5″, Acropolis Museum, Athens.

The abdominal muscles of the kouros and particularly the face of the calf have been treated with an attention to naturalism and modeled with skill and sensitivity. The face also reflects the archaic grin typical of sculptures from this period.

The marble Kroisos kouros from Anavysos, not far from Athens, marks further development in the style of the kouros. The figure is more natural in stance and pose, and the abdominal muscles reveal a sense of underlying anatomy and flesh. The stance remains Egyptian in influence but the arms now bend slightly back and away from the body, and the shoulders are more rounded and muscled.

This kouros functioned as a grave marker for a young man named Kroisos, who died in battle. The base of the work is inscribed "Stay and mourn at the tomb of Dead Kroisos whom raging Ares destroyed one day as he fought in the foremost ranks."

The figure is not intended to be read as a portrait of Kroisos but rather as an ideal image of the beautiful youthful male. Notice that the kouros still retains traces of its original paint, particularly in the hair.

The Kroisos kouros also reveals the developmental trend of kouroi toward a more natural depiction of the human figure. The same progression toward a more natural figure is evident in archaic period korai as well.

Like kouroi, korai could function either as votive offerings or grave markers, and they too were an example of the wealth and status of the donor.

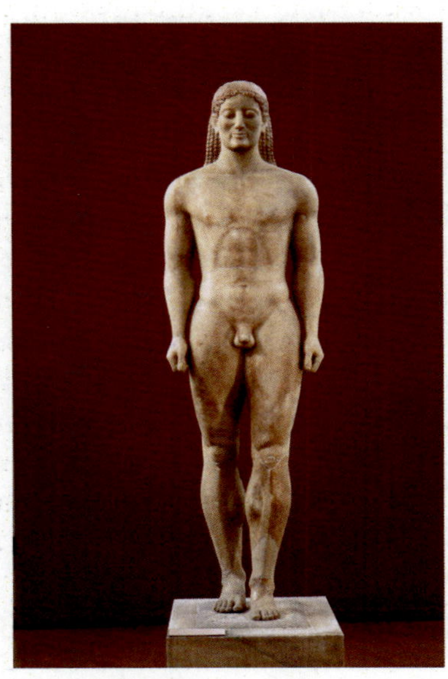

**5-7:** Kroisos, from Anavysos, Greece, c. 530 BCE, marble, 6′4″.

This kore, given as a dedication on the Acropolis in Athens, wears a Peplos, a simple long woolen belted garment. She too has the archaic smile.

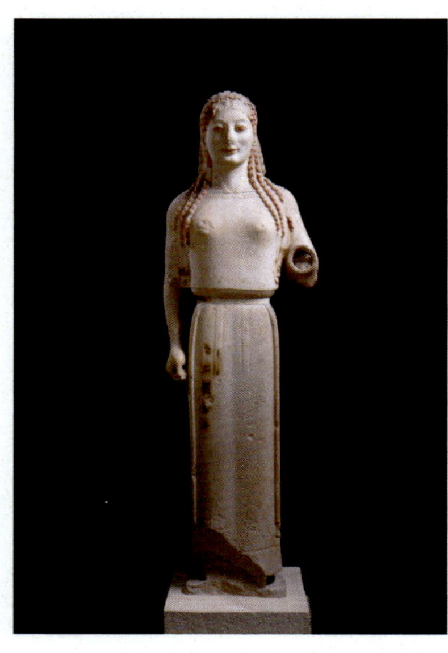

**5-8:** Peplos Kore, marble, c. 530 BCE, 4'Acropolis Museum, Athens.

She is smaller than life size and was richly decorated with paint, some of which is still preserved.

Her left forearm arm, now lost, was extended in front of her, in the act of making an offering.

Her female form is hinted at by the indication of her breasts under her garment. Though these figures are never shown nude the Greeks did have a way of concealing and yet revealing the female an ingenus body.

## Archaic Architecture

### Greek Temple Building: Houses for the Gods

From as early as the Orientalizing period the influence of monumental stone architecture, like that constructed in Egypt, is recognized in the Greek shift away from mud-brick and wood architecture to the use of stone.

Stone was a more suitable and permanent material for the worship of the gods. Temples were built to house the cult statue of the god or goddess but the sacrifices and ceremonies dedicated to them actually took place outside the temple proper.

The external colonnade, or *pteron*, which appeared as early as the 7th century BCE, is one of the most important innovations in Greek architectural design.

Greek architecture, though found in many variations, is all based on a few core principals, particularly the importance of proportional order or relations.

### Basic Temple Plan Description

Essentially the general plan of the temple consisted of a core composed of a rectangular room, called the *cella* or *naos*, with projecting walls, called *antae*, at either end.

The projecting walls created a porch or *pronaos* at the front end, and at the back an *opisthodomos*. The pronaos allowed for entry into the naos while the opisthodomos was used mostly as a storehouse or treasury.

The porches were often fronted by a pair of columns set between the projecting walls; these are called *columns in antis*.

The cella or *naos*, at the core of the temple, is where the cult statue was housed. It had no windows, and had access at only one end.

The building itself (the level the columns stand on) sits on top of a low stepped platform called a *stylobate*.

A colonnade, or row of columns, was placed all the way around the cella and the porches, creating a peristyle. The peristyle made the temple seem solid yet transparent, formidable yet still accessible.

A temple with a single peristyle is called a *peripteral* style temple. If the temple has two peristyles it is called a *dipteral* temple. The peripteral style is by far the most common.

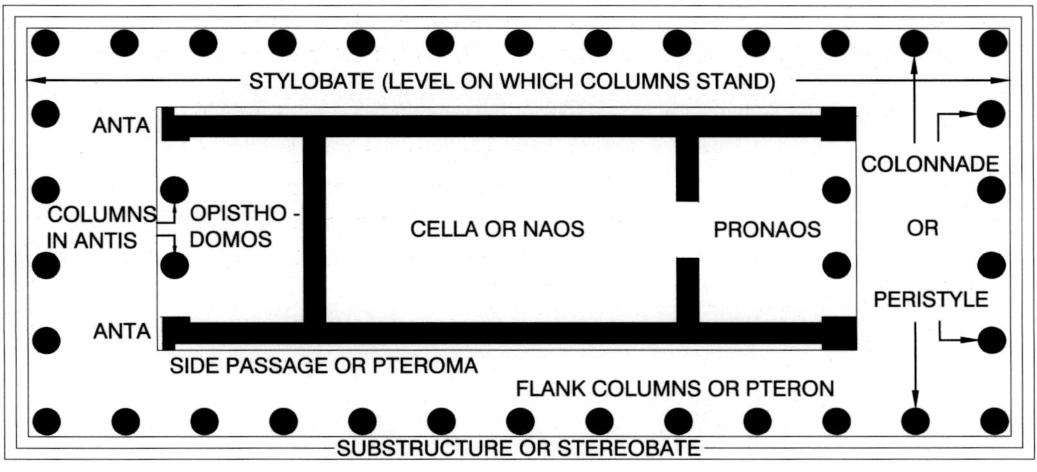


**5-9:** Plan of typical Greek temple.

Temples were, however, built in a variety of configurations. A temple with a colonnade just across the front is a *prostyle* temple and a temple with a colonnade at the front and back is an *amphiprostyle* temple.

## Proportions

The proportions of Greek temples were systematized and most often were based on a mathematical system of proportion relating each individual component or part to the whole. The diameter of the columns often served as the primary unit of measure to determine the rest of the temple's proportions.

As a general rule, the external colonnade used twice as many columns along the long side than along the short side, plus one. So that, if there were six columns used across the short end there would be thirteen along the side. Although the number of columns across the short side varies, depending on the size of the temple, they are usually of an even number. An even number is practical so that, in terms of symmetry, there would be an open space, not a column, at the direct center of the façade.

## Worship and Site

Public worship was carried on outside the temple; therefore the geographical location was chosen for impact in the context of the surrounding landscape. In most cases the main or temples is located at the high point of the city, or on its *acropolis* (literally the high point of the city). Also, at least eighty percent of all Greek temples face east, so that the cult idol (with the cella doors open) could face the rising sun.

## Elevation

The elevation of a Greek temple is usually discussed or described in terms of three major components: the platform, colonnade, and entablature.

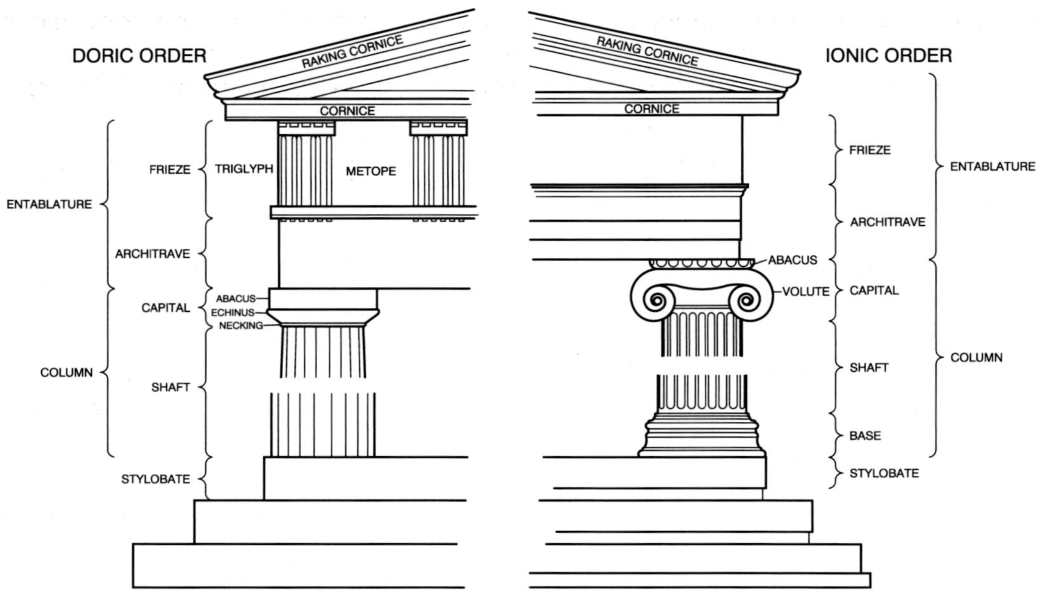


**5-10:** Elevation of Doric and Ionic Orders.

## Platform

The platform is the substructure or foundation on which a building is erected. The stylobate is the top or uppermost step of the platform and the level on which the building stands. The steps, or *stereobate,* that lead to the stylobate, often wrap all the way around the temple allowing for access from all sides.

## Colonnade

The colonnade is generally composed of individual free-standing columns. A column consists of three main elements: the base, the shaft, and the capital.

The columns of the temple support the entablature (everything above the level of the columns). The entablature also consists of three main elements: the architrave, the frieze, and the cornice.

Greek temple architecture was the most important architecture in ancient Greece because the gods were of primary importance. The Greeks believed that no action and no victory were achieved without their assistance. For this reason there was little attention paid to domestic architecture.

During the Archaic period, temples were built in one of two established orders or styles; the Doric and the Ionic.

The Doric order or style, which originated in mainland Greece, is more massive in appearance, with sturdy columns planted directly on the stylobate. The Ionic order, which originated in the East, appears lighter and more ornamental with columns that are more slender in proportion and rise from decorated bases. The capitals of the two orders are quite distinctive; the Doric order employs a round simple capital, while the Ionic order capital is characterized by two volutes or scrolls.

The two orders are often discussed or addressed in terms of their differences.

1. **The capitals are distinctly different:**
   The Doric column capital is simpler: it is divided into two parts, the echinus (cushion shape that extends upward from the shaft of the column) and the abacus (square flat slab) that joins to the architrave.

   The Ionic capital is more ornamental and terminates in scroll-like spirals or volutes and its abacus is often decorated.
2. **The bases are different:**
   Doric columns rarely have a base and the shaft simply rests directly on the stylobate. Ionic columns separate the shaft of the column from the stylobate with a base that is often ornamented with horizontal fluting.
3. **The column shafts are different:**
   Doric shafts are thicker and heavier and the flutes (20 often in total) are separated by sharp ridges, called *arrises*. Ionic columns have more fluting (24 total) than Doric columns, and the flutes are separated by a flat *fillet*. The whole column shaft is also more slender in proportion to its height than the Doric column.
4. **The architrave is different:**
   The Doric architrave is usually left blank and unadorned. The Ionic architrave is usually divided into 3 horizontal bands called *fasciae*.
5. **The frieze is different:**
   The Doric frieze consists of an alternating series of *triglyphs* (3 upright bars) and *metopes*. The square metopes are flat surfaces that were frequently decorated with relief sculpture. The Ionic frieze is generally left unadorned. If it does carry decoration it appears in the form of continuous frieze element.

One of the best surviving examples of a Greek Doric temple is found in Italy. The Greeks, it should be noted, had colonized southern Italy by as early as 700 BCE.

This temple in Paestum, south of Naples, was built at a site the Greeks called Poseidonia, named for the god of the sea. Several large temples survive here, the most impressive of which is the Archaic Doric temple dedicated to Hera.

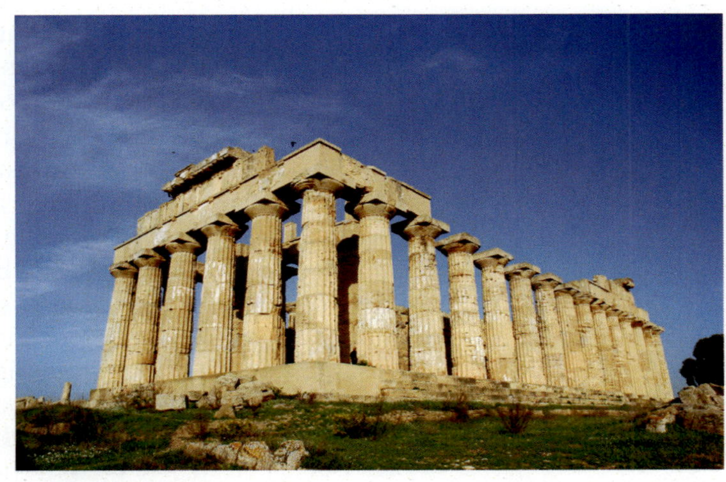

**5-11:** Temple of Hera I, Paestum, Italy, c. 550 BCE.

This enormous sandstone temple measures 80 by 170 feet and has an unusual peripteral colonnade configuration of nine columns on the short sides and eighteen on the long. It has a cella with seven columns down the middle and a pronaos with three columns in antis.

Its entire peripteral colonnade and some of its architrave survive but almost all of the rest is gone.

The temple has heavy Doric columns that are spaced closely together and have a pronounced swelling at the middle of the shaft; this swelling or tapering is called *entasis*.

The columns, so massive and closely spaced, seem to underscore their load-bearing function. In a progression similar to that in kouroi figures, columns will become slender and more graceful.

At the sanctuaries where these enormous temples were built, there were also a number of other smaller buildings that were constructed. This included shrines and altars, and at the more famous sanctuaries, there were also treasury buildings.

Treasury buildings were generally small rectangular buildings preceeded by a two-column porch and were often highly decorated. These impressive treasuries were set up for the safe storage of votive offerings. The citizens of many of the major cities in Greece built treasuries at major sanctuaries including the Athenians, Sikyonians, and the Siphnians.

The most celebrated treasury, erected by the citizens of the island of Siphnos, was located at the sanctuary in Delphi, a site famous for its oracle.

The tiny Ionic order building was constructed entirely of marble, measuring only 20 by 28 feet with a small porch with two columns in antis; however the columns in this case take the form of clothed female figures, or *caryatids*. *Caryatids* are fairly rarely used in Ionic architecture but never in Doric.

The tiny treasury had pedimental sculptures as well as sculptures on the roof, or *akroteria*. It also had a continuous painted relief frieze that ran around the entire building.

The pediment sculpture depicted Zeus at the center arbitrating between Apollo and Herakles, who fight over a tripod. The tripod, a three-footed seat or stand, was sacred to Apollo and particularly associated with the oracle at Delphi.

On the frieze are scenes from the god's battle against the giants, and a battle scene from Troy.

This detail of the frieze depicts the Gigantomachy, a battle between the gods and giants. It is also a common allegorical scene meant to represent the battle between the good and civilized (gods) against the evil and uncivilized. In this section Apollo

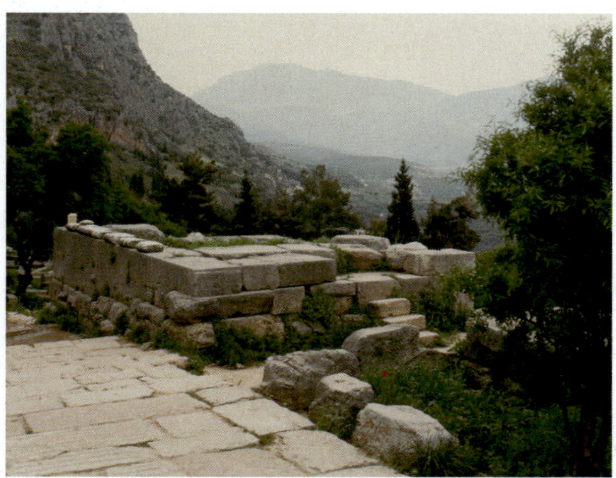

**5-12:** Treasury of the Siphnians, Delphi, Greece, c. 530 BCE.

and his twin sister Artemis chase a fleeing giant. Behind them a potion of another scene shows a lion pulling a chariot, biting a giant. The whole scene would have been painted, including the labels provided to identify the participants. Metal detail would also have been included for objects such as swords and shields.

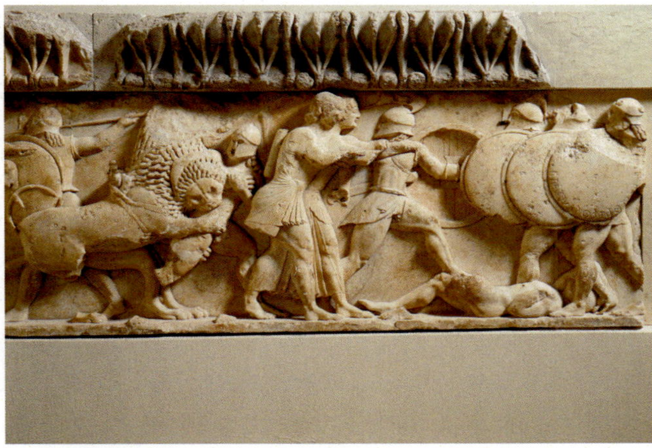

**5-13:** Gigantomachy, North frieze, Siphnians treasury, Delphi, Greece, 530 BCE, 2′1″, Archaeological Museum, Delphi.

## Archaic Pottery

By the 6th century BCE the Greeks, and particularly the Athenians, had become master potters and painters. The quality of the Athenian black-figure technique and the type of clay in the area, which turns a deep orange when fired, helped bring Attica to the forefront of Greek archaic vase painting.

There are basically two types or methods used for figural painting for vases of this period. The earlier form is called **black-figure style**, in which the figures are depicted in black silhouette against the reddish clay. Details were added by incising designs into the black paint with a fine sharp tool such as a needle or stylus. The results of black figure decoration were often very decorative.

The later style, or **red-figure style**, began to replace the earlier black-figure style around 520 BCE. The red-figure style paints the background black and leaves the figures red, the color of the clay. The addition of details is added in paint since incising was no longer the most common decorative technique.

Often both the potter, the one who created the vase, and the painter, who decorated it, would sign their work. They were sometimes but not always the same person.

Both styles of pottery were expensive and often used primarily for special occasions. These pots were also highly sought after and were exported, particularly to the colonies in Italy, in vast numbers.

The Francois Vase is a large volute krater (it has handles that terminate in large scrolls) named for its Italian discoverer Alessandro Francois, who found it in an Etruscan tomb in 1844.

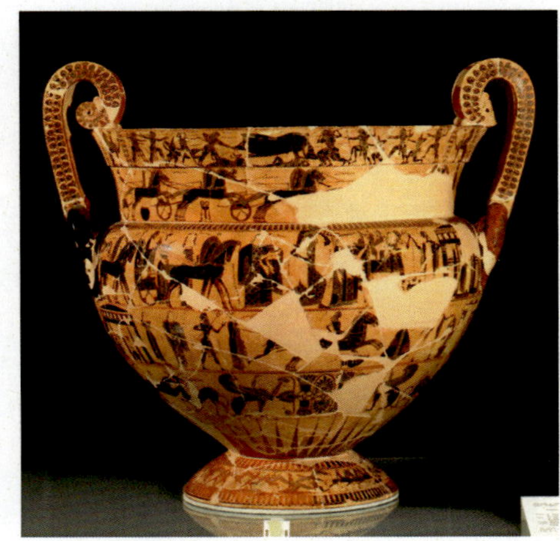

**5-14:** Francois Vase, Attic Black Figure Krater, Chiusi, Italy, 570 BCE, 2′2″, National Archaeological Museum, Florence.

The krater is decorated with over 200 figural scenes in six separate friezes, on both sides of the vase and on the handles. The vase is signed (twice) by both the potter Ergotimos and the painter Kleitias.

The most prominent frieze, the one at the top of the body of the vessel, depicts a procession of gods and goddess to the wedding of the Greek hero Peleus to the beautiful nereid Thetis. The wedding, seemingly a happy event, is actually, and unfortunately, partly responsible for the Trojan War.

Most of the rest of the decoration relates to the heroes Achilles, the son of Peleus and Thetis, and Theseus. Inscriptions, included all over the vase, help identify the major players and scenes.

## Art is an Endangered Species:

In 1900 a disgruntled museum employee, who had been dismissed for neglecting his duties, threw a stool at the case containing the vase shattering the krater into 638 pieces. It was restored, in 1902, by Pietro Zei, who used a piece that did not belong to this vase (called the Strozzi fragment) into his reconstruction. Another piece, which did belong to the Francois vase, was also stolen, though that piece was returned to the museum in 1904. In 1973 the vase was deconstructed so that it could be re-reconstructed to remove the errant fragment and replace the returned one.

By the mid 6th century BCE Athens and its immediate neighbors were the undisputed leaders in the making and decorating of pottery in the Greek world.

Some of the most recognized and finely executed attic black-figure vessels are the work of the painter Exekias (active c. 550–530 BCE). At least sixteen extant vessels are signed by him and his work is considered the pinnacle of the black-figure style with mature compositions and extremely minute detail.

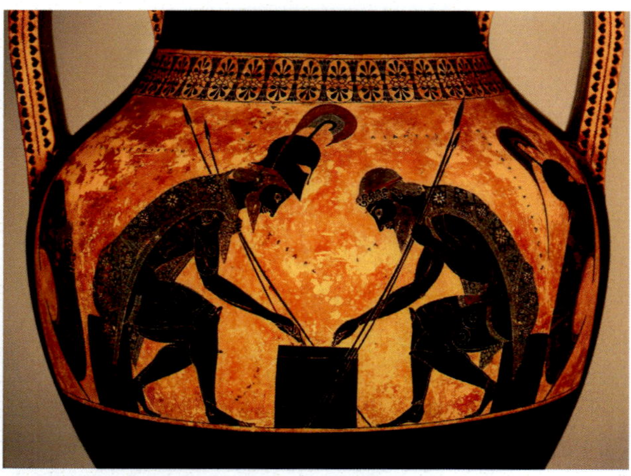

**5-15:** Black figure Amphora, Achilles and Ajax playing dice, Exekias, 540–530 BCE, 2′, Vatican Museums.

Exekias was often both the potter and the painter of his vessels, and they were highly sought after and both exported and copied a great deal. He also dispensed with the use of registers or bands for his decoration, and instead used monumental sized figures that fill a single large panel on the body of the vessel.

Perhaps his best recognized vessel is an amphora that depicts Achilles and Ajax playing a game on one side, and the twins Castor and Pollux, known as the Dioscuri, on the other.

The scene depicts two warriors, Achilles on the left and Ajax on the right, as they sit for a game of dice. They are not relaxed since they are armed and have their shields at the ready. The scene is at Troy, where the two take a break from the battle. Ajax's helmet is resting on his shield behind him, ready to be donned swiftly should they come under attack. Holding their spears in one hand, and fingering the dice with the other, there is a pent-up tension as the men seem never to be able to let their guard down completely.

As they play, Achilles says the word *tessera* (four), inscribed as if the word falls from his mouth, while Ajax says *tria* (three). This is perhaps the earliest known depiction of a gaming scene in art.

The scene is full of quiet power and foreboding, the sort of calm before the storm. Viewers would have recognized the scene and known the violence of the events yet to come; both men will die, Achilles in battle, and Ajax by his own hand. All ancient Greeks, familiar with the story of the Iliad, find the scene bittersweet, and it would serve to underscore their belief in fate.

The Exekias painter was a master craftsman. The quality of his vessels and the precision of his lines were incomparable. His balance of positive and negative space as well as his ability to create drama made his works not only sought after but extremely influential. However, he still does retain some of the old fashioned traditions since the figures are shown in profile yet are still drawn with a frontal eye.

By the late sixth century c. 510 BCE, painters using the new red-figure technique, now comfortable with it and its decorative possibilities, began experimenting with more complex compositions and poses for figures.

One such painter was Euphronios, also an Athenian, who like Exekias before him; both potted and painted many of his vessels.

One of his best recognized and most influential works is a red figure calyx krater depicting the battle between the Libyan giant Antaios and the hero Herakles. A calyx krater has low handles that protrude from the base of the vessel.

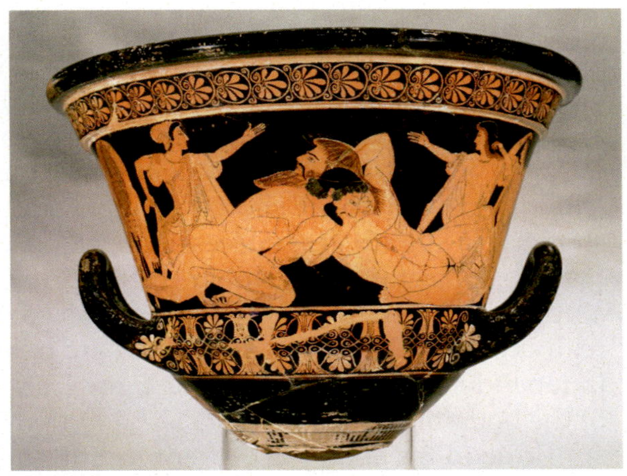

**5-16:** Red Figure Krater, Antaios and Herakles, Euphronios, from Cerveteri, Italy, c. 510 BCE, 1′7″, Louvre, Paris.

Antaios was a Libyan giant; a son of the earth, whose strength and power was dependent on his contact with the earth. In order to defeat him Herakles had to lift him off the ground and crush him. But this is not a scene of the victory of Herakles over the giant but is instead a scene of the struggle between the two as Antaios tries to keep their wrestling low to the ground.

The giant is shown in an extremely contorted pose with his head twisted back and his nude body twisted flat with picture plane. The giant's arm hangs limp next to his body and he actually grits his teeth against the pain. The hero Herakles with the darker hair and groomed beard appears to be gaining the upper hand.

The contorted poses and use of foreshortening reveals Euphronios' skill and inventiveness, particularly the front view of the giant's thigh as it is situated parallel to the picture plane.

The new poses and large scale of the figures represent a radical break with what had come before. Euphronios is seen as a revolutionary artist for his daring new compositions.

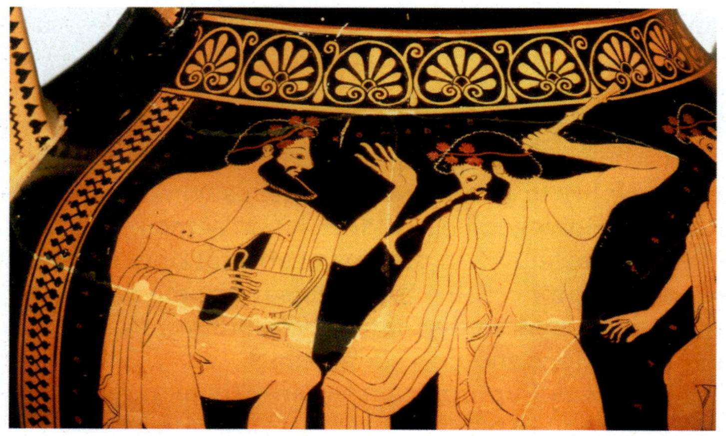

**5-17:** Red figure Amphora, Three Revelers, Euthymides, c. 510–500 BCE, 2′, Antiker Kleinkunst, Munich.

An example of another exceptional and innovative red-figure amphora was executed by the painter Euthymides, a rival of Euphronios.

The Athenian artist Euthymides experimented with the pose of the human figure in space. In one of his best recognized works he depicts three nude revelers, each in a unique pose. Two are shown in rather successful three-quarter pose, and another is shown in a slightly less successful back pose.

The subject of three rather drunken revelers is appropriate for the vessel, as an amphora is often used for wine storage. Notice how the bodies to do not overlap, or really come close to each other, they are treated less like a group and more like three independent figural studies. The figures are also quite large in proportion to the size of the body of the vessel.

Pride in his ability is evident in Euthymides signature on the vase. He not only signed his name but also added "as Euphronios never could."

The painter Euthymides, and his rival Euphronios, are often referred to as "pioneers" because of their experimental and daring innovation.

More than just innovators, these artists represent a spirit of competition and a desire for recognition that fueled artistic innovation and advances in Ancient Greece.

## The Early Classical period: 480–450 BCE

The early Classical period begins when Athens and her allies defeat the Persian invaders of Greece. The decisive battle was the battle at Salamis, in 480 BCE, at which the Greeks were severely outnumbered and yet defeated the Persians and captured a number of their ships.

The defeat of the Persian forces solidified the concept of a truly Hellenic identity and the power, strength, and supremacy of Athens within greater Greece.

It is important to remember that as Athenian pride and position grew in strength, her enemies became more bitter. She had defeated the Persians but enemies much closer to home would be the next biggest problem. Cities like Syracuse on the island of Sicily, and the Athenian rival city of Sparta, on the Peloponnese, watched with disdain as Athens began to rule the Greek world more like an empire than a democracy.

An example of an architectural monument of the Early Classical Period is the Temple of Zeus at Olympia, the original site of the Olympic Games.

The temple, built by a local architect named Libon of Elis, is now in ruins, but was well known in the classical world.

It was the biggest temple in Greece at the time measuring approximately 210 feet on the long side. The Doric 6 × 13 peripteral temple was built of limestone covered with stucco and marble. The interior cella had two rows, of Doric columns, that divided the cella into 3 aisles. Inside the cella was a colossal chryselephantine (made of gold and ivory) cult statue of Zeus, created by the sculptor Phidias.

The temple was lavishly adorned with decorated metopes on the interior above the pronaos and opisthodomos and both pediments were filled with three-dimensional sculpture.

The East pedimental sculpture shows the preparation for a chariot race between Pelops (from whom the Peloponnesus takes its name) and King Oinomaos.

The subject chosen had particular local significance in terms of both subject and location. The story revolves around a chariot race between Pelops and the King, and like all other Greek myths, it is dark and tragic and wrought with irony.

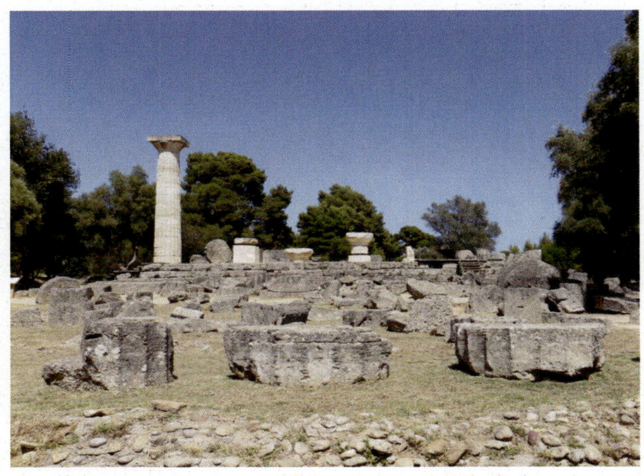

**5-18:** Temple of Zeus, Olympia, Greece, c. 470–456 BCE.

The choice for a scene that involves a chariot race must have seemed appropriate for the site, since this was the location of the Olympic Games and chariot racing was an event.

As the story goes, the King had a daughter, named Hippodameia, and it had been foretold to the King that he would die if she ever married. So the King would challenge anyone who asked for her hand to a chariot race. He of course knew that he would always win because his chariot was drawn by horses that his father, the god Ares, gave to him. Peplos, the new suitor for the hand of Hippodameia, knew of this deceit and therefore bribed the King's horseman, Myrtilos, to manipulate the King's chariot so that it would break down during the race. The horseman did, and Pelops won the race. But Pelops was a cad and rather than pay the bribe he owed to Myrtilos, he drowned him. So, just before his death Myrtilos cursed Pelops and all his descendants. The curse worked! The generations of descendants of Pelops all died horrible tragic deaths: Pelops' son Atreus was murdered; his grandson, the son of Atreus, was Agamemnon, who murdered his own daughter (Iphigenia) and then was killed by his wife (Clytemnestra). Pelops' great grandson son, Orestes (son of Agamemnon and Clytemnestra) killed his mother and her lover Aegisthus (probably with the help of his sister Electra) in revenge for the death of his father and sister.

It should be noted that the east end, with the pedimental sculptures relating to the story of Pelops and the King, actually faced the location of the start of all the Olympic chariot races. Perhaps then the sculptures could be read as a cautionary tale against cheating.

The East pediment depicts the god Zeus, larger than all the other figures, standing at the center. On one side are King Oinomaos and his wife and on the other are Pelops and Hippodameia. Behind the two couples are their respective chariots. Notice all the central figures stand calmly, poised, and facing outward. It is the calm before the storm. The drama is implied in what is to come but is not shown.

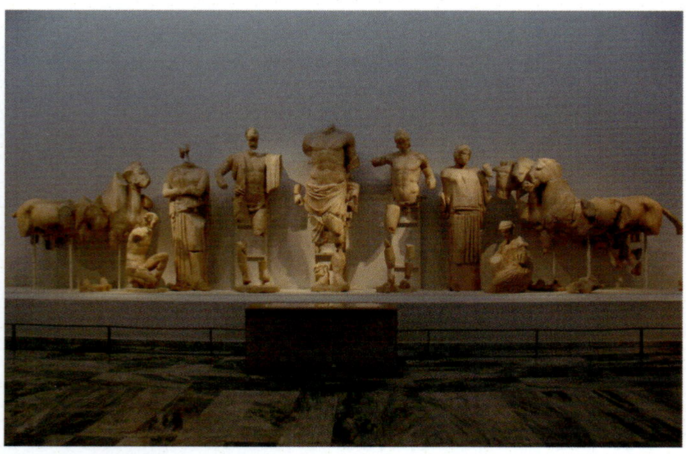

**5-19:** East Pediment, Temple of Zeus, Olympia, Greece, ca. 470 – 456 BCE, 88′ wide, marble, Archaeological Museum, Olympia.

The only figure in a non-frontal static pose is the figure of the seer, located to Zeus' left. A seer is an individual who can see the future. His pose, like the others toward the ends of the triangular pediment, is forced into a reclining position. The artist uses the positions of the bodies to fill the awkward

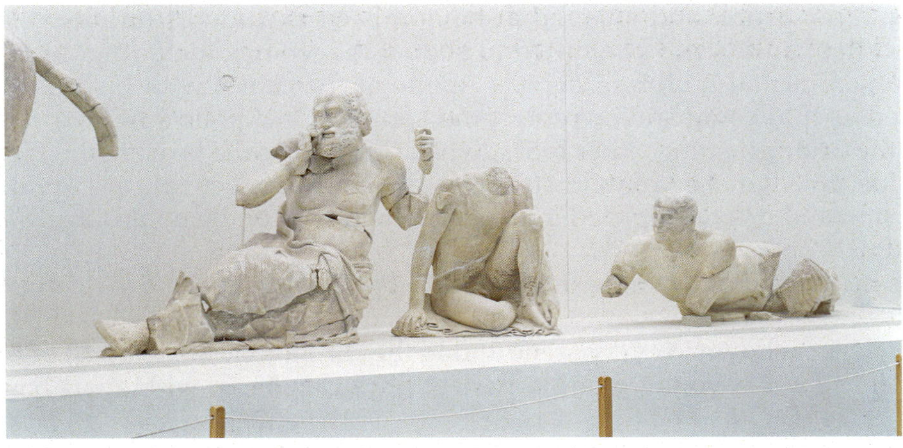

**5-20:** Seer, from East Pediment, Temple of Zeus, Olympia, Greece, c. 470–456 BCE, marble, Archaeological Museum, Olympia.

triangular section with figures or parts of figures that continue to decrease in size as they reach toward the end.

Here the seer, a prophet from the king's house, seems to recoil at the upcoming events. He is an expressive figure who clearly reacts to the story. He is also shown unlike the others because he is not a god or a hero but rather old, wrinkled, and balding. His moustache and other portions were left flat to better retain the paint that would have been applied.

In all of the figures there is a play of the surface to add interest and drama. The smoothness of flesh is contrasted with heavy folds of drapery, or the detail of the locks of hair.

This turn toward expressiveness is new in Greek sculpture and is at the leading edge of a revolution.

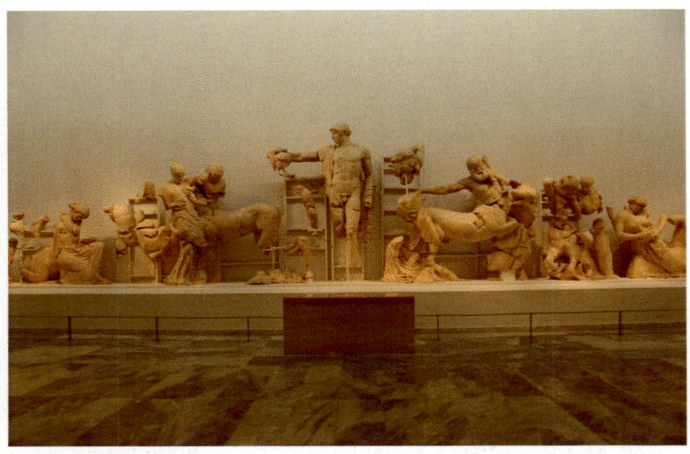

**5-21:** West Pediment, Temple of Zeus, Olympia, Greece, c. 470–456 BCE, 88′ wide, marble, Archaeological Museum, Olympia.

The west pediment depicts the story of the battle between the Lapiths (a Greek clan from Thessaly) and the Centaurs (half man half horse); a battle with centaurs is called a centauromachy. The battle occurred at the wedding of Perithus the king of the Lapiths, and Hippodameia (not the same wife of Pelops). According to one version, the Centaurs, drunk and angered at having been excluded from the celebration, attacked the Lapiths and attempted to abduct the women including the bride.

The pedimental sculpture depicts Apollo at the center with his right arm outstretched as if to command or protect the Lapiths. On Apollo's right, a centaur has seized the bride grasping at her breast while she elbows the beast in the face. On the other side, an anguished centaur struggles against a stronger calmer Lapith. There is both action and drama depicted in the faces and poses of the noble Greeks and their half-animal combatants.

The metopes that decorate the front and back porch depict the twelve labors of Herakles.

Herakles is shown in every scene and in the chronologically earliest of the scenes he is depicted as a young man, in perfect physical shape, with short hair and no beard.

In one of the metopes Herakles, with the help of Athena, takes on the task of holding up the sky for Atlas. (Atlas meanwhile will go and fetch the apples of the Hesperides.) The nude hero Herakles, at the center of the metope, is depicted with his arms folded back above his head steadying the sky as it rests on the pillow that he has doubled on his shoulders. Behind him stands Athena who calmly lends him a hand. In front of Herakles is Atlas, who approaches the hero with his arms outstretched in front of him to reveal that he has, in fact, retrieved the golden apples. All three figures stand calmly and in contrast to one another; the clothed female figure of Athena is shown frontally, contrasted against the profile view of Herakles and Atlas.

Herakles is important to the site because in some legends he is the founder of the Olympic Games. Further, his determination and athletic skill and power make him a suitable subject for temples on the site of the Olympic Games.

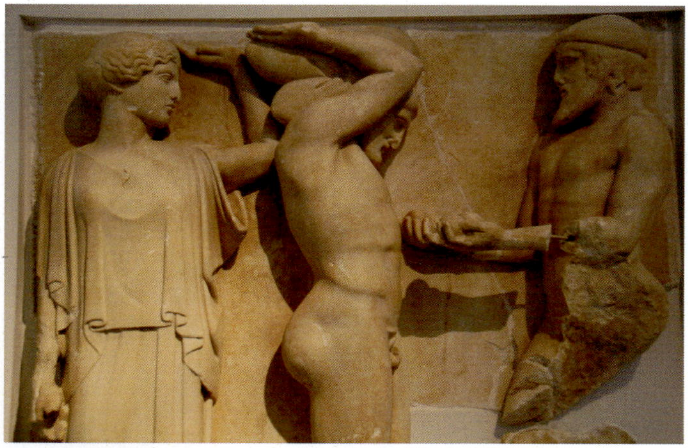

**5-22:** Metope, Athena, Herakles, and Atlas, Temple of Zeus, Olympia, Greece, c. 470–456 BCE, 5′3″, marble, Archaeological Museum, Olympia.

The most remarkable sculpture at the temple was Phidias' cult statue of the god Zeus. The statue, considered one of the seven ancient wonders of the world, depicted a seated Zeus holding a scepter, symbol of authority in his left hand, and in his outstretched right hand, a statue of Nike (symbol of Victory). The statue reached the interior roof of the temple and measured over 40 feet tall. No part of the statue remains, but ancient authors recounted its appearance and grandeur.

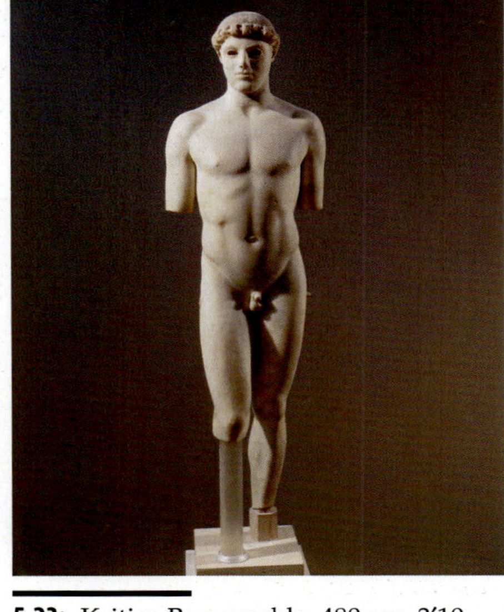

**5-23:** Kritios Boy, marble, 480 BCE, 3'10, Acropolis Museum, Athens.

## Early Classical Statuary

A true revolution in free standing three dimensional sculpture occurred during this period. That revolution is often represented by one sculpture: the Kritios Boy.

This marble sculpture, considered by many scholars to be one of the most beautiful of all Greek sculptures, was discovered in 1866 on the Acropolis in Athens. The sculpture is often attributed to the 5th century BCE artist Kritios, from whom the sculpture takes its name.

The revolutionary aspect of the sculpture is found in the posture of the figure. The stance of the figure, for the first time in art, is organic, natural, and reflects a desire on the part of the artist to depict what he observes, and to show the natural movement of the human body.

The figure does not stand in the very stiff and extremely unnatural pose of earlier Egyptian figures but instead reflects how people actually stand.

This naturalism is seen particularly in the shift in weight onto one leg. The figure stands so that his right hip dips slightly which indicates that there is a weight shift onto the left leg. His right leg is slightly bent. His head also turns slightly to the right. The body curves very slightly.

This weight shift is described by the term *contrapposto*, (literally "set against"). It is this use of contrapposto that separates this sculpture from not only earlier archaic Greek sculpture but from all sculpture that came before it.

While this figure is a break or step away from the past, it is not a leap. The contrapposto here is very slight. It will of course become much more pronounced and, by the Hellenistic period, exaggerated.

Perhaps then the single most important aspect of this classical revolution represented by Kritios boy is the clear, definable, and total break with the Egyptian inspired pose for standing figures.

The Kritios boy has a fairly square chin, flat smooth cheeks and thick upper and lower eyelids. He has a unique hairstyle in which the hair is pushed forward from the crown and then rolled up around a band worn on the head. The lack of expression in the figure, notice he has lost the archaic smile, puts it in a category of early classical works that are often described as part of the Severe Style.

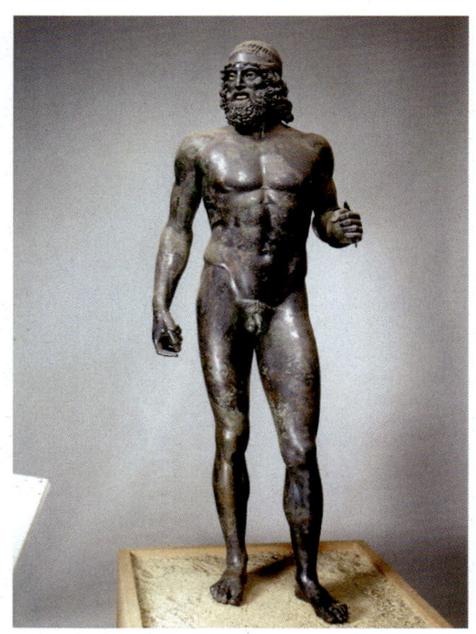

**5-24:** Warrior, bronze, Riace, Italy, 460–450 BCE, 6′6″, Museo Archeologico, Reggio Calabria, Italy.

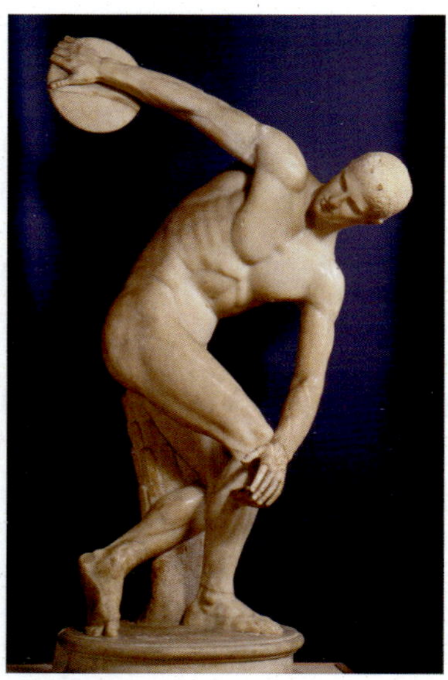

**5-25:** Diskobolos, Myron, Roman marble copy of Greek bronze original, c. 450 BCE, 5′1″, Museo Nazionale Romano, Palazzo Massimo alle Terme, Rome.

An example of more developed contrapposto is found in a pair of bronze statues found off the coast near Riace, Italy.

In 1972 two larger-than-life sized bronze statues were discovered in the sea near Riace, Calabria, in southern Italy. It is still unclear if the statues were made in Greece and in route to Italy, or vice versa.

Both statues (one called Warrior A and the other Warrior B) are hollow cast bronze with copper and silver inlay for details. They have eyes inlaid with ivory and glass paste, copper lips and nipples, and Warrior A even has silver teeth.

The two standing nude male warriors, also called the Riace Bronzes, formerly held spears and shields, and perhaps wore helmets though those articles are lost.

The warriors display contrapposto in a much more pronounced way than the Kritios boy. The heads turn more forcefully and the level of the shoulders is much more tilted, the weight bearing leg is strong while the shift in the hip that releases the weight on the front leg is much more pronounced. The relaxed leg has moved further away from the body as have the arms.

There is clearly an advance in the understanding not only of anatomy but of motion and the turning of the body on its vertical axis. It is an expression of natural human motion.

The Riace bronzes took over nine years to conserve and restore, in work that was done in Florence where they were first displayed in 1981. The two sculptures serve as major additions to the surviving examples of over life size three-dimensional Greek bronze sculptures.

The statues are an exquisite example of the indirect lost wax, or *cire perdue*, technique of bronze casting. This technique, developed by the Greeks in the 8th century BCE, is a relatively complex process that involves forming a clay mould around a core model covered with wax, which is then subsequently melted and drained away.

An excellent example of the classical interest in the natural motion of the human body is evident in a work by Myron called the Diskobolos, or Discus Thrower.

Myron was a Greek sculptor of the middle 5th century BCE who worked almost exclusively in bronze. Bronze was, at that time, the preferred medium of choice. Myron created statues of gods and heroes, but his fame rested principally on his representations of nude male athletes. Myron is attributed with real innovation and revolution in the depiction of action achieved by his figures' bold and active poses.

The discus thrower is represented at the moment when he has swung back the discus with the full stretch of his arm, and is about to hurl it with the full weight of his body. Notice that the head of the athlete is turned away from the viewer, instead of facing the viewer directly. The athlete is depicted as focused on his own internal actions.

The date of the Diskobolos places it at the cusp between the early and high classical periods. The active pose and graceful movement suggest the high classical period while the hair style and severe expression suggest the early classical.

### Roman copies

The demand for classical Greek sculpture, throughout Greece and Italy was remarkable. Freestanding statues were particularly sought after, and many copies were often made of the most celebrated statues. To keep costs down and supply up, these copies were generally made from less expensive marble, instead of the original and more highly prized material of bronze. The more fragile nature of marble, compared with bronze, also meant that the Roman copies were fitted with supports and struts to help strengthen the marble. This in many cases meant the addition, not found in the original bronze, of a strategically placed, though illogical, tree trunk.

## The High Classical Period: 450–400 BCE

One of the best recognized and most frequently copied statues from ancient Greece was the Doryphoros (spear bearer) by Polykleitos.

Polykleitos was considered, even in ancient times, to be one of the most important sculptors of classical antiquity.

Polykleitos consciously created an entirely new approach to sculpture. He described this new approach in a treatise he wrote called, the *Kanon*, long since lost. However, Polykleitos also created a sculpture that would serve to illustrate or demonstrate by example his aesthetic theories. The Doryphoros is the visual exemplar of his written treatise.

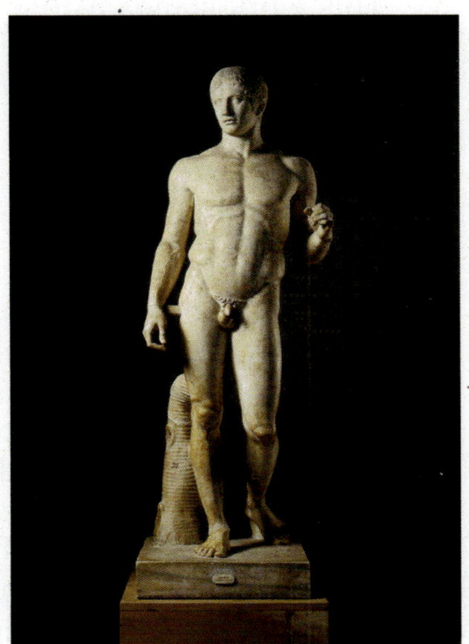

**5-26:** Doryphoros, Polykleitos, Roman marble copy of Greek bronze original, 450–440 BCE, 6′11″, National archaeological museum, Naples.

His treatise was essentially a prescription or description of the proportions that should be used to create the ideal statue of a nude male athlete.

To achieve ideal beauty was dependent upon a concept of *symmetria* which involves an interrelated proportional order and balance or harmony of all the parts, singly and as a whole.

The figure of the Doryphoros also stands in a much more pronounced contrapposto than we have seen thus far with his bent leg farther behind the body with the heel raised. This natural looking stance is sometimes called the walking stance.

The Doryphoros also demonstrates a concept of cross or counterbalance, called *chiastic*. *Chiasma* is a Greek word that refers to a crisscross or X pattern.

The stance of the statue, while it appears natural and casual, is in fact composed of a complex and subtle organization of the various parts as they balance or counter balance each other. Notice how the standing tensed right leg is counter balanced by the flexed arm that held the spear. Yet notice too how the verticality of the standing tensed leg is echoed by the straight hanging arm. All of this counter balance is best describes as chiastic.

It should be remembered that Polykleitos was aiming for more than a natural pose; he searched to impose an order and perfection to the movement of the human figure based on a system of mathematical proportions, based at least in part on the work of the 6th century BCE Greek philosopher Pythagoras.

The Doryphoros ultimately serves as the embodiment of the classical ideal; natural and yet perfected by mathematical proportion.

This work stands as the culmination of the evolution of the nude, male figure from the early archaic static daedalic kouros figures through the revolution represented by the Kritios boy to this, now fully developed, logical, and perfected depiction of the nude male form.

## Pericles and the Acropolis

The High Classical period is perhaps best exemplified by the massive construction project on the Acropolis in Athens.

Athens was by the mid 5th century the self proclaimed capital of Greece and had the strength, power, money, and pride to undertake an expensive and revolutionary building campaign on the Acropolis.

While the Athenian building campaign was meant to glorify and embellish the city of Athens, with a population of roughly 150,000, it was accomplished through what today would probably be considered an illegal misappropriation of funds.

The beauty of the buildings should not obscure the fact that the monies used to pay for this extensive building project were in fact monies that had been collected by the Delian League. The Delian League was an alliance formed in 478 BCE after the Persians were chased from Greece in order to fund protection of the cities if needed from any further invasions. The seat of the league was the island of Delos, and its treasury, holding monies given by all the allies, was there as well. In 454 BCE the Athenians decided that the treasury should be moved to Athens, ostensibly for its protection, but really so that it could be used to fund the great building campaign in the city.

This is important because the buildings on the Acropolis are often cited as an example of the beauty and result of democracy when really they are a reflection of Athens' bold abuse of power and tyrannical decision making not for the good of the demos (all the people) but instead for the good of Athens and the Athenians.

The leader and director of the building project on the Acropolis was the Athenian statesman Pericles. Pericles was born in Athens in about 495 BCE to a family of wealth and position. His father was also a statesman, and his mother, Agariste, was a member of a politically powerful family. Pericles, a *strategos*, (military general) was elected to public office some fifteen times.

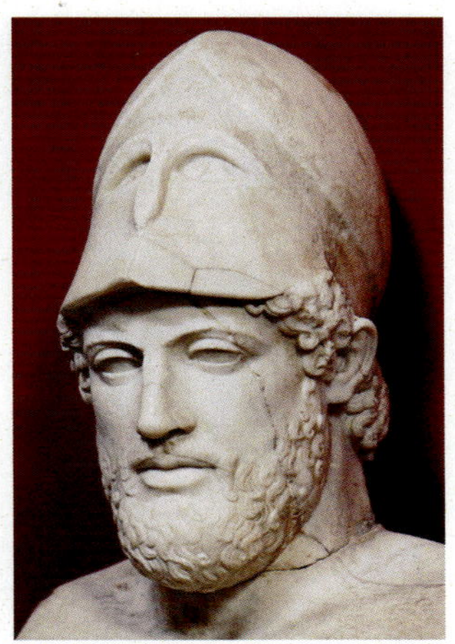

**5-27:** Bust of Pericles, Kresilas, Roman marble copy of Greek bronze original, c.429 BCE, 4′6″, Vatican Museums, Rome.

This Roman copy reproduces only the head of the original free standing nude bronze. The Romans used the portrait in the form of a *herm*, a Greek invention and popular Roman format. A herm is a portrait bust on top of a square or tapered pillar. The herm is inscribed in Greek in three lines of text. It reads in translation, "Pericles, son of Xanthippos, the Athenian."

The portrait depicts a bearded and mature Pericles wearing the helmet of a general. The portrait with its serene expression and flawless features is clearly an idealized portrait of the statesman.

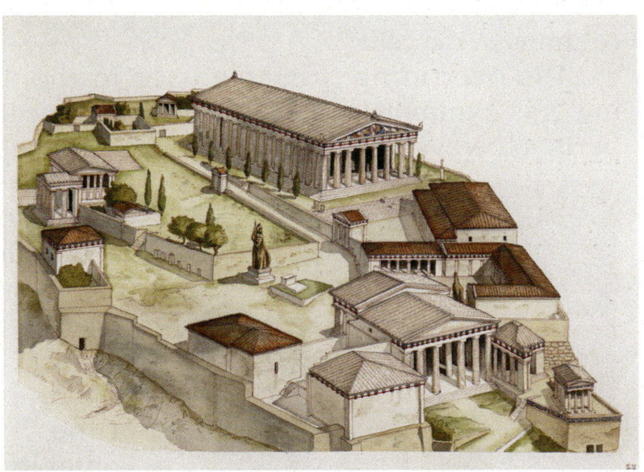

**5-28:** Reconstruction of the Acropolis, 5th cen BCE.

### The Athenian Acropolis

During the High Classical period four major structures were built on the Acropolis. They were built either under the direction supervision of Pericles or after his death according to his plan. The sculptor Phidias (c. 480–430 BCE), who had created the cult statue of Zeus for the temple of Olympia, served as overseer of all the temples decorations.

The buildings erected on the Acropolis at this time were:

The Parthenon 447–438 BCE, the Propylaia 437–432 BCE, the Temple to Athena Nike, 427–424 BCE, and the Erechtheion, 421–405 BCE.

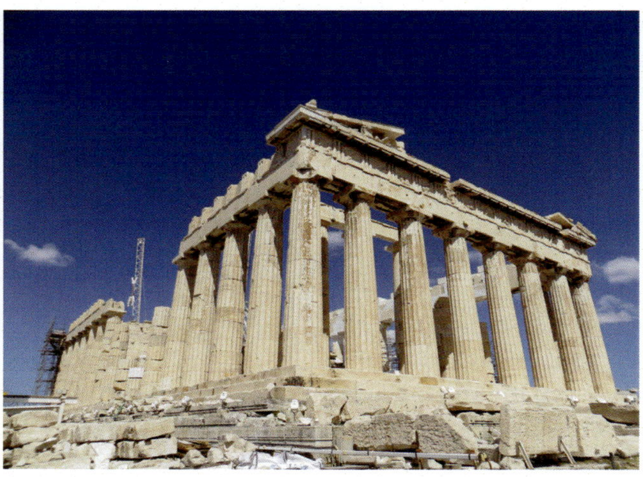

**5-29:** The Parthenon, Iktinos and Kallikrates, Acropolis, Athens, 447–438 BCE, 228′ × 101′.

The Parthenon is the main temple on the Acropolis and was built to house the cult statue dedicated to Athena Parthenos (the Virgin Athena). The architects, recorded in contemporary documents and named in a biography of Pericles, were Iktinos and Kallikrates, although beyond that very little information about them survives.

The Parthenon is best and most succinctly described as a Doric, octastyle, peripteral; which means its external colonnade is in the Doric style. It has eight columns on the short sides, and a single peristyle. It has a rather unusual plan; unusual because it has no pronaos, and it has an internal horseshoe arrangement of columns in the cella.

The overriding principle used in the design and dimensions of the building was symmetria; a logical mathematical basis for the proportions of all the parts. However, even embracing the concept of symmetria the building is actually quite irregular.

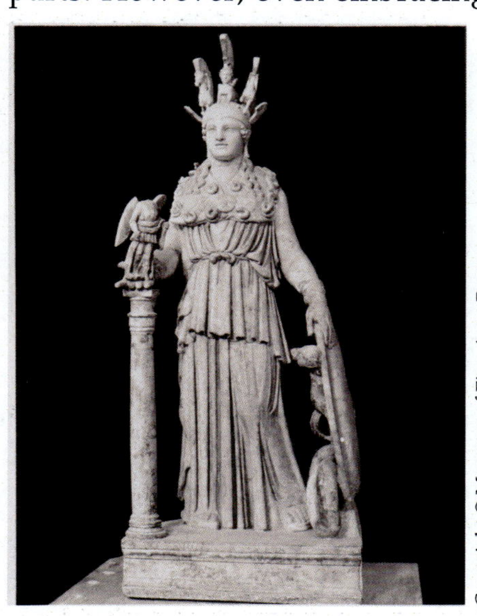



**5-30:** Athena Parthenos, Phidias, cella of Parthenon, Acropolis, Athens, Greece, 438 BCE. Model of lost original.

The irregularity is in compensation for optical illusions, so that there are no true right angles in the building, no true horizontals and no true verticals; nothing is perfectly plumb, straight, or square.

For example the stylobate curves upward at the center because a row of parallel horizontal lines appears to sink in the middle. The peristyle leans inward slightly from bottom to top because parallel vertical lines appear to lean outward. The columns at the ends of the peristyle are also about two inches thicker in diameter than all the rest. Indeed, because of their location on the corner, those columns receive more light which makes them appear thinner. The architects understood perfection but in order to see the temple as perfect, changes were made to compensate for optical illusions.

On the interior of the two-story cella was the monumental cult statute of the goddess Athena Parthenos by the sculptor Phidias.

The statue, long since lost, was a 40 foot chryselephantine representation of the goddess fully armed with a shield, spear, and helmet. In her outstretched right hand she held a Nike; a winged female personification of victory. On her sandals was a representation of a Centauromachy and on her shield an Amazonomachy. The symbolism in the sculpture of the Nike and other decorative elements were intended to reinforce, and celebrate the victory of the Athenians over the Persians in 479 BCE.

## Plan of the Parthenon

The Parthenon is not an example of a pure Doric temple because the four columns of the opisthodomos are Ionic. Also unusual is that the Parthenon has a typical Doric entablature with a blank architrave and a frieze of alternating triglyphs and metopes, but it also has an internal continuous frieze that runs around the exterior wall of the cella.

## The pediments and decoration

The decorative program at the Parthenon was the most lavish decorative program ever conceived or executed for a Greek temple. It had 92 decorated metopes, elaborate pedimental sculpture, and an internal continuous frieze that was over 500 feet in length.

The two pediments, some 90 feet in length, at the east and west end of the Parthenon, were each filled with dozens of over life size figures in dramatic poses. The subjects of the two pediments are appropriate for the temple and include Athena as the protagonist in both.

On the East side the pedimental sculptures depict the Birth of Athena. On the West, the pediment sculptures depict the contest between Athena and Poseidon. This mythical contest was held in order to determine who would be the patron of the city

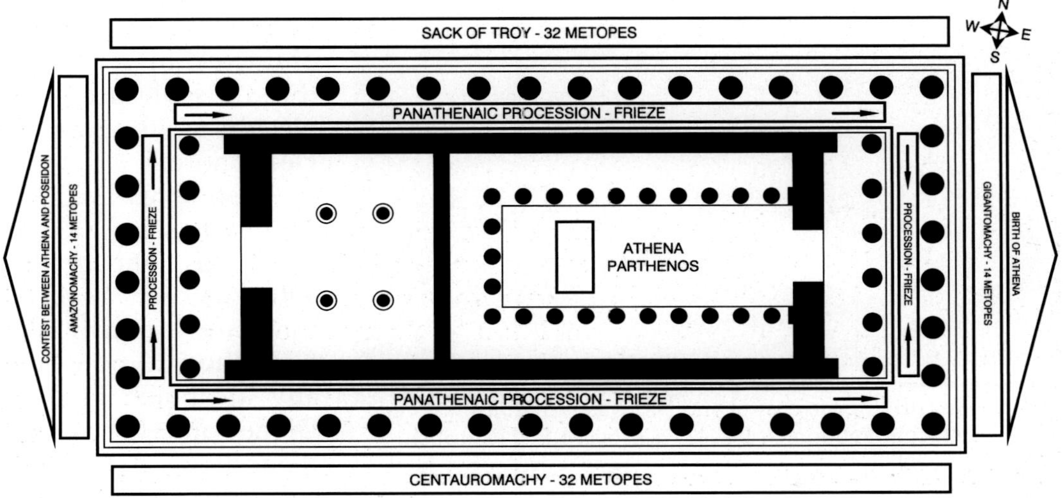


**5-31:** Parthenon Plan with Sculptural Program, 447–432 BCE, Acropolis, Athens.

and would worship at that site. Poseidon struck a rock and gave saltwater, Athena struck the ground and an olive tree grew, the citizens then awarded her the victory. She is therefore the patron goddess of the city, to whom she gave her name, and it is to her the main temple on the Acropolis is dedicated.

Unfortunately, very little of the original sculptures remain at the Parthenon. What was not damaged or destroyed by time, occupation, and war, was sold.

## Art is an Endangered Species:

Two major events greatly affected the condition of the Parthenon and its sculptures. The first occurred in 1687 when the Venetian commander Francesco Morosini accidently struck the Parthenon with cannon fire while attempting to oust the occupying Ottoman Turks.

The second event occurred between 1801 and 1803 when Thomas Bruce, the British Earl of Elgin purchased (although there is some doubt about this ) and then dismantled the pedimental sculptures and other sculptures and architectural fragments. He then had them shipped them to London. In 1816 the British government bought the sculptures, and they were put on display in the British Museum, where they remain. The legality of the original purchase remains a subject of debate and the Greek government continues to push for the return of the sculptures.

Two of the best preserved sections from the East pediment give us a glimpse of the sculptures original beauty, splendor, and technical virtuosity.

`From the far left corner of the east pediment is the sun god Helios and his chariot pulled by horses as it emerges into the scene. This is intended to represent the beginning of the story as Helios brings the sun and light to the subject. Just to the right is the reclining nude male figure of a god, perhaps Dionysius. The strong contrapposto of the reclining figure and the musculature resembles the ideal figure of the Doryphoros.

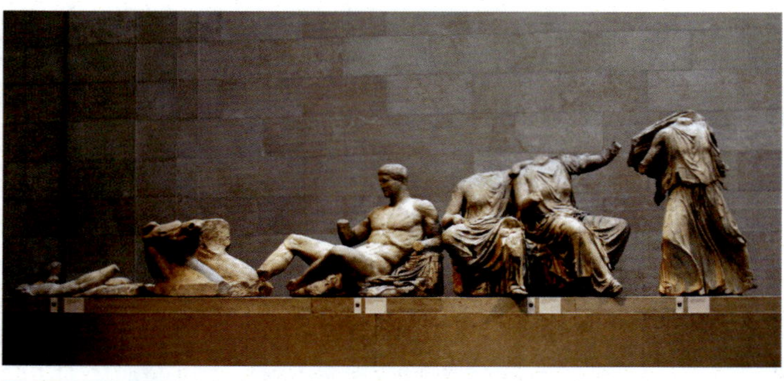

**5-32:** Helios driving his chariot and Dionysios, marble, East Pediment, Parthenon, Acropolis, 438–432 BCE, over life size, British Museum, London.

Also preserved from the east side are three goddesses, though none still has her head. The three are variously identified, though now generally attributed as Hestia, Dione, and her daughter the reclining Aphrodite.

The figures are wrapped in heavy garments that bunch and fold to create impressive knots and swags. The drapery is sheer and clinging, like wet fabric that both conceals and reveals their female form. The deeply cut folds of drapery also create shadow and interest emphasizing their three dimensional quality.

The figures in the pediments are all brilliantly composed and organized to show the potential of movement and grace and physical beauty while contained within the small and very awkward slanting shape of the pediment.

## The Panathenaic Frieze

The sculpted Ionic frieze that decorates the external cella wall is in many ways the most remarkable of all the Parthenon's decoration. This is due in part because here the decoration honors the Athenian people and depicts one of their most revered events. This is an event in which the gods are actually the viewers and not the primary focus. This tribute is another example of Athenian pride, in their city, their festivals, and themselves.

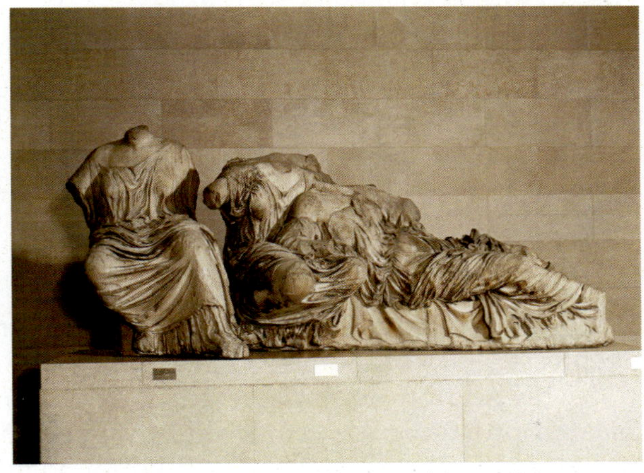

**5-33:** Three goddesses, marble, East Pediment, Parthenon, Acropolis, 438–432 BCE, over life size, British Museum, London.

The subject of the frieze is the Panathenaic procession; the most ancient and important festival of the Athenians. The festival was celebrated every four years in honor of the patron deity **Athena**, and it lasted more than eight days.

The procession began at the **Dipylon** *gate* and following the Panathenaic way, crossed through the Agora, and ended on the Acropolis. The procession was the formal delivery of a new *peplos* **(a long tunic)** made by the women of Athens to Athena.

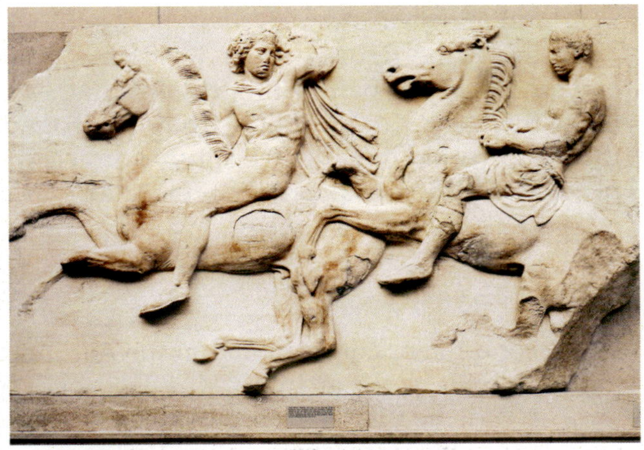

**5-34:** Horseman, Parthenon frieze, marble, 440–432 BCE, height 43″, British Museum, London.

The frieze depicts this procession in incredible detail and

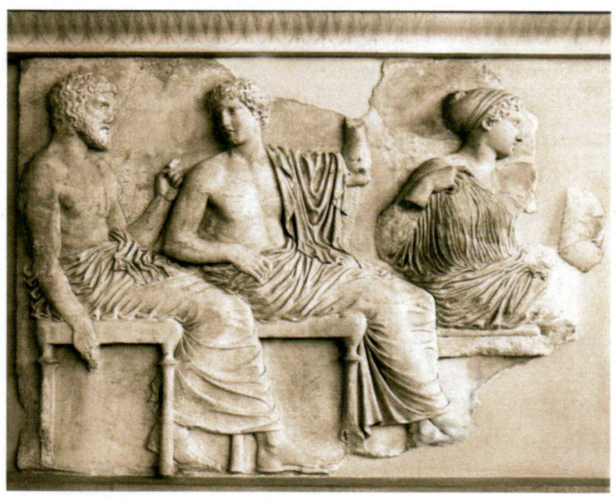

**5-35:** Seated deities, Parthenon frieze, marble, 440–432 BCE, height 43″, Acropolis Museum, Athens.

includes depictions of all the major activities of the festival including the mounted riders, the young maidens, the elders, and even the gods seated at the front awaiting the arrival of the procession.

The frieze of the riders depicts the beginning of the procession while the maidens and elders represent a portion nearer the end.

From the east side a procession of women moves slowly forward toward the center. These are not gods or goddesses but instead are Athenian women. They converge toward the center and are met by male officials who continue to lead the procession to the twelve Olympian deities who sit on either side of the scene of the delivery of the peplos.

This section depicts the gods, Poseidon, Apollo and Artemis. The gods are seated on stools; each one slightly overlaps the chair in front to suggest space and depth. The gods, depicted larger than the standing figures, turn and twist in their chairs, some watching the event and others turning to chat with their neighbor.

The execution and skill of the work is paramount. The figures are balanced, proportioned and reveal a contrapposto pose as well as an intimate understanding of male and female anatomy.

Because the figured frieze is some 40 feet off the ground the sculptors have carved the upper half of the frieze in higher relief than the lower half in order to make the images more legible from the ground. Also to aid in visibility and drama, the frieze would have been brightly painted with metals, like iron, bronze, and copper used for the metal details in the frieze.

## The Propylaia

The second major construction on the Acropolis was the Propylaia, or monumental gateway, built by the architect Mnesikles between 437 and 432 BCE.

The Pentelic marble structure erected at the western end of Acropolis was begun even before the decoration on the Parthenon was complete. The site was awkward because it sits on a steep slope so the architect disguised this by building a split level gateway with a five door entranceway. Four of which had steps and one with a ramp for animals.

The entrance resembles a classic Doric temple façade with six columns. The spacing of the columns is adjusted at the center, between the fourth and fifth columns, for a wider central entrance.

Two asymmetrical structures or wings flank the gateway to the right and to the left. The larger one, to the north, contained a *pinakotheke* or painting gallery. Here paintings, most often done on wood panels, would have been displayed. The function of the smaller wing is still unclear. Due to the outbreak of the Peloponnesian war the building was never completed as designed. Visitors still enter the acropolis through the Propylaia.

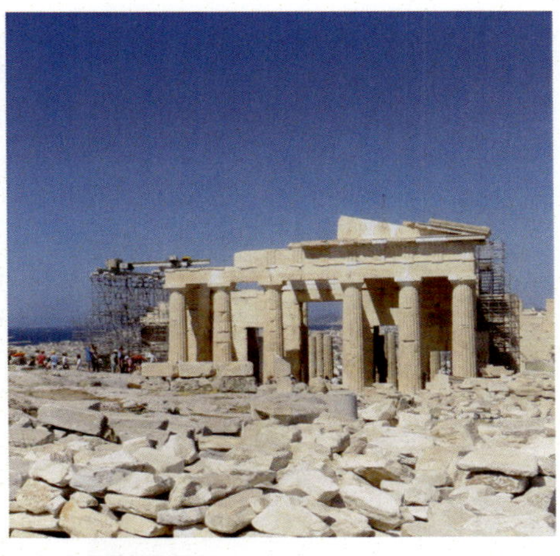

**5-36:** Propylaia, Mnesikles, East face, 437–432, BCE, Acropolis, Athens.

## The Temple to Athena Nike

The small temple to Athena Nike, (victorious Athena) was designed and built by the architect Kallikrates.

Located to the south of the Propylaia it is an Ionic tetrastyle amphiprostyle temple; which means that it has four Ionic columns only at its front and back (east and west ends). It is dedicated to the goddess Athena in her aspect as victorious in battle and is precariously situated on a little outcropping of rock that juts out from the Acropolis on the west end.

The temple had a decorative figural frieze that encircled the entire external wall depicting battle scenes and depictions of the gods. It also had a carved balustrade or parapet (a low protective wall) that was added sometime around 410 BCE. The parapet was less than four feet high and encircled the temple on the north, south, and west sides. It was decorated with high reliefs depicting a parade

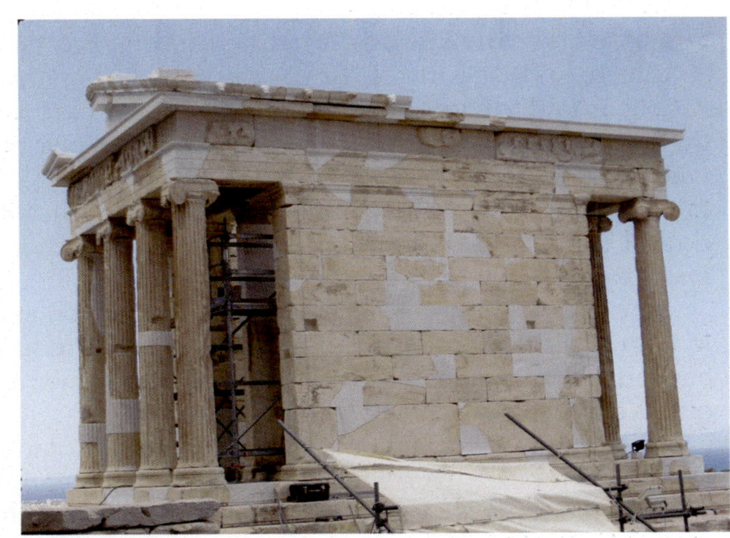

**5-37:** Temple to Athena Nike, Acropolis, Athens, marble, c. 427–424 BCE, 27′ × 19′.

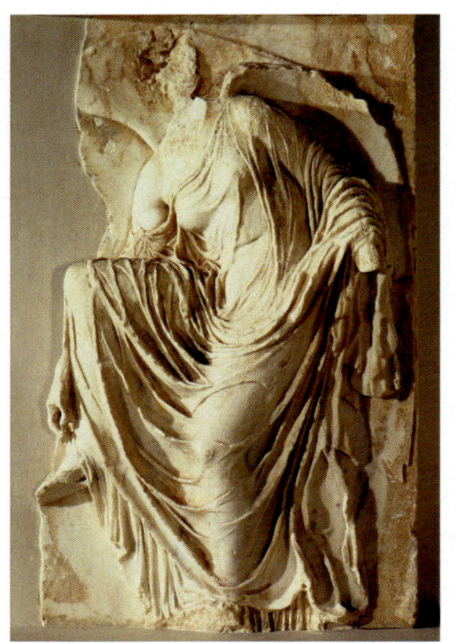

**5-38:** Nike adjusting her sandal, Temple of Athena Nike, marble, 410 BCE, 3′6″, Acropolis Museum, Athens.

of Nikes toward a seated figure of Athena. Here the decoration reflects the purpose of the building, to celebrate victory.

The procession of Nikes depicted the winged females in a variety of poses and activities; some were shown walking, others carrying water jugs, and some leading sacrificial animals. One of the most graceful images depicts a Nike who has paused to adjust the strap of her sandal. The figure shows the artist's fascination with the twist of the figure and reveals the high point of classical drapery at its most clinging and transparent. The thick and deeply carved patterns in the drapery create ridges and shadows that contrast with the highly polished and light reflecting flat surfaces elsewhere.

## The Erechtheion

The last building to be erected on the Acropolis was the Erechtheion, built in the Ionic style between 421 and 405 BCE. The architect may have been Mnesikles, but that is not certain.

The building, built to replace an earlier archaic temple, is a multiple shrine temple with an unusual plan. It was built to house not only the cult statue of Athena, polias the wooden one that was the object of the Panathenaic procession, but also statues of Poseidon and early kings of Athens, including Erectheus and Kekrops.

Erectheus was King of Athens during whose reign the ancient wooden statue of Athena is said to have fallen from the sky, and Kekrops was the king who ruled when the competition between Athena and Poseidon took place. He was one of the judges who decided the contest.

The actual site of the temple was chosen because it encloses the spots where the contest took place. Both the imprint of Poseidon's triton in the rock and Athena's olive tree are included within the temple's confines.

The temple, built to the north of the Parthenon and facing east, is asymmetrical in plan and therefore different from the norm in terms of balance and symmetria. It has four distinct sides, each different from the other and each of the four sides rests on different levels.

The temple with its varying levels and odd plan is, however, most recognized for its south porch. The south porch uses six caryatids instead of Ionic columns to support the roof. The caryatids are weight bearing and serve the same function as columns. The caryatids, clothed and elegant stand in contrapposto.

The caryatids are exceptional in the way that their form beautifully and elegantly reflects their dual nature. They reflect both the verticality and strength needed from a supporting column and yet the grace and naturalness needed to convey them as living creatures, or *kore*.

The vertical flutelike drapery of their garments on the weight bearing side underscores their function as a column, but the sheer drapery and soft folds against the relaxed leg underscore their femaleness.

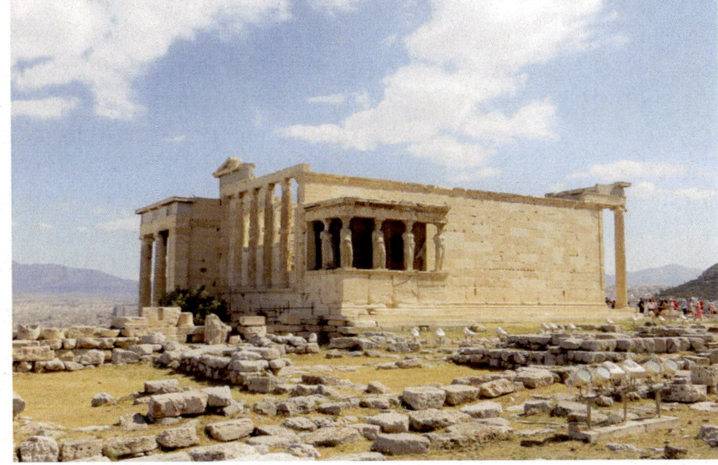

**5-39:** The Erechtheion, Mnesikles? Acropolis, Athens, 421–405 BCE.

## Stelae

In addition to the civic purposed sculptures of the Athenian acropolis the production of private works reached a zenith in the classical period. Private works such as large scale grave stele were produced for the elite and set an impressive tone for funerary monuments. These *stelae*, often carved in high relief, were intended to honor the deceased and record the names for posterity. The best preserved examples come from the Dipylon cemetery in Athens.

One of the most elegant examples of this type of grave marker is the stele erected to commemorate the death of Hegeso, the daughter of Proxenos. The information about the deceased is given in the inscription on the cornice of the pediment.

Here a young woman, Hegeso, is seated on a *klismos* (a classical chair with curved tapered legs that sweep forward and backward) with her feet resting on a small footstool. She has been brought a small box from which she selects a piece

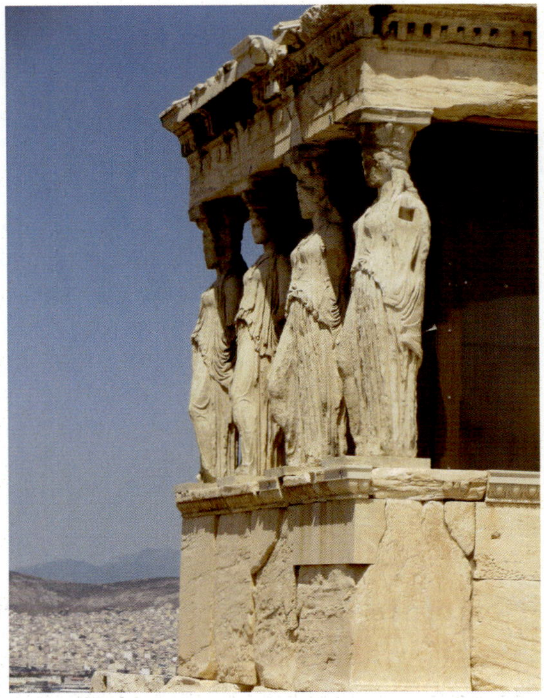

**5-40:** Caryatids, marble, South Porch of the Erechtheion, 421–405 BCE, 7′7″.

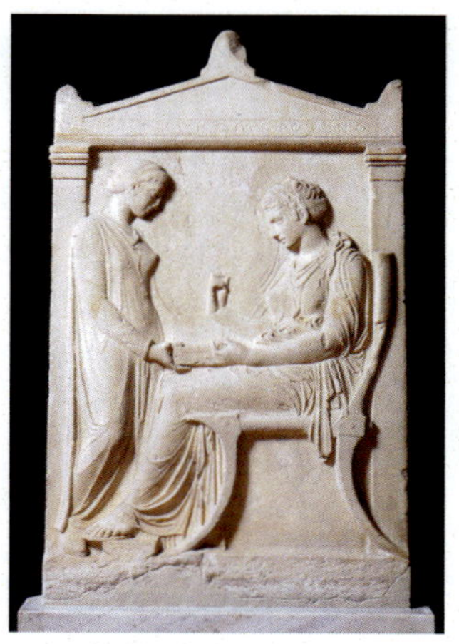

**5-41:** Grave Stele of Hegeso, Dipylon Cemetery, Athens, Greece, 400 BCE, 5′2, Archaeological museum, Athens.

of jewelry. Her young maid, dressed in a simple garment, stands in front of her.

The young women are enclosed in a classical architectural framework, suggesting an interior scene. The drapery is elegant and revealing of the forms underneath. The maid's simple garment contrasts with the rich and elegant drapery of Hegeso's garments. The women appear engaged in a simple domestic act that they would have been engaged in on a daily basis.

Notice that the faces are serene but not sad, and nothing but the inscription reveals to the viewer that this has a funerary context.

A grave stele of this size and quality reflects the wealth of the donor. To be sure it is a statement about the wealth of the father Proxenos, who had the lovely daughter, whom he supplied with the jewelry, and slaves, and who had the money to erect this monument to her. The monument speaks to the cloistered and sheltered existence of women in the classical period and that the young woman is best identified through her male family members.

## The Late Classical Period: 400–323 BCE

Two important historical events impacted the art of the late classical period: the defeat of Athens by her rival Sparta in 404 BCE and then, in 338 BCE, the defeat of Greece by the Macedonian king, Phillip II.

The Peloponnesian War began in 431 BCE between the Athenian Empire (or The Delian League) and the Peloponnesian League which included Sparta and Corinth. The war, documented by Thucydides in his work *History of the Peloponnesian War*, lasted 26 years and left Athens and the whole of Greece disillusioned and weak.

Then in 338 BCE, Greece suffered another crushing defeat, this time to an enemy from outside its borders. Though the Greeks managed to unite against the common enemy, they were simply too strained and weakened to defend against the Macedonian insurgence. Two years later, in 336 BCE King Phillip was assassinated in Macedon, and was succeeded by his 21-year-old son Alexander III; better known as Alexander the Great.

### Sculpture in the Late Classical Period

The fourth century was essentially a time of upheaval and defeats in battle, and both had a profound effect on the Greek psyche and therefore on the art of the period.

During the mid-fifth century BCE the Greeks, the supreme power in the ancient world, looked to perfect nature. They had searched for the correct and true mathematical proportions that could reflect the order of their universe. Their art reflected their world, their way of life, and their victories

The fourth century, however, brought an end to that idealism. The standing nude male athlete remained the dominant subject but there were new innovations in movement and balance and the physical space around sculptures, as well as the integration of an emotional component.

This new style and approach to art is apparent in the work of the sculptor Praxiteles, one of the great masters of the fourth century. His works were invested with a solemnity, and a new sensuality, even his depictions of the gods seemed less dynamic and more humanized.

This humanization and sensuality is clearly visible in his most famous work, the Aphrodite of Knidos.

The Aphrodite of Knidos is considered to be the first life size three dimensional sculpture of the nude female figure in western art, setting a new standard for the depiction of women in Greek art.

In this work Praxiteles has humanized the goddess of love, she is completely nude, not the way one generally depicted the gods, and she is caught in a vulnerable moment. That the goddess has a vulnerable moment at all is impressive, moreover she is caught in the act of doing something quite banal; she is about to take a bath.

According to an account by Pliny the Elder (a first century CE Roman author), Praxiteles received a commission from the citizens of Kos for a statue of the goddess Aphrodite so Praxiteles created two versions–one fully clothed, and the other completely nude. The shocked citizens of Kos rejected the nude statue and purchased the clothed version. The rejected nude version was purchased by the citizens of nearby Knidos and set up in a round open-air temple that permitted viewing of the statue from all sides.

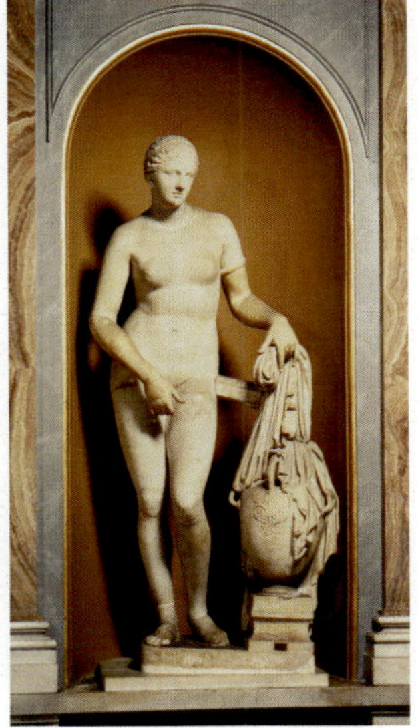

**5-42:** Aphrodite of Knidos, Praxiteles, Roman marble copy of Greek marble original, 350–340 BCE, 6′8, Vatican Museums.

It quickly became one of the most famous works in the ancient world and was praised for its bold depiction of Aphrodite as proudly and sensually nude.

According to legend, the statue became so widely known and copied that the goddess Aphrodite herself supposedly came to Knidos to see it. Upon viewing the work the goddess asked "where did Praxiteles see me naked?"

According to Pliny it was the most beautiful sculpture in the world and that many visitors who came to Knidos to see it were "overcome with love" for the statue.

The sculpture depicts the goddess just after she has removed her garment and laid it on top of a large hydria (water pitcher). She is about to step into the bath and seems to, perhaps unconsciously, cover herself in a pose that reflects

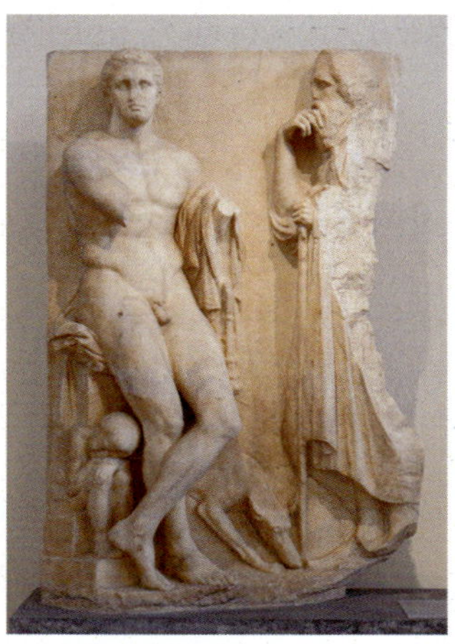

**5-43:** Grave Stele of a Young Hunter, marble, 340–330 BCE, 5′6, Archaeological Museum, Athens.

her modesty. She is not therefore considered erotic but is instead described as sensual. This particular pose of the figure, with one hand covering the pubic area, is called the "Venus Pudica" pose. The pose is often copied and quite popular during the Italian Renaissance, and its asymmetry often serves to draw attention to the very spot being obscured.

The figure has long legs, a small head, and a rather dreamy expression. The soft or dreamy expression is created in part by the deeply set eyes and projecting brow bone that casts a shadow just above the eye.

This pose of the figure, with the exaggerated contrapposto, bowed position of the body, and standing hip pushed markedly upward is called the Praxiteles S curve. This S-curve of the body is a clear feature in all of Praxiteles works and was extremely influential for other artists.

The solemnity and added emotion and sentimentality in these late works are also reflected in funerary sculpture.

Emotion is also evident in Late Classical stelae, like the Illissos stele, found in 1874, near the Illissos river in Athens.

The stele was originally set in an architectural frame like that of the Hegeso stele but that framework is now lost. This monument, however, is very different from that earlier one. Not only is this work carved in much higher relief, it depicts much more emotion. This stele immediately conveys a sense of time, sorrow, and even perhaps regret.

The deceased is the young nude male who leans on a column and looks out of the scene addressing his gaze to the viewer. His gaze seems to invite the viewer to contemplate his death and the sorrow and despair it has caused. A young boy, perhaps his son, brother, or even slave weeps (or perhaps sleeps) at his feet, and even his dog bows his head and seems to have a sad expression. The old man, perhaps the young man's father gazes at the youth. His heavy brow and melancholy pose, with his hand to his face, reveal a contemplative quality as if the old man wonders why death chose a youthful strong man instead of an old frail one.

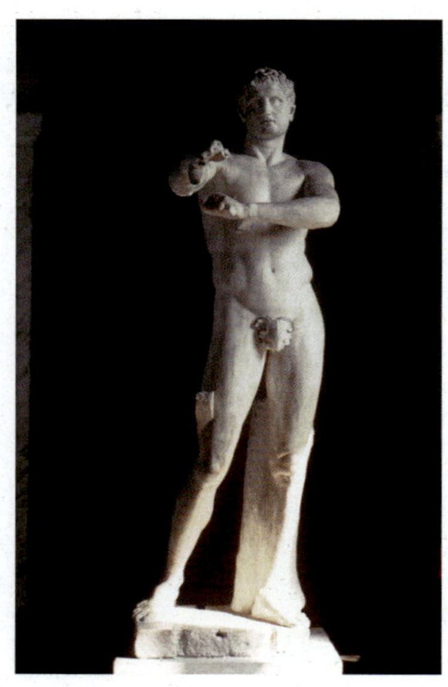

**5-44:** Apoxyomenos, Lysippos, Roman marble copy of Greek Bronze original, 330 BCE, 6′9″, Vatican Museums.

The emphasis on mourning in this stele is overt and dramatic while the earlier grave stele of Hegeso was reserved and remote.

The new, more graceful and slender proportions and added emotional content are clearly evident in the work of another late classical sculptor, Lysippos of Sikyon.

Lysippos, unlike Praxiteles, is closely identified with Alexander the Great, and is recorded as having created several official portraits of him. Alexander believed that only Lysippos was able to capture him and his essence in a portrait.

Lysippos is generally credited with establishing a new cannon of proportion, different from the earlier canon by Polykleitos, because his figures were more slender and taller in proportion, the head is now 1/8th instead of 1/7th of the body's height.

The Apoxyomenos is perhaps Lysippos' most recognized and copied work. Apoxyomenos means "the scraper" which describes the action depicted.

The nude athlete is depicted holding a strigil (a curved metal object used by athletes to remove dirt from the body) in his left hand and scraping it down his right arm to remove oil and dirt from his body. It appears as if he is about to switch hands and continue the motion to the other arm at any second. This part of the inclusion of a concept of a fleeting moment that is characteristic of some late classical works. The position of the arms raised and with one thrusting forward, essentially blocking the torso, is also new.

What is even more revolutionary about this work, and others from this period, is that the conventional frontal approach no longer satisfies the viewer. Instead this unusual pose of the figure invites the viewer to move all the way around the sculpture in order to gain several views. Each angle of the sculpture offers a very different perspective, and it is perhaps only through a profile or three quarter position that the viewer is satisfied. The earlier rigidly frontal poses for statuary are no longer satisfying; statuary is now conceived in three dimensions and the viewer is now expected to move around it in order to experience it fully.

## The Hellenistic period: 323–31 BCE

The Hellenistic period in Greek art begins in 323 BCE with the death of Alexander the Great and ends in 31 BCE with the Roman conquest of Egypt.

Alexander the Great, or Megas Alexandros as he is known in Greek, ruled from 336 BCE until his death in 323 BCE. He was the single most successful military commander of the whole of ancient history, conquering most of the known world before his death.

Alexander was the son of King Philip II of Macedon and of a Greek Epirote princess named Olympias.

According to Plutarch (a 1st century CE Greek historian) Olympias was impregnated not by her husband Philip, who was afraid of her and her affinity for sleeping with snakes, but by Zeus. Plutarch also records that both Phillip and Olympias had

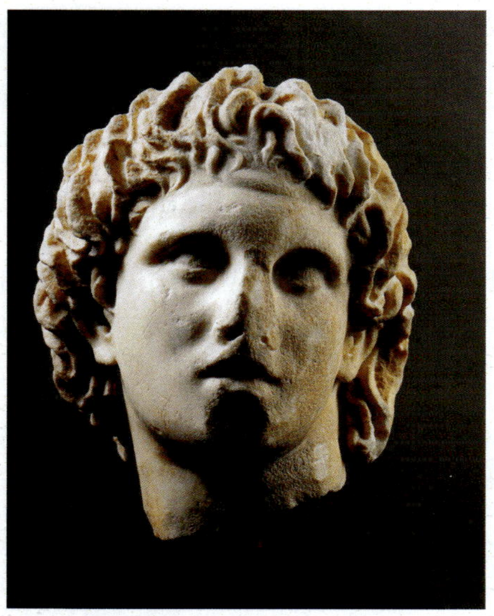

**5-45:** Head of Alexander the Great, marble, Pella, Greece, 200–150 BCE 1'high, Archaeological Museum, Pella.

dreams about their unborn child that he would be born with the qualities of a lion.

The Greek philosopher Aristotle was Alexander's tutor, and he provided Alexander a thorough training in rhetoric and literature, stimulating his interest in science, medicine, and philosophy. Alexander's favorite book was the *Iliad* by Homer and he was fascinated with stories the gods and battles described in it.

During his military campaigns, Alexander conquered the Persian Empire, including Anatolia, Syria, Phoenicia, Gaza, Egypt, and Mesopotamia. He extended the boundaries of the empire as far as the Punjab, the area between Pakistan and India.

Alexander integrated non-Greeks into his army and administration, leading some scholars to credit him with a "policy of fusion." He encouraged marriage between Greeks and non-Greeks, and practiced it himself (he married a Bactrian princess named Roxanne).

After twelve years of constant military campaigning, Alexander died of a mysterious illness (perhaps malaria, typhoid, or viral encephalitis) in the palace of Nebuchadrezzar II of Babylon in 323BCE; he was only 33 years old.

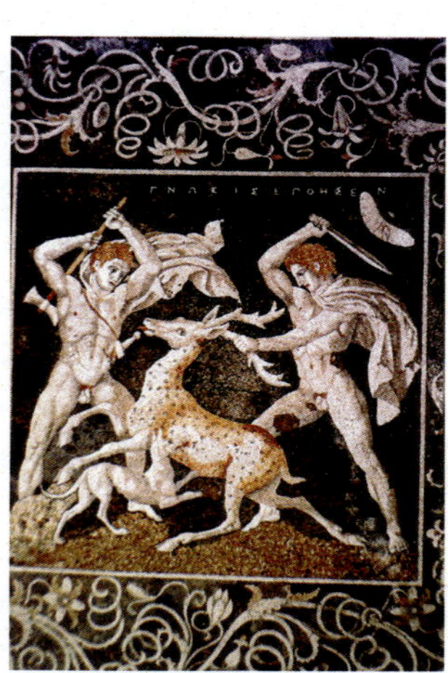

**5-46:** Stag Hunt, Gnosis, pebble mosaic, from Pella, Greece, c. 300 BCE, central panel 10'2" height, Archaeological Museum, Pella.

As early as 330 BCE a large number of portraits of Alexander the Great were produced, due in part to Alexander's request that Lysippos create a formal portrait of him. It seems the young general was quite aware of the propagandistic value or portraiture. Although his portraits vary in style, medium, and location many share similar features, such as a twisting neck with upturned face, deep set eyes, slightly parted lips, and thick wavy hair.

Full, thick, leonine hair is a particular attribute of Alexander's, and his hairstyle, or *anastole,* frames his face and creates two distinct curls at his forehead.

This portrait head displays all the key ingredients first captured by Lyssipos' original portraits of Alexander. It is likely then that this head is a close copy of one of those lost originals.

Although Alexander's palace in Pella (the ancient capital of Macedonia) has never been excavated, we do get some sense of the beauty and style of Macedonian art from other extant examples.

Pella is particularly famous for the mosaics found decorating the floors of wealthy homes. The mosaics at Pella are pebble mosaics; pebble mosaics are made up of small stones of various sizes and colors. The pebbles are then set into thick cement to create a decorative and durable floor mosaic.

There are two types of mosaics found at Pella, those with geometric decoration that cover the entire surface of the floor, and those with figural or narrative subjects, such as hunts, and battle scenes. The narrative mosaics have borders around the edge and a framed central panel, called an *emblema*.

The large *emblem,* framed by a border of scrolling vines with leaves and flowers, depicts a stag hunt. The choice of subject though not mythological is still heroic. The action depicts two nude male figures and their hunting dog killing a large stag. The active poses of the figures, their flowing drapery, and the implied motion of the dog and steer combine for a violent scene filled with tension and drama. There is a masterful use of gradation of light and dark to suggest volume, light, and shadow. This use of shading is called *skiagraphia,* or shadow writing, and would have been a feature of Greek panel painting in the period as well. The artist was clearly proud of his work as he signed it prominently across the top "Gnosis epoesen" or "Gnosis made it." Not only is this signature an example of artistic pride, but it is also important because this is the earliest known signature of a mosaicist in the history of art.

Another remarkable example of mosaic art is found in Pompeii.

This large mosaic, often called the Alexander mosaic, is estimated to contain 1 million tesserae. *Tesserae* are small cubes of stone or glass cut to a desired size. This use of smaller more precise stones allows for much greater detail and intricacy than is found in pebble mosaics. The mosaic originally decorated the floor of the House of the Faun in Pompeii.

The subject of the mosaic is the battle between Alexander the Great and his armies and that of the Persian King Darius and his forces on the battlefield in Issus, Turkey.

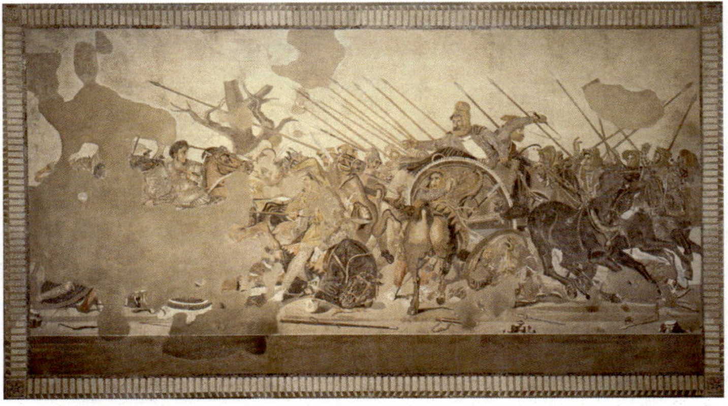

**5-47:** Battle of Issus, Roman mosaic copy of Greek panel painting, original panel painting by Philoxenos of Eretria, c. 310 BCE, mosaic 8′10 x 16′9, National Archaeological Museum, Naples.

It shows a particularly dramatic moment in the battle when the Persian King Darius is turning his chariot to run from the approaching Alexander.

The mosaic is thought to be a reasonably faithful copy of a panel painting by Philoxenos of Eretria, who made the painting for King Cassander one of Alexander's successors who was actually with him at that famous battle.

The mosaic reflects, at least in part, the style of the original painting. In the mosaic, like in the original panel, the artist has employed the use complex poses, twisting of figures, foreshortening, and the illusion of recession in space. Foreshortening is an implied perspective achieved through the apparent visual contraction of an object that extends back in space at an angle from the picture plane. Also exceptional is the masterful use of skiagraphia.

The composition of the mosaic is dominated by diagonals which heighten the drama. The drama is evident in the confusion and the push and pull of figures rushing in from the right and others countering from the left. Just to the right of center, the fleeing chariot moves away while the king leans forward and gestures toward his fallen companion. The drama and confusion is also highlighted by the fallen horses in their twisted poses and the scattered battle ground with lances and swords and shields and other articles cluttering the ground.

As impressive as the illusionist advances in the technique of the original painting is the impact created by the emotional content of the work.

There is a psychological intensity in the work as the drama of the battle unfolds. From the left we see Alexander, with no helmet, riding his famous horse Busephalus, leading his troops toward the Persian King. Alexander is driving his spear through the body of one of Darius' men but never looks at him; instead he gazes directly at Darius. Darius gazes back with a look of surprise and fear.

After Alexander's unexpected death in 323 BCE his generals divided up the empire and then began to battle each other for control. Without a center or clear ruler to guide it, the empire began to break apart. In this weakened condition the empire would succumb to the growing Roman Empire. Roman armies began to make their way into Greece by 210 BCE and by 146 BCE the Greek peninsula, including Macedonia, finally came under Roman rule.

## Hellenistic Period

Diversity in subject matter, psychological intensity and drama, and brutal realism are some of the main characteristics of Hellenistic art. The heightened sense of drama was also connected to a more evident interest in eroticism and sexuality.

Statues like those that decorated a Greek victory monument clearly reflect this new interest in drama.

The original bronzes were part of a group of works created to commemorate the victory of King Attalos I (241–297 BCE) of Pergamon (a Greek city in Western Asia Minor) over the Gauls (a tribe from an area in France).

This sculpture depicts the Gallic warrior at the moment of his own suicide; something he chooses over surrender, captivity, and execution. He has also already chosen to kill his own wife, who hangs limply from his left hand, rather than to have her taken captive, abused, and sold as a slave.

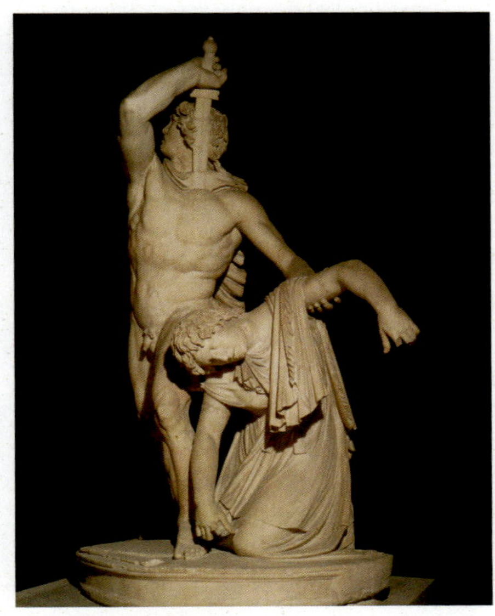

**5-48:** Gallic Chieftain killing himself and his wife, Roman marble copy of a Greek bronze original, c. 230–220 BCE, 6′11, National Museum, Rome.

The Hellenistic sculptor did not choose to depict a moment from the battle but rather chose to focus on the defiant act of a barbarian. This both glorifies and extols the dignity of the barbarian warrior as well as the brilliance and strength of the Pergemenes who defeated them.

The group, carved completely in the round, must be viewed from all sides. From one viewpoint the observer can see the expression of the warrior and from another he can see the face of the wife, but not both at the same time. The figures are expressive and bold; the nude, tensed, muscular body of the warrior is a stark contrast to the clothed, limp, lifeless body of his wife.

This is a sculpture that epitomizes the Hellenistic aesthetic; it is a sculptural group, there is a complexity of pose, grand gestures, and a focus on emotional intensity and drama.

From the same victory monument is another sculpture of a Gallic warrior.

This sculpture was part of the same group as the Gallic Chieftain. This warrior, however, is wounded and dying.

He was a trumpeter, evidenced by the curled instrument at his feet. He has fallen on top of his shield, as blood seeps from the wound in his side. His wavy thick hair, moustache, and the jewelry he wears around his neck, called a torque, all signal his ethnicity. He is clearly not Greek! His muscles are still taught and tense from the battle and we can see the blood course through his veins; it is clear that he has just been wounded.

As one moves around the work it is apparent that the warrior is staring down, not at the ground, but at his own sword. One wonders whether he is contemplating his own suicide.

The writer Pliny the Elder, in his work *Natural History*, mentions an artist named Epigonos and credits him with a work called The Trumpeter. Epigonos' name appears on several extant bases from works at Pergamon, so it is possible he is the sculptor for this work, and the Chieftain, among others.

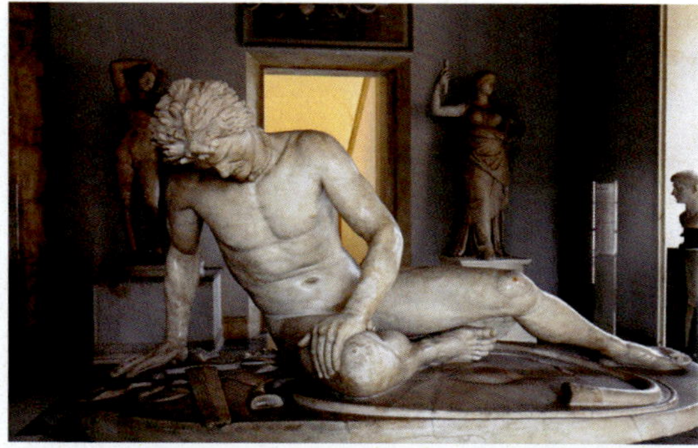

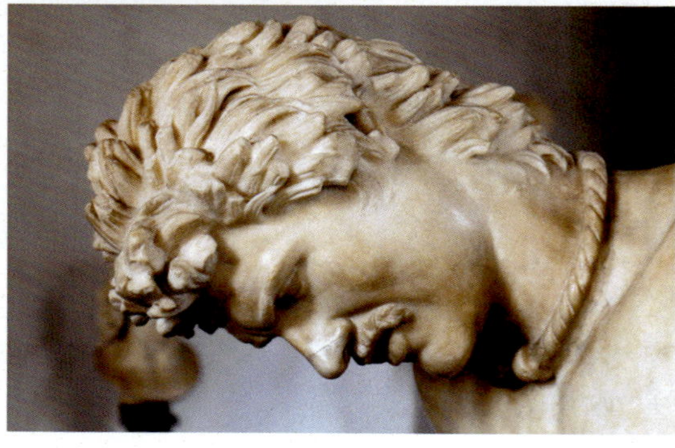

**5-49 a and b:** Dying Gaul, Roman marble copy of a Greek bronze original, c. 230–220 BC, life-size, Capitoline Museum, Rome.

This same interest with vitality and motion and drama are found in another Hellenistic masterpiece, the Nike of Samothrace.

The sculpture, made by the sculptor Pythokritos of Rhodes, was originally set up in the Sanctuary of the Great Gods on the Aegean island of Samothrace.

The monumental figure of Nike, the goddess of victory, is depicted just as she is landing on the prow of a Greek warship. Her wings are still outspread and her drapery is a swirling whipping mass of fabric that spirals around her legs and pulls tight across her abdomen. Her torso twists as she plants her leg firmly in front of her and braces against the wind. The curve of her body still conforming to the Praxiteles S curve, though now much more exaggerated.

The base of the Nike represented the prow of the ship and the whole ensemble was then placed in a basin that included water and large boulders.

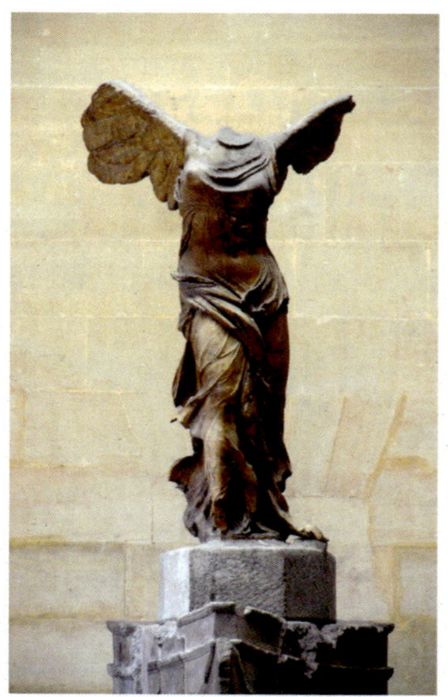

**5-50:** The Nike of Samothrace, marble, c. 190 BCE, 8′ 1″, Louvre, Paris.

Water would have splashed at the prow of the ship as if it was in rough waters and the Nike was guiding it. The sound of the rushing water and the inclusion of the aspect of reflections in the water would all have contributed to the dynamism and theatricality of the work. It is even erotic in the way it involves all of the senses.

The sculpture, discovered in 1863 and immediately sent to the Louvre, is a great example of how far removed Hellenistic sculpture is from the serene and classically structured frontal images of the Archaic and early Classical periods.

The impact of Praxiteles' Aphrodite of Knidos on later depictions of the female nude is clear, however, in the Hellenistic period artists will include an element of teasing and sexuality not found in Praxiteles work.

When the sculpture of Aphrodite was found on the Greek island of Melos in 1820 it was found with a part of its original base. That base, now lost, was signed by the sculptor Alexandros of Antioch on the Meander. It is likely, but not certain, that he was the artist.

The goddess of love is depicted in a state of undress with her drapery just below her hips; in her right hand she once held the top edge of her drapery, and in her outstretched left hand she once held an apple.

The apple is the 'apple of discord' which she was awarded by Paris after she promised him the love of the most beautiful woman in the world. This is a particularly appropriate representation of the goddess because *Melos* in Greek means apple. A fragment of her forearm and hand with an apple were found near the statue but in such damaged condition neither was ever restored.

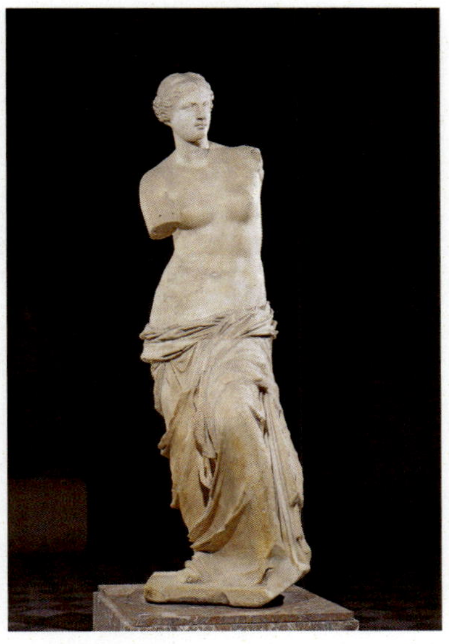

**5-51:** Aphrodite of Melos (Venus di Milo), marble, c. 150–125 BCE, 6′7″, Louvre, Paris.

The explicitly teasing quality of the statue is evident when the viewer sees the work from the back. The back reveals that her drapery has slipped low enough to reveal the whole of her lower back and just the top of her buttocks. Even her hair has come undone from its tight bun and leaves curls on the back of her neck. Also teasing is that of her rather aloof expression which seems to suggest that she does not to mind her present state of undress.

While the nude male athelete remained an important subject during the Hellenistic period, it was often quite different from earlier examples.

The athlete is not the perfect, youthful, heroic nude of the Classical period; instead he is a mature, battered man who has been utterly defeated.

The boxer sits, hands still wrapped in leather straps, with his shoulders slumped forward and his arms resting on his thighs. The face of the boxer is swollen and bruised, his nose and teeth are broken and his ears have become puffed and thick. Blood, depicted in inlaid copper, oozes from the cuts on his face and body.

This work, like other Hellenistic works we have seen, focuses on drama and explores emotion, both the part of the subject and the viewer. It is an example of a kind of brutal reality that Hellenistic artists often explored.

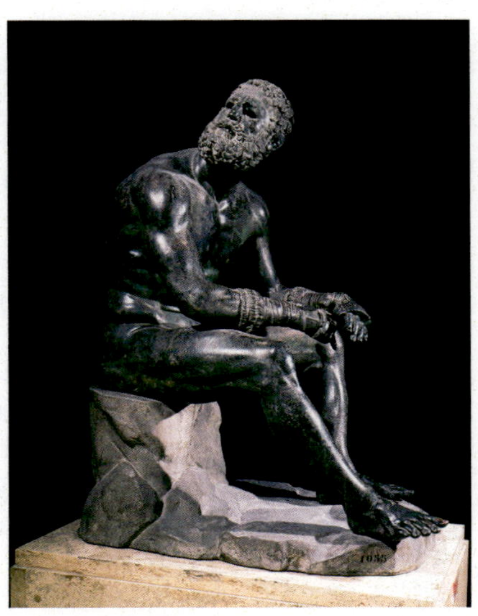

**5-52:** Seated Boxer, bronze, Rome, c. 100–50 BCE, life-size, Palazzo Massimo Terme, Rome.

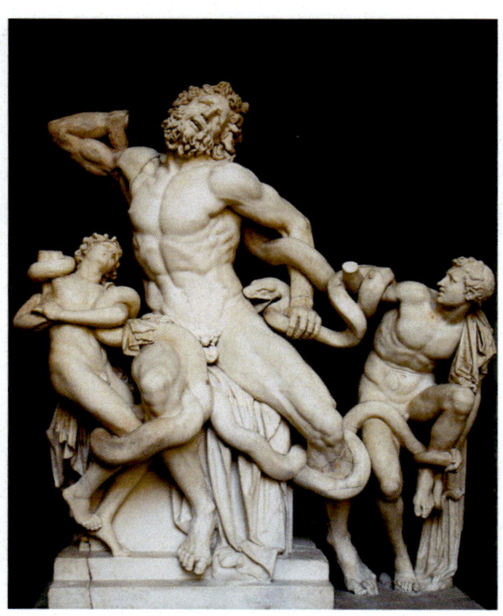

**5-53:** Laocoön, Athanadoros, Hagesandros, and Polydoros of Rhodes, marble, 1st cen BCE, 7'10", Vatican Museums, Rome.

The is a style of art that no longer reflects the beautiful ideal world but instead focuses on the harshness and brutality of existence.

This hollow cast bronze, found in Rome 1885, may originally have been part of a group. If he were part of a group it might help to explain why he looks so forcefully over his shoulder; perhaps he sees his younger victorious opponent standing above him.

Perhaps the single most influential sculpture from the Hellenistic period is the Laocoön.

This celebrated sculptural group depicts the Trojan priest Laocoön and his sons, Antiphantes and Thymbraeus, being strangled to death by sea serpents.

The event is described in Vergil's *Aeneid* as the result of Poseidon's wrath for Laocoön's attempt to expose the gift of the horse as a trap. Laocoön attempted to warn his fellow Trojans against accepting the horse from the Greeks with the words "Do not trust the horse whatever it is, I fear the Greeks, even when they bring gifts." His advice was not heeded, and in his anger he hurled a spear against the horse. His warning, however, sealed his fate, for both Poseidon and Athena favored the Greeks in the war and so they sent the serpents to kill him and his two sons.

The statue depicts the heroic yet futile struggle of the priest and his sons.

The muscular Laocoön with his face turned upward clearly writhes in agony as one of serpents bites him in the hip. He twists and contorts and strains every muscle in his body. He and his sons, it should be noted, are attacked on their father's altar; ironic that the priest and his sons are now the sacrifice.

The son on his left looks at his father and the snake in disbelief as he tries to wrestle his leg free. The younger son, on his right, has thrown his head back succumbing to the serpent's hold. The three men are utterly powerless as they struggle against their certain death.

The sculpture was discovered in Rome in 1506 in what were the remains of the palace of the Emperor Nero. Among the witnesses who saw the piece unearthed was the artist Sangallo and a young Michelangelo newly arrived in Rome. Immediately after its excavation it was brought to the Belvedere Courtyard at the Vatican where it remains.

## Art is an Endangered Species:

The Laocoön was one of the hundreds of works of art stolen from the Vatican in 1799 by Napoleon and his troops. He had it and thousands of other looted art objects from across Europe shipped back to France, to be exhibited in the Louvre. Napoleon even presented the Pope with a bill to pay for the shipping. After the fall of Napoleon at Waterloo in 1815, the Laocoön and many other works, though not all, were returned by the British to the Vatican.

Name ______________________________ Date ______________

## Chapter 5

# Art and Architecture of Greece

1. What was the original purpose of the Delian League?

2. What is the term for a standing nude sculpture of a young man? Young female figure?

3. The Orientalizing period developed from the early Greek's exposure to which two cultures?

4. What was the artist's intent in utilizing the archaic smile?

5. What form of architectural support was utilized on the south porch of the Erechtheion?

6. What is the term for a sculpture made of gold and ivory? Provide an example from this chapter of where this term applies.

7. During which period was contrapposto introduced to Greek sculpture?

8. What impact did the Pelopnnesian War have on Greek art? Who won the war?

9. The Parthenon is a fusion of which two architectural styles? What are the subjects of its pediments?

10. What is the difference between black figure and red figure pottery?

# THE ART AND ARCHITECTURE OF ROME

## Chapter 6

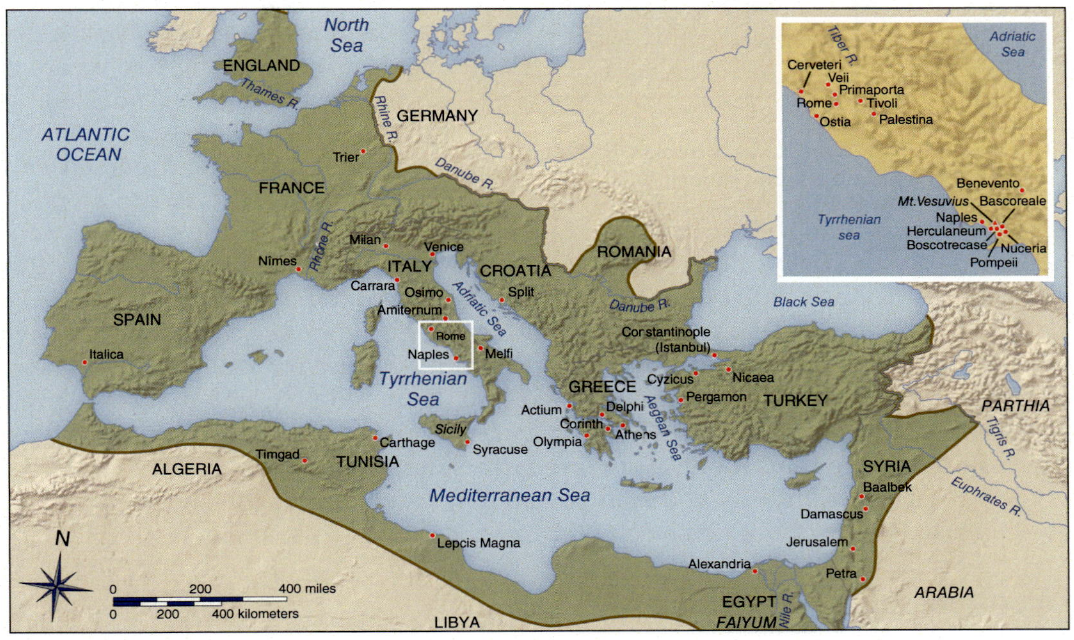


The Roman Empire c. 120 CE.

The long history of classical Rome is often divided into three major time periods; the Monarchy, the Republic, and the Empire.

| | |
|---|---|
| **Monarchy:** | 753–509 BCE (Etruscan Kings–Republic) |
| **Republic:** | 509–27 BCE (Republic–Octavian) |
| **Empire:** | 27 BCE–337 CE (Augustus–Constantine) |

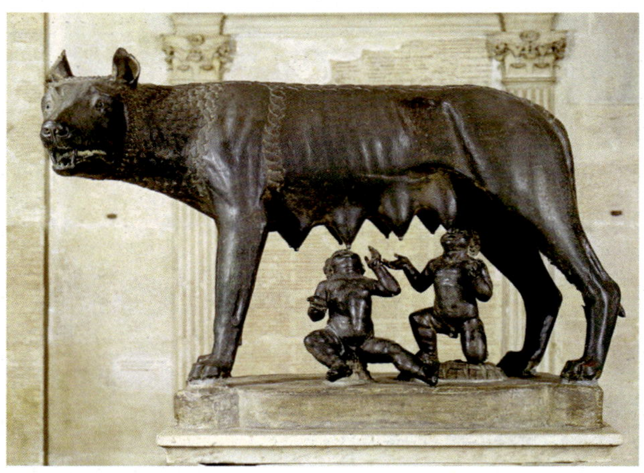

**6-1:** Capitoline She–Wolf, Rome, Bronze, 2′9″ height, c. 500 BCE, Capitoline Museum, Rome.

The traditional date of the founding of the city of Rome is April 21, 753 BCE. The founding of the city is explained by the legend of the twins Romulus and Remus. Romulus and Remus were the twin sons of the god Mars and the vestal virgin Rhea Silvia. Rhea's uncle, angered by the disgrace of their birth, put them in a basket and set them afloat on the Tiber River. The basket came aground under a fig tree where the twins were found and suckled by a she-wolf. Later they were found and raised by a shepherd named Faustulus and his wife, Acca Larentia.

When the brothers grew up, they decided to found a city on the site where they had been found. The brothers could not agree who was the rightful founder of this new city and so they both begin to build one. Romulus, who chose the Palatine Hill for his city, built a wall to mark the boundary of his new metropolis. Remus, who built on the Aventine Hill, jumped over Romulus' boundary wall, an act that was considered an invasion, so Romulus killed him. It should be noted that some myths say Remus was not killed by his brother but only exiled. As the founder of the new city, Romulus gave it his name and served as its first King.

The image of Romulus and Remus as babies suckling at the she-wolf was frequently, used as a symbol for the city of Rome.

## Archaeological Evidence

In the 8th century BCE Rome was just a collection of small huts located on the Palatine Hill; one of the seven hills that make up Rome. The others are the Capitoline, Quirinal, Viminal, Esquiline, Caelian, and the Aventine.

In 509 BCE, the Romans expelled the last Etruscan King, Lucius Tarquinius Superbus who ruled from 535–509 BCE, and replaced him with a republican form of government.

The new republic put power in the hands of two consuls who were elected annually. The consuls were advised by a senate, or council of elders. All leaders of the republic, senators and consuls, were elected from among the wealthy elite called patricians. The rest of the citizen population, including farmers, merchants, crafts people, and freed slaves were the plebeians.

## Greek Influence

In 211 BCE the Roman desire for and admiration of all things Greek intensified due in part to the Roman defeat of the Greek city of Syracusa on the island of Sicily. At that time numerous art objects were brought into the city of Rome fueling the artistic desires and imaginations of rulers and artists. This influx was further intensified in 146 BCE when the Greek peninsula (the Aegean Islands did not succumb to Roman rule until 133 BCE) finally came under Roman rule.

The Greek influence on Roman culture cannot be overstated. The Greeks had settled in southern Italy and Sicily as early as the 8th century BCE and therefore influenced the earliest Italian tribes, particularly the Etruscans. Greek culture, gods, art, and architecture greatly influenced all aspects of Roman culture. The Romans adopted and adapted Greek culture, learning, customs, and beliefs to suit their needs and even the most learned of Roman men were expected to speak and read Greek.

## Republican Art and Architecture

The art and architecture of Republican period Rome is a mixture of Greek and Etruscan art forms and styles blended with new and innovative Roman taste. This is best seen in one of the oldest and best preserved early temples in Rome, The Temple of Portunus.

Often misidentified as the Temple of Fortuna Virils (manly fortune) this tiny temple is located in what was the ancient Roman Forum Boarium. The temple is a great example of the mixing of Greek, Etruscan, and Roman styles. The temple sits on a high platform (Etruscan) accessed by a flight of steps at the front (Etruscan). The deep front porch is comprised of ionic columns (Greek). However, the cella has been extended and the columns on the flank are engaged; the result is a *pseudoperipteral* temple. Another Roman feature is the choice of local stone as the primary building material and the use of white stucco to mimic marble.

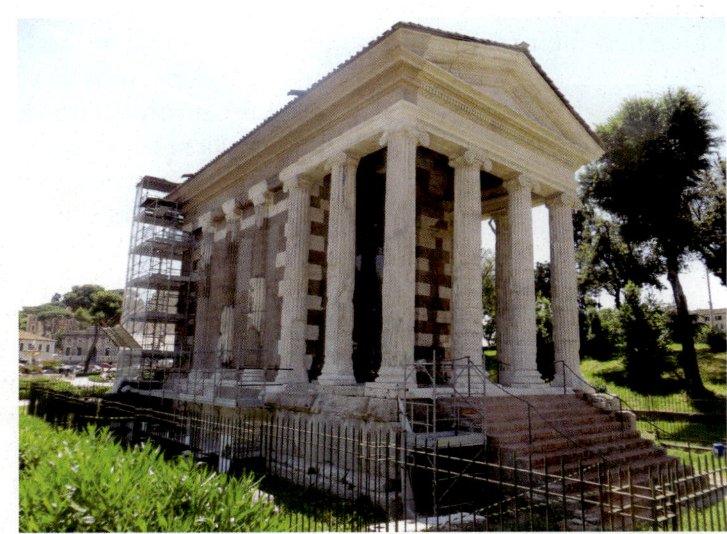

**6-2:** Temple of Portunus, Rome, Italy ca. 75 BCE, 70′ long, 40′ wide, 40′ high.

### Portraiture

Roman art focused, from the very beginning, on portraiture, due primarily to the importance that the Romans placed on family lineage.

Likenesses or *imagines* were ancestral masks or portrait busts that Romans kept in cupboards in the home. These *imagines* would be taken out and carried by family members to major events such as festivities

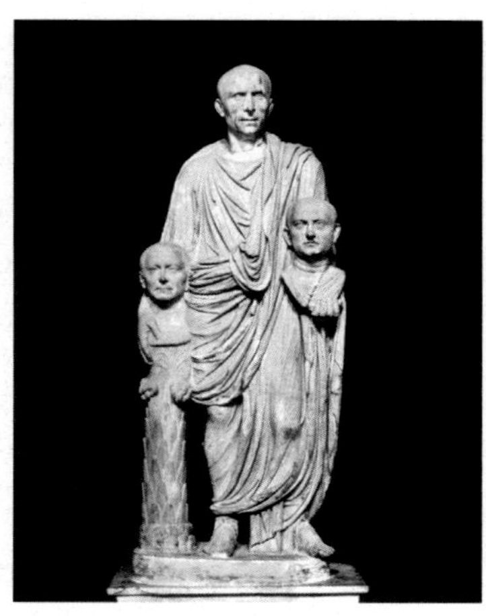

**6-3:** Patrician carrying portrait heads, marble, 1st cen. CE marble 5′5″.

and funerals. This was a way for Romans to include their deceased ancestors in current events and to publicly display distinguished lineage.

This honoring of ancestors was critical to patrician Romans. It should also be noted that slaves were forbidden to posses family portraits because they and their ancestors were not seen as people but as property.

Portraiture during the Roman republic was not about idealized beauty and heroic youth, as it had been in classical Greece. Instead, it focused mostly on images of mature men, and occasionally women, and it delighted in showing age and sternness, or gravitas. These images with their brutally realistic details represent a trend in portraiture called *verism* or truth in portraiture.

The portrait bust as an art form is also essentially a Roman invention; it was used in both private and public contexts, as well as in a funerary context. Portrait busts often decorated funerary altars, tombs, and cinerary urns.

This image of a mature, stern, wrinkled man was, in Rome, ultimately a portrait of power. There were numerous types of these portraits made, all done in the veristic style with every wrinkle, bump, and crevice depicted.

Prominent citizens who requested a portrait bust had achieved a level of success and their furrowed brow, wrinkled face, and taut mouth were understood as expressions of their wisdom, intelligence, and experience. Experience, perhaps above all other virtues, was valued by the Romans; therefore men and women appreciated and glorified their mature faces because they had earned them.

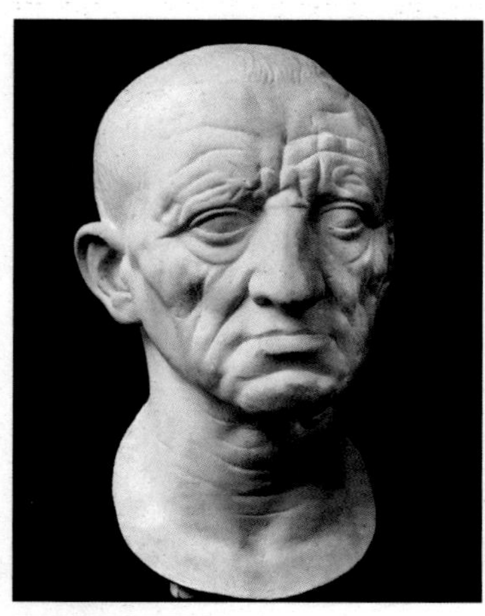

**6-4:** Head of anoldman, marble, Otricoli, Italy, 75–50 BCE,.

These portrait busts express the virtues considered most important in republican Rome; particularly *gravitas*: a serious and dignified demeanor, a dignity in form, behavior, and appearance.

The importance of the portrait extended not only to sculpture but also to coinage in ancient Rome. Unlike the Greeks who had put bust portraits of the gods on their coins, in republican Rome coinage showed ancestral portraits.

The importance, power, and propagandistic value of the veristic portrait was fully recognized by one of Rome's early rulers, Julius Caesar.

**Gaius Julius Caesar** was born July 12, 100 BCE and was assasinated on March 15, 44 BCE. He was a Roman military and political leader whose early conquest of Gaul extended throughout the Roman world all the way to the Atlantic Ocean. He is widely considered to be one of the greatest military geniuses of all time, as well as a brilliant politician. In 42 BCE, two years after his death, the Roman Senate officially proclaimed him one of the Roman gods. This act of elevating a person to the status of a god is called *deification*.

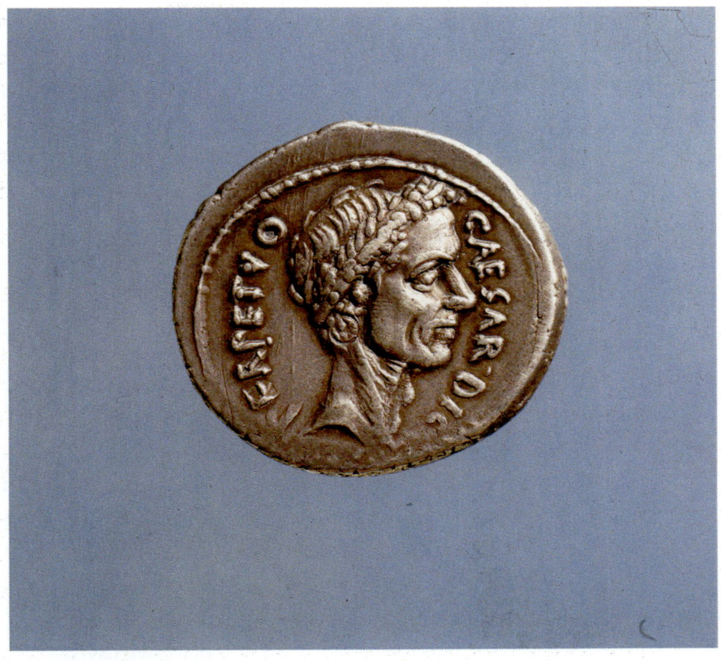


**6-5:** Denarius with portrait of Julius Caesar, silver denarius, 44 BCE.

Julius Caesar greatly influenced Roman art and portraiture because shortly before his assassination he had coins minted with his own portrait on them. This was the first time in history that a Roman coin had been struck with a portrait of a living person on it.

This coin features a bust portrait of Caesar, wearing a crown of laurel leaves. It includes his title Dictator Perpetuus (dictator for life). His aging face, pointy chin, long aquiline nose and receding hairline are portrayed in the typical veristic style.

The importance and propagandistic value of portrait coinage, as well as its value for transmitting information was recognized by all later rulers; each of whom would use their own portraits on their coinage. The reverse was reserved for the use of allegories, symbols, and personifications. In the years immediately after Caesar's assassination Brutus, Mark Antony, and Cleopatra all had coins minted with their images on them.

After the death of Julius Caesar there were 13 years of fighting over the empire. Brutus was killed at the Battle of Phillipi by the forces of Marc Antony, and then Marc Antony and Cleopatra were defeated by Caesar's adopted son and heir Octavian in a huge naval battle at Actium.

In 27 BCE the Senate of Rome conferred the title of Augustus to Octavian; he was 31. The conferring of the title Augustus, which means venerable or majestic, marks the end of the Republic and the beginning of the Empire.

Augustus' titles included *princeps* (first citizen), sole consul, *Imperator* (commander in chief) and *Pontifex Maximus* (chief priest of the state religion). Augustus was, therefore, in total control of all aspects of Roman life: social, sacred, secular, and militaristic.

Luckily, Augustus was a good and smart man, who brought about a reign of peace in Rome, called the Pax Romana, and this peace lasted for almost 200 years!

Augustus commissioned countless public works including roads, bridges, forums, temples, basilicas, theaters, amphitheaters, markets, and baths. He commissioned them all on a huge scale. It was often said that Augustus found Rome a city of bricks and left it a city of marble.

In fact, during the 1st century BCE the marble quarries at Carrara (Luna) were opened providing a wealth of pristine white marble for building and statuary in Rome.

## Augustus (c. 63 BCE–14 CE)

As a young man and now sole ruler of Rome and her empire, the rule and the image of the old Roman republican patrician came to an end. Augustus was young and handsome, and since Caesar had been deified a god after his death, he was also the son of a god.

His portraits needed to reflect his youth so he turned to classical Greece for his model. Therefore we find a conscious shift away from the veristic portraiture of the Republican period to a new idealized classical beauty in Augustus' empire.

This free-standing marble portrait statue of Augustus was found at his wife Livia's villa at Primaporta just outside Rome.

The standing figure represents the emperor Augustus as a young, idealized, heroically beautiful general. The work is clearly based, in pose and proportion, on the Doryphorous by Polykleitos.

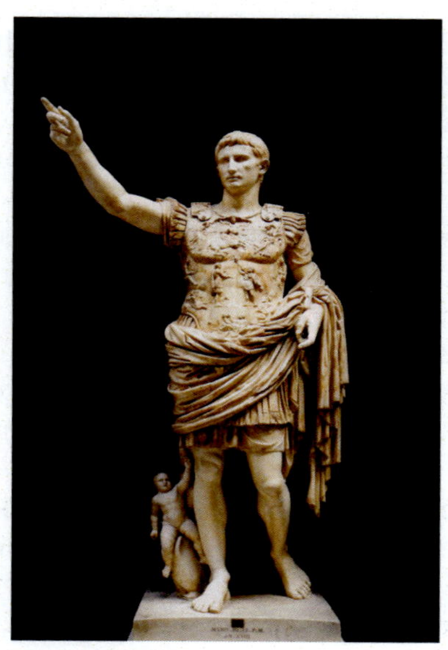

**6-6:** Augustus of Primaporta, marble, 1st century CE copy of 20 CE bronze original, 6'8, Vatican Museums, Rome.

The emperor, with short hair and idealized features, raises his right hand to address his troops. His garments express his role as emperor and general; he wears a toga around his waist over a moulded cuirass (breastplate). At one time he may have held a commander's baton or spear in his left hand. The decorated heroic cuirass he wears accentuates and exaggerates his torso and was often, like this one, ornamented or decorated. This one, worn by Augustus, is used to display some of the emperor's great deeds. The cupid at his feet suggests his ancestry as a descendant of the goddess Venus through her son Aeneas while the dolphin may be an allusion to his great naval battle at Actium

At the center of the cuirass is a depiction of the return of the Roman military standard. This momentous occasion occurred in c. 20 BCE when the emperor Augustus negotiated the return of the captured Roman military standards from the Parthians. Other decoration includes personifications of the provinces at the sides of the cuirass as well as sphinxes on the shoulder flaps. At the top just below the neck is a personification of the universe in the form of the bearded Caelus with billowing drapery over his head. Notice too that Augustus is depicted barefoot; typical for the Greek athlete but here perhaps an illusion to his divinity, as the son of the deified Caesar.

Ultimately, we find that the statue has been created not only as a work of art but of political propaganda. The symbols, messages, and ideas related in the sculpture and on the breastplate are all intended to reflect the glory of the emperor; they portray his rank, nobility, diplomacy, beauty, courage, and victories.

This work is a prime and early example of the power of images to display and project messages and the masterful way Roman emperors used their portraits to represent the messages they deemed most important. Like its classical predecessors, it would have been brightly painted.

One of Augustus' most important monuments, as art and propaganda, was the Ara Pacis, or Altar of Peace.

The altar was dedicated in 9 BCE to celebrate the peace initiated by the reign of Augustus. The Ara, or altar, consists of a rectangular enclosure inside of which is an altar.

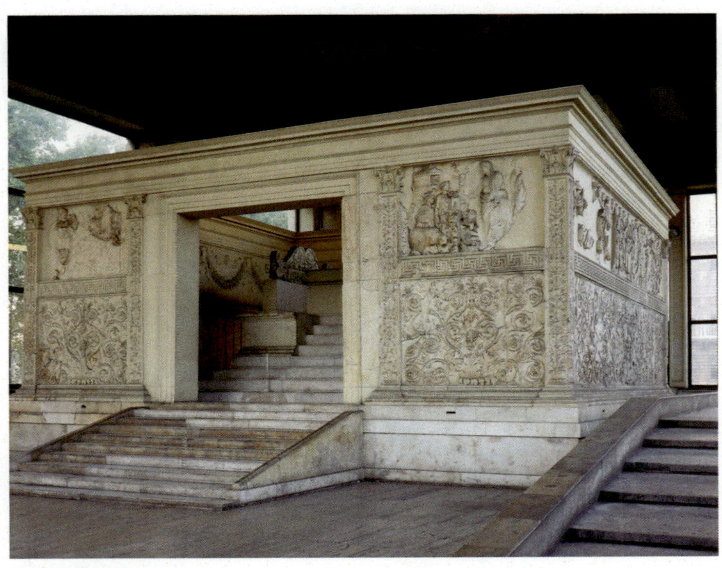

**6-7:** Ara Pacis Augustae (Altar of Augustan Peace) marble, Rome, Italy, 13–9 BCE, 34.5′ × 38′, Ara Pacis Museum, Rome.

In this monument, like in his portrait statue, he continues to stress those messages that are important to him. Here, particularly his lineage, not just from Julius Caesar but from the goddess Venus through her son Aeneas (founder of Italy) is stressed.

This lineage is described in the most important literary work of the period the *Aenead*.

The *Aenead*, is a Latin epic poem written by the poet Virgil in the 1st century BCE, sometime between 29 and 19 BCE.

The poem, written in a style similar to the *Iliad*, recounts how the young Prince Aeneas, a Trojan prince and son of Venus, escapes the burning city of Troy with his aging father Anchises and his young son Ascanius and then journeys to the shores of Italy. This mythological tale makes Aeneas the founder of the Roman race and it also makes a clear association between classical Greece and Rome such that the Romans are the heroic and favored descendants of princes.

Many of the decorative relief panels on the Ara Pacis refer to this mythology yet others speak more specifically to Augustan rule and the Imperial family.

On the east façade of the altar enclosure is a relief panel showing a monumental seated female figure with two male babies on her lap. On either side of her are personifications of the winds, one over land and the other over the sea. The mature female figure, with her head covered, is perhaps meant to represent Tellus (mother earth) or Roma or even Peace. Her ample bosom and the fact that she is surrounded by livestock and grains suggest the bounty of the peaceful land as it exists under the rule of Augustus. The whole scene is a microcosm of the Augustan universe, with beauty and bounty and peace on land and at sea.

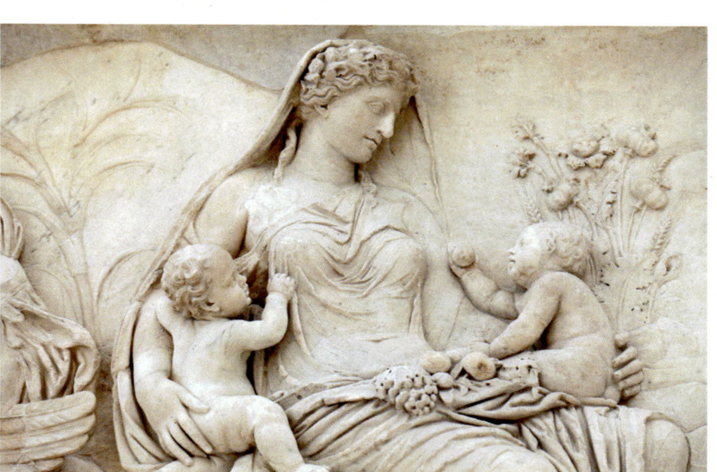

**6-8:** Female Personification (Tellus?), marble, Ara Pacis, 13–9 BCE, height 5′3″, Ara Pacis Museum, Rome.

On the long sides of the monument are scenes that show processions; on the north are senators and magistrates and on the south are priests, Augustus, and the Imperial family.

The format of the long processional frieze is indebted to Greek art; in particular to the Panathenaic frieze on the Parthenon.

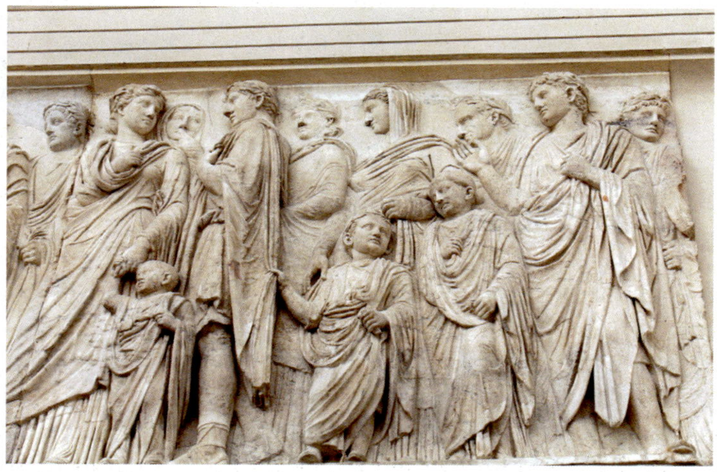

**6-9:** Procession of the Imperial Family, marble, south frieze, 13–9 BCE, height, 5′3″, Ara Pacis Museum, Rome.

The south procession includes Augustus, at the front of the procession, followed by his wife and immediate family. The surprising inclusion of children here is not without significance since Augustus had recently enacted a series of laws intended to promote marriage, fidelity, and children. These laws were a way to ensure the population of the Roman nobility, and to populate the empire with Romans. The decoration of the Ara Pacis then serves to visually underscore Augustus’

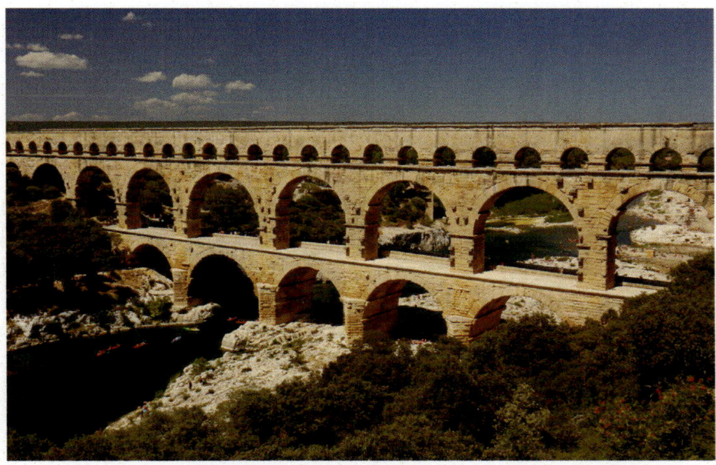

**6-10:** Pont du Gard, Nimes France, height 160′, length 900′.

political and social reforms, as well as concepts of family lineage, duty, and piety. Significant too is that this is the first time children have appeared on any state sanctioned monument in classical Greece or Rome.

Augustus building campaign was not restricted to the city of Rome but was evident throughout the empire. An excellent example of Rome's growing architectural and building skills, is the enormous Pont-du Gard, an aqueduct and bridge in Southern France.

An aqueduct (from the words *aqua*-water and *ducere*-to lead) carries water underground, over ground, and across gaps. It is built so that gravity does the work as the water flows on a declining gradient. The aqueduct provided water from a source some 30 miles away to the center of the town of Nimes. The uppermost level, comprised of small arches, is the level that carried the water channel.

The Pont du Gard is a three level structure that is constructed from blocks that weigh as much as 6 tons and it was constructed entirely without the use of mortar. The masonry was lifted into place by block and tackle with a massive human-powered treadmill providing the power.

The bridge reflects not only the incredible skill of the Roman engineers and builders but also of their desire for order in design and for functionality. The bridge is functional, practical, and yet still pleasing visually.

## Note

It is that at this point in the text that we have left BCE dates and enter the ce. This period coincides with the birth and execution of Jesus of Nazareth; who was born c. 6–4 BCE while Augustus was emperor and was executed c. 30 CE during the rule of the emperor Tiberius.

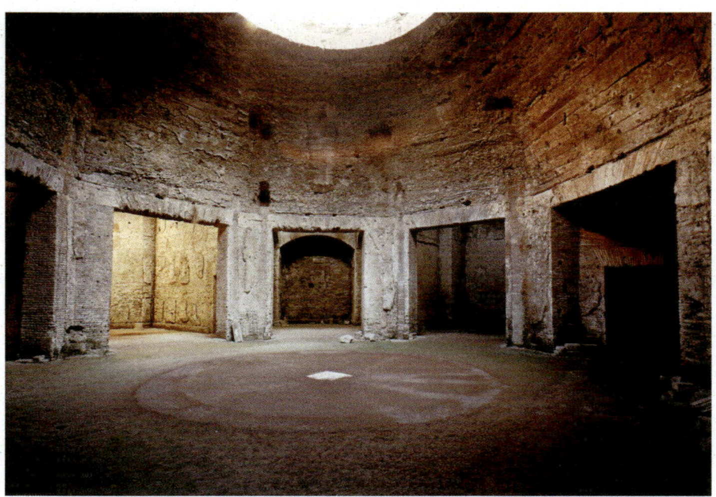

**6-11:** Severus and Celer, octagonal hall of the Domus Aurea, concrete, Rome, 64–68 CE, Rome.

Nero Claudius Drusus Germanicus was the fifth and last Roman Emperor from the Julio-Claudian dynasty to rule. He ruled from 54–68 CE. He was crazy, paranoid, and deluded into thinking of himself as a great artist, actor, and musician. He had both his adopted father and own mother murdered, among others.

Nero is remembered for a couple of reasons: he was the ruler of Rome during the great fire, he demanded the first real organized persecutions of the Christians (he ordered the execution of saints Peter and Paul), and he built one of the most luxurious and opulent palaces ever built by a Roman emperor.

In July of the year 64 CE a great fire erupted in the center of Rome. It began in the very the center of the city in a densely populated area where many *insulae* (wooden dwellings built on three or four floors) were located. Rumors circulated that Nero played his lyre and sang, on top of Quirinal Hill, watching while the city burned. This may be legend but what is true is that the suspicious fire and its demolition of crowded areas in the center of the city provided land and space for Nero to begin construction of his own new city palace. Nero also needed a scapegoat for the fire, so he blamed the Christians, having many of them thrown to the lions in the Colosseum or crucified.

Nero hired two architects, Severus and Celer, to build a new palace for him in the center of the city; the place complex was called the Domus Aurea or Golden House. Extant descriptions testify to the enormity and extreme luxury of the palace.

The most impressive room in the palace may have been the huge octagonal concrete domed hall that reached to a circular opening at the top.

This structure would not have been possible without one of the most important architectural achievements of the Romans; concrete. Concrete is a building material invented by the Romans in the c. 2nd century BCE that consists of various portions of lime, mortar, volcanic sand called pozzolana, water, and stones. Together the mixture forms a thick and workable material that when dry is incredibly durable. The Romans saw the opportunity for the combination of traditional building techniques such as the vault and the new material of concrete to create architectural possibilities that had been previously impossible.

Radiating off the central domed hall were five other smaller rooms also covered with concrete vaults. The rooms and decoration were elaborate including fountains, wall mosaics, and a thin veneer or sheathing of colored marble on the interiors of the walls. Accounts say the marble was so highly polished that it reflected like mirrors; important to the paranoid Nero so that he could see in front and behind him at all times.

Some accounts even say that the room actually spun and that during parties or special dinners, perfume and flower petals would rain down through the opening. There is no archaeological evidence that the room itself spun but it may have appeared to spin with slats placed in or below the oculus regulating the light entering the room.

In 68 CE the senate deposed Nero shortly after which he committed suicide.

## The Flavian Dynasty: 69–96 CE

After Nero's death, and following a year of civil unrest, the next ruler of the empire was Vespasian, a general who had served under Nero.

Titus Flavius Vespasianus (9–79 CE), called Vespasian, restored peace and stability to an empire in disarray following the death of Nero. In the process he established the Flavian dynasty securing imperial rule for his two sons, Titus and Domitian.

## Portrait of Vespasian c. 75–79 CE, marble

Vespasian was a good soldier and a good ruler who tried to restore order and dignity to Rome through his actions. By his own example of simplicity in his life, he put to shame the luxury and extravagance of the Roman nobles and initiated in many respects a marked improvement in the general tone of society. Much money was spent on public works and the restoration and beautifying of Rome including the construction of a new forum, new public baths, and new amphitheatre.

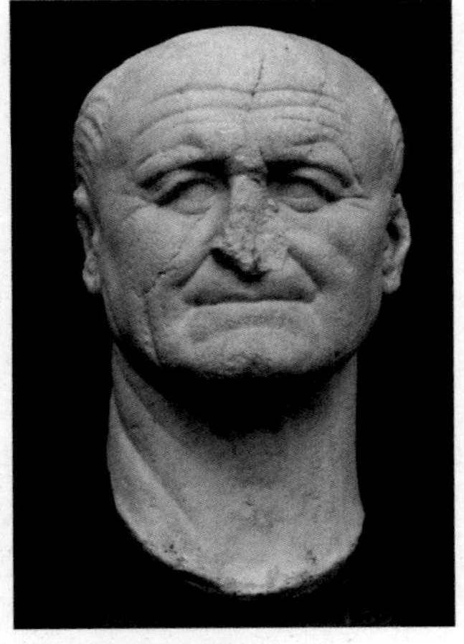

**6-12:** Portrait bust of Vespasian, marble, c. 70 CE, Carlsberg Glyptotek Museum, Copenhagen.

His portrait exhibits a return to the veristic style of portraiture. He is not depicted as Augustus and other emperors had been, as idealized gods on earth, but instead he is portrayed as aged, experienced, and serious.

The single most impressive monument left to the city of Rome by Vespasian was the Flavian amphitheater begun in c. 70 CE and completed and inaugurated by his son Titus in 80 CE.

The Flavian amphitheater was built on the site of an artificial lake on the grounds of Nero's enormous palace, the Domus Aurea. The location of the site was a shrewd political decision; Vespasian was seen as building a huge public monument on a site that had been taken by Nero. The ampitheatre was seen as a gesture of returning public land and space to the Roman people.

The building was the largest ampitheater ever built and could hold more than 50,000 spectators. It was built for the express purpose of entertaining the Roman public with galditorial battles and lavish spectacles. The colosseum gets its nickname not from its enormous size but rather from a *colossus* (a very tall statue) of Nero which stood nearby.

The exterior travertine shell is 160 feet high and there are 76 numbered entrances that lead to the cavea (seating sections). There are actually 80 entrances at ground level, 76 for spectators and four on the main axis for the imperial family, guests, and gladiators.

The emperor had a special covered box, and seating was decided by class. Generals and guests sat closest, then ruling families, then soldiers, and finally at the top level were slaves and women.

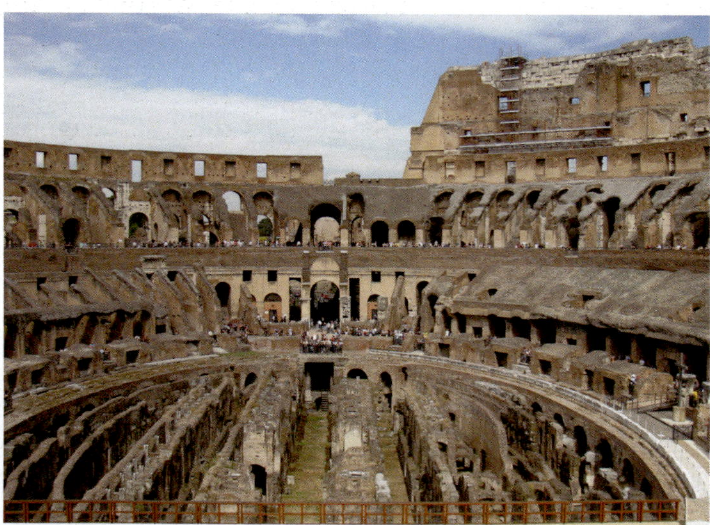

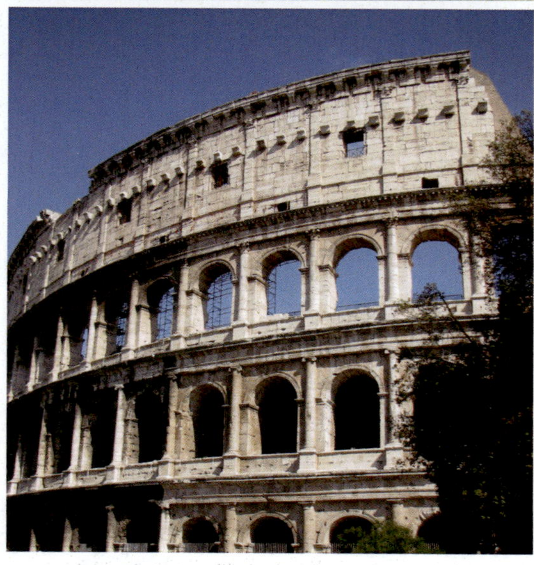

**6-13 a and b:** Flavian Amphitheater (Colosseum), Rome, 70–80 CE.

The Colosseum measures 615 feet long by 510 feet wide. The huge oval wooden floor or arena (*arena* is the Latin word for sand) was originally covered by sand to soak up the blood. Its elliptical shape was important because it allowed the spectators to be closer to the action than a circle would have allowed.

The exterior facade is divided into four registers or bands, with large arches piercing the lower three levels. Ornamental Greek orders acsend with the registers so that the lower floor uses Doric, second Ionic, third Corinthian, and the fourth Corinthian pilasters.

The upper story also has protruding brackets between the pilasters that supported poles (240) that held up the large velarium, a cloth awning that could be rolled out to cover the spectators and shelter them from sun and rain.

Underneath the arena floor was the basement or hypogeum. It was a hidden underground network of tunnels and cages where gladiators and animals were held before contests began. There were also numerous trap doors in the arena floor to be used for the arrival of various wild animals.

The arena floor no longer exists, and the *hypogeum* is visible in the ruins of the building.

The inaugural games for the building lasted 100 days and some records say some 90 animals a day were slaughtered.

The Colosseum hosted large-scale spectacular games that included fights between animals (*venationes*), the killing of prisoners by animals and other executions (*noxii*), mock naval battles (*naumachiae*), and combats between gladiators (*munera*). It has been estimated that about 500,000 people died in the Colosseum games.

The galditorial combats were the most popular of the shows, often taking place in the evening when the heat of the day had subsided. The killing of prisoners, slaves, and Christians took place in the morning.

Gladiatorial games and executions continued until Christianity was adopted in the empire in 313. The spectacles and animal hunts continued until 524 CE.

In the Middle Ages, the Colosseum was severely damaged by an earthquake in 847, and was then converted into a fortress. During the Renaissance and Baroque periods the ruling Roman families used the colosseum as a marble quarry, simply removing the marble blocks as they needed. Many of the Renaissance palaces of Rome were built using stone taken from the Colosseum.

In more modern times the building has become the symbol of Rome and in many cases, the whole of the ancient world. A 7th century Anglo-Saxon proverb suggests that if the Colosseum ever falls, so too will Rome, and then the world.

After the death of Vespasian in 79 CE, his son Titus became the next emperor; though he would only live two years in that role. Domitian, Titus' younger brother, ruled after him.

The Arch of Titus is a memorial monument in the form of a monumental single passageway triumphal arch. It was erected to the emperor Titus by his brother Domitian, after 81 CE, to celebrate Titus' victory over the Jewish revolts in 70 CE.

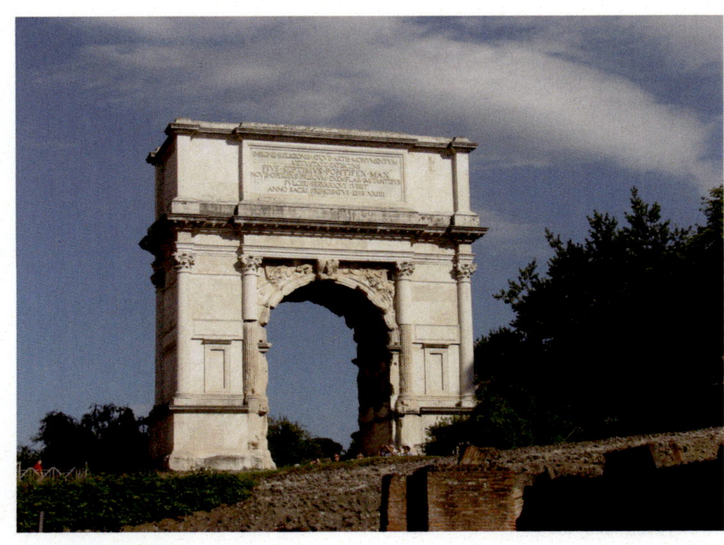

**6-14:** Arch of Titus, marble, Rome, Italy, after 81 CE, height 50′ × width 44′ × 15′5″ deep.

The arch was erected on the sacred way or *sacra via* leading into the Republican forum. The monument is decorated on the interior and exterior with relief decoration and would have been topped by a gilded bronze statue of the emperor riding in a horse-drawn chariot (now lost).

The arch has engaged composite columns (a Roman invention of a column capital that combines Ionic volutes and Corinthian leaves) flanking the large central archway. In the spandrels (area between the arch's curve and the framing columns and entablature) are relief sculptures of flying victories.

An enormous dedicatory inscription fills the attic space and declares that the monument was erected by the senate and people of Rome (Senatus Populesque Romanus/SPQR) to the god Titus, son of the god Vespasian.

Depicted in marble relief, on the left and right wall of the inside of the passageway, are two important scenes from Titus' triumph. They both represent an actual event; the triumphal parade of Titus on the sacred way after his return from his victorious conquest in Judea at the end of the Jewish war in 70 CE. (In 66 CE the Jewish people revolted against the Roman control of Jerusalem, the uprising was crushed, and the Temple in Jerusalem destroyed.)

One relief depicts Roman soldiers carrying the spoils of war, including the sacred seven-branched Menorah, silver trumpets, and the table of Sacred Breads all taken from the Temple in Jerusalem. The parade is moving towards the *porta triumphalis* (the principal gate into the walled city) which is depicted just at the front of the relief. We also see soldiers carrying *tabulae ansatae*, or "announcement boards" on which information about the soldier's units would be displayed.

On the other side is the Emperor Titus riding in a triumphal chariot (*quadriga)* accompanied by lictors (civil servants who protect the Emperor) and priests. Behind Titus, riding in the chariot with him, is the winged goddess Victory who holds a laurel wreath above his head. Just in front of the quadriga is a bare-chested male figure, perhaps meant to represent Honor. A large female figure, perhaps a personification of Valor, leads the horses.

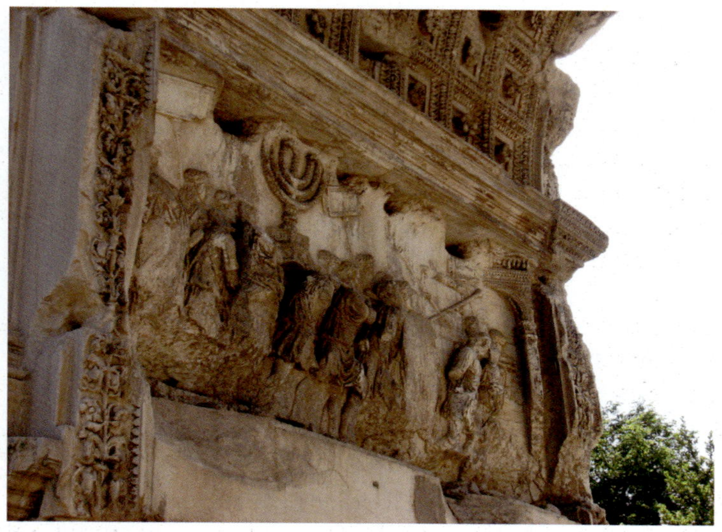

**6-15:** Spoils of Jerusalem, relief panel, Arch of Titus, after 81 CE 7'10.

In the soffit at the center of the interior of the arch is an image of the *apotheosis* of Titus. An apotheosis is literally the ascent into heaven of the deified person. Here Titus is depicted riding on the back of a large eagle, suggesting his ascent.

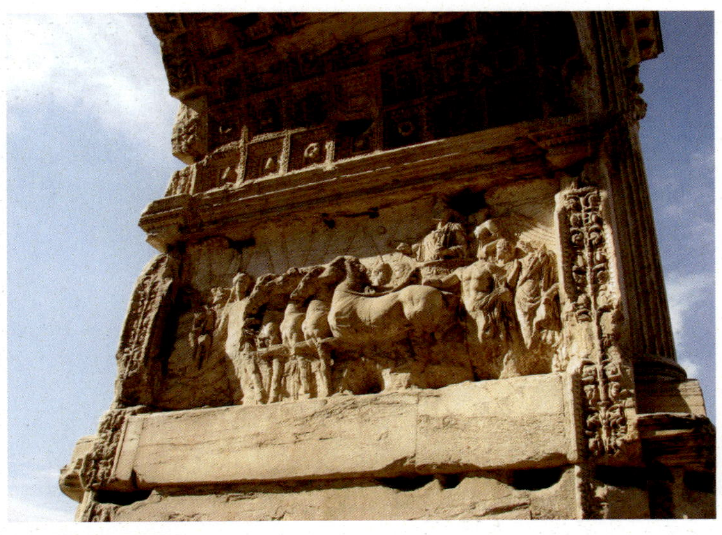

**6-16:** Triumph of Titus, relief panel, Arch of Titus, after 81 CE 7′10.

By depicting scenes from his actual triumphal procession on the interior of the arch there is an added aspect of timelessness and perpetuity. The idea is that Titus will forever pass in triumph since the actual act is now symbolically reenacted every minute of every day. The processions in the passageway even move in the direction that the actual procession would have moved.

The monument is meant to honor the deified Titus and record his political victories, while the inscription makes clear that all of his actions were sanctioned by the senate and people of Rome. It should be noted, however, that just as the arch of Titus serves as a monument to mark a great victory in the history of Rome, it also marks one of the saddest and most tragic events in the history of Judea.

Titus' brother, Domitian, was the next to rule Rome; unfortunately he was insane and an ego-maniac. He demanded to be addressed as *dominus et deus* (lord and god) and was so paranoid that he constantly had senate members and members of his own guard killed. It should also be noted that it was under Domitian that the Jews and the Christians were most heavily persecuted. It is not surprising that the senate had him assassinated in 96 CE, bringing an end to the Flavian dynasty.

Under the next ruler Nerva, Domitian suffered a fate worse than his own death; he was declared *Damnatio Memoriae* (condemnation from memory). This decree was intended to dishonor a person and to remove them from memory, to the extent that the person's name, title, and face would be removed, even coinage recalled and melted. Nerva was succeeded by his adopted son Trajan.

During the 2nd century CE, under emperors like Nerva, Trajan, Hadrian, Antononius Pius, and Marcus Aurelius, the empire flourished. The period is sometimes referred to as the period of Five Good Emperors. During this period the boundaries and borders were mostly secure and the empire was still flourishing under the Pax Romana established by Augustus.

Trajan (98–117 CE), born in Italica, Spain, was the first non-Italian to rule Rome. He was extremely popular, so much so that the SPQR granted him the title Optimus (the best), a title usually reserved for the god Jupiter.

Under Trajan, the Roman Empire reached its largest geographical extent stretching from northern England to North Africa to Syria and Egypt. Trajan instituted many Roman reforms and social programs and established cities all around the empire.

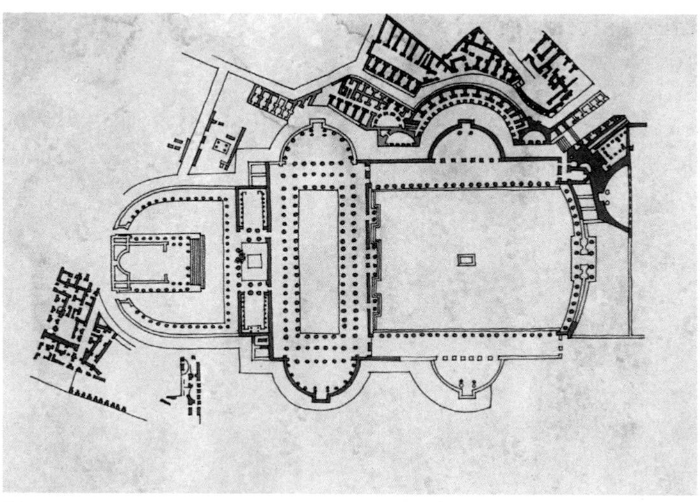

**6-17:** Forum of Trajan, Apollodorus of Damascus, Rome, Italy, dedicated 112 CE.

These cities were established and built to the same plan, a plan usually used for the building of a Roman military encampment or *castrum.*

A castrum was designed on a grid plan and based on the crossing of two major axis roads, the Cardo (north to south) and the Decumanus (east to west). The plans of the cities were extremely well designed and organized. They were established in the same manner whether they were built in England or Africa. These castrums served as tangible and physical examples of Roman rule, authority, and the desire for order. They also helped establish a sense of continuity in an empire that had almost none.

Trajan's most impressive building campaign, however, was in the center of Rome where he built an enormous new forum, twice the size of the earlier forum built by Augustus, and a massive marketplace.

Trajan's forum, now mostly destroyed and paved over, included among other monuments, two libraries, a temple, a column, a basilica, and an equestrian statue.

The new forum was built in part to glorify Trajan's greatest military victories; his victories against the Dacians (Romania). His booty from those battles paid for the expensive building project.

Trajan hired Apollodorus of Damascus, to build his forum. Apollodorus had been with Trajan during both Dacian campaigns and served as his chief military engineer.

The forum space was dominated by a huge basilica, the Basilica Ulpia that measured some 400 feet long and 200 feet wide with semicircular recesses or apses at both ends. It also had a clerestory that allowed light into the interior. The huge basilica stood at one end of a large colonnaded courtyard. In the center of the courtyard stood a larger than life size gilded bronze equestrian statue of the Emperor. Behind the basilica in another small courtyard was a temple dedicated to the deified Trajan (completed after his death).

Between the temple and the basilica were two large libraries, one Latin one Greek, that flanked a courtyard focused around a giant commemorative column.

The ornamental column, covered entirely with narrative relief sculpture, was a type of monument first invented here by Apollodorus. It was certainly not something that had ever been used in classical Greece.

The column, 128 feet in height including the pedestal, is composed of 18 colossal Carrara marble drums, each weighing about 40 tons, with a diameter of about 15 ft. Inside the shaft, a spiral staircase of 185 stairs provides access to the top, and small windows can be seen on the exterior on one side of the column. A frieze carved in low relief winds around the exterior of the shaft 23 times, with the bands getting larger as they reach the top.

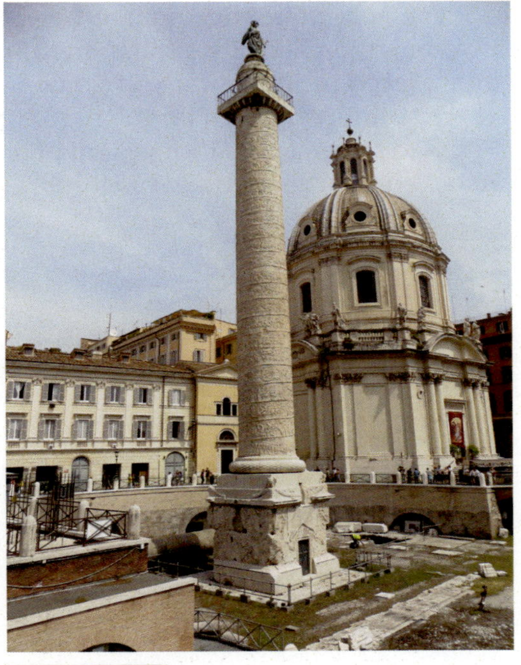

**6-18:** Column of Trajan, Apollodorus of Damascus, Rome, Italy, dedicated 112 CE, 128′ with base.

The narrative scenes of the frieze depict Trajan's two victorious campaigns against the Dacians. The scenes spiral up from the bottom toward the top and incorporate a method of representation called continuous narrative. Continuous narrative is a method of representation in which separate episodes in a story are shown in a unified pictorial field. There are over 150 different episodes and over 2,500 figures on the column.

The scenes are wonderfully detailed and depict specific events of many of the battles; they also offer historians great insight into Roman military procedures and techniques. Scenes include: Trajan addressing his troops, Trajan sacrificing to the gods, Romans storming towers, Roman fighting the enemy, and even specific Roman military techniques. Scenes also include classical personifications like the scene of the Romans crossing the Danube River, where the river is depicted as a huge bearded naked river god.

It is clear from all the scenes on the column that the Romans spent more time travelling, building roads and bridges, transporting equipment, and founding cities and forts than they did actually fighting. It seems that their victories were due as much to their organizational skills as their military ones.

Originally, the column was topped by a heroic nude portrait statue of Trajan (now lost). Today a sculpture of St. Peter is on the top.

The column's huge square base, which is decorated with images of captured Dacian armor, served as Trajan's tomb. His ashes and those of his wife Plotinus were both placed inside the base in golden urns.

A Latin inscription on the base explains that the monument was erected by the SPQR to Trajan in his 17th year of office to demonstrate the height of the hill that was removed in order to build his forum.

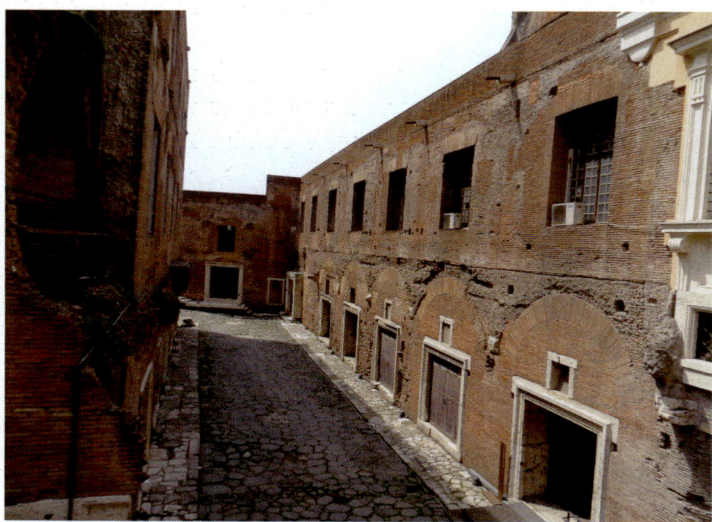

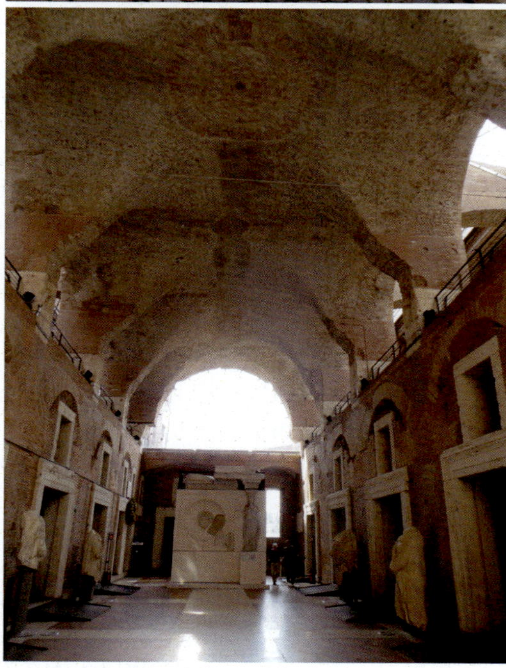

**6-19 a and b:** Markets of Trajan, Apollodorus of Damascus, Rome, 100–112 CE.

The monument successfully serves several purposes: it is commemorative, honorific, historical, artistic, and serves as both a geographical marker, a grave marker, and a tomb.

On the Quirinal Hill, just above and overlooking the vast Forum of Trajan, are Trajan's markets.

The markets, used to house numerous shops and administrative offices, were built into the slope of the hill in order to support the terraces of shops on several levels.

The rows of shops either opened onto the large hemispherical façade on the exterior or onto a large indoor market hall or small avenues on the ground level. The shops were each designed as single shop spaces or *tabernaes,* with a barrel vault and a post and lintel marble doorway with a small window above.

The markets represent the ancient equivalent of the modern shopping center, housing no less than 150 shops and offices. They were hugely popular and proved to the Roman citizen that Trajan was working hard to organize and help make their daily lives better and more efficient.

Trajan is remembered in history as one of the best of all the Roman emperors. He was a good soldier and a good general. He expanded the empire and retained the Peace. He built a forum, markets, roads and bridges, and he rebuilt the Circus Maximus in Rome where chariot races are held.

Trajan died, on August 9, 117 CE and on his deathbed, he named Hadrian, another Spaniard, as his successor.

Hadrain (117–138 CE) was a good soldier and had served under Trajan, but his reign is not marked by any major wars. Instead, Hadrian was famous as a patron of the arts. He was also a true *hellenophile,* a lover of all things Greek. He was a writer and an architect, and he even designed some of the domes built at his country home in Tivoli. We know from the writings of the historian Dio Cassius that after Hadrian had some verbal altercations with Trajan's architect Apollodorus of Damascus, he had him killed.

## Hadrian

Hadrian is perhaps best known for a wall he commissioned. In 122 CE Hadrian initiated the building of a wall to safeguard the frontier province of Britain from invasions from the northern country of Caledonia (now modern day Scotland). The wall is 73 miles long and is built across the width of Great Britian.

The wall took Hadrian's army over 6 years to build. It also kept an otherwise idle military very busy and very far from Rome.

Hadrian traveled a great deal during his reign, and everywhere that he went statues and arches were erected in his honor. More portraits of Hadrian exist than any other emperor except Augustus. His portraits always show him as a mature man with a beard.

It is significant that Hadrian is shown with a beard, something that the mature men of Greece, particularly the philosophers wore, but not something common in Rome. This influenced the rulers that followed him because for the next 150 years or so emperors wore beards. Hadrian was still looking to classical models for inspiration, though he chose not the idealized youthful athlete as a model but the mature philosopher.

The single most important and lasting commission of Hadrian's reign was the rebuilding of a temple dedicated to all the Roman gods.

The Pantheon was a temple dedicated to all the gods built by Marcus Vispanius Agrippa in 27 BCE, though that building was destroyed by fire in 80 CE. Hadrian rebuilt the temple between 118–125 CE and

**6-20:** Portrait Bust of Hadrian, marble, 2nd cen. CE, 2′16, Galleria degli Uffizi, Florence.

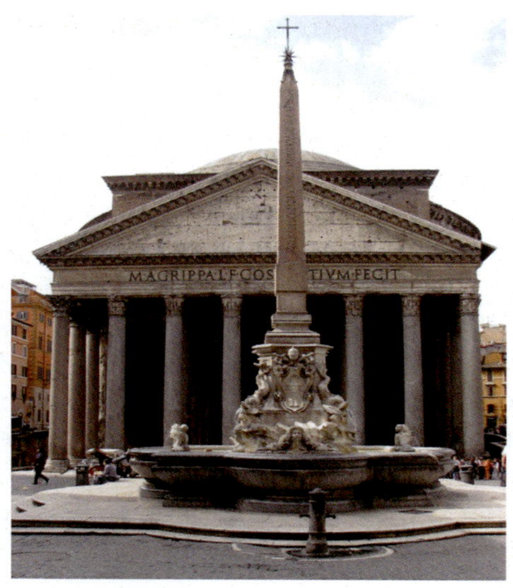


**6-21:** The Pantheon, Rome, Italy, 118–125 CE.

left the original dedicatory inscription, perhaps as an homage to Agrippa. The inscription reads M·AGRIPPA·L·F·COS·TERTIUM·FECIT, "Marcus Agrippa, son of Lucius, consul for the third time, built this."

The Pantheon is one of the best preserved buildings from antiquity and reveals the full potential of concrete both as a building material and as a material for shaping space. It is also considered one of the single most influential designs in architectural history.

The temple was originally approached through a colonnaded courtyard. The temple front reveals a Classical Greek inspired façade using eight 40 foot Corinthian columns across the front. Although the porch is clearly a reference to ancient Greece, everything else about the building is revolutionary.

Behind the porch is shallow vestibule that links the façade to an immense concrete cylinder covered by a huge concrete hemispherical dome 142 feet in diameter. The interior height of the building is also 142 feet. The spherical proportions of the building may have been intended to reflect the orb or globe (*globus* in Latin) held by Jupiter and the emperors symbolizing the world or the universe.

The dome rests on the walls of the 20 foot thick cylinder and is composed of concrete whose weight decreases in stages as it nears the great oculus (from about 20 feet thick at the bottom to about 4 feet thick at the oculus). At its base the concrete is denser and heavier to support the weight but as it reaches the upper part near the oculus the concrete is thinner and lighter having been mixed with pumice. The oculus at the top is 30 feet in diameter and serves as the only source of light for the building.

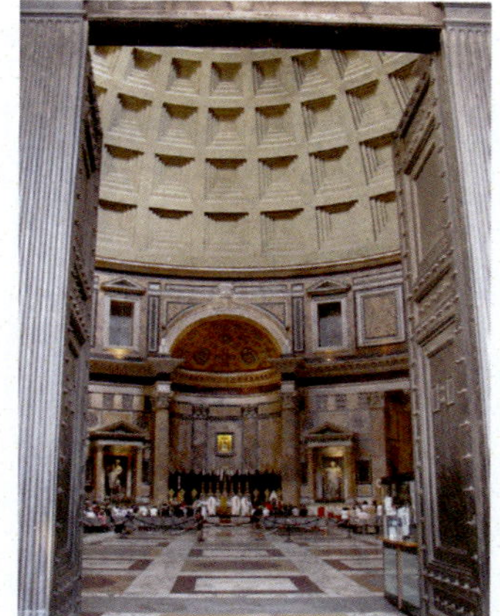

**6-22:** Pantheon, interior through door, Rome, Italy, 118–125 CE.

The immense weight of the huge vault was lessened by the inclusion of 5 rows each comprised of 28 square coffers, or sunken decorative relief panels. The coffers were critical to the construction because they lessened the weight of the great dome, but they also served a decorative function providing a pattern of recessed squares in a completely round building.

Much of the Pantheon's original interior marble veneer on the floor and walls is preserved and gives a glimpse of the splendor of ancient Roman interiors. The design

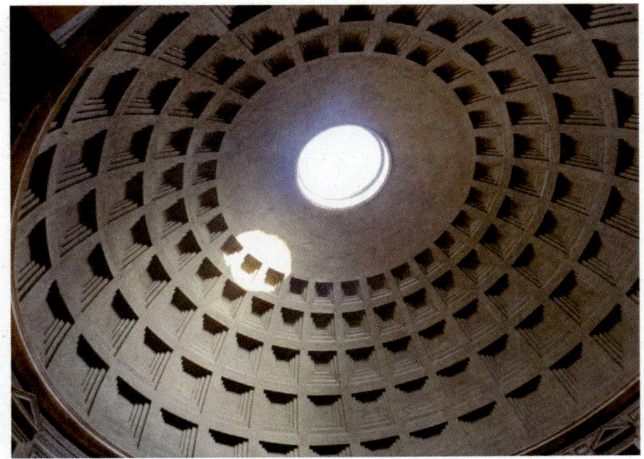

**6-23:** Pantheon, interior, oculus, Rome, Italy, 118–125 CE.

of the marble floor echoes the circles and squares represented in the dome. The floor also reveals drain holes that allow the water in the building to escape.

The Pantheon is truly remarkable for its sense of uninterrupted unified space with no supporting piers or columns to interrupt it. The sky and clouds can be seen from inside and the sun enters the space creating a circular beam that marks a path along the interior reinforcing its spherical shape and creating a sort of cosmic sense of continuity and timelessness.

In 609 CE the Pantheon was converted into a Christian church consecrated to Santa Maria dei Martiri (Holy Mary of the Martyrs) and it is still used as a church today.

In 138 CE Hadrian, who had no legitimate heirs, adopted the 51 year old Antonius Pius as his heir, and at the same time he required Antoninus to adopt Marcus Aurelius and Lucius Verus as a way to ensure a peaceful succession for at least the next generation or more.

At his death in 139 CE Hadrian was deified a god and Antoninus Pius became Emperor. Antoninus ruled for 23 years and he too was deified at his death; at which time Marcus Aurelius and Lucius Verus became Rome's first co-ruling emperors. This initiated the Antonine Dynasty (138–192 CE).

In 161 CE the co-emperors Marcus Aurelius and Lucius Verus erected a commemorative column to their adoptive father Antoninus Pius. The column does not survive but its massive base does.

The pedestal is decorated on all four sides; on one side is a dedicatory inscription, on the opposite side is a relief depicting the apotheosis of Antoninus Pius and his wife Faustina. On the other two sides is the same scene depicting a *decursio*, or ritual circling of the imperial funeral pyre.

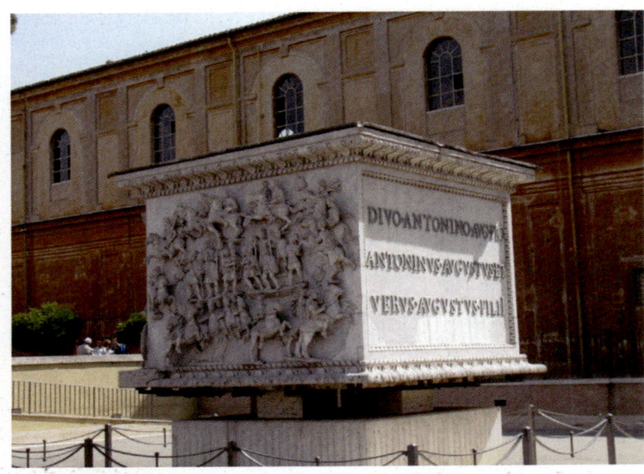


**6-24:** Pedestal of the Column of Antoninus Pius, marble ca. 161 CE, height 8′1″, Vatican Museums, Rome.

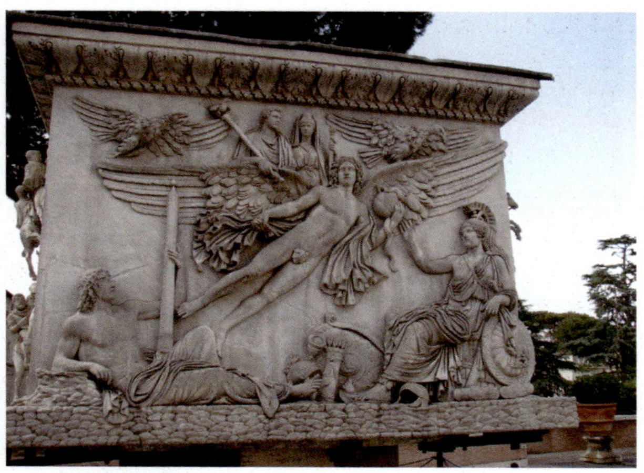

**6-25:** Apotheosis of Antoninus Pius and Faustina, Pedestal of the Column of Antoninus Pius, marble c. 161 CE, height 8′1″, Vatican Museums, Rome.

Interestingly the two relief scenes, the apotheosis and the *decursio,* are markedly different in style.

In the apotheosis relief a heroic nude winged male personification of Fame (or perhaps Aion a personification of eternity) lifts the Imperial couple into the heavens on his back. The couple is shown in half length, Antoninus holds an imperial standard and Faustina's head is covered; they are accompanied on either side by eagles.

Below, a female personification of Roma, dressed in armor and reclining on her shield, watches and acknowledges this ascent.

On the left is semi-nude reclining male figure that personifies the Campus Martius (field of Mars) holding an Egyptian obelisk. Augustus had placed an obelisk in the Campus Martius as part of a great sundial and it was there that the rituals of imperial deification were held.

There is an interesting conflation of time in the scene because Antoninus' wife had died 20 years prior to this but that they are shown here suggesting that Antoninus and his wife would be reunited and revered as they spend eternity in the heavens together.

The *decursio* panel is treated in a very different style. Rather than classically inspired monumental figures, the figures are smaller and stockier.

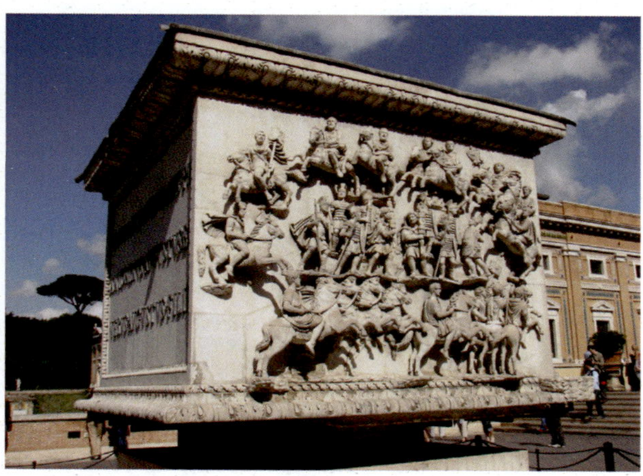

**6-26:** Decursio, pedestal, Column of Antoninus Pius, marble 161 AD, 8′1″.

There is no ground line, so horses and soldiers float on little independent scraps of earth. The figures are meant to be understood as encircling the soldiers at the center.

This style of art, less classically inspired was the style favored by the general public, not the elite patrician class; it was clearer, more direct, and more easily understood. This style lent itself to a more narrative even documentary style.

The monument proves then to be a very interesting mix of elite classical inspired art and the art of the common folk used together in the decoration of a state-sanctioned public monument. It also shows Roman artists pulling away from classical established ideals and following their own aesthetic.

Another break with the classical Greek tradition is found in the imperial portraits commissioned by Marcus Aurelius. (Lucius died in 169 CE and Marcus Aurelius became sole ruler).

The portraits of Marcus Aurelius are not classically idealized or beautiful, instead they reflect a more personal and individual quality. Portraits of Marcus Aurelius show him as appearing less stoic and more benevolent and compassionate. In some works the Emperor he even looks weary, perhaps worried.

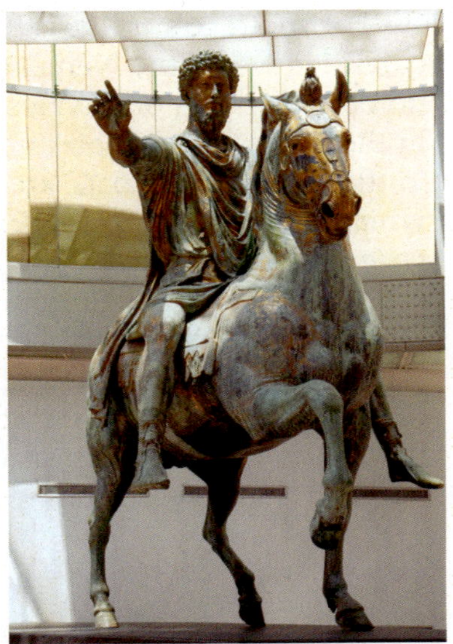

**6-27:** Equestrian Statue of Marcus Aurelius, Bronze, Rome, ca. 175 CE, 11′ 6″, Capitoline Museum, Rome.

In this larger-than-life sized gilded bronze equestrian statue, Marcus Aurelius is seated atop a striding horse, with his right arm outstretched in a gesture that is reflective both of greeting and of offering clemency. His expression is calm and serious.

The emperor does not wear any imperial armor and has no weapon; instead he wears a tunic and heavy cloak and sports a beard like Hadrian. This image of him clearly associates him with a Greek philosopher, a fitting description since he is often referred to as the Philosopher Emperor.

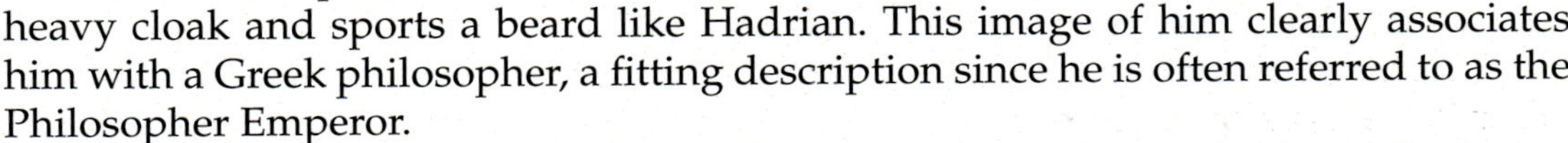

The Emperor, however, is depicted exceptionally large in relation to the horse. Hierarchy of scale makes clear that this is a portrait of a powerful emperor, not of his majestic horse. The sculpture manages to depict him as an incredibly powerful man who is commanding yet does so without being overtly militaristic.

This statue is the only ancient equestrian bronze to survive from antiquity. It was preserved primarily because of the mistaken belief in the early Christian and Medieval periods that the sculpture actually represented the first *Christian* emperor Constantine.

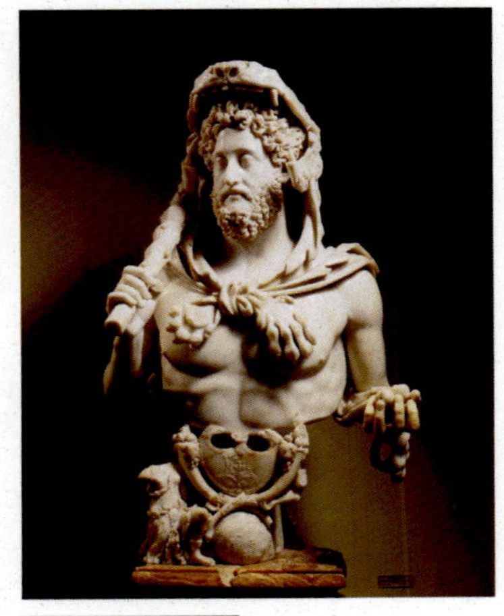

**6-28:** Commodus as Hercules, marble, c. 191 CE, 3′9″, Capitoline Museum, Rome.

Marcus Aurelius' son Commodus (r. 180–192 CE) was the next to rule; unfortunately he was, by all accounts, crazy. He liked to dress up as his favorite mythological figures, especially Hercules, and he liked to pretend he was a gladiator. He was, perhaps not surprisingly, assassinated by his own wrestling coach while in the bath; he was then declared Damnatio Memoriae. His murder ended the rule of the Antonine dynasty.

Fortunate to survive is this exquisite sculpture, which depicts Commodus as Hercules. He wears the Nemean lion skin, carries the distinctive gnarled club, and even holds the apples of the Hesperides in his left hand. The skill of the artist is evident in the finely drilled hair and beard as well as in the extremely finely chiseled details in the base. On the base an Amazon (there were once two) kneels next to a globe on which the zodiac is carved. Two cornucopias cross each other and flank a decorated *pelta*, an Amazonian shield.

After the rule of Commodus, the Roman Empire was clearly in decline. The far-flung empire was stretched too thin, and the cities on the fringes were beginning to clash; Imperial rule was beginning to look much more like military rule.

The next ruling dynasty began with African-born general named Septimius Severus who was elected emperor by his own troops. He founded the Severan dynasty that ruled from 193–235 CE.

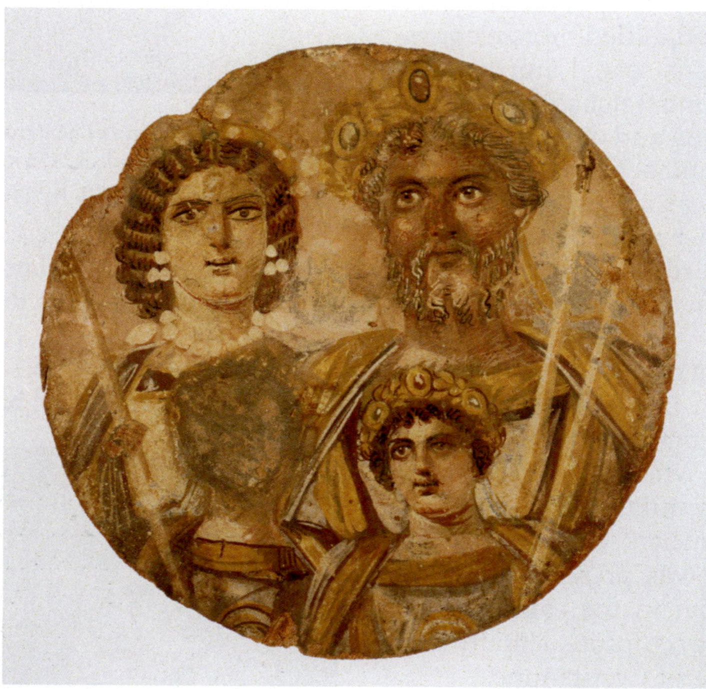

**6-29:** Tondo of Septemius Severus and family, tempera on wood, from Egypt ca. 200 CE, 13′ diameter, Staatliche Museum, Berlin.

Several extant portraits of Severus and his family survive. Many show him with his Syrian wife Julia Domna and their two sons Caracalla and Geta.

This small wooden *tondo* (circular format) is painted in tempera (pigment mixed with a binder) and is considered the ONLY surviving painted likeness of any emperor that exists to the present. The family is presented here in imperial regalia with Septimius in an impressive crown and Julia Domna wearing large pearl earrings and a choker; both young sons wear crowns. The style of the painting, with its particularly stylized and formal approach, represents a type found in the region of the Fayum in Egypt.

The face of the youngest son, Geta, has clearly been erased; a fine example of his having been declared damnatio memoriae. Geta was murdered and then declared damnatio by his older brother Caracalla in 212 CE. Caracalla, described by many as cold and ruthless, is remembered best for building a huge bath complex in Rome that covered some 50 acres.

## Funerary Sculpture

During the 3rd century CE the custom of burying the dead, instead of cremation, had become the dominant form of burial in Rome. This was a trend that had begun around the time of Hadrian and persisted, perhaps reflecting an influence from Christianity or other Eastern religions in the empire. This trend in Roman burial customs led to an increase in the production of large-scale sculpted sarcophagi (containers for the dead).

This elaborately carved marble sarcophagus depicts a vivid battle scene of Roman soldiers fighting barbarians, probably the Northern Goths, a Germanic tribe. The entire surface of the sarcophagus is covered with figures, with no attempt or illusion of any space between or around them.

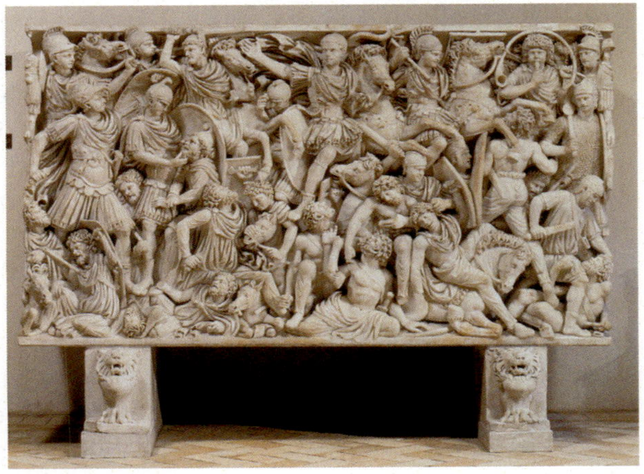

**6-30:** Battle between Romans and Barbarians, the Ludovisi Sarcophagus, marble, c. 250 CE, 5′ high, National Museum, Rome.

The style shows a clear rejection of the classical concepts of three-dimensional space and proportion in favor of a more dramatic and descriptive style. The style is similar to that found in the decursio scene on the pedestal of the Column of Antoninus Pius, though here much more compact.. The figures are deeply carved in high relief, with many parts almost completely in the round creating deep crevasses and shadows that further animate the surface.

Although the scene is chaotic, we can discern some of what is happening. A figure, larger than the rest, is on horseback at the center of the chaos. He has no helmet and carries no weapons and seems to be gesturing either to the other soldiers for the attack, or to show that he is capable of this victory without much effort at all. All around him armed Roman soldiers defeat the bearded and helmetless barbarians. Notice the figure at the top blowing into a large curling horn just like the one depicted in the sculpture of the dying Gaul.

The theme, which was very popular at the time, is appropriate for its location; suggesting victory, in battle, in life, and in death.

By the end of the 3rd century CE the empire was collapsing and emperors and generals were willing to make bold moves in an attempt to gain or retain control. One such move, a last ditch effort, was made by the Emperor Diocletian.

The Roman general Diocletian (r. 284–305), who was elected Emperor by his own troops, decided that in the interest of keeping the peace in the Empire that he would share rulership. In 293 CE he decided to share control with three of his rivals; thereby establishing a *tetrarchy* (rule of four).

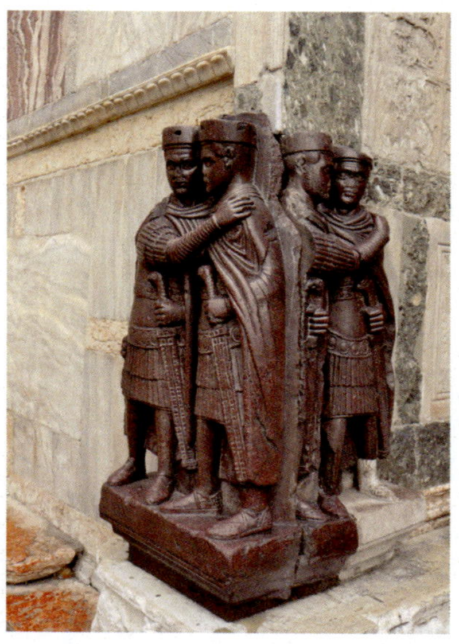

**6-31:** Tetrarchs, porphyry, ca. 305 CE , 4'3", now in St. Mark's square, Venice, Italy.

In this compact sculpture the rulers of the tetrarchy are portrayed together with no individuality given to their portraits. They each wear a cuirass and a long cloak and each carries a sheathed sword. There is no individuality and no sense of individual portraiture. The emotionless figures are rather short and squat with thick necks and stiff poses; even the drapery has been simplified and reduced to a system of lines. The figures are depicted as physically and philosophically inseparable. The sculpture does not attempt to depict four individuals, rather it attempts to show the nature of equal and shared power of the tetrarchy. This sculpture is not about the image but instead is about the message.

The sculpture also stands out, now at the end of the Roman Empire, as the antithesis of all that Greek art had managed to achieve; it denies naturalism and denies the idealized beauty of the human form. It is, however, something completely different with a different goal and a different purpose.

The tetrarchy remained intact until 305 when Diocletian decided to abdicate his power and retire to his palace at Split in Dalmatia on the Yugoslavian coast (Croatia).

## Constantine: (r. 306–337 CE)

The three remaining rulers fought for control of the empire until the whole system ultimately collapsed. After a period of struggle between the remaining rulers and later their sons, Constantine emerged victorious.

In 312 CE, in a decisive battle at the Milvian Bridge in Rome, Constantine defeated Maxentius and took control of the Capital becoming Emperor of the West.

Legend says that the night before the battle Constantine had a vision in which he saw a brilliant sign in the sky and heard a voice say "in this sign you shall conquer" (*in hoc signo vinces)* The following morning he made all his soldiers put the sign that he saw in the sky on their shields. Constantine and his soldiers using their new symbol won the battle and the new Emperor attributed his victory to the Christian God.

The sign he saw, called a Chi Rho, is formed by the first two letters of Christ's name written in Greek, ΧΡΙΣΤΟΣ, superimposed.

In 313 CE, as a result of his victory, Constantine (along with Licinius the ruler in the East) wrote a document called the Edict of Milan in which he legalized Christianity throughout the empire. Another reason for his acceptance of Christianity may be that his mother, Helen, was already a devout Christian.

In 325 CE Constantine proclaimed Christianity as the official religion of the empire, and in 330 CE he founded a new city on the ancient Greek site of Byzantium, and named it Constantinople. In 337 CE on his deathbed, as was the usual custom, Constantine was baptized.

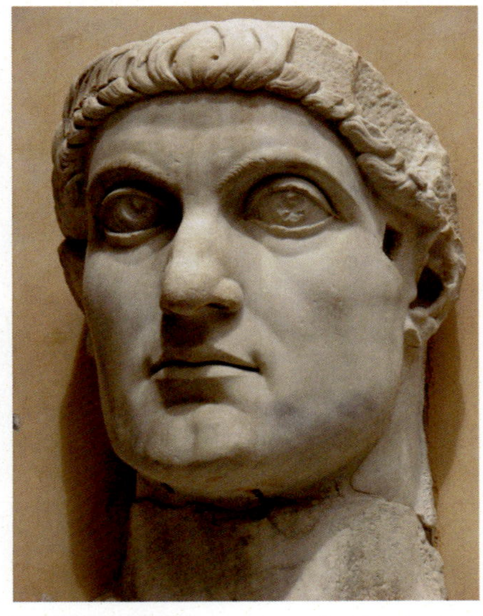

**6-32:** Constantine, Basilica Nova, Italy, marble, height 8′6″ 315—330 CE, Capitoline Museum, Rome.

The art produced during this transitional period in Roman history reflects the changes in the empire. Constantine had to balance his Christian beliefs with his responsibilities to the Roman sate religion, and in the early years he commissioned art that seemed to reflect both pagan and Christian ideals.

Constantine had many official portraits and statues of himself created, and most reflect a return to a more classical style in which the emperor is shown idealized and eternally youthful.

One fabulous example is attested to in the remains of what was a colossal enthroned portrait of the emperor approximately 40 feet tall. The sculpture, now in pieces, depicted the Emperor with his right arm raised, index finger pointing upward, and holding an orb in his left. The statue was so large that the torso was made of wood and then covered with relief sculpted bronze while the head and limbs were all carved in marble.

Unlike earlier imperial portraits, the eyes do not gaze at the observer or at anything in this world but instead gaze upward. This was done perhaps to reflect his vision, both literal and figural. These large eyes are a constant part of images of Constantine throughout his life.

One of Constantine's his first major architectural commissions was the completion of a massive basilica that had already been begun by Maxentius.

The Basilica Nova was an enormous building, 300 feet long and 215 feet wide, with brick faced walls 20 feet thick. The walls were built so thick in order to support the massive coffered barrel vaults of the side aisles and the 115 foot groin vaults in the nave.

The interior would have been richly ornamented with stucco and painted and the floors would have been covered with colored marbles. Located at the west end in a large recessed niche, would have sat the colossal portrait of Constantine.

Three of the enormous barrel vaults survive today and are by far the largest structures in the forum.

After his victory in 312 CE the SPQR erected a monumental triple-way triumphal arch to Constantine. The arch, located just next to the Flavian Amphitheatre, was intended to commemorate his victory, but unlike previous arches, some of the

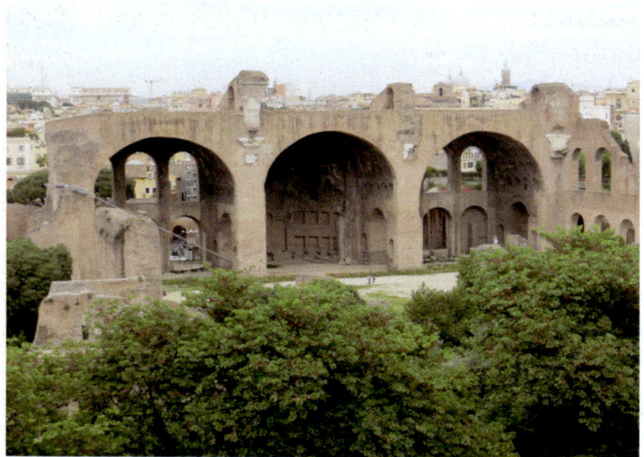

**6-33:** Basilica Nova, or Basilica of Constantine, 306–312 CE, Rome, Italy.

decoration was taken from earlier monuments. The decoration was taken from monuments originally erected to Trajan, Hadrian, and Marcus Aurelius, suggesting a kind of visual correlation between the new Emperor Constantine and those past good emperors, all of whom had been deified.

The arch has different images on its two faces; so that the South side facing away from the city shows images of battle while the North side facing toward the center shows images of peace and Constantine as a benevolent ruler. Many of the panels have been recut and the head of Constantine are either damaged or destroyed. It should be noted that the external ends of the arch depict the gods Sol and Luna and there is no Christian symbolism on the arch anywhere.

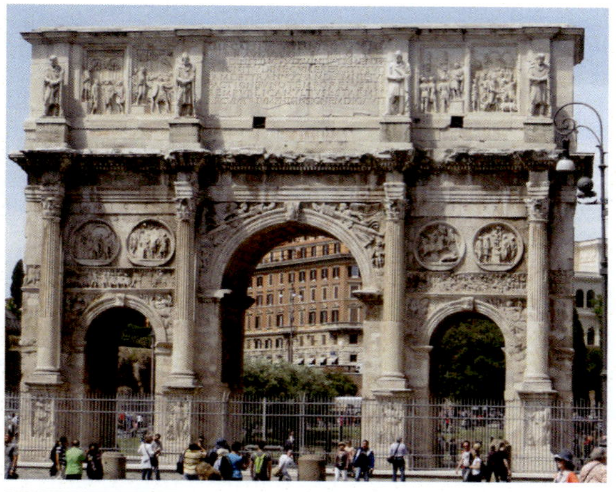

**6-34:** Arch of Constantine, North Side, marble, 312–315 CE, height 68′8, Rome, Italy.

The reuse of sculpture on the arch is sometimes cited as an example of the decline of Roman artistic abilities in this period. However, it should be seen as a conscious and shrewd decision by Constantine to make sure, visually and historically, that he is associated with the good emperors of the past. This new style, with its rejection of classical proportion and a focus on the message, is not necessarily better or worse than what came before; it is simply different. The new art of the empire had its own new set of pictorial values and compositional formality, and it is that style, and focus on messaging that will impact Christian art and the art of the Middle Ages.

Name ______________________________ Date ______________

## Chapter 6

# Art and Architecture of Rome

1. What style of portraiture was preferred in the Roman Republic? What is the term used for this style?

2. What event does the Arch of Titus commemorate?

3. What structure incorporates coffers and an oculus?

4. Under which emperor did the empire reach its greatest geographical extent?

5. Which structure reveals the full potential of concrete in Roman architecture?

6. What terms can be used to describe the Temple of *Portunus?*

7. Which emperor established a pattern of succession by adoption with his adoption of Trajan?

8. Which ruler established Christianity as the official religion of Rome in 313 CE?

9. How did Roman funerary practices evolve over time?

10. Compare Roman portraiture during the Republic and Imperial periods. Cite two examples.

# EARLY CHRISTIAN ART AND ARCHITECTURE

## Chapter 7

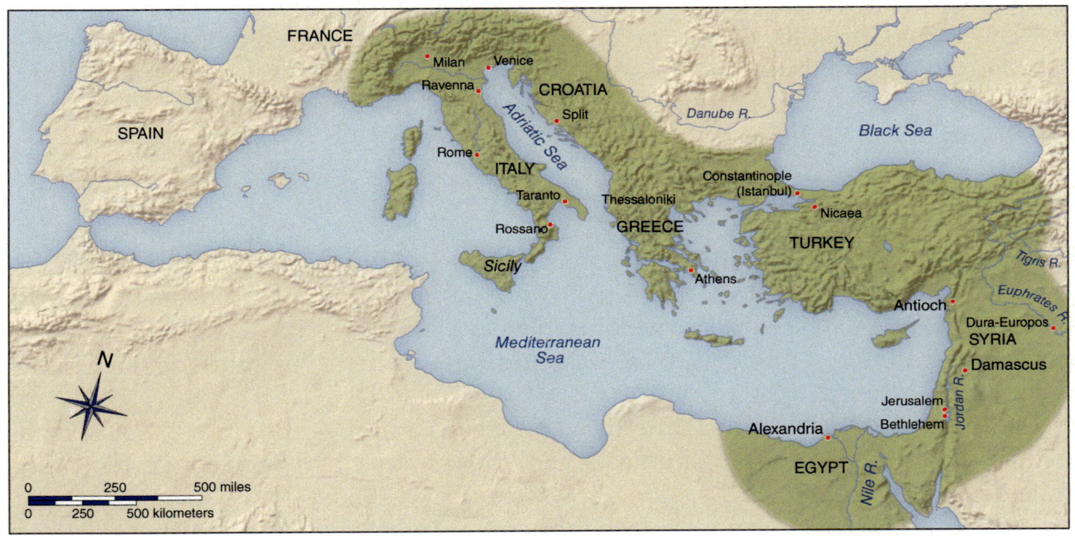


Expansion of Christianity c. 250 CE.

Early Christian art is, generally, art produced in the service of or reflecting Christian faith, made between the 2nd and 6th centuries CE. There is almost no extant Christian art from the period of the first century CE and art made after 525 CE is generally referred to as Byzantine art.

From this point forward all dates, unless otherwise noted, are Common Era.

*Christian* is a general term given to followers of Jesus of Nazareth, who according to history was crucified in the year 30, during the reign of the Emperor Tiberius (r. 14–37) under Pontius Pilate (r. 26–36), the governor of Judea.

Concentrated persecution of the members of the new religion began around 64 when the Emperor Nero blamed the fire of Rome on the Christians; and then ordered the execution of both St. Peter and St. Paul. Christians were executed primarily because they refused to worship the Emperor or to take part in the rites of the state's imperial cult. This defiance of the state made them appear dangerous and a threat to imperial authority.

The persecution of Christians did not stop until 313 when Constantine wrote his Edict of Milan. It is only after that date that Christians were free to worship and to create public works of art and architecture in honor of their faith.

Very little is known about Christian art in the first century in part because the early Christians, having come from a faith whose basis was Judaism, shared a reluctance to make figural art. However, graven images, expressly prohibited by the second commandment, were interpreted by Christians to mean carved in wood or stone, so images were often made in paint and mosaic but rarely in three dimensions.

The early Christian desire for image making seems to have been in part motivated by the desire to use images as teaching tools. Images were, particularly for the mostly illiterate, the best and most impactful way to express tenets of faith and tell the stories of the Bible.

## Dura Europas

One of the earliest Christian churches yet discovered was located near the Euphrates river in Syria at a site called Dura-Europas. The small Roman outpost was destroyed by the Sassanians in 256 and abandoned. Excavations there have led to the discovery of several different cult worship sites, including a Jewish synagogue and a Christian community house.

In the early years of the Church, when it was still illegal to practice, Christians, like Jews, gathered in private homes. Often these homes had been converted to serve the needs of the faithful.

At Dura Europas, the community house was built like other Roman houses with small rooms (*cubiculas*) surrounding a courtyard. The space was large enough to hold approximately 70 worshippers and had a small recess or niche that contained a baptismal font, over which was an image of Christ as the Good Shepherd' as well as an image of Adam and Eve.

The font is significant as evidence of the importance of the rite of Baptism for Christians, as they were washed of their sins and initiated into the faith.

There was also a communal dining room in which the Christians practiced the celebration of the Eucharist; the ritual consumption of bread and wine recognized by Christians as Christ's bo dy and blood.

Though badly damaged, the decoration of the house included mural scenes such as the three Marys visiting Christ's tomb, Christ healing, and David and Goliath.

## The Catacombs

Most of our examples of early Christian art date to the 3rd and 4th centuries and come from the underground cemeteries or *catacombs* located just on the outskirts of Rome.

The catacombs are a vast subterranean network of galleries and chambers, carved out of the tufa rock, designed as cemeteries in which to bury the Christian dead. They

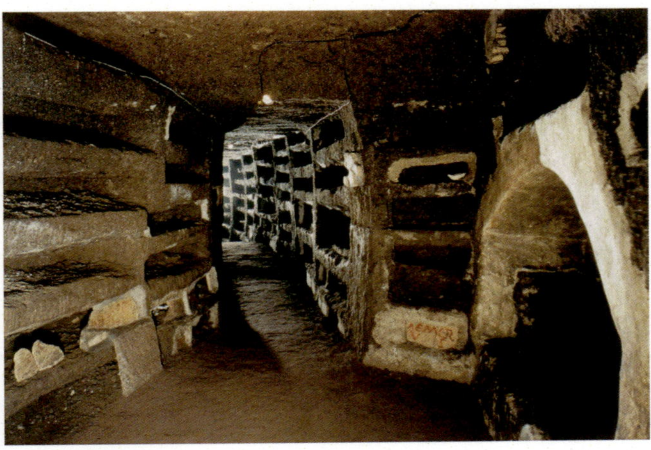

7-1: Catacombs of Priscilla, gallery with loculi, Rome, Italy.

were in keeping with Roman laws by being located outside the old *pomerium,* or sacred boundary of the city proper.

The catacombs, in constant use between the 2nd and 4th centuries, consist of varying levels of narrow street-like tunnels with niches, or larger cubiculas, cut in the walls. The catacombs were dug by professional men called *fossores* who served as grave-diggers, tunnelers, and guides to visiting families and pilgrims. While actively in use, between 500,000 and 750,000 Christian dead may have been buried in the catacombs.

There are two main types of burial spaces within the catacombs: the *loculi* which are shelf-like openings in the walls of the galleries placed one above the other, and the *cubicula* which are small rooms carved out of the rock that could contain a number of loculi, often used for a family burial, like a mortuary chapel.

The Romans did not have a need for catacombs, because they cremated their dead and deposited their remains into small urns or containers that were housed in a *columbarium.* Christians, on the other hand, believed in the eventual resurrection of the dead, and therefore believed it a sin to cremate the dead, so they practiced inhumation, burial as opposed to cremation.

After the legalization of Christianity in 313, churches were often located near or over parts of the catacombs and chapels designated for worship of some of the martyrs were designed in the catacombs themselves.

## Decoration

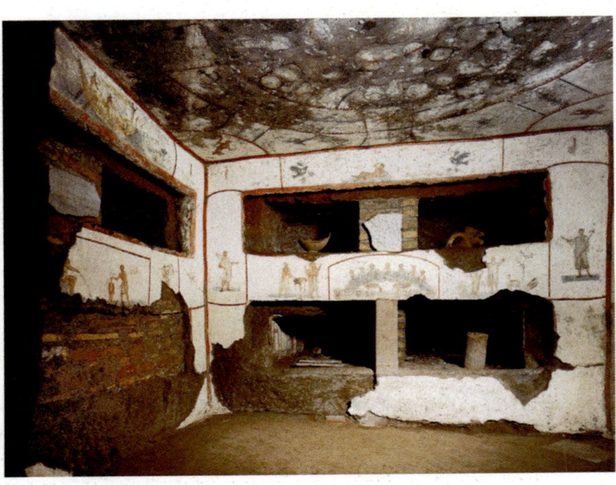

7-2: Catacombs of St. Callixtus, cubicula, Rome, Italy.

The decoration in the catacombs was often not figural but instead made up of a series of symbols meant to represent Christ and Christian beliefs. This included various inscriptions like the Chi Rho, the Christogram, the alpha and omega, the symbol of a fish, or acrostics such as IXΘYC. The Greek word 'fish' is an acrostic composed from the initial letters if the Greek phrase J' esus Christ Son of

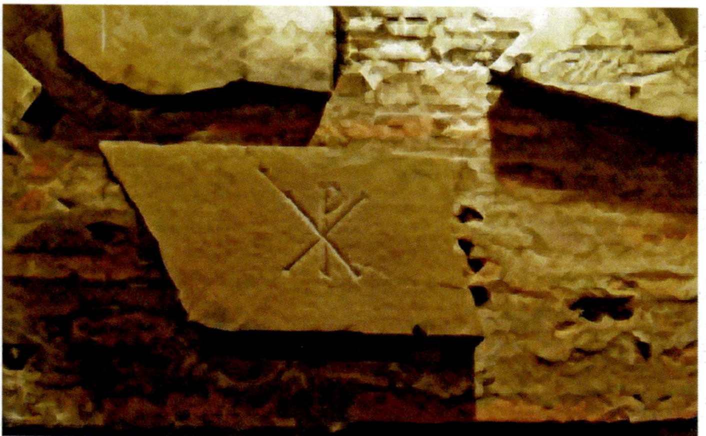

7-3: Early Christian symbols, Catacombs of St. Callixtus, Rome, Italy.

God Savior." Simple symbols like the dove, fish, peacock, lamb, grapevine, and anchor were recognized as symbolic of larger Christian themes and messages.

The figural art of the early Christian period is Roman in style but Christian in context. This borrowing and assimilating of imagery and providing it with new meaning is called *syncretism*.

In one example from a painted cubicula the ceiling fresco depicts an image of Christ as the Good Shepherd. He is shown youthful and beardless, carrying a sheep on his shoulders. The type of image is based on an already established form, the moscophoros, but here imbued with Christian meaning.

The Good Shepherd image takes as its source the *New Testament*, in which Christ describes himself as the Good Shepherd, who would give his life for his sheep. Christ portrayed as a shepherd or a teacher is a common depiction for him until after Christianity becomes the official religion of the Empire. Only after Christianity is legalized do we find Christ depicted wearing imperial robes and a halo.

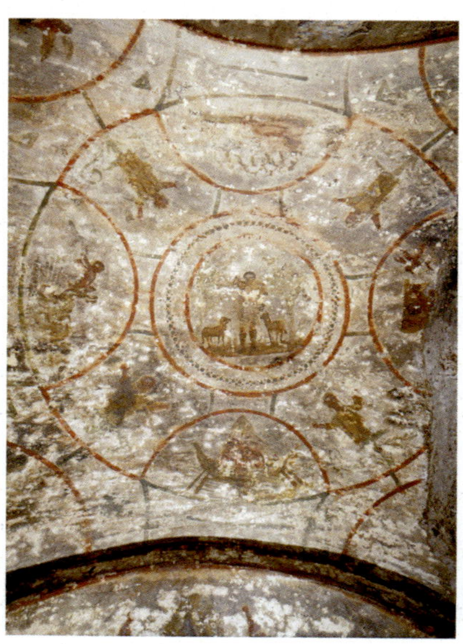

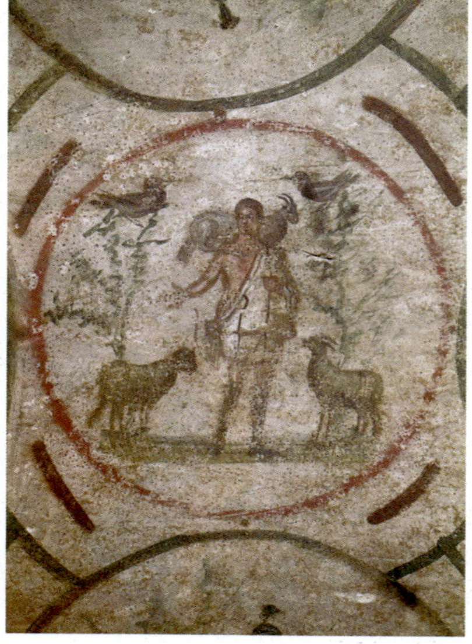

7-4: Christ as Good Shepherd, ceiling painting from two different cubicula, Catacombs, Rome, 4th cen.

In the spaces between the lunettes are standing *orant* figures, both male and female. "Orant" in Latin means "praying" and the early Christian attitude of prayer was one with arms outstretched and palms raised upward.

In the lunettes, around the edges, are scenes from the *Old Testament* story of Jonah. In one scene sailors throw Jonah from a boat, in another we see the whale, or sea dragon as he is described in the *New Testament*, regurgitate the thankful Jonah. In another lunette, Jonah reclines under an arbor. The story of Jonah and the whale is considered a prefiguration (a prophetic forerunner) of Christ's death and resurrection. Jonah spent three days in darkness (as Christ spent three days in the tomb) and then was resurrected to a new life.

Many *Old Testament* stories can be read as prefigurations of events in the *New Testament,* and the iconographical pairing or coupling of *Old* with *New Testament* imagery is called *typology*.

The images found in the catacombs were painted by anonymous artists, and were done with a minimum of color, usually only reds, greens, browns, and some yellows. The medium is a mixture of fresco techniques, using both dry and wet pigment on wet and dry plaster.

Commonly found in the catacombs are images such as Jonah, Daniel in the lion's den, the three hebrews in the fiery furnace, and Moses striking the rock. These images all share a specific message, a message crucial to the persecuted Christians; it was the message of salvation. Interestingly, an image not found in the catacombs is the crucifixion. The crucifixion scene was too violent and perhaps too present in the everyday world of the early Christian faithful and so it was unnecessary to show.

The catacombs have been called the "archives of the early church" and they contained the most important and extensive collection of early Christian art that exists in the world.

## Sarcophagi

Because of the Christian's rejection of cremation there was a development in the art of the sculpted sarcophagus. A sarcophagus is a coffin, or container for the dead body, usually made of stone. It was not a new art form, but was adopted and adapted by the Christians for their use, and therefore tended to be decorated with the same types of subjects that were found in the catacombs.

One of the most important surviving early Christian works of art is a marble sarcophagus that belonged to a Roman official named Junius Bassus, who died on Aug 25, 359 at the age of 42.

According to the inscription on the sarcophagus, he was baptized just before his death, as was common practice. Junius Bassus was an aristocratic, wealthy, politically powerful man, and his public and demonstrative celebration of his Christian faith is impressive at this early date. The sarcophagus was originally buried near the tomb of St. Peter.

It is carved on three sides with a flat back side that would have stood against a wall in a mausoleum. The lid is badly damaged and little remains, but it appears to

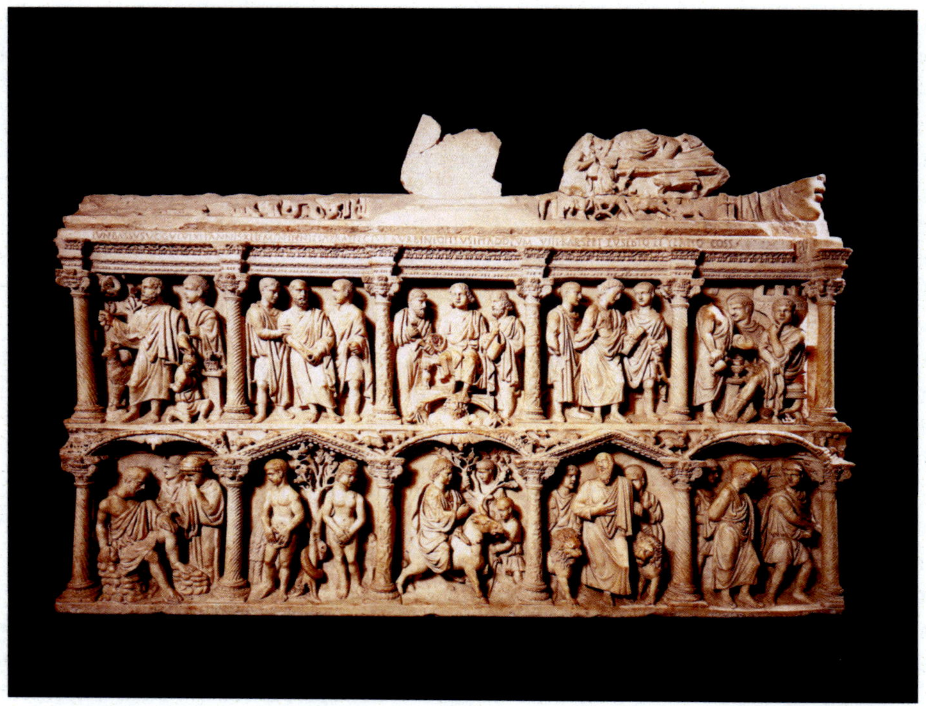

**7-5:** Sarcophagus of Junius Bassus, marble, Rome, Italy, c. 359, 3′10″ × 8′, Vatican Treasury.

have depicted masks at either end and a reclining portrait of the deceased (typical of images found on Roman sarcophagi), as well as a dedicatory plaque at the center. The sides depict *putti* (a putto is a young cherub-like figure with wings) harvesting grapes, and other seasonal imagery.

On the front are two horizontal registers with ten small scenes, five on each register. The scenes are separated by ornamental columns that create independent niches for each of the scenes. The scenes are from both the *Old Testament* and the *New Testament*.

On the upper register, reading from left to right are Abraham and Isaac, St. Peter taken prisoner, Christ enthroned between Peter and Paul, Christ under arrest, and Christ before Pilate.

On the lower register, reading from left to right are Job on the dunghill, Adam and Eve, Christ entering Jerusalem, Daniel in the lion's den, and St. Paul being led to his martyrdom.

Christ, youthful and beardless, is prominent in the work, and takes up the central niche on both registers. In the upper section he is robed and seated on a throne like an Emperor supported by a personification of the universe. The personification, depicted as a semi-nude bearded man holding a billowing sail above his head, is meant to signify that the seated ruler above is ruler of the entire universe. Christ is seated between

Saints Peter and Paul to whom he hands his law; this is an adaptation of a Roman scene called the *traditio legis*, in which the Emperor is depicted handing down laws. Below, in the corresponding position, we see a humble Christ, not seated on a throne but on a donkey, which he rides into Jerusalem.

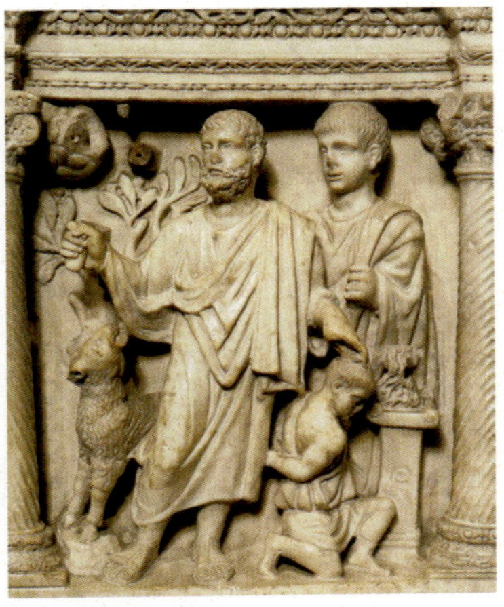

**7-6:** Sarcophagus of Junius Bassus, detail of Sacrifice of Isaac, marble, Rome, Italy, 359, Vatican Treasury.

Scenes relate to one another and make connections and prefigurations, just like those in the catacombs, so that in the upper left is a scene of Abraham and Isaac. Abraham was called on by God to sacrifice his only son, and was going to do so obediently; this scene is often seen as a prefiguration of God's sacrifice of his own son. Adam and Eve are here because it was their action and fall that precipitated the need for salvation. Notice too Daniel in the lion's den on the right, another popular scene of salvation.

Again, there is no depiction of the Crucifixion, here, like in the catacombs, Christ's role as law giver and savior is emphasized over his suffering and death.

Once Christianity was legal it could emerge from the shadows and the darkness of the catacombs, and with this emergence rose the need and desire for large-scale public places of worship.

Constantine's role as Roman emperor and as a Christian was reflected in his commissioning and support of the building of a large number of Christian churches, memorials, and mausoleums, in Rome, in Constantinople, and in Jerusalem. Therefore, Constantine was the first major patron of Christian architecture.

The greatest of the Christian churches erected by Constantine was Saint Peter's begun c. 319. This massive basilica was built on the west side of the Tiber river, literally on top of the site of Peter's burial.

Peter was an apostle of Jesus, a martyr, and a saint, and is considered Rome's first Bishop and therefore the first Pope. Peter had been crucified upside down during the reign of the Emperor Nero, and after his death a small altar was erected over his tomb. It was over his physical tomb that Constantine decided to build the largest Christian church in the Empire.

The new Constantinian church needed to be glorious, and large enough to house the growing multitudes of the faithful; it also needed to signify the house of God. The design for the structure also needed to be based on an imposing architectural model that did not previously have any strong pagan religious significance. That meant that the typical pagan peripteral style temple plan would not be acceptable. So architects turned to Roman civic architecture, specifically the basilica, for inspiration.

The basilica was a large rectangular hall that served primarily as a public gathering space, especially for law courts, markets, and reception halls. The Roman basilica was ideal for the needs of the Christians: it simply needed to be adopted and then adapted.

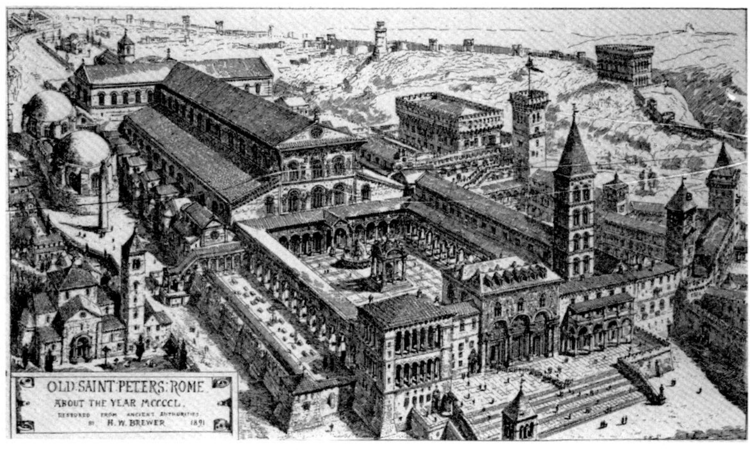


**7-7:** Reconstruction drawing of Old St. Peter's, Rome Italy, begun c. 319.

Saint Peter's was designed with a wide central *nave* (center aisle) with double flanking side aisles, and a semicircular niche or *apse* at one end (usually the east end). The structure was preceded by a large open colonnaded courtyard called an *atrium*. Worshipers entered the basilica through the *narthex* (vestibule) at the front of the church, and then into the nave, providing them with a long unobstructed view of the altar in the apse. The altar was framed by an architectural feature called a triumphal arch that divided the apse from the *transept*. The transept, or transverse arm, was an aisle set perpendicular to the nave at the apse end. The transept, which became a standard element in western church architecture, symbolically altered the basilica form into a shape that mimics the cross. This transept arm was unique to Christian architecture and was a specifically Constantinian innovation. The transverse arm added additional space that could be used for smaller altars, to house relics, and to hold additional faithful. This new innovation was created to suit the needs of the expanding congregation and more complex liturgical services.

Another way in which the Christian basilica differed from the Roman civic basilica, was that the entrance was moved from the long flank (as it had been in Roman structures like the Basilica Nova), to the short side, providing singular access to the atrium.

St. Peter's was 300-feet in length and 215-feet wide. It had four rows of 22 columns that supported an entablature, and clerestory windows above. The trussed wooden roof may have been about 125-feet tall.

The exterior of the building was simple and austere, but the inside was richly adorned with murals, mosaics, and exquisite marble columns, and gold and silver objects. There was also a huge marble canopy (*baldachino*) supported by four spiral columns, to mark the altar just above the sacred spot of the burial of St. Peter.

Our knowledge of that early basilica built under Constantine survives in written descriptions of the building, but the basilica was completely torn down in the

16th century to accommodate the new, enormous, largely Baroque, basilica (begun 1506) that we recognize today as St. Peter's.

Although the basilica plan was the most common and generally preferred type of building plan, early Christian architects did use another type: the central plan. A central plan structure is a circular domed building; central refers to the fact that the buildings parts are equally dispersed around the center. The central plan building has the ancient tholos tomb as its inspiration.

The central plan was generally reserved for smaller buildings like *martyriums* (a small building intended to mark the site of a burial of an early Christian martyr); *mausoleums* (large tombs); baptisteries; and private chapels.

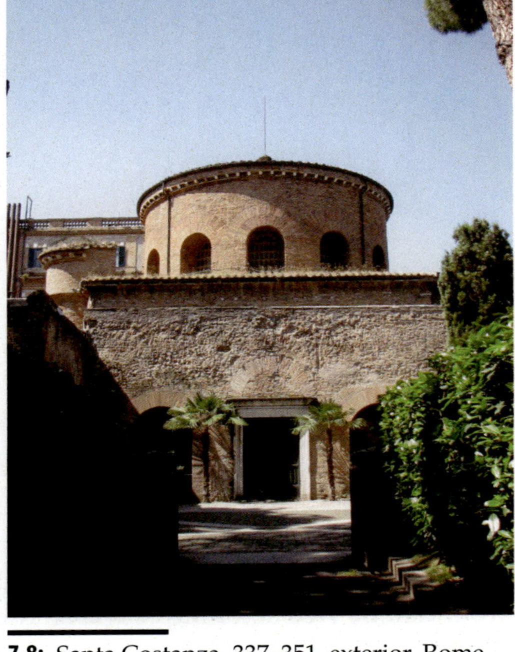

**7-8:** Santa Costanza, 337–351, exterior, Rome, Italy.

One of the earliest central plan churches built in Rome was that of Santa Costanza. Santa Costanza was originally built as the mausoleum for Constantine's eldest daughter Constantina (Costanza). The mausoleum, which did in fact once contain her elaborate porphyry sarcophagus, was then later converted into a church.

The interior of the central plan building, because of its shape, does not have a nave and side aisles, but instead has an ambulatory. An ambulatory is a ring-like barrel-vaulted corridor or aisle, that is often separated from the central domed space by a ring of columns. At Santa Costanza there is a ring of columns composed of 12 pairs of columns.

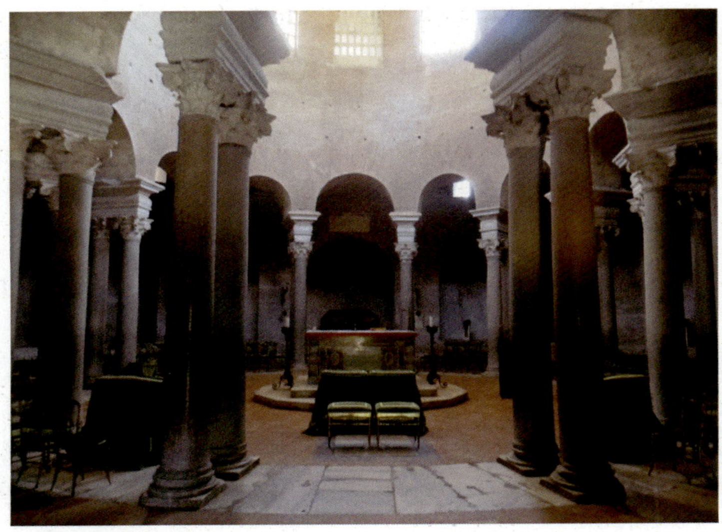

**7-9:** Santa Costanza, 337–351, interior, Rome, Italy.

Like most basilica plan churches, the exterior of the building was unremarkable and unadorned,

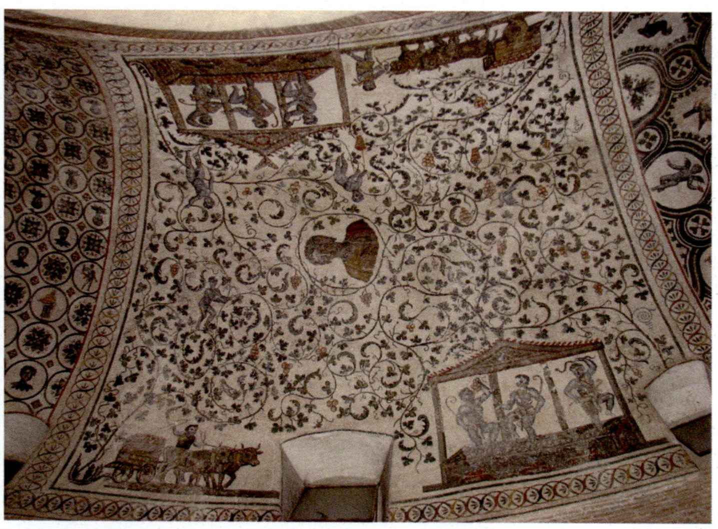

**7-10:** Santa Costanza, 337–351, ambulatory mosaic, Rome, Italy.

but the interior was richly decorated. The interior would have been sheathed in rich marbles and both the floor and ceiling were covered with mosaics. The mosaics display a variety of subject matter including bust portraits, decorative coffers, and scenes reminiscent of the catacombs and sarcophagi.

On the barrel vaulted ceiling of the ambulatory, mosaic decoration depicts images that include both pagan and Christian elements.

At the center of one panel is a bust portrait of a woman, perhaps Costanza, surrounded by rich scrolling vines. At the corners are scenes of putti harvesting grapes and producing wine. Wine in the pagan world was associated with the god Bacchus, but for Christians it represented the blood of Christ. The scenes and style are Roman in nature, but the meaning and context is now Christian.

Mosaic decoration was a favorite method of decoration during the early Christian period. It was adopted from the classical past, but used in another manner: in the classical world mosaic had traditionally served as a floor decoration, but the Christian adaptation was to transfer mosaics upward to the walls and vaults.

## Santa Maria Maggiore

An early and impressive cycle of mosaic imagery is preserved in the early Christian basilica of Santa Maria Maggiore in Rome. This was the first major church dedicated to the Virgin Mary in the West.

The church was begun in the year 432. The year is significant because it was during the same year that, at an ecumenical council in Ephesus, the Virgin Mary had been officially given the title, *Theotokos*, or “Bearer of God.” An ecumenical council is a meeting of Church officials in which they discuss, decide, or settle matters of Christian doctrine or practice.

The nave of the huge church is decorated with mosaics on the entablature (wall portion above the columns) with scenes from the Old Testament. Originally there were 42 panels, but now only 36 survive. One example is the panel depicting Lot and Abraham.

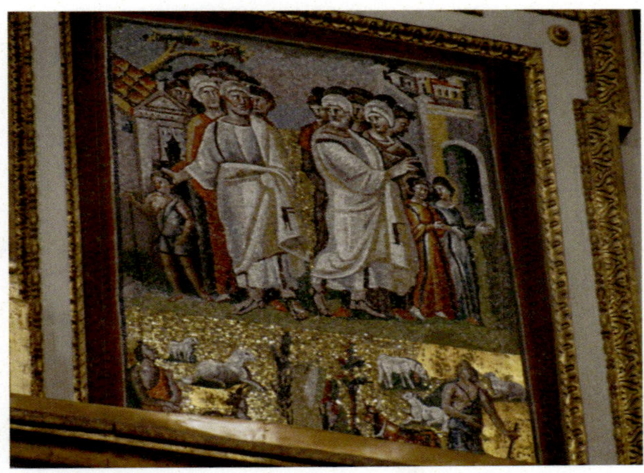

**7-11:** Parting of Lot and Abraham, mosaic, nave arcade, Santa Maria Maggiore, Rome, Italy, 432–440, panel approximate height 3′5.

This Old Testament scene (Genesis 13: 1–12) represents the separating of Abraham and his nephew Lot. The scene is an allegory for the separation of good from evil.

Abraham represents good. He moves to the right toward a temple in Canaan (Palestine), where God had foretold that the descendants of Abraham would rule. His son Isaac is in from of him.

Lot, who on the other hand symbolizes evil, moves off to the left in the direction of the city of Sodom. In front of him are his two daughters.

The separation of the two is evidenced and heightened in the mosaic by the physical rift between the two groups of figures. Lot and Abraham turn and look at one another as each goes his very separate way. The image is simplified in order to focus on the message; one chooses wisely and righteously; the other did not.

The composition is simplified and reduced to its most basic elements in order to capture the story in such a small panel. The groups are reduced to head clusters, a simplified artistic choice that depicts a group of people without having to depict every part of them. The use of gesture is strong and clear as Abraham motions to the right, with his torso open, frontal, and unobstructed, while Lot gestures to the left with his right arm blocking his torso; literally turning his back to Abraham. The use of broad gestures and simplified motion is characteristic of early Christian art. The work is simplified but powerful in its clarity.

The mosaic decoration still retains some classical qualities; like the use of shading, movement of the figures, and the suggestion of architectural settings, all elements that will soon disappear altogether.

## Ravenna

In 395 Emperor Theodosius I split the Empire in half, dividing it among his sons, with the East ruled by Arcadius and the West ruled by Honorious.

Honorius moved the capital of the West from Rome to Milan, and then again to Ravenna, a small provincial town on the Adriatic coast. The move was necessitated by the rapidly declining conditions in Rome and the onslaught of marauding tribes of Goths who were invading Italy from the North. In 404 the Visigoths attacked Rome and in 410 Rome essentially fell.

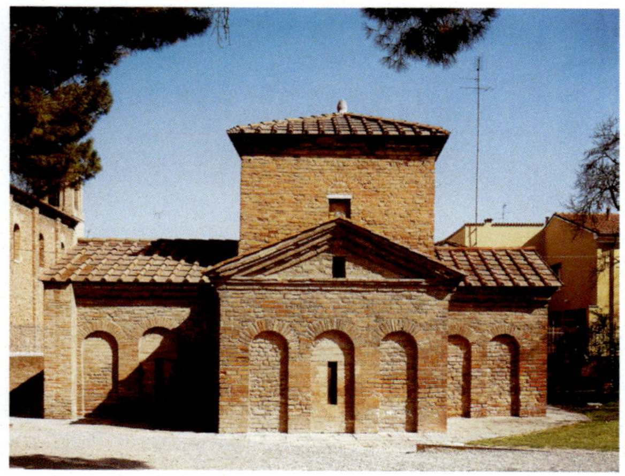

**7-12:** Mausoleum of Galla Placidia, exterior, Ravenna, Italy, 425.

When Honorius died in 423, his position was briefly filled by his half-sister Galla Placidia, who ruled until her death in 450.

In 425 Gall Placidia commissioned a tiny cruciform (cross-shaped) structure with barrel-vaulted arms and a small crossing tower. The building was originally attached to the Imperial Palace, and may have initially been dedicated to Saint Lawrence, but was later adapted to serve as the Imperial funerary chapel.

This little chapel is often cited as one of the earliest examples of the architectural fusion of the longitudinal basilica and vertically oriented central plan. It has four short barrel-vaulted arms and a dome over the crossing (the intersection of the nave and transept). An external tower demarcates the crossing and disguises the internal dome. This combination style will be very influential in later church architecture.

Like Santa Costanza, the chapel's exterior is extremely plain, with simple brick walls with blind arcades and gabled roofs. The inside, however, is exquisitely and richly covered in brilliant glass mosaics. Glass mosaics are composed of small cubes of colored glass cut to desired size and shape; these tesserae are then set into wet plaster and oriented to achieve maximum reflection. The process was arduous and extremely costly.

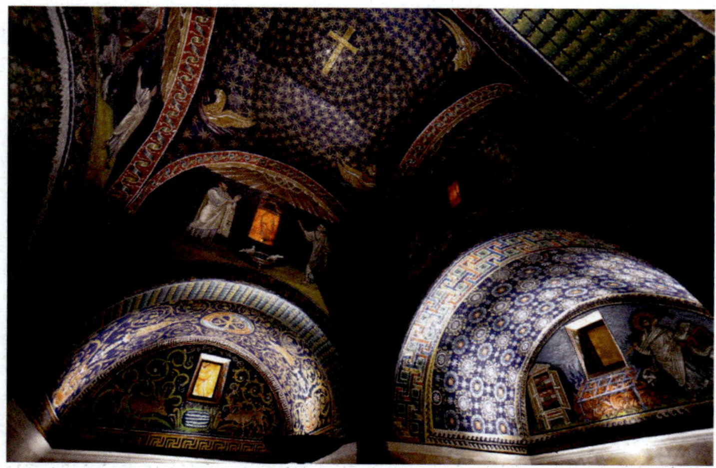

**7-13:** Mausoleum of Galla Placidia, interior, Ravenna, Italy, 425.

The interior of the chapel glitters with colorful vibrant mosaics, some figural and some purely decorative. Much of the decoration is set on a dark blue background adorned with decorative medallions that resemble stars and snowflakes. The crossing vault mosaic has a large gold cross at the center, set against a star-filled sky; in the corners are symbols of the evangelists.

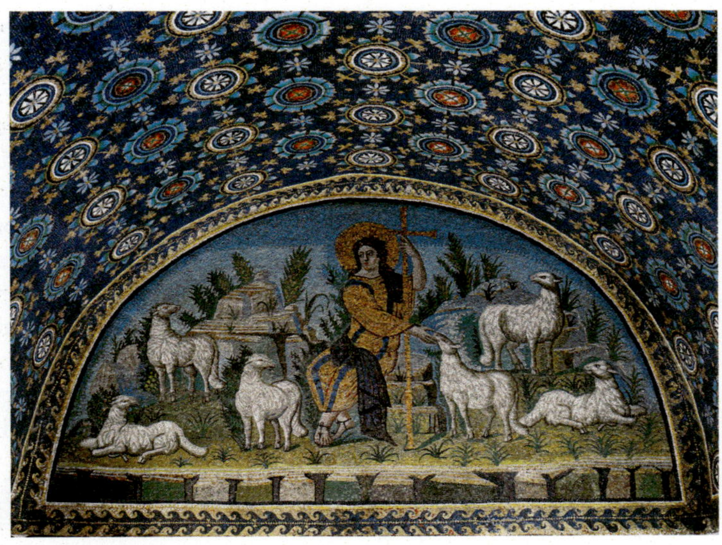

**7-14:** Christ as the Good Shepherd, mosaic, Mausoleum of Galla Placida, Ravenna, Italy, c. 425.

The symbols for the evangelists are: the winged man for Matthew; the winged lion for Mark; the winged ox for Luke; and the eagle for John. These symbols occur often in early Christian art and are derived from the *Old Testament* vision of Ezekiel (Ezekiel 1:1–3:27), in which he saw the throne of God surrounded by these four creatures.

In the lunette, above the entrance, is a mosaic depicting Christ as the Good Shepherd. Unlike the image from the catacombs, in this depiction Christ is regal and imperial looking, wearing a gold-striped tunic and purple mantle. He sits on a rock surrounded by his flock of sheep, and has a huge golden halo. He also holds a long Latin cross staff. The sheep, arranged in groups of three on either side of him, all turn to look at him; as if for guidance and direction. The rocky landscape is green and populated with rocks, plants, and grasses.

Christ and the sheep have a real sense of mass and weight and even cast shadows. The artist is still using Greco-Roman illusionist painting techniques but the conception and depiction of Christ has evolved from simple shepherd to regal enthroned ruler.

## Manuscripts

Another costly art form that dominated the early Christian period was the codex.

At the end of the first century CE a new format for collecting or containing the written word and its accompanying decoration was developed; it was called the codex. The codex is essentially the ancestor of the modern book; it is composed of separate leaves or pages, called folios, that are enclosed together within a cover and bound together at one side. This new format essentially replaced the *rotulus* or scroll format.

The scroll format had been used by the ancient Egyptians, Greeks, Etruscans and early Romans. Scrolls were often about 10-yards in length and were made primarily of papyrus, which was expensive and tended to be fairly brittle. Scrolls were also difficult to manage, as they had to be continually rolled and unrolled, and they were difficult to store.

The codex was a much more practical and easy-to-manage format. Its pages were flat and made of sturdy vellum (calfskin) or parchment (lambskin). The pages provided a better surface for writing and painting and could be decorated on both sides.

The art historical term for an early decorated codex is an illuminated manuscript. Illuminated, which refers specifically to the decoration, is derived from the Latin word *illuminare* which means to adorn, ornament or brighten. Manuscript comes from the Latin *manus* meaning hand and *scribere* meaning to write. The illuminations in a codex are called miniatures (a term derived from *minium*, the Latin word for a red mineral pigment used to decorate early manuscripts).

Illuminated manuscripts, or codices, were incredibly expensive and time consuming to produce. The very beginning of the process required the raising of the animals, then the curing, cutting, and in some cases dying of the skin, then the planning and plotting of each page for the location of text and illumination, then the actual lettering and illuminating. Finally the folios needed binding and then the addition of a decorated cover. The process could take years depending upon the length of the text and the intricacy and number of illuminations.

The Vatican Virgil, or Vergilius Vaticanus, is a codex that contains fragments of Virgil's *Aeneid* and *Georgics*. It is the oldest extant preserved illuminated manuscript containing classical literature.

The miniatures, of which only 50 survive from what must have originally been over 200, depict a variety of subjects including landscapes, seascapes, architectural views, humans, and animals. Each of the miniatures is painted in a classical style and contained within a frame.

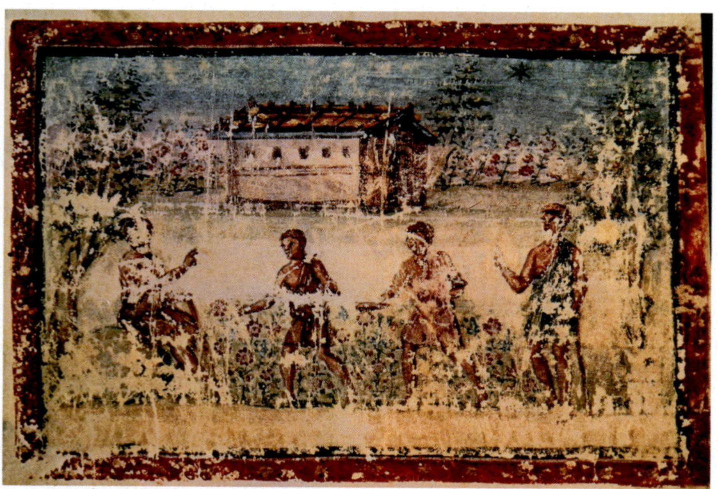

**7-15:** The Old Farmer, miniature in the Vatican Vergil, tempera on parchment, 400–420 AD, Vatican Library, Rome.

The illuminated manuscript was adopted by the Christians as the preferred medium for scripture. Not only was it easier to read and store but it made a visual connection between the Gospels and the rest of the *New Testament* that was in stark contrast to the scroll format which was always and only used for the Torah.

The oldest, best-preserved illuminated manuscript containing scenes from the Bible, is the early sixth century manuscript called the Vienna Genesis. (The name is simply a combination of its subject matter; the *Old Testament* book of Genesis and its current location in Vienna.)

The pages of the Vienna Genesis are vellum, that was died purple and the text, in Greek, was written in silver ink. Both aspects reveal the luxury nature of this manuscript.

The illumination depicts an episode found in the Old Testament Book of Genesis (24: 15–61).

Eliezer was the servant of Abraham, and was sent out to find a wife for Abraham's son Isaac. Eliezer chooses Rebecca because when they meet at a well outside of her city she offers water to both him and his camels.

Two different episodes appear in the scene; this is another example of the use of continuous narrative.

At the left we see the lovely Rebecca, dressed in pink, with her head covered by a white veil, carrying a water jug on her shoulder. She is walking away from her city, the little walled town of Nahor, to fetch water from the well. In the lower portion we see Rebecca again giving water to Eliezer and his camels.

Though this is a biblical text, there are a number of specifically Roman artistic devises used in the illumination: most prominently the semi-nude reclining female that appears to lie on the ground in front of Rebecca. The figure leans over an overturned amphora, and serves here as a personification of the spring or river that is the source of the well water. The tiny white columns suggest a colonnaded walkway, but are diminished in size so as not to detract from the subject.

Although the image is simplified, it does have little details that make it more convincing, such as the way Rebecca puts her foot up on the edge of the well to steady herself or the way Eliezer leans forward to drink from her upturned jug, or the way one thirsty camel has already started drinking.

Like the mosaic decoration at Santa Maria Maggiore, these illuminations are depicted with a minimum of detail in order to keep the message clear and simple.

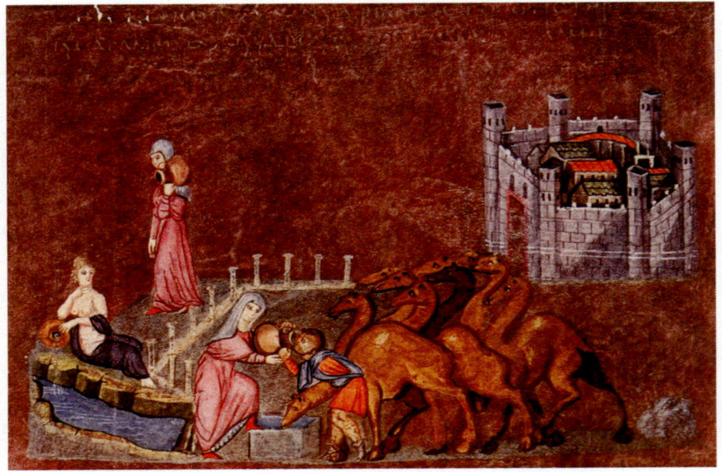

**7-16:** Rebecca and Eliezer at the Well, miniature in the Vienna Genesis, early 6th century, tempera gold and silver on purple vellum, 12 in × 9 in, Osterreichische Nationalbibliothek, Vienna.

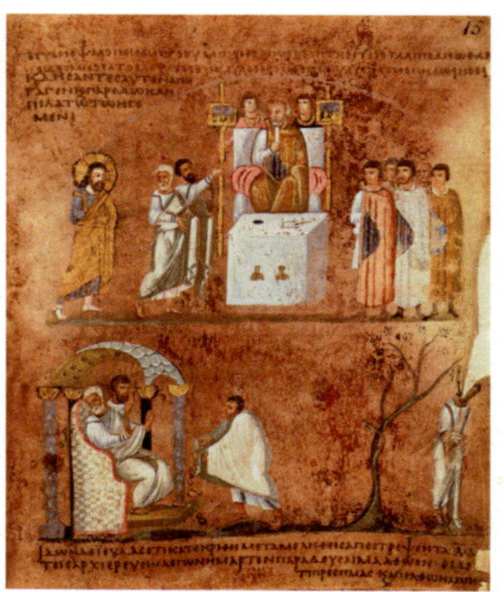

**7-17:** Christ before Pilate and Suicide of Judas, miniature in the Rossano Gospels, early sixth century, purple vellum, 11 × 10, Museo Diocesano d' Arte Sacra, Rossano.

Another early 6th century illuminated manuscript similar to the Vienna Genesis is the **Rossano Gospels**.

Like the Vienna Genesis, it is a purple vellum manuscript with Greek text in silver ink. However, as the name implies, its subjects come from the GOSPELS of the New Testament. The Rossano Gospels is the earliest preserved illuminated manuscript of the *New Testament.*

The illumination depicts a scene from the Trial of Christ (Matthew 27: 2–26). It shows Jesus brought by soldiers before Pontius Pilate who sits on a *dais* (a raised platform) decorated with imperial portraits. Standing next to the dais, are accusers and imperial gaurds.

In the lower portion, divided neatly from the scene above, Judas repentant, tries to return the pieces of silver he was paid to betray Jesus but cannot. At the far right we see the suicide of Judas.

Once again there is a desire to illuminate the actual text, but to do so with clarity and an emphasis on the message, as opposed to artistic convention and landscape details.

Another early Christian image that illustrates a very powerful image in the simplest of details, is an ivory carving from the 5th century.

This small ivory plaque is considered the earliest known example of the Crucifixion in the history of Western art.

The plaque is actually part of a series of four plaques depicting the suffering and triumph of Christ that were made for a small ivory box.

This scene depicts two separate but related events. At the far left we see the suicide of Judas. Judas, filled with remorse for having betrayed Jesus, tried in vain to return the money he had accepted, but could not, so in an act of despair he hung himself from a tree. At his feet we see the money bag filled with the 30 pieces of silver. Notice how the strap to tie the bag mimics a snake at the feet of Judas.

On the right is the image of the Crucifixion. In the center Jesus is nailed on the cross. On either side of him stand three figures. On his right, his mother Mary and John the Evangelist (both present at the crucifixion). On his left is the Roman centurion, Longinus, who pierces him in the side with his sword. Above Christ's head is the superscription REX IUD, which is a shortened form in Latin for Rex Iudica, or King of the Jews.

In this image of the Crucifixion there is still a message of hope. Christ, though nailed to the cross, is still alive. He is muscular and heroic, his eyes are wide open and he does not hang limply from the cross; instead he is shown triumphant over death. The term for this type of image is a *Christus Triumphans*, (Christ triumphant) a term that refers to the image of Christ alive on the cross.

This image is contrasted in art with the *Christus Patiens*; an image of the tortured Christ dead on the cross.

Christ's triumph over death is visually and theologically contrasted with the lifeless body of Judas. His head is thrown back and his eyes are closed, his hands and feet hang limp. His dead weight pulls on the branch of the tree that supports him. This is a dramatic visual contrast between Christ's triumph over death and Judas'de ath.

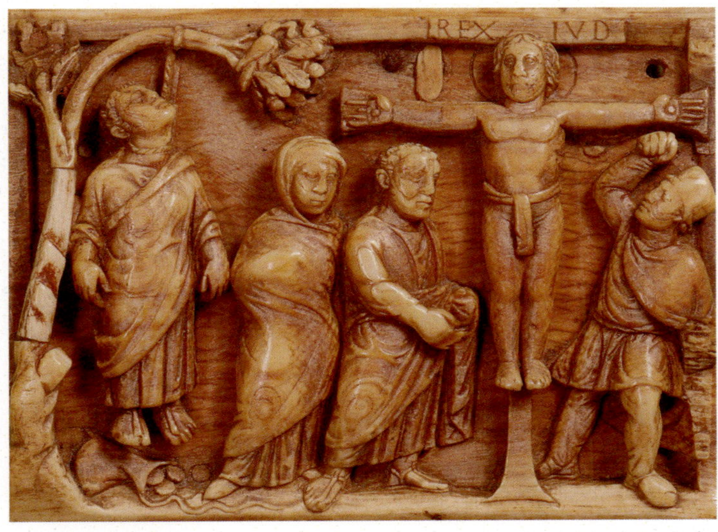


**7-18:** Suicide of Judas and Crucifixion of Christ, ivory, c. 420, 2.8 × 3.9 inches, British Museum, London.

The image is simple and without a great deal of detail yet it carries a very strong, clear message.

Name ______________________________ Date ______________

## Chapter 7

# Early Christian Art and Architecture

1. What is a Chi Rho? Describe it and explain where it first appears?

2. What is the earliest extant illuminated manuscript with scenes from the *New Testament*?

3. What is the term for the vast network of subterranean galleries that contain a great number of early Christian art works?

4. What is the date of the earliest depiction of the crucifixion scene in the history of Western art? Describe it. What is the medium?

5. Who commissioned St. Peter's Basilica? Describe its design and location.

6. What is the term for the biblical interpretation in which individuals and events from the Old Testament serve as prefigurations of New Testament individuals and events?

7. Where did Honorius, the Emperor of the West, move the capital?

8. What is the term for the architectural design of *Santa Constanza?*

9. What is the title of the oldest preserved manuscript and what is its subject?

10. What is difference between *vellum* and *parchment*?

# THE ART AND ARCHITECTURE OF BYZANTIUM

# Chapter 8

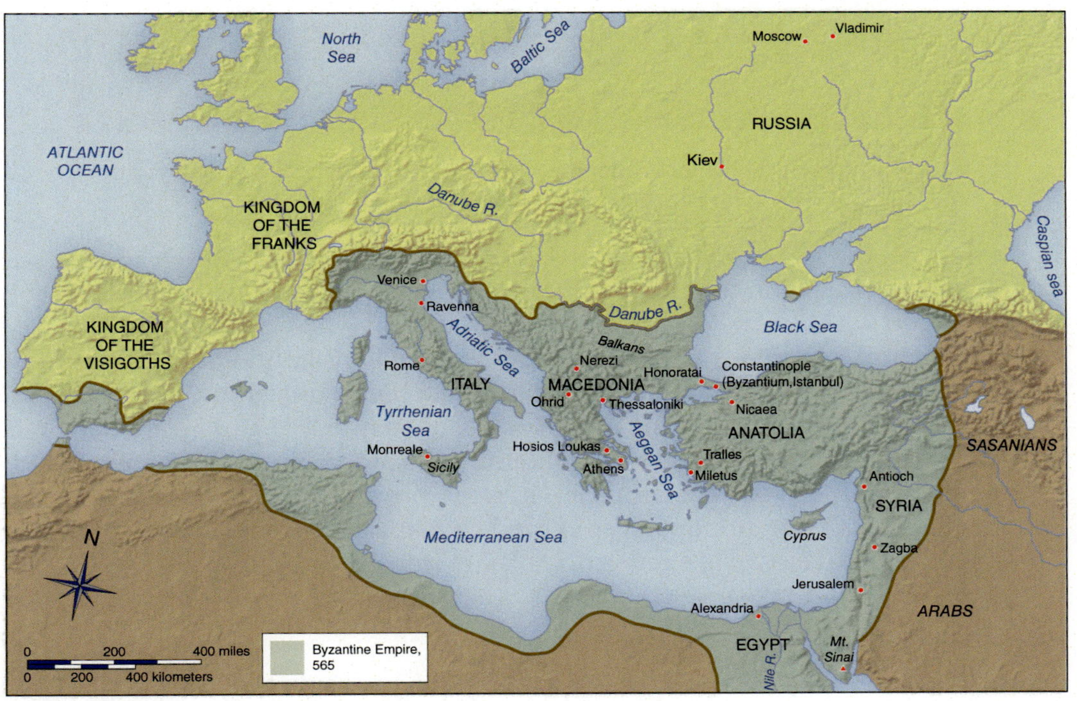


Byzantine Empire c. 565 CE.

The name for the Eastern Christian Roman Empire, also called the Byzantine Empire, comes from the name of the ancient Greek site of Byzantium on which Constantine built his new eponymous capital, Constantinople.

The city, often called the "New Rome" was founded by Constantine in 330.

With the sack of Rome in 410 and the virtual collapse of that city by 476, the last Roman emperor, Romulus Augustus, left sole imperial authority to the Emperor in the East. These "Byzantine" Emperors were the legitimate and rightful heirs or successors to the ancient Roman Emperors.

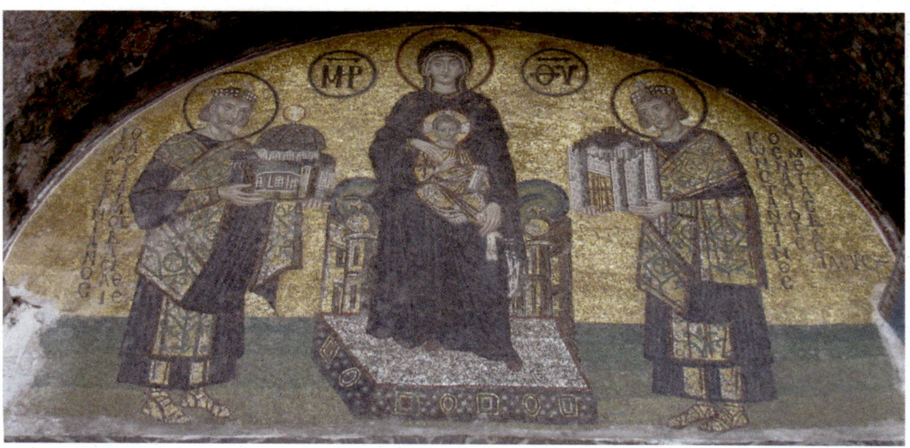

**8-1:** Constantine and Justinian offer the city and church respectively to the Virgin and Child, mosaic, Hagia Sophia, c. 944, Constantinople (Istanbul).

In the East the Byzantine emperor was the ruler of both the church and the state, exerting all spiritual and temporal authority; aspects that the Western empire would keep separate.

The Byzantine Empire survived until 1453 when Constantinople finally fell to the Ottoman Turks, an Islamic group from eastern Anatolia, whose empire lasted until 1923.

The geographical location of the city of Constantinople, today modern Istanbul, was extremely important. The city literally sits at the physical juncture between Europe and Asia. It was, therefore, a strategic position for commerce, for travel, and for defense. Constantinople also served as a kind of geographical, cultural and Christian barrier against the expansion of Islam into central Europe.

## Justinian I

One of the most important early Byzantine rulers was Justinian I (483–565) who reigned between 527 and 565. The period during his rule is also often called the Golden Age of Byzantium.

Justinian was ambitious and saw himself as a reformer in the fashion of Augustus. He sought to bring about a new peace for his empire and to restore the Empire to its former glory and geographical extent.

Perhaps one of his greatest accomplishments was the revision and codification of Roman law. Justinian created a commission of sixteen men to bring order out of all the old Roman laws. These men worked for six years and studied more than 2000 texts. In 534, the commission produced the **Corpus Juris Civilis**, the Code of Civil Law; a work, written in Latin, that became the foundation for western law.

Justinian, in his ambitions and obsessions, was aided by his wife, the Empress Theodora (c.500–548). Theodora was the daughter of an animal trainer at the Hippodrome and an actress. Very little is known about her except what was written by the historian Procopius (c. 500 – 565).

According to Procopius, in his work the Secret History, Theodora was a courtesan, and prior to her role as Empress, she had performed some extremely lively and pornographic stage productions. One such theatrical event even involved a vulgar display of agility involving grains of barley strategically placed on and about her naked body, which were then pecked at and eaten by geese.

In addition to her dramatic skills as an actress Theodora was extremely intelligent and skilled in law and diplomacy. Some writers have described her as being even more ambitious than her husband.

The image of Justinian as a triumphant and imperial ruler who seeks to recall Old Rome in his rulership and patronage is made clear in an ivory plaque called the Barberini Ivory; named for Francesco Barberini who was a 17th century cardinal in Rome who at one time owned the work.

This ivory plaque, carved originally of five separate parts (one small panel is lost) is the largest extant Byzantine ivory and was once a part of an even larger diptych (a two paneled painting, altarpiece, or ivory that is hinged on one side).

In the center, the emperor Justinian is depicted in military armor riding on a rearing horse. Notice how large Justinian is in comparison to the horse. Justinian wears an imperial crown and holds a long spear-like standard in his right hand. Just behind him we see the raised hand of a vanquished barbarian.

Beneath the horse is a female personification of the earth who touches the foot of the emperor, notice her full bosom and the abundance of fruit in her lap. Just in front of him is a Nike (winged figure) standing on a small orb who offers him a palm and a crown (now lost) of victory.

On either side of the central panel are smaller vertical panels (one now lost) that show a military general offering a small statue of the Nike to the emperor.

Beneath the central panel in a horizontal strip are various barbarians who carry offerings to the emperor. That they come from various far off regions of the empire is accentuated by the fact that we see images of a lion, a tiger and an elephant among them. Each of their costumes and the gifts that they carry also suggest that they are from different regions in the empire. The barbarians move inward toward the center where another Nike reaches upward.

At the top, in a horizontal panel, is a bust portrait of Christ in a gesture of blessing. He seems to be blessing Justinian indicating approval of him and his actions. Christ holds a cross-topped scepter and is enclosed in a medallion in which we see symbols for a star, the moon, and the sun. The medallion is held aloft by two winged angels or victories in flowing robes.

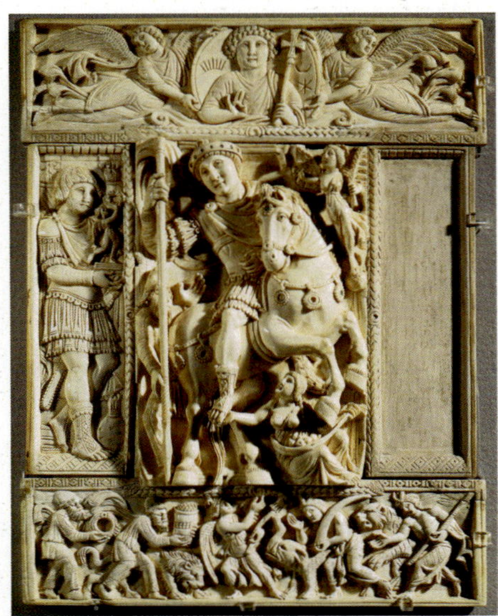

**8-2:** Justinian as World Conqueror, ivory plaque, mid sixth century, 13″ x 10″, Louvre, Paris.

## Hagia Sofia

The emperor Justinian was responsible for the construction of at least thirty churches in the empire, the most famous and largest of all, was the church of Hagia Sophia (Church of the Holy Wisdom) in Constantinople.

Justinian chose two men, neither an architect, to design and construct the church: Anthemius of Tralles, a Greek mathematician and Isidorus of Miletus, a professor of physics. It is believed that Justinian chose these men so that they would overcome or transcend the limits of contemporary architecture and instead envision and then succeed in building something entirely new and emblematic of the glory of the new capital. This of course all plays into Justinian's desire to make Constantinople as the new Rome overshadow the old.

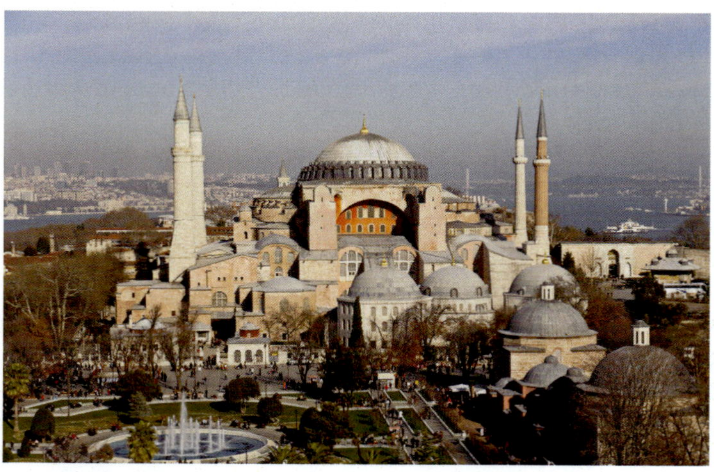

**8-3:** Hagia Sophia, Anthemius of Tralles and Isidorus of Miletus, Constantinople (Istanbul), Turkey, 532–537 (minarets added after 1453).

The massive structure measures roughly 270 feet long and 240 feet wide with a central dome 108 feet in diameter that rises 180 feet above the ground.

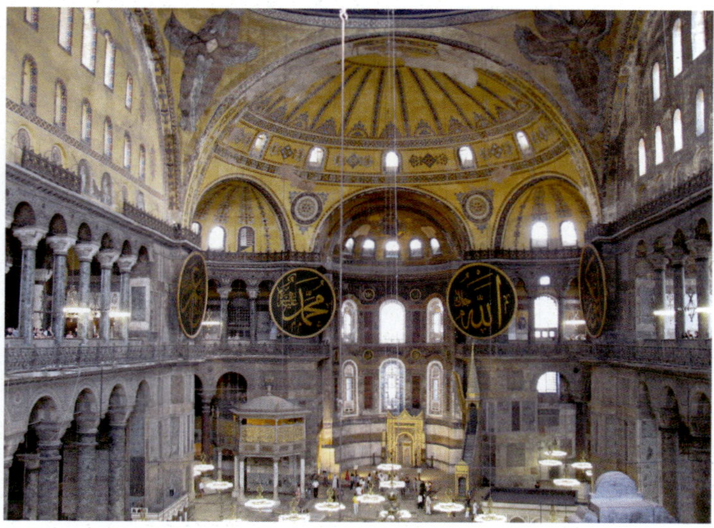

**8-4:** Interior of Hagia Sophia, Constantinople, Istanbul, Turkey, 532–537.

## Plan of Hagia Sophia

What the architects managed to achieve with their building design is the consolidation or union of the longitudinal basilica plan with the vertically oriented central plan.

Thus the design is a completely new structure that encapsulates the needs of the church and its space requirements with the ethereal quality provided by a massive dome that serves as a symbol of heaven itself.

The dome was achieved through the architectural innovation of the pendentive. A pendentive is a triangular shaped section of vaulting that is employed when a circular dome is placed over a square structure. Pendentives are used to join the two structures lifting the dome above the top of the walls and carrying the weight down at the corners into the supporting piers.

The interior of Hagia Sophia was lavishly decorated with colored marbles and mosaics. Early authors tried to capture the sense of beauty and awe as they described how the interior of the walls were sheathed in gold mosaics and the columns were made of purple and green marbles.

Perhaps more astounding than its luxurious decoration or even its sheer size was the church's light-filled interior. The light enters, rather streams, into the church through 40 large windows located at the base of the dome. This pierced lower portion of the dome creates the illusion that the enormous dome is suspended above the light or hovers just above it.

Light was an extremely important feature in a church since light was seen as a visual manifestation of God; the more light, the more filled with God.

It seems that Justinian had achieved his goal to build the largest most awe-inspiring church in the known world. Legend says that when he entered the newly completed church for its consecration on Christmas Day 537, he is said to have exclaimed "Solomon, I have surpassed thee."

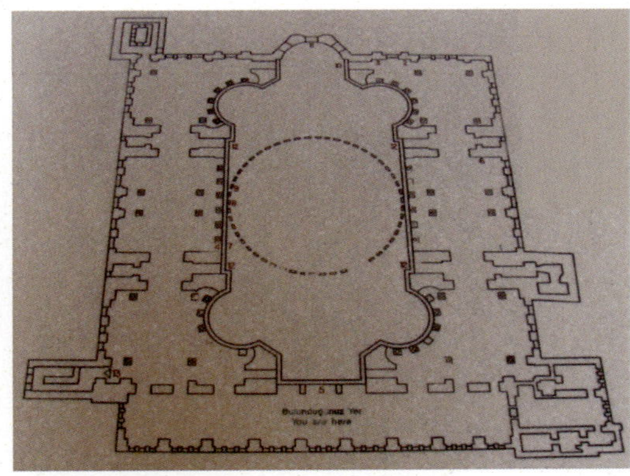

**8-5:** Hagia Sophia, Plan, 532 – 537, Constantinople (Istanbul), Turkey.

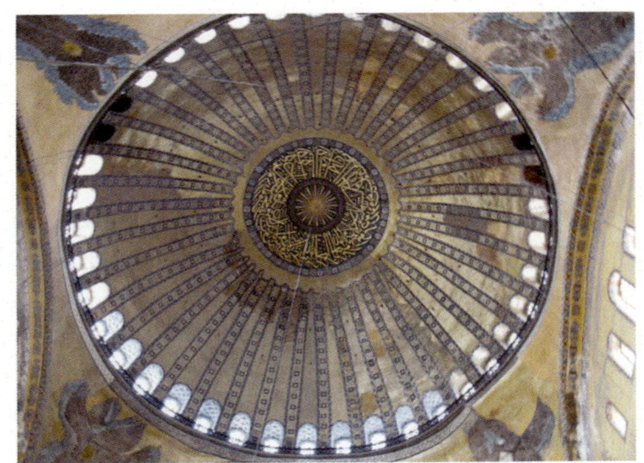

**8-6:** Hagia Sophia, Interior, Dome, 532–537, Constantinople (Istanbul), Turkey.

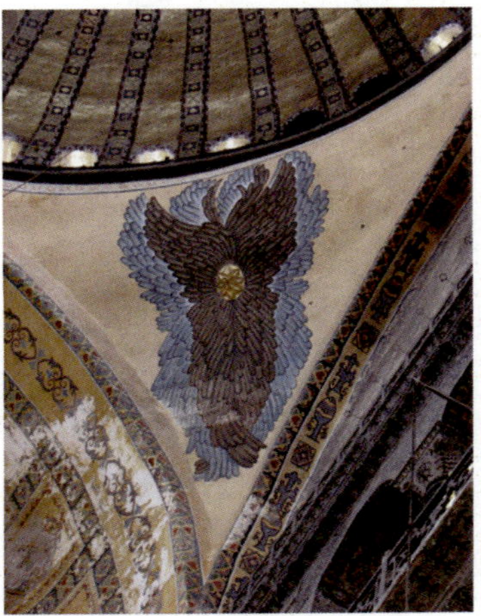

**8-7:** Hagia Sophia, pendentive, 532–537, Constantinople (Istanbul), Turkey.

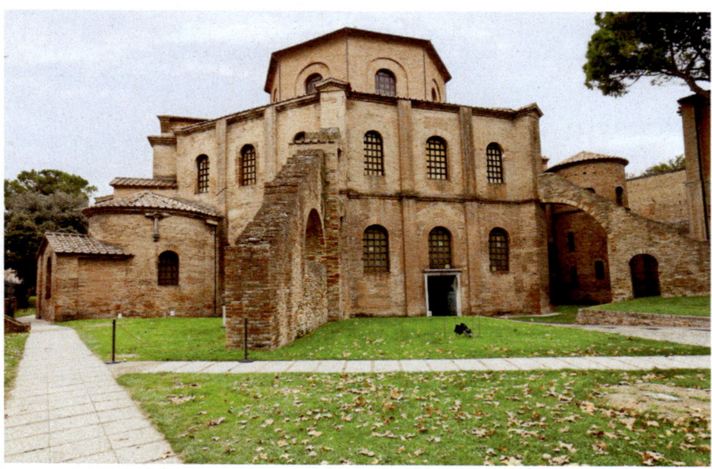

**8-8:** San Vitale, Ravenna, Italy, 526–547.

## Ravenna

The city of Ravenna, once briefly the capital of the Empire, was seen as an important extension of Byzantine rule in Italy and not surprisingly Justinian embellished the city with lavish structures and imperial decoration.

Perhaps the most important church built during this period was the Church of San Vitale. The church was begun in 526 by an unknown architect and completed in 547 by the archbishop of Ravenna, Maximianus. It was dedicated to Saint Vitalis, a second century saint from Ravenna. Like other early christian structure it is austere on the exterior and lavishly decorated on the interior.

The church has a central plan with a polygonal apse, and an off-center narthex. The design is centered on two concentric octagons. A dome-covered octagon in the center and an outer octagonal wall pierced with windows to add light. The central space has eight large piers that alternate with curved niches or exedrae that animate the two-story ambulatory. The *exedrae* create an intricate design that unites the inner and outer spaces permitting light to suffuse the interior.

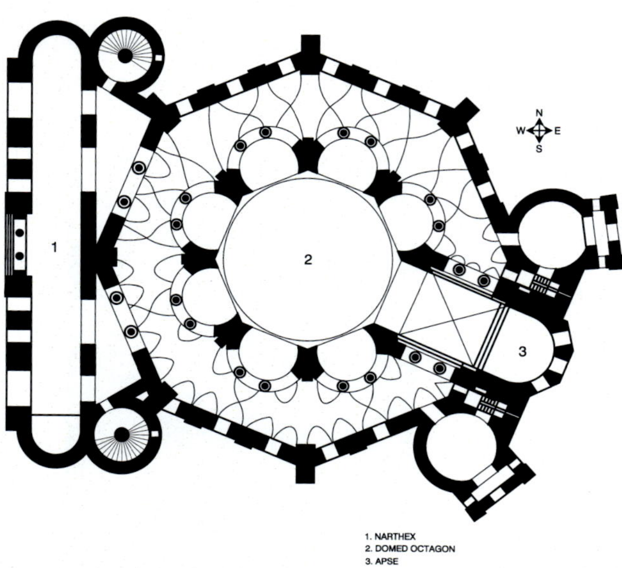


**8-9:** Plan of San Vitale, Ravenna, Italy, 526–547.

In the presbytery (choir/sanctuary) vault, a youthful and beardless Christ sits on the orb of the world. He holds the scroll with the seven seals in his left hand and a martyr's wreath in his right. The four rivers of paradise flow from the rock beneath the orb.

On Christ's right an angel cloaked in white robes presents Saint Vitalis to Christ who offers him a crown of martyrdom. Saint

Vitalis reaches forward, with his left hand to accept it. The saint is labeled above.

On the other side another angel presents the bishop of Ravenna, Ecclesius (in whose time the foundations for the church were laid) to Christ. The bishop holds in his hands a little model of the church of San Vitale, which he offers to Christ. He is also labeled above.

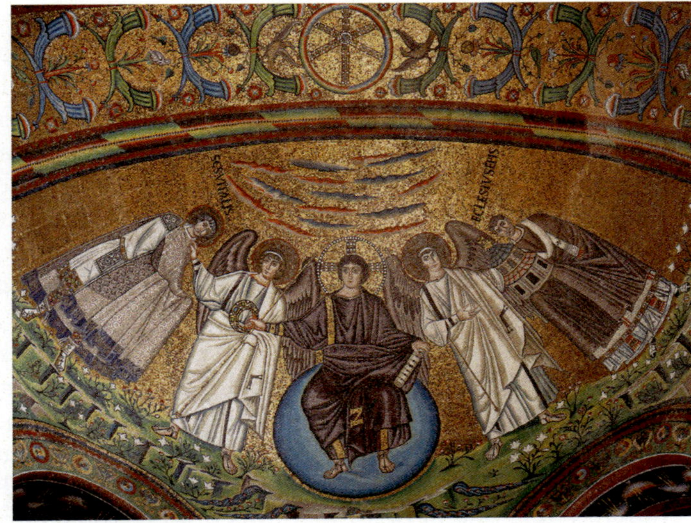

**8-10:** Christ between Angels, mosaic, apse of San Vitale, 526–547.

Directly below the apse mosaic are three windows that allow light into the sanctuary. Just adjacent to them, on the left and the right, are imperial mosaics depicting the Emperor Justinian and his wife, and co-regent, Theodora.

In this large mosaic the emperor is shown wearing a purple robe and a jeweled crown holding, with his covered hands, a golden paten (a paten is the bowl for holding the Eucharistic bread). The emperor, shown with a halo, has a large jeweled pin at his shoulder and even jeweled shoes. His halo is intended not to depict him as a saint but to symbolize the divine origin of his rulership. He is depicted larger than all the other figures and moves in a direction that reflects the actual placement of the altar in the apse. Justinian's purple robes even echo the robes worn by Christ in the mosaic above.

Next to Justinian stands the Bishop Maximianus, the man responsible for the church's completion. Maximianus is depicted as a slender balding man with a short beard. He holds a large jeweled cross in his hands and is the only figure labeled. Next to the bishop, two more clergy members carry instruments used in

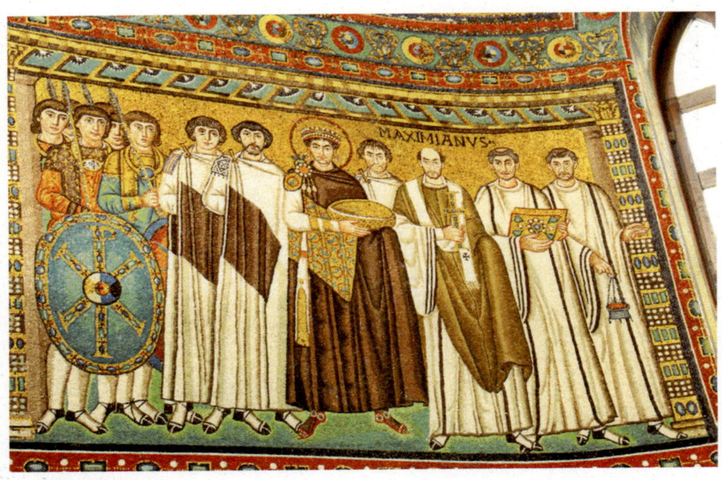


**8-11:** Justinian, Maximianus, and Attendants, mosaic, Apse, north wall, San Vitale, Ravenna, c. 547, 8′8″x 12′.

the liturgical services, a jeweled gospel book and a censor. Behind Justinian are members of the imperial guard who hold a shield emblazoned with the *chi rho*. Justinian is literally flanked by men who represent his authority in the church and state.

Each of the three groups of men, the clergy, the Emperor and his retinue, and the soldiers each have a member standing on the foot of another. This is not only a way to indicate a recession in space, but seems to imply a specific hierarchy. Justinian is largest and steps on the foot of one of his advisors, Maximianus, who in turn steps on the foot of the clergymen next to him, and so on. The whole scene also serves as a visual representation of the liturgical procession of the offering of gifts. Here the emperor takes part in the actual mass.

Directly opposite the Justinian mosaic is the mosaic depicting Theodora and her attendants. Theodora wears a jeweled crown and purple robe and, like Justinian, has a halo. In her hands she carries a gold and jewel-encrusted chalice. The chalice was used to hold the wine during the mass and is a counterpart to Justinian's paten used to hold the bread. The Empress stands beneath a shell-shaped canopy, as if outside the church, while one of her attendants holds open a curtain for her to pass through. The fountain may indicate that she is in the atrium of the church and not yet inside it. She is accompanied by seven ladies, each in elaborate and vibrantly patterned gowns, and two imperial guards.

The significance of Justinian and Theodora's participation in the mass is hinted at in the embroidered image on the hem of her robe. Visible in the bottom quarter of the garment, in gold against the purple, is the image of three exotically attired figures carrying gifts. The three figures represent the Magi, who were eastern kings who brought gifts to the Christ child; an act imitated by the eastern emperor and empress who carry their gifts to the altar!

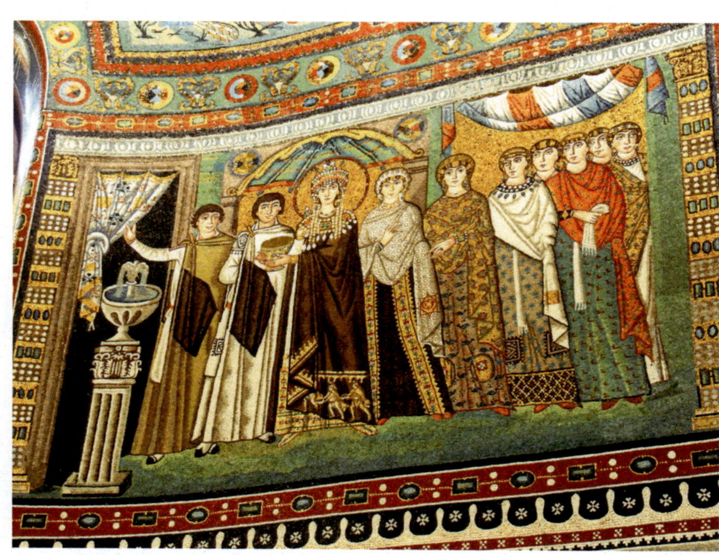

**8-12:** Theodora and Attendants, mosaic, Apse, south wall, San Vitale, Ravenna, c. 547, 8'8"x 12'.

The presence of the imperial couple in the sanctuary is also significant as it suggests that the emperor and empress are perpetually in attendance at the church participating in the mass. This is noteworthy for Ravenna and the church of San Vitale since, it appears, neither Justinian nor Theodora ever visited Ravenna nor did they ever step foot in the church of San Vitale.

Notice the difference in style from early classical imagery and even that of some early Christian imagery. The figures are elongated and all are depicted in a frontal pose. The figures seem to have no weight or volume and do not ever really stand flat on their feet but seem to stand on their tiptoes. They cast no shadow, and there is no use of contrapposto. The drapery has lost all sense of real fabric or movement and there is no sense of the body beneath.

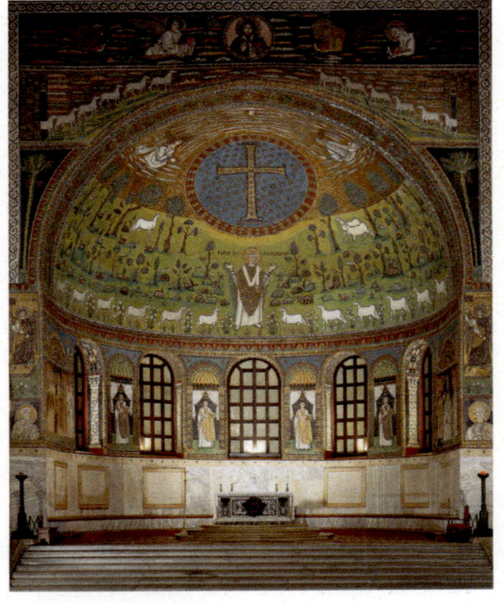

**8-13:** Transfiguration and Saint Apollinaris, apse mosaic Sant' Apollinare in Classe, Ravenna, Italy, 533–549.

## Sant'Apollinare in Classe

Another, yet very different, mosaic comes from a large basilica plan church just outside the city of Ravenna in the port city of Classe.

The church is dedicated to the 2nd century CE saint, Apollinaris, who was martyred there and was the first Bishop of Ravenna. The exterior, like the others we have seen, is very plain, but the interior has impressive mosaic decoration. In the vault of the presbytery is an enormous mosaic that depicts two separate scenes or events in one large composition.

At the center of the mosaic is an enormous jeweled cross set against a blue background filled with gold stars, all contained in a jeweled mandorla. At the very center of the cross is a tiny medallion portrait of Christ and just beneath the cross are the words *Salvus Mundi* (savior of the world). On either side of the cross are the Greek initials Alpha and Omega and above it is the acrostic ΙΧΘΥC.

Directly above the cross, emerging from the dramatically colored clouds, is the hand of God. On either side of the cross are two figures, dressed in white, who appear to emerge from the clouds; they are the *Old Testament* prophets Moses and Elijah (both labeled). On either side just below the prophets are three sheep; one below the figure of Moses, and two below Elijah.

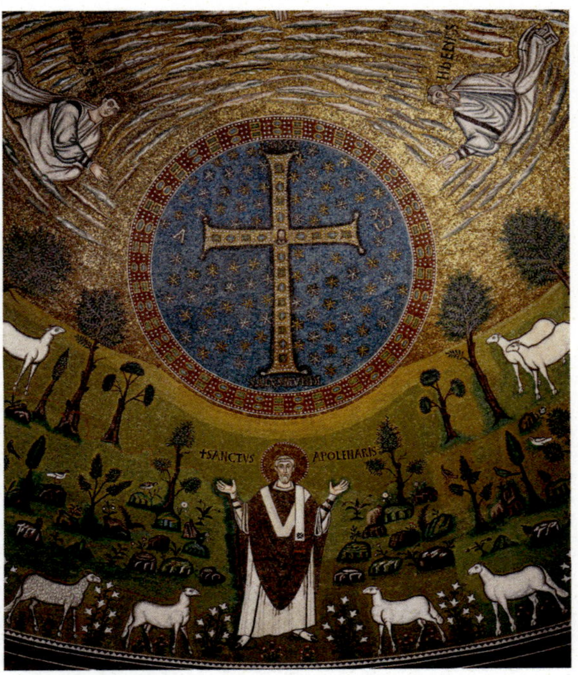


**8-14:** Transfiguration, detail, Sant' Apollinare in Classe, 533–549, Ravenna, Italy.

The event depicted in the upper portion of the mosaic is the Transfiguration. The event, described in three of the four gospels is the occasion at which Christ manifests his divine nature to three of his disciples. The event occurs just after Christ ascended Mount Tabor with three of his disciples (Peter, James, and John the Evangelist) at which time his face shone with light and his clothes became radiant white, and Elijah and Moses appear at his side to converse with him. Then a voice came from the heavens and exclaimed, "This is my son." In this image Christ is represented by the large jeweled cross and the disciples by the three sheep.

Below this very distinctive representation of the Transfiguration is the figure of Saint Apollinaris, clearly labeled. He stands in the center directly beneath the jeweled cross in a green field strewn with flowers and birds. He is shown in an orant pose and is flanked by twelve sheep; sheep here likely representing the faithful.

Apollinaris, however, does not look up at the vision above him instead he looks directly out at the viewer. Here the martyr raises his hands in prayer to God and recalls Christ's triumph over death on the cross. This is significant because Apollinaris as a martyr was triumphant over death and now serves as intercessor for his faithful followers. It is significant too that directly below the figure of Apollinaris is the altar and directly below the altar is the original location of the relics of the saint.

Justinian did not just build and embellish buildings in his capital Constantinople or in the newly recaptured city of Ravenna but he did so all across the empire.

At the same time the mosaics were being completed in Ravenna, Justinian's architects were rebuilding a very important monastery at Mount Sinai in Egypt. The tiny monastery, dedicated to Saint Catherine, was rebuilt and enclosed in defensive walls between 548 and 565.

Mount Sinai is the biblical location of two important events from the *Old Testament*. It is where Moses received the ten commandments and is the place where Moses heard the voice of God in a burning bush.

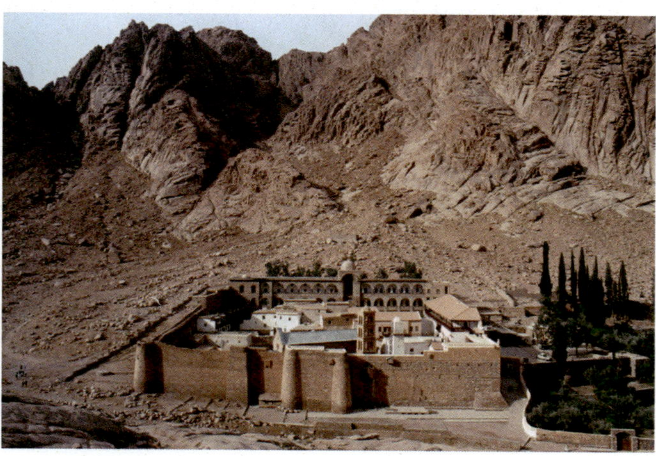

**8-15:** Monastery of St. Catherine, Mount Sinai, Egypt, 548–565.

Due in part to its remote location, the monastery preserved from destruction a number of exquisite and rare treasures.

One of the works preserved at the monastery of Saint Catherine is an icon of the Virgin.

An icon (*icon* comes from the Greek word for 'image') is generally a small, usually flat, portable painted image depicting Christ, the Virgin Mary, and/or saints. An icon is not an object of veneration, or an object to be worshipped, instead it is an aid to contemplation and devotion of the divine. The icon is then a sort of channel for communication between worshipper and divinity.

Icons are an important aspect in worship in the Eastern Orthodox Church.

This icon is particularly rare because very few icons survived the period of Iconoclasm in the 8th century CE when the destruction of images was promoted.

This icon depicts the Virgin and child enthroned. The Christ child holds a scroll in his left hand and blesses with his right. Mary is so large that she almost completely obscures the decorated throne on which she sits. This imagery derives from the Byzantine type called a *Chora tou Achoretou* or the Container of the Uncontainable, in Latin she is the *Sedes Sapientiae* or *Seat of Wisdom.* These types of images are intended to stress her role as intercessor and Mother of God.

Standing on either side of her are the dragon-slaying warrior saints Theodore (with the beard) and George. Behind them two ethereal angels look upward to witness a beam of light from which the hand of God appears.

There is no depiction of space in the picture, and no dimensionality as the figures seem pushed up almost to the edge of the picture plane. The figures are completely removed from time and space. The wide eyed and direct stare, particularly of the two saints, seems to echo the stare or devotion with which a worshipper would approach these images.

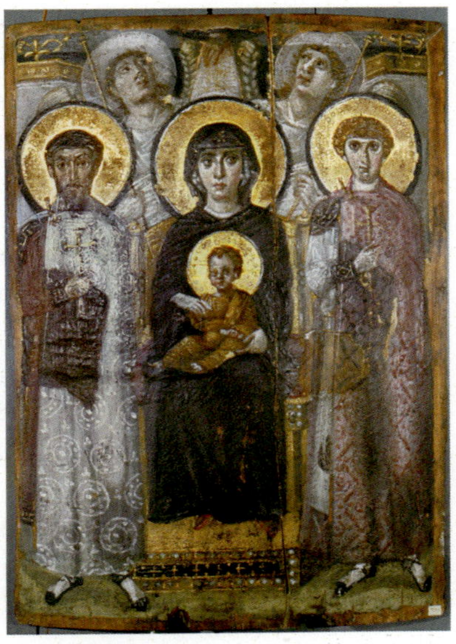

**8-16:** Virgin and Child between Saints, Icon, encaustic on wood, Monastery of St. Catherine, Mount Sinai, Egypt, 6th century, 27″ x 19″.

## Byzantine Manuscript Illumination

An event from after Christ's Crucifixion and Resurrection is the subject of a full page illumination in the Rabbula Gospels.

The manuscript, dated 586, contains the four gospels and was signed by a calligrapher named Rabbula at the Monastery of St. John the Evangelist in Beth Zagba, Syria.

The event of the Ascension of Christ into heaven took place 40 days after his Resurrection. According to the Gospels the event was witnessed by his mother the Virgin Mary and the apostles.

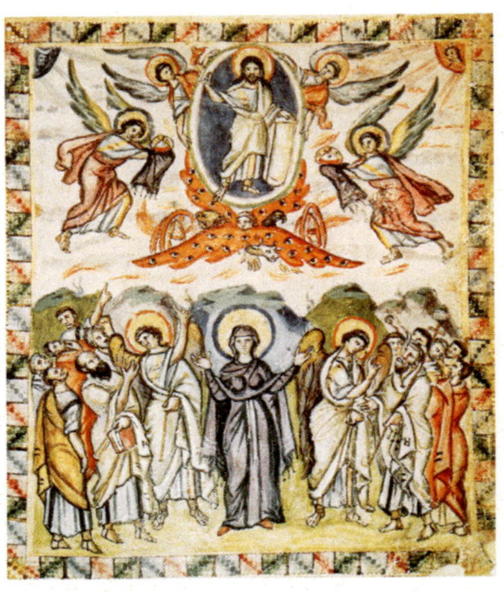

**8-17:** Ascension, Rabbula Gospels, Manuscript Illumination, tempera on vellum, Syria, 586, 13″ x 10″, Biblioteca Medicea Laurenziana, Florence, Italy.

In the illumination we see the figure of Christ, bearded and carrying a scroll in his left hand and blessing with his right. He is completely enclosed in a mandorla that is supported by angels, flaming chariot wheels, and four beasts with eye-studded wings. The four beasts, also associated with the four symbols of the Evangelists, were described in the vision of Ezekiel as surrounding the throne of God. Emerging from below the *tetramorph* (the four beasts seen together) is the hand of God.

Two angels approach Christ bearing crowns in their cloth-covered hands. At the upper left and right corners are classical personifications of the sun and the moon.

Below, the Virgin Mary and the apostles witness the event. Mary is depicted exactly in the center of the page, directly beneath the figure of Christ. She stands in an orant pose. She does not look upward but instead seems to gaze outward at the viewer. On either side of her, very large angels direct the gazes of the astonished apostles upward.

The event takes place, unlike in Byzantine mosaics, in temporal time and space. The sky is filled with pinkish clouds and there is a hilly landscape in the distance.

Name ______________________________ Date ______________

# Chapter 8

## Art and Architecture of Byzantium

1. Explain pendentives. How and where are they used?

2. The Barberini Ivory draws inspiration from which antique Roman imperial portrait?

3. Where are some of the finest early Byzantine icons preserved?

4. How did the dome of Hagia Sophia differ from previously constructed domes?

5. Which church's mosaic program underscores the dual imperial and religious roles of the Byzantine emperor?

6. What events characterize the Transfiguration and where is this scene depicted?

7. What is the subject of the mosaics in the sanctuary at the church of San Vitale?

8. Which Byzantine emperor commissioned Hagia Sophia?

9. Name the individuals that designed and constructed Hagia Sophia. What does Hagia Sophia mean?

10. What is the date of the fall of Constantinople? To whom did it fall?

# EARLY MEDIEVAL ART AND ARCHITECTURE

Chapter 9

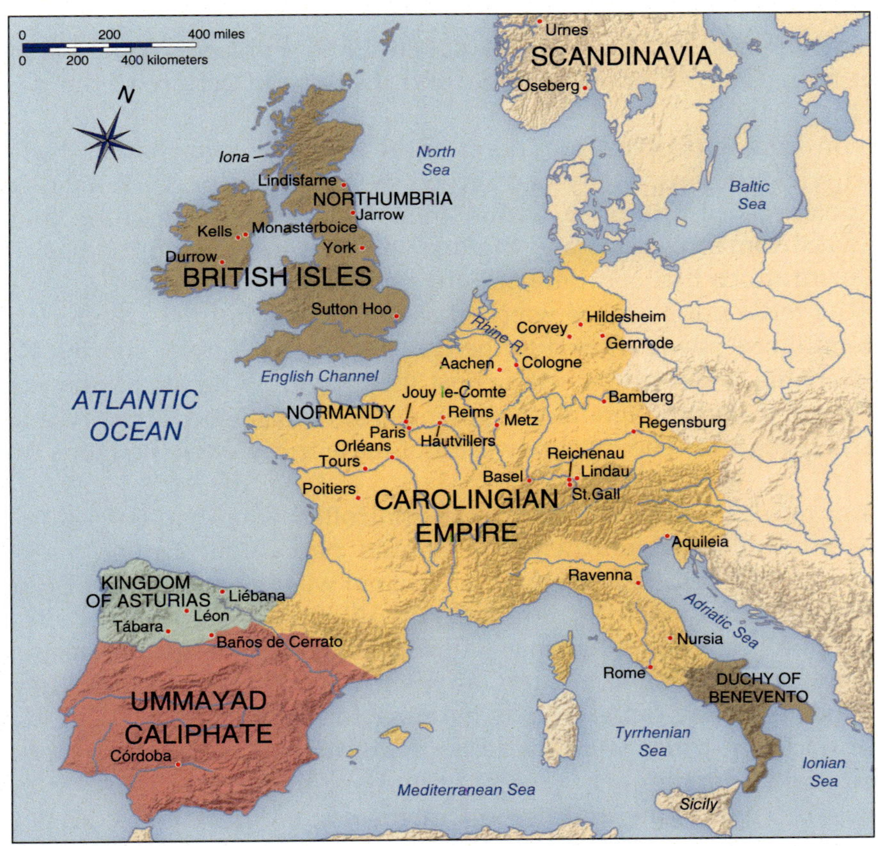


Western Europe in the Age of Charlemagne, c. 814.

## The Middle Ages

The terms *Middle Ages* and *Dark Ages* are used by historians to refer to the period from about 400–1400; or roughly the 1000 years or so between the classical ancient world of Greece and Rome and the dawn of the Renaissance.

The term *Dark Ages,* is however, misleading. The term implies that the period was in some way lost or dark. The term further implies that artistically the entire period was crude, primitive, and uncivilized. It suggests that the period lacked the production of artistic masterpieces or treasures.

Art Historians have long since realized that this is not the case. Rather, it is noted, that the art and cultures that flourished in some of the remote regions of Western Europe, particularly north of the Alps, were anything but dark and were instead quite colorful and spectacular.

The early period in Medieval art, c. 500–1000, represents a period of fusion of Christian faith, Greco-Roman heritage, and the art and culture of the peoples from north of the Alps.

The non-Roman peoples from north of the Alps, however, had had a fair amount of contact with Romans. Many had served in the armies of the Romans some even gaining positions of authority within their local areas. Over time these peoples merged with Roman citizens and melded together to develop the basic social and political institutions that continue into the modern period.

Many of these non-Romans watched as the Roman Empire and her army waned and its centralized power moved to the east in Constantinople. This left Rome weakened and unable to defend herself against the ever growing list of non-Roman tribes moving south: including Vandals, Merovingians, Franks, and Goths (West) Visigoths, and (East) Ostrogoths. The most powerful of these tribes were the Huns from Central Asia.

Further north the Anglo-Saxon tribes controlled what had been Roman Britain, and the Celts inhabited northern France and part of the British Isles, including Ireland. Ireland (called *Hibernia* by the Romans) was the one area of Britain that the Romans never colonized. In Scandinavia, the Vikings held power.

It is important to note that many of these non-Roman groups, beginning with Goths, were actually converted to Christianity fairly early, though they practiced various, and according to the church, heretical forms of it.

These northern tribes were made up of hunters, shepherds, farmers, and warriors who came from highly organized cultures with complex religious and cultural traditions. They had a long tradition of oral history and poetry, but did not develop a written history or literature until after their contact with the Latin language.

The art production of these northern peoples, or at least what remains to us, was predominantly, small scale. These small-scale, portable objects include weapons and status symbols such as such as crowns, scepters, shields, jewelry, fibula, belt buckles, swords, and sword hilts.

Evidence reveals that they often buried their dead in elaborate and rich ceremonies that included the inclusion of grave goods: a practice that suggests an already developed and sophisticated concept of an afterlife.

The small-scale objects they often produced show a very high degree of sophistication in terms of design and technique, and represent an artistic aesthetic quite different from the figural-based art of the Greeks and Romans.

Northern artists focused on linear patterns and designs, rather than on figural representation. They tended to concentrate on zoomorphic, or animal shapes, and intricate interlace and interwoven patterns and designs.

These northern tribes were masters of the *cloisonné* technique. The term cloisonné comes from a French word that means *partition*. The technique involves creating a metallic cavity or small compartment, usually with threads of metal, and then filling that cavity with molten glass, or molten semiprecious stones that when hardened forms a permanent part of the metal object.

The term *enamel* is also used for this technique, though enamel is more accurately the molten colored-glass that fills the cloisonné.

## Sutton Hoo

In 1939 an exceptional archaeological discovery was made at Sutton Hoo in Suffolk, England. Buried beneath a large circular earthen mound, or *barrow*, was a completely intact and undisturbed Anglo-Saxon ship burial.

This magnificent find was due not because of the expert efforts of archaeologists in the area, but because of the vivid and persistent dreams of a widow named Mrs. Edith May Pretty.

Mrs. Pretty was the owner of the estate in Suffolk where the discovery was made. It seems that she had noticed that the property had an interesting terrain which included a number of curious, unnatural mounds. Mrs. Pretty became convinced that the mounds held buried treasure. She was convinced of this in large part due to a series of dreams in which she saw and heard a large and grand funeral procession. She also told of dreaming about the figure of an armed warrior standing on the largest of the mounds in the twilight. Finally, after several attempts and letters, she wrote to the Ipswich Museum, requesting the services of an archaeologist. He sent her Mr. Basil Brown, and together they discovered the ship burial and some 27 other mounds, not all of which have been excavated.

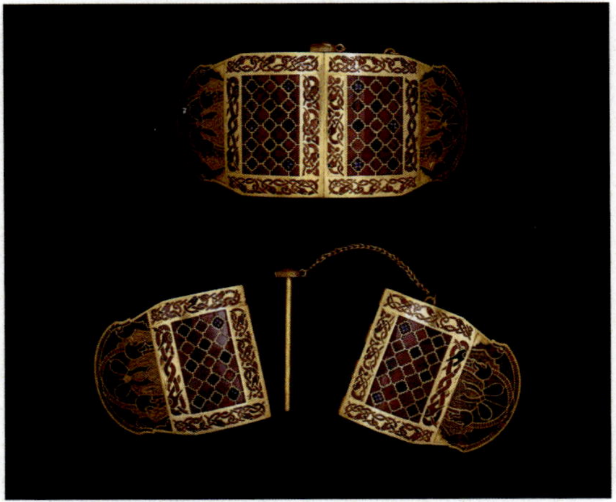

**9-1:** Hinged shoulder clasps (fibulae), gold, cloisonné garnet, and glass, Sutton Hoo ship burial, c.625, 5″ in length, British Museum, London.

The ship, powered by 40 oarsmen, was 27-meters (89-feet) long and 4.2-meters (14-feet) wide. It was placed in the mound with the bow facing away from the river and had a burial chamber constructed mid-deck.

In the burial space was the body of a man, laid out on a bier, surrounded by incredibly rich grave goods, many of which were clearly symbols of his power. The items found included a

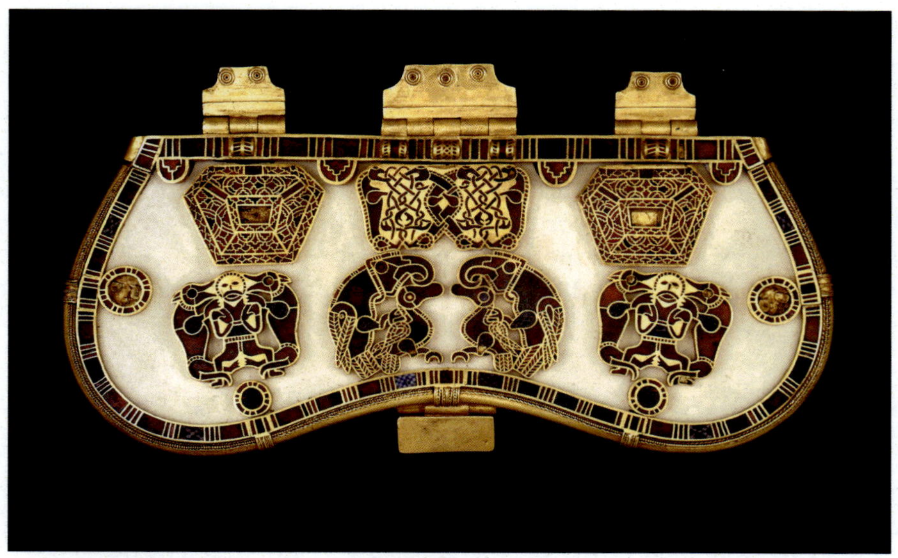

**9-2:** Purse Cover, Cloisonné, Sutton Hoo ship burial, Suffolk, England, c. 625 CE, 7″ in length, British Museum, London.

scepter, elaborately decorated armor including a shield and a helmet, as well as jewelry, two silver spoons, an exquisite gold belt buckle, two cloisonné and gold fibulae (a fibula is a decorative pin), 10 silver bowls, and even a purse full of 40 gold coins.

The spoons were inscribed with the names Saulus and Paulus and seem to indicate that perhaps the person buried with these items had been baptized (Saul is the name of the apostle Paul before his conversion to Christianity.) This has led scholars to suggest that the man buried was an East Anglian king named Raedwald; who according to legend was baptized before his death in 625.

The Sutton Hoo purse cover is decorated with four symmetrically arranged groups of figures on the lower portion. The two end designs show a heraldic-style composition of a man, shown frontally, in the center flanked by two beasts, perhaps wolves, shown in profile. The two central images show two large eagles or hook-beaked birds attacking a smaller bird, perhaps a duck. Above these are three geometric designs. The two outer ones are symmetrical and serve as mirror images, while the central image has an interlocking interlace pattern that terminates in stylized animal forms. Above are hinges that attached the cover to the actual purse, and below is the clasp for locking it.

This combination of interlacing pattern and animal forms was particular to the arts of the early Middle Ages and the tribes from the north and is found throughout the art of the Middle Ages in jewelry, book illumination, and sculpture in wood and stone, and even architecture.

## Hiberno Saxon Art

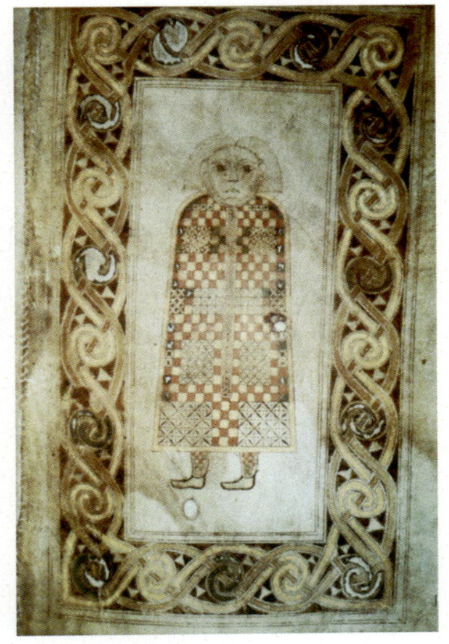

**9-3:** Man (symbol for Saint Matthew), *Book of Durrow*, tempera on parchment, Scotland, c. 660–680 CE, 9–5/8 x 6–1/8, Trinity College Library, Dublin.

The term Hiberno-Saxon refers generally to the arts of Britain, Scotland, and Ireland: Hibernia-Ireland/ Saxon-Britain. Insular, a term that describes the British Isles, is also used to describe the art of this region

In 432 Saint Patrick established the first Christian church in Ireland, and began the work of converting and Christianizing the Celts. Because of its isolation the church in Ireland and Britain was less dependent on and less controlled by the Pope in Rome. This independence and geographical seclusion often resulted in some local variation in liturgical practices, methods and art forms; this is especially true in terms of monastic establishments.

In the inaccessible and inhospitable cold northern regions there was a particular missionary zeal that developed. Irish monks began to organize and develop a distinctly northern form of monasticism that depended on their isolation. This isolation kept the monks focused on their work and prayer, and ultimately on the careful transcription and illumination of manuscripts.

Many of the manuscripts were made in scriptoria, or writing houses, attached to monasteries or major churches.

This new, northern Christian development was occurring at the same time that Rome and the Church were in great danger from the onslaught of invading Gothic-tribes and warfare. Some historians have even attributed these Hiberno-Saxon monks with literally saving western Christianity.

Among the earliest surviving Hiberno-Saxon illuminated manuscripts is the *Book of Durrow.*

*The Book of Durrow* is an illuminated Gospel book written in Latin. In the book each of the four Gospels (Matthew, Mark, Luke, and John) is preceded by a full-page illumination of the symbol of the evangelist who wrote that Gospel. This type of page, with the image of the evangelist or his symbol preceding the text of his gospel, is called an author portrait.

In this page, the Man, the symbol of Matthew, is depicted. It is a highly simplified and highly stylized design. There is no background and no sense of illusion, space or volume in the figure. Here the human figure is reduced to a frontal head (notice he wears a tonsure—a hairstyle for monks) and profile feet that emerge from a large bell-shaped cloak.

Both the cloak and the substantial border on the page reflect interlace and interwoven linear patterns typical of insular art. The depiction of the cloak reflects a

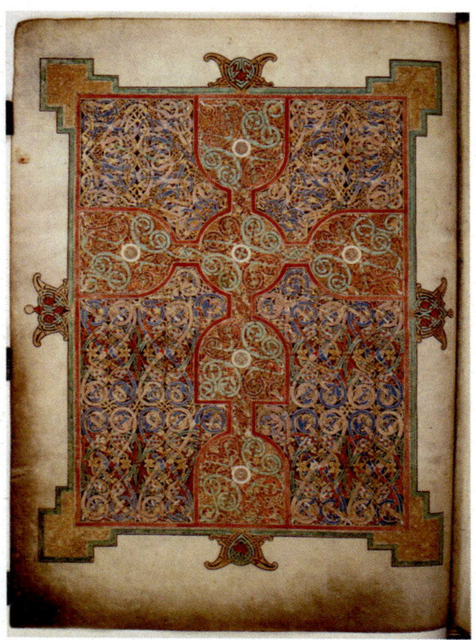

**9-4:** Carpet Page, Lindisfarne Gospels, tempera on vellum, England, 698–721 CE, 13 ½ x 9 ¼″, British Library, London.

cloisonné technique here translated from metal work onto parchment. The border or frame around the figure is a fine example of zoomorphic and linear interlace pattern.

Clearly the artist seems much more comfortable with the intricate patterns and design of the cloak and the border done in a more traditional style than with that of the more foreign tradition of the depiction of the human figure.

*The Book of Durrow* is also an exceptional example of **Art is an Endangered Species**.

It seems that sometime in the 16th century, after the monastery was dissolved, the manuscript or a portion of it ended up in the hands of a local farmer. The farmer for whatever reason believed that the book had curative properties and either poured water or submerged the book in a trough in order to cure his sick cows. The book was eventually discovered and in the 17th century donated by the Bishop of Meath to Trinity College in Dublin.

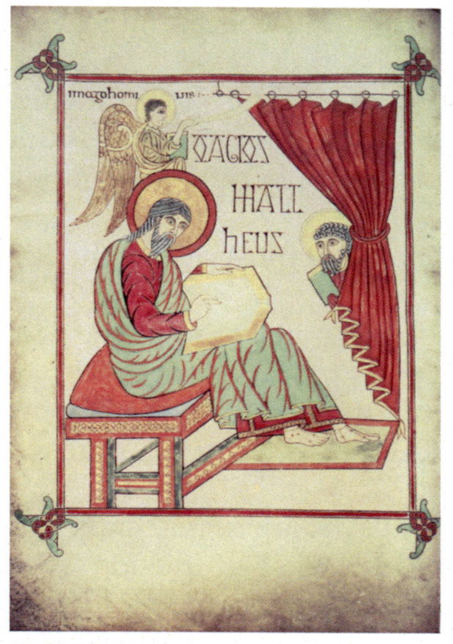

**9-5:** Saint Matthew, Lindisfarne Gospels, tempera on v ellum, England, 698–721 CE, 13 ½ x 9 ¼″, British Library, London.

In another Insular manuscript, the Lindisfarne Gospels, we find a popular type of illumination common in early Insular manuscripts: the *carpet page*.

The manuscript contains the four Gospels, written in Latin, and includes 15 fully-decorated pages with additional minor decoration and decorated initials throughout.

A carpet page is an ornamental page with decoration that covers the entire page, like a carpet. The design of the page is made up of complex patterns and designs that often resemble cloisonné work and textile patterns.

These types of decorative pages have no precedent in Western manuscript decoration and point to the genius and artistic independence of early Insular artists.

Each Gospel is preceded by an author portrait and a carpet page. This carpet page reveals a large Latin-style cross composed of a central circle and five bell shapes, each of which has at the center a circle that resembles a metal rivet. The design represents a union and melding of western Christian symbolism with local artistic tradition: the Christian cross and the insular tradition of metal design and interlace patterns.

However, for all its intricacy and apparent confusion, it should be noted that the work is highly organized. The design proves to be an intricate pattern of inversions, reversals, and repetitions of forms and designs that cover the surface of the page.

Also from the Lindisfarne Gospels is an author portrait of Saint Matthew.

Matthew is depicted in his study writing his Gospel. He sits on a decorated bench with a big red pillow on it, with his feet resting on an oddly slanted footrest. Above him is his symbol: the winged man. In case the reader is unclear about who is represented, the illuminator has included labels. In Latin, above the head of the symbol for Matthew, it reads *"Imago hominus"* or "image of the man." The figure of Matthew is also labeled for clarity, *Hagios Mattheus,* though it is written in both Greek and Latin. *Hagios* means Saint in Greek and *Mattheus* is Matthew in Latin.

The reason for this unusual mixing of languages is unclear, though it has been suggested that it was done as homage to the *New Testament* since it was originally written in Greek but then translated (in the late 4th century by St. Jerome) into Latin.

St. Matthew is seated in front of a curtain, which appears to be slightly drawn back. Peering out from behind the curtain is a curly-haired bearded man wearing a halo and holding a book. The figure is not identified though some scholars have suggested Moses and Christ as possibilities. If it were Moses the figure should hold a scroll, a common identifier for *Old Testament* figures and if it were Christ, he would surely be larger and have a larger halo than Matthew. An alternative, and more plausible suggestion, is that it represents the Gospel writer Mark whose text follows Matthew's. Mark, it seems, rather impatiently appears from behind the curtain to see if Mathew (or the reader, perhaps) is ready to move forward and on to his Gospel.

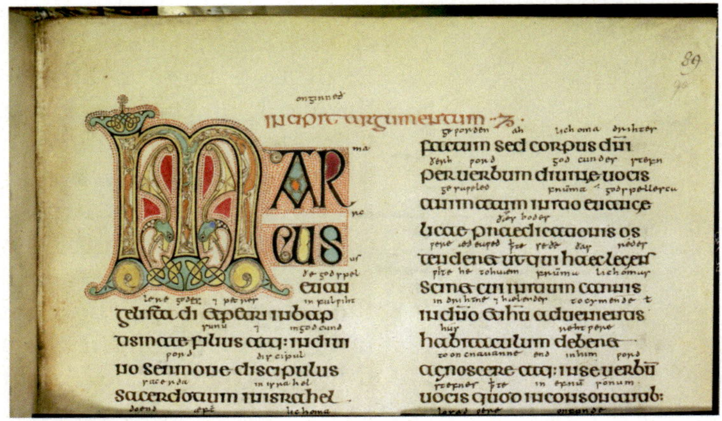

**9-6:** Lindisfarne Gospels, Page from Gospel of St. Mark shows interlinear gloss, tempera on vellum, England, 698–721, 13 ½" x 9 ¼", British Library, London.

In addition to the splendid illuminations, some very interesting and rare information survives about the Lindesfarne Gospels. This information comes from the *colophon* at the back of the book. A *colophon* is an inscription or entry usually found on the last page of a manuscript that provides information about the books production.

The Lindisfarne Gospel has a colophon that was added to the book in the 10th century, by a monk named Aldred. Aldred wrote that the book was both written and drawn by Eadfrith, Bishop of Lindisfarne between 698–721. He also writes that the Bishop wrote the book in honor of St. Cuthbert (d. 689), who was the founder of the community at Lindesfarne.

Aldred states that a monk named Ethelwald bound the book and another named Billfrith adorned the cover of the book with ornaments of gold and jewels.

Aldred, our narrator, also includes some information about his contribution to the manuscript, explaining that he *glossed* the text in English between the lines, with the help from God and Saint Cuthbert. A *gloss* is a brief explanatory note or even a full translation of a difficult or technical expression or text usually inserted in the margin, or between lines of a text or manuscript. Aldred's gloss was done between the original lines of text and is therefore called an interlinear gloss.

The interlinear gloss in the Lindisfarne Gospels is the earliest surviving translation of the four Gospels into any form of the English language.

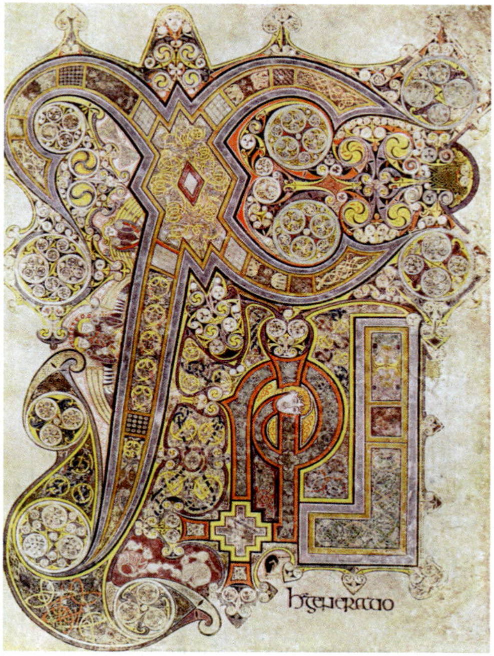

Larger and more lavishly illustrate than the Lindisfarne Gospels is the Book of Kells.

The book, now in Trinity College in Dublin, is considered the most elaborately decorated of all Insular manuscripts. The Book of Kells is a Latin text of the four Gospels written and decorated either in Iona, Scotland or Ireland. It has a total of 680 pages of which only two are without color.

It is a large book, larger than both the Book of Durrow and the Lindisfarne Gospels. It also includes more full-page illuminations that any other insular manuscript. It includes carpet pages, author portraits, initial pages, canon tables, and even illustrated pages within the text of the Gospels, depicting crucial moments in the story, including the arrest of Christ, the Crucifixion, the Temptation, and the Resurrection.

One of the most remarkable pages is the opening page for the Gospel of Matthew.

The three Greek letters , XPI, represent the first three letters of the Greek word

**9-7:** Chi Rho Iota page, Book of Kells, Pigment on vellum, Iona, Scotland, 8th–9th cen. CE, 13 x 91/2", Trinity College Library, Dublin.

(CHRIST – **X** = CH **P** = Rho **I** = Iota). The monogram starts the text of the nativity of Jesus in the Gospel of Matthew. This page is an *incipit* page: an incipit page (incipit from the Latin meaning *it begins*) is a page that begins a text, usually with just the first few words of the beginning of the text.

The decoration of the monogram is so monumental that only three words actually fit onto the page. "Christo (XPI)" which takes up most of the whole page and then at the bottom right are *autem* (abbreviated as h) *generatio*" translated as *Now the generations of Christ.* This is the opening of the text that is read during the mass on Christmas day.

The letter rho ends in a tiny male head; the head has a beard and bright red hair. The head may represent Christ, who now appears with a more northern physiognomy. Remember, art is a reflection of the culture that made it. Also tucked into the elaborate details of the page are blond angels and even cats and mice.

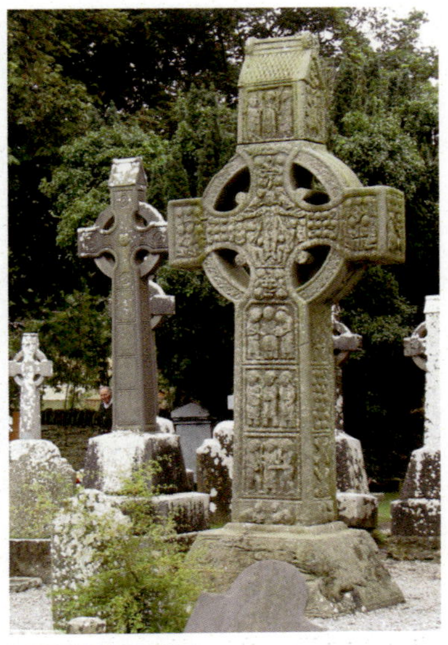

**9-8:** High Cross of Muiredach, sandstone, Monasterboice, Ireland, 923 CE, 19′ including base, Monasterboice, Ireland.

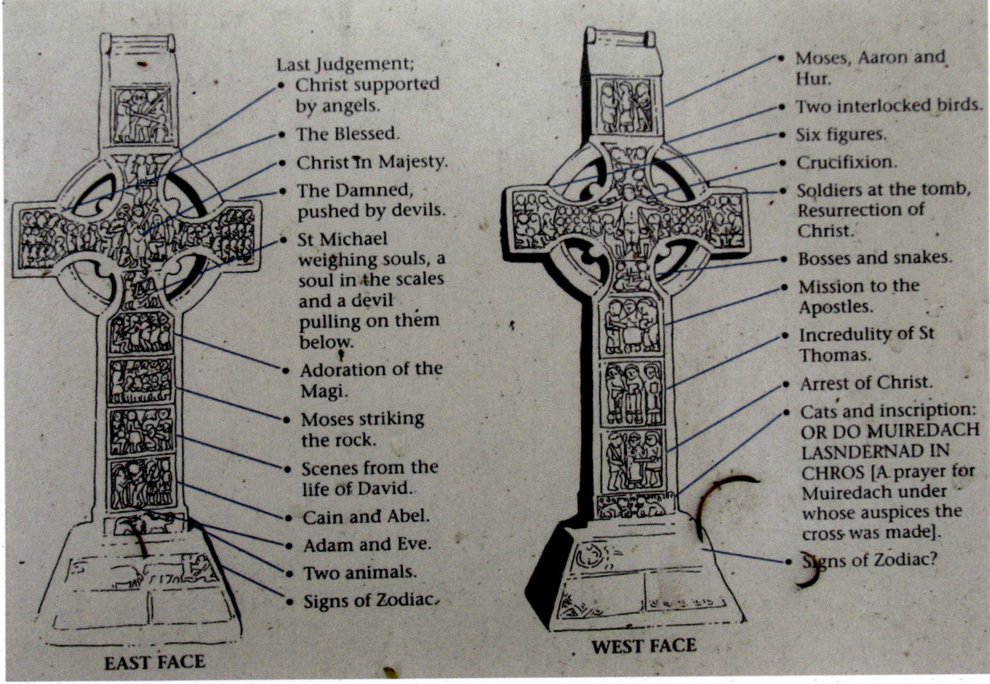


**9-9:** Plan showing East and West face, High Cross of Muiredach, sandstone, 19′ including base, 923, Monasterboice, Ireland.

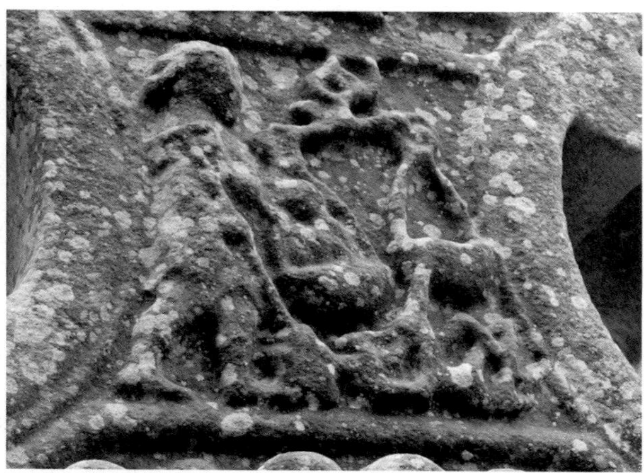

**9-10:** Weighing of the soul (psychostasis), detail East face, High Cross of Muiredach, sandstone, 19′ including base, 923, Monasterboice, Ireland.

This single page is considered one of the most lavishly decorated pages in all of Hiberno-Saxon manuscript illumination, and is often cited as the supreme example of this art form.

## Celtic Crosses

An example of an early insular art form that is not small in scale and not from a manuscript are Celtic high crosses.

These crosses were erected almost exclusively in Ireland (with a few in Britain) between the 8th and 10th centuries. The crosses are free-standing three-dimensional stone monuments that range from 5–25 feet in height. Most are located on monastic sites in burial grounds and serve as grave markers.

The design of the cross identifies it as a Celtic cross. This is a Latin cross with a central circle that connects the four arms. The central wheel is called a 'wheel of glory' and may represent a crown or wreath. This particular design may have originated from very early crosses made in wood that would have needed a central support.

This exceptional example is one of the largest and best preserved Celtic crosses in Ireland. An inscription at the bottom of the west-face asks for prayers to be said for a man named Muiredach. Scholars believe that this was the Abbott of Monasterboice, one of Ireland's oldest monasteries, who died here in 923.

The cross is intricately carved with both interlace patterns and figural decoration on all four sides. 124 figures in various costumes are represented and the subjects include scenes from the *Old Testament, the New Testament* and more indigenous subject matter. At the center on the East side is an image of Christ as judge of the world, while on the west is an image of the crucifixion.

Just below the scene of Christ as judge is an image of the souls of the dead weighed in a scale. This scene is called a *psychostasis* (weighing of the soul) and represents the literal weighing of the soul before judgment is passed. It is a subject that will appear in Romanesque art with some frequency.

In terms of Christian theology, the *psychostasis* symbolizes God's judgment of the individual, and proves that no single human soul is insignificant in God's eyes. It can symbolize judgment and personal responsibility, both themes that were very important in the Medieval church.

The figures are simply rendered and rather short and squat. There is no desire by the artist for perfect harmonious figural proportions, but instead on a clarity and simplicity needed to relate the story and the message.

## Carolingian

In the 8th century Charles Martel (688–741), a Frankish ruler, established the Carolingian dynasty. His grandson was Charles the Great, or *Charlemagne* (742–814).

On Christmas Day 800, Charlemagne, King of the Franks and Italy, was crowned Roman Emperor by Pope Leo III, in St. Peter's basilica in Rome. He was the first Emperor elected since the fall of Rome.

Charlemagne proved himself a brilliant military strategist and administrator, promoting art and education, while waging war from Saxony to the Mediterranean. He could read and speak Latin fluently as well as understand Greek, though he never totally mastered writing. He studied rhetoric, theology, astronomy and mathematics, and filled his court with the greatest known scholars in the empire.

One of his goals as a Christian ruler was the recovery of the true text of the Bible, which had become filled with errors due to copying. He was a true *bibliophile* (a lover of books) and commissioned numerous illuminated manuscripts from the many scriptoria in the empire.

There are several contemporary biographies of Charlemagne that provide a great deal of information about him and his life, even his appearance. His biographer, Einhardt (c. 775–840) described him as merry, stately, lofty of stature, and a ruler who defended and beautified his empire. He even describes how Charlemagne adored his children and educated the boys and the girls equally.

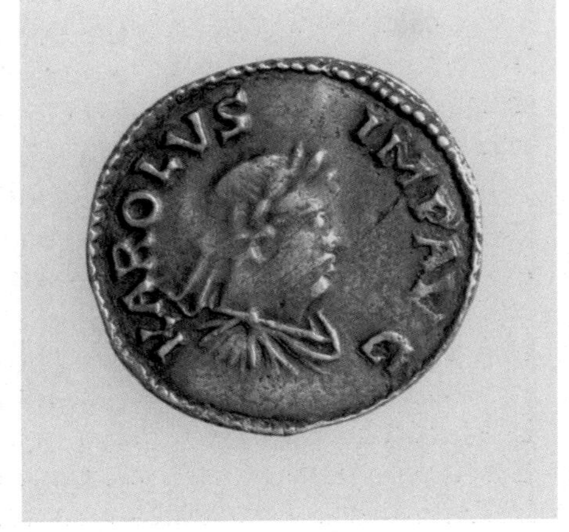


**9-11:** Denier of Charlemagne, Obverse, Portrait of Charlemagne, silver, c. ½", 768–814, Fitzwilliam Museum, Cambridge, UK.

Charlemagne's desires, dreams, and ambitions for his rule were made explicit in his official seal, which read *"renovatio imperii Romani"*, the renewal of the Roman Empire! His goal, explicitly stated, was to bring together a Christian empire as large and glorious as the empire of Trajan had been.

Charlemagne, as part of his grand design for the renovation of the empire, emulated the art, style, glory, scale, culture, learning, culture and political ideals of the empire; though infused with and inspired by Christian faith.

He instituted what historians have deemed a Carolingian Renaissance in the late 8th early 9th century.

After Charlemagne's return from his coronation in Rome, he ordered the transfer of a large equestrian statue of the Emperor Theodoric from

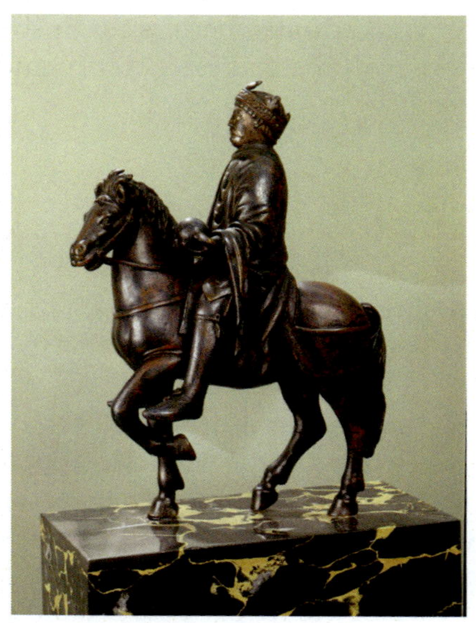

**9-12:** Equestrian portrait of Charlemagne, bronze, 9th cen. CE, bronze, 9 ½″ tall, Louvre Museum, Paris.

Ravenna to his new capital at Aachen, Germany. Though that statue is now lost, there is a small statuette of an equestrian image of Charlemagne that survives.

This small bronze statuette reveals just how much Charlemagne was modeling not only his empire, but much of his art, on classical models.

Charlemagne is depicted seated upright, gazing straight ahead. He wears imperial robes, an imperial crown, and in his left hand he carries an orb symbolizing power or dominion.

This small-scale work is clearly influenced by the larger-than-life size bronze equestrian statue of Marcus Aurelius in Rome. By modeling this small bronze statuette on that one, Charlemagne associates himself with the first Christian Emperor.

As part of his love and support of manuscript illumination, there are a number of particularly impressive manuscripts that date from the Carolingian period.

One of the best examples is the Gospel Book of Charlemagne; an Imperial purple manuscript written in Latin in gold ink. The style of the illuminations in the manuscript represents a shift from earlier insular manuscripts, reflecting a Hiberno-Saxon influence, to a now much more classical, or Byzantine model.

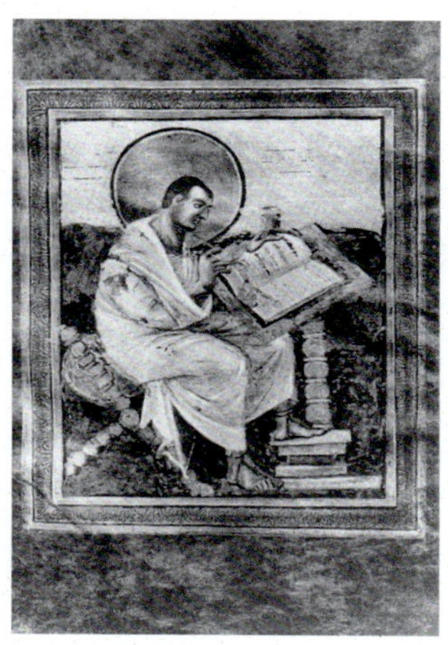

**9-13:** Saint Matthew, Gospel Book of Charlemagne (Coronation Gospels), gold ink and tempera on vellum, Aachen, Germany, 800–810 CE, 12 x 10″ Kunsthistorisches Museum, Vienna.

This page is one of the four author portraits found in the book and represents St. Matthew. The Evangelist sits on a cross-legged stool with a red pillow on it. In front of him his Gospel rests on a lectern while he holds a writing instrument in his right hand and an ink horn in his left. He wears an enormous gold halo and seems intent on his writing. The background, though damaged, reveals a high horizon line which pushes the figure to the front edge of the picture pane.

The artist is clearly familiar with an illusionist style of painting that includes an understanding of classical drapery, perspective, and the use of shadow and modulated colors to create shadows and depth. Even the frame reveals its classical influences, as it is decorated with a pattern of acanthus leaves.

On the first page of the Gospel of Luke, written in gold in the margin, is the Greek name *Demetrius presbyter* (presbyter indicates that he was a member of the clergy or an administrative church official). We do not know exactly who he was, but it is possible that he was either the scribe or the illuminator of the book. If so, it would indicate that there were Byzantine artists at work in the court of Charlemagne.

The manuscript, much like all that Charlemagne commissioned, was surely an attempt to establish and promote a western classical style of art at the new Imperial court in Aachen.

The Gospel Book of Charlemagne was re-discovered in the year 1000, when the Ottonian Emperor Otto III opened the tomb of Charlemagne and found it resting on his knees. He took the book and it was then used by later German Emperors at their coronations; that is how it came to be known as the *Coronation Gospels*.

The western classical style was however not the only artistic style that emerged from Charlemagne's court.

This author portrait from the Ebbo Gospels clearly reflects a different style altogether.

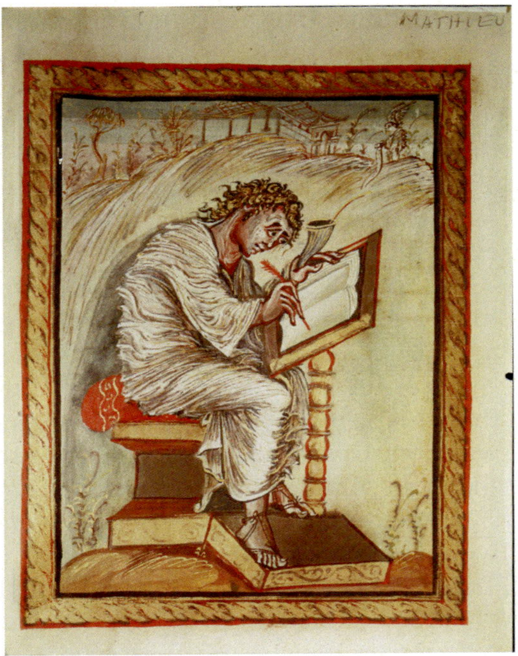


**9-14:** Saint Matthew, Ebbo Gospels, ink and tempera on vellum, 816–835 CE, 10″ × 8″, Bibliotheque Municipale, Epernay.

This author portrait comes from a Gospel book made for Archbishop Ebbo, of Reims, France. Notice that this portrait very closely follows the model of the author portrait from the Coronation Gospels but does so in a very different style.

Like the earlier example, the Evangelist sits at a lectern, with the book open as he records his Gospel. He rests one foot higher than the other on the footstool and even holds the pen and ink horn in the same manner.

But this representation is quite different. Here, unlike the Coronation Gospel image, the illuminator has included the symbol for the evangelist in the upper right corner, and he has also included a landscape and even two small buildings in the distance.

The big difference is in the style. The Coronation Gospel illumination reads as calm and serene, regal even in its refined and dignified composition. This illumination, however, is filled with energy

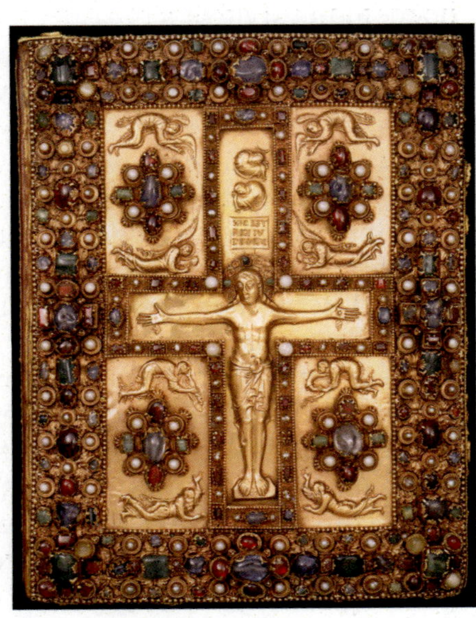

**9-15:** Crucifixion, The Lindau Gospels Cover, gold, precious stones and pearls, Saint Gall, Switzerland, c. 870 CE, 13″ × 10″, The Pierpont Morgan Library, New York.

and motion. Lines are jagged and tightly compressed and seem to move and vibrate on the page. Brushstrokes are quick, short, and clearly visible. It reads somewhat as if the Evangelist is so infused with the word of God that he cannot possibly write it all down fast enough. Look at his eyebrows, he seems frantic to get the words down on the page.

There is truly a frenetic and energetic quality to the whole image that is unmistakable and quite remarkable, leading some scholars to refer to this as an "inspired evangelist" portrait.

What is also remarkable is that this style was permitted to flourish at the same time as the more classically-inspired styles; it seems there was a kind of freedom of artistic expression that is extraordinary at such an early date.

In order to express the sacred nature and preciousness of the words written inside these luxurious manuscripts the covers were often adorned and made precious. This was done in part to protect the manuscript but also in order to reflect the beauty and the glory of the words and the illuminations contained inside.

The covers of the manuscripts were intended to make clear, even to a person who would never see inside it, that what was contained inside was extremely precious. This would be one of the rare times that one is intended to judge a book "by its cover."

The Lindau Gospels cover is perhaps the most luxurious of all Carolingian manuscript covers and was probably made during the reign of Charles the Bald, Charlemagne's grandson.

The cover takes its name from the Gospels to which it was later added.

The cover shows a crucifixion scene with Christ nailed to the cross with his eyes open, in the style of a *Christus Triumphans*. Notice that blood drips from the wounds in his hands. Above him is the superscription 'HIC EST REX IUDEORUM" in translation "This is the King of the Jews." Above that are personifications of the sun and moon.

In the four corners of the cover are figures that gesture and twist and curl in a kind of frenzy reminiscent of the Ebbo Gospel illumination. They seem to express their inner turmoil in their exterior posture and gesture.

The two top compartments reveal four angels, two each, surrounding a central jeweled decoration. Below, on the left and right' are the figures of the Virgin Mary (mantle covering her head) and St John the Evangelist. Below them are two more figures, perhaps Joseph of Aramathea and Mary Magdalene; both of whom were present and often depicted in scenes of the crucifixion.

The figures are created by a technique called *repoussé*. *Repoussé* is a technique of hammering or pushing metal out from behind to create a raised image. We have seen this technique before in the Mycenaean mask of Agamemnon.

The whole surface is encrusted with gems and pearls that catch and reflect the light and cover the surface with the same brilliant jewel-tone colors that illuminate the pages on the inside.

As in all other art forms, the Carolingian empire looked to the Roman Empire for inspiration in architecture.

# Carolingian Architecture

At Aachen, Charlemagne had his architect, Odo of Metz, design and build an extensive palace complex based on classical models. The complex consisted of a palace chapel on one side of a large open forum and a residence and audience hall at the other.

For his palace chapel, or Palatine Chapel, Charlemagne looked to Rome and specifically Ravenna for inspiration. He even imported porphyry columns from Ravenna which he used to decorate his chapel.

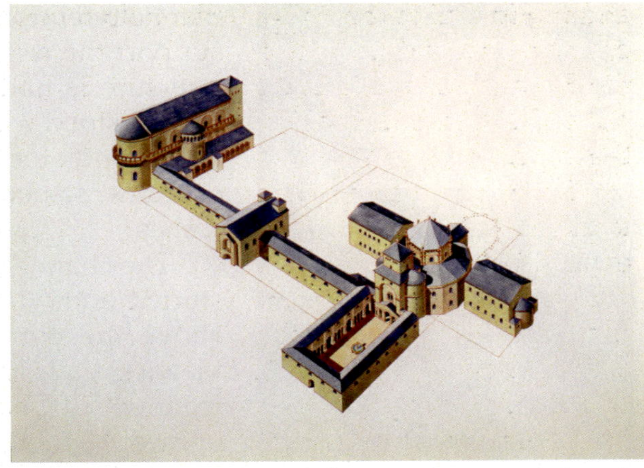

**9-16:** Palace complex and Palatine Chapel, Odo of Metz, Plan, Aachen Germany, 792–805 CE.

The plan for the Palatine Chapel is closely based on the church of San Vitale in Ravenna. Like that structure, it is a central plan building based on a design of concentric octagons.

This building is, however, also very independent and stands as its own invention. It is much sturdier, more massive, and clearer in design than San Vitale, and it is also much more vertical in conception.

Also new and influential here is the use or incorporation of twin cylindrical towers flanking the west entrance portal This innovative architectural approach to elaborate the west end is called a *westwork*. This design element greatly influences the dual-tower facades of later Romanesque and Gothic churches.

The interior space is defined by massive piers

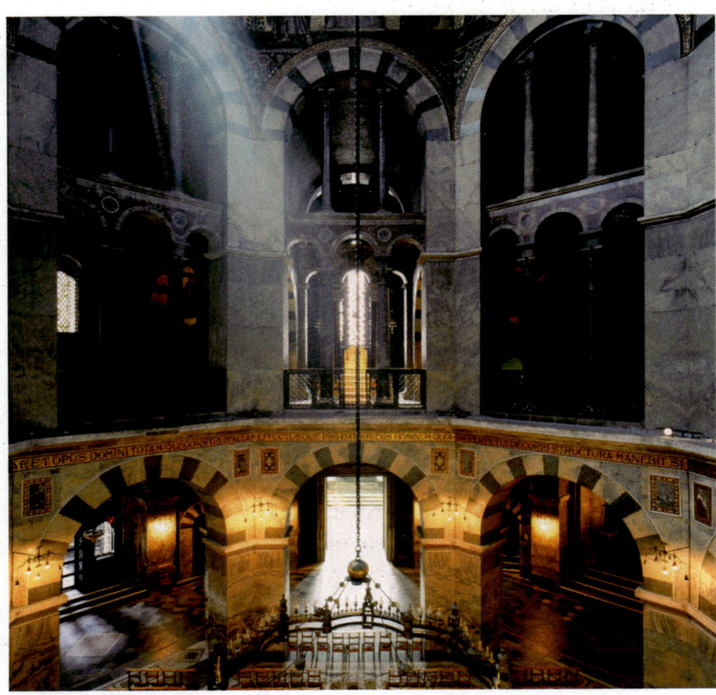

**9-17:** Interior of the Palatine Chapel, Odo of Metz, Aachen Germany, 792–805 CE.

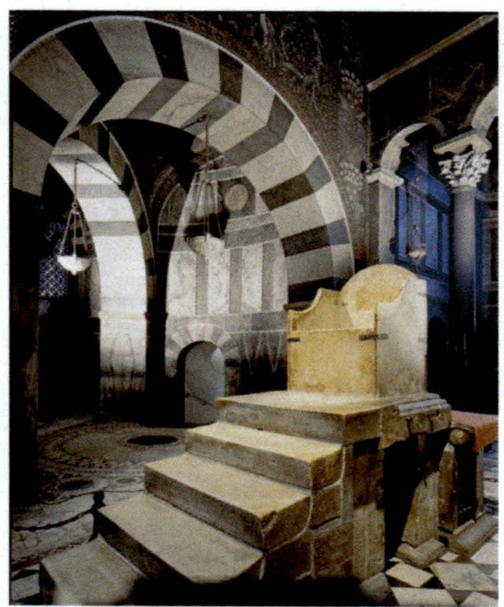

**9-18:** Throne of Charlemagne, Palatine Chapel, Aachen, Germany.

that help reinforce the building's octagonal shape, and support the weight of the dome. The verticality of the structure is underscored in part by the height of the second story, which is twice the height of the first. The tall second story arches are ornamented with pairs of columns, stacked one above the other, set within the arches.

The chapel also had (now much altered) a double-storied entryway that provided a large framing arch above the entrance. This space provided a special viewing gallery within the *westwork* called a *tribune*, from which Charlemagne could appear to the masses of people in the atrium below. The tribune is also where Charlemagne's throne was located, a feature influenced from earlier Byzantine churches.

The palatine chapel was built and designed to serve as a royal chapel. The choice for a central plan building may reflect the function of the building to also serve as a martyrium for relics, a court chapel, and an Imperial mausoleum.

In 814 Charlemagne was buried in a vault in the chapel, and his son Louis the Pious was crowned emperor here.

## Monasticism

Monasticism is generally defined as a way of life in which monks and /or nuns withdraw entirely or in part from society, to a monastery or convent, in order to devote themselves to prayer and solitude. Monasticism was an integral part of the medieval church, and many monasteries were built and supported by Charlemagne and his descendants.

Most of these institutions were, in the West, governed by a particular set of rules and regulations. Those rules were laid out in the 6th century by St. Benedict. St. Benedict (c. 480–543 CE) was born at Nursia (Norcia), Italy, and is considered the founder of western monasticism. His work, entitled *regula sancti Benedicti*, or *Rule of St. Benedict*, is composed of 73 short chapters that address spirituality and administrative concerns. The work was widely used by the 9th century.

Not only were these monastic institutions ordered and strictly governed by a set of rules, but in the best case scenario, they were also totally self sufficient.

The plan, originally drawn on five sheets of parchment sewn together, was intended as a design to rebuild a monastery at St. Gall in Switzerland. The plan, which was never completed to the design, was commissioned by Abbott Haito of Reichenau for Abbot Gozbert at St. Gall.

At its most basic, the plan reveals itself as an organized and coherent arrangement of buildings, intended to serve two main purposes: to be self-sufficient and to separate the clergy from the laity.

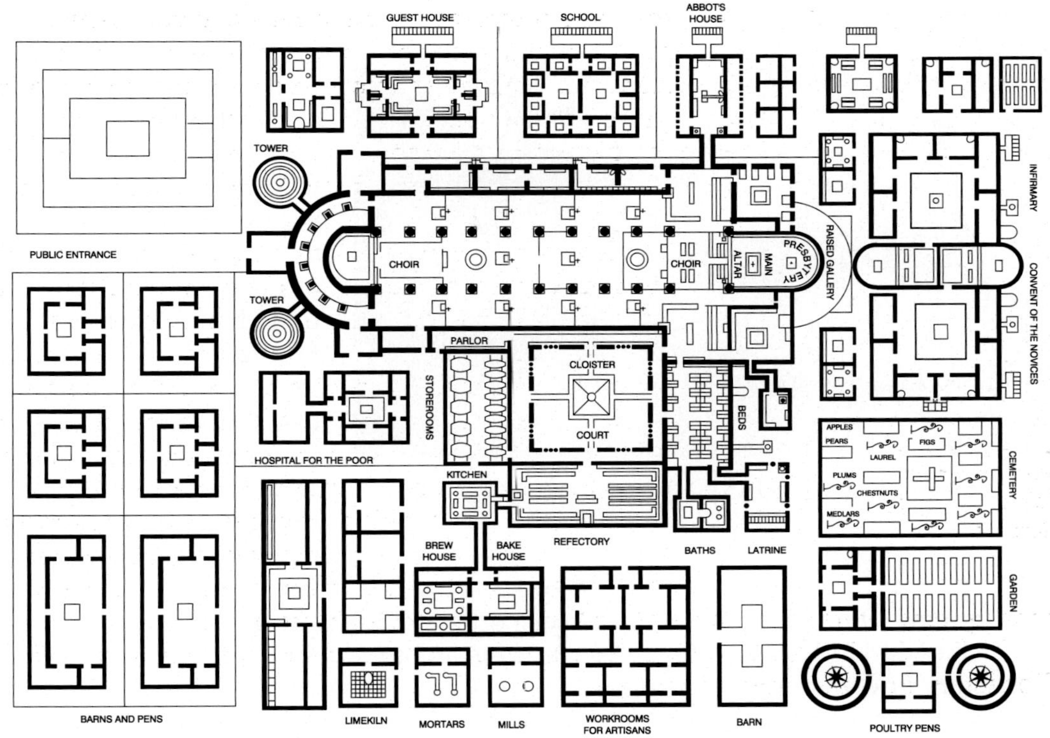


**9-19:** Modern drawing based on original plan for a Monastery at St. Gall, Switzerland, original parchment c. 819, 28"x 44 1/8", Stiftsbibliothek, St. Gall.

At the heart of the plan is a large basilica-plan church with an apse at both ends, and two cylindrical towers flanking the entrance.

The large church is flanked on one side by the school and guest houses, and on the other side by the cloister. The cloister is a colonnaded courtyard that is reserved for the monks, and off the cloister is the *refectory* or dining hall. Arranged in an organized and efficient plan are all the other buildings that make the monastery totally self sufficient, including the chapel, hospital, bakery, mill, cooper, brewery, and others.

## Ottonian Art

After the death of Charlemagne in 814, and then the death of his son Louis the Pious in 840, the empire was divided between Charlemagne's grandsons. The three signed a treaty in 843 (called the Treaty of Verdun) which split the empire so that Charles the Bald ruled in the West, Lothair took the title Holy Roman Emperor, and Louis the German ruled in the East. These divisions, which essentially correspond with modern France, Germany/ and the Netherlands/Belgium, weakened the empire leaving it vulnerable to Moslem and Viking invasions.

Not until the mid 10th century, after some 100 years of battles and Viking invasions, was there another attempt at a renewal of Empire. This renewal came through a new

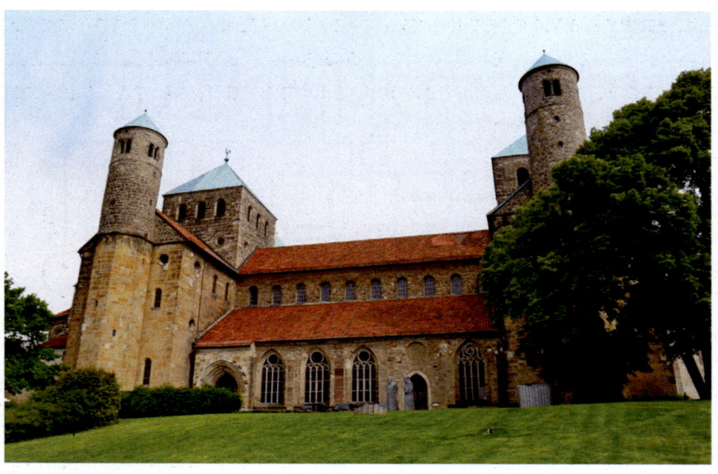

**9-20:** Abbey Church of Saint Michael's, Hildesheim, Germany, 1001–1031 CE.

Saxon line of German emperors, the first three of which were named Otto. Otto I, also called "the Great", was crowned Roman Emperor in Rome by Pope John XII in 962. With Otto's coronation as Emperor, the kingdoms of Germany and Italy were united into the Holy Roman Empire.

Ottonian architects, like Ottonian artists, were inspired by Carolingian and Western models but reinterpreted those models to create their own individual style.

The new Ottonian architectural style is best evidenced in the abbey church of St. Michael at Hildesheim. An *abbey church* is a church that is or was once part of a monastery or convent.

This church was built under the direction of Bishop Bernward who consecrated the crypt in 1015. Bernard was chaplain at the Imperial court and tutor to the young Otto III, then six years of age, before becoming Bishop and then founder of the church at Hildesheim.

Bernward spent nearly thirty years at Hildesheim focusing his attention on the building and decoration of the church. Thangmar of Heidelberg, his biographer, described how Bernward would visit the various workshops connected with the cathedral school and with his own hands manufacture gold and silver vessels for the altars.

The church, constructed between 1001 and 1031, is a double-transept plan with double-crossing towers and double-flanking cylindrical towers. The building also has double entrances on the lateral sides. The long nave serves to connect the two distinct ends of the church. The plan and arrangement of the church is very different from traditional western Christian basilica-plan churches, and is perhaps closer to Roman Imperial basilicas. This may be due in part to Bernward's visit to Rome in 1001.

The building is very rational and geometrically proportioned so that one unit of measure, or module, is used throughout the entire space. This is called a *modular* approach. In this church the crossing square is the basic unit of measure and the nave is equal to three crossing squares long and one wide.

The design is very proportional and rational. There is not only a clear and ordered arrangement of the architectural elements, but there is a palpable clarity and severity that typifies the entire structure both inside and out.

The exterior is an organized arrangement of geometric masses of stone that make clear from the exterior the masses on the interior. The interior decoration is austere and reduced to the interplay of repetitive lines and arches, including a nave arcade of alternating square pillars and round columns.

## Art is an Endangered Species

The church has unfortunately suffered severe damage including several fires: it was restored or rebuilt in the 11th, 12th, and 17th centuries. The building was almost completely destroyed by a bomb during the air raids over Germany in 1945. In 1950 it was completely restored and is now a UNESCO World Heritage Site.

For the decoration of this church, Bishop Bernward commissioned two exceptional works of bronze: a colossal set of doors and a monumental bronze column.

The particular choice of decoration reflects Bishop Bernward's visit to Rome with Otto III for his coronation in 1001. In Rome, Bernward would have been able to see the great carved wooden doors at the basilica of Santa Sabina and the monumental carved marble columns of Trajan and Marcus Aurelius.

The monumental bronze doors of the church were commissioned by Bernward in 1001 and took some 14 years to complete. The doors are 16 feet 6 inches tall, and each door was cast in one piece. They are exceptional examples of the lost wax technique of bronze casting and are considered the first monumental cast bronze sculptures created in Northern Europe. They are also considered the first monumental cast bronze sculptures created since antiquity.

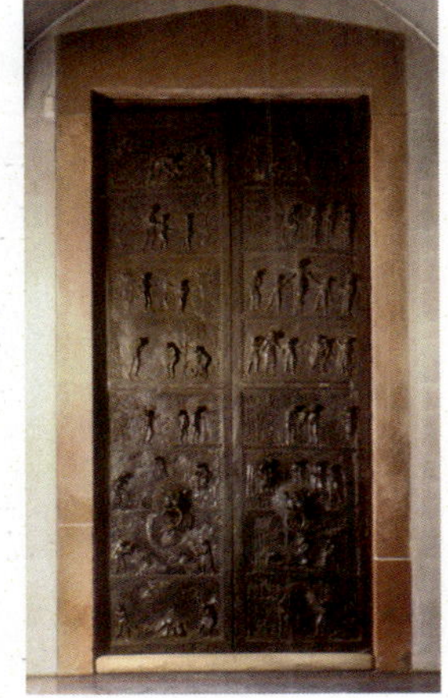

**9-21:** Doors of Bishop Bernward, bronze, St. Michael's, Hildesheim, Germany, 1015 CE, 16′6″ height, Dom-Museum, Hildesheim.

The doors are decorated with 16 narrative scenes, eight on each door, from the *Old* and the *New Testament*. The eight panels on the left are taken from the *Old Testament* book of Genesis, beginning with the creation of Adam and ending with the murder of Abel. The scenes are read from the top down.

On the right side there are eight scenes taken from the *New Testament* accounts of Christ's life. The scenes begin with the Annunciation, and end with the appearance of Christ to Mary Magdalene after his resurrection. The scenes on this side are read from the bottom up.

The decoration, in a series of complex typological pairings, ultimately recounts the history of salvation from the fall through the resurrection.

At the center of the doors is a wide strip that carries a dedicatory inscription. It reads *"In the year of the Lord 1015, Bishop Bernward, in divine memory, had these cast door (win)s) suspended on the façade of the Angels' Temple, for his remembrance."* The inscription was added in 1035.

It is interesting that these magnificent doors were not originally located on the front entrance doors to the church but were instead located at the entrance to the church from the cloister. That means that they were placed where only the monks would have had the opportunity to see them. It seems that they were intended to be devotional and private, not demonstrative or public.

The typological pairings provide for a reading of the scenes that follows both a thematic progression and a parallel one. This subtle yet complex iconographical arrangement was probably designed by Bernward himself.

The pairing of the scenes, for those fortunate enough to see them, act as mini devotionals that demand to be read and meditated upon.

The narrative scenes are reduced to their most basic elements. The stories are presented in a clear and legible manner that focuses on the message and the emotion. The images are almost stark in their simplicity but are unforgettably powerful in their message.

The image of Cain killing his brother Abel is an example of drama and emotion. The scene is reduced to the raw and dramatic moment when Cain strikes his brother with a large stick and Abel tumbles to the ground.

One of the most remarkable and powerful scenes is God's rebuke of Adam and Eve.

This scene depicts God pointing his finger at the couple who has just eaten from the Tree of Knowledge. God jabs his finger at the couple with such emotion and such anger that he actually leans forward with his shoulders hunched up near his ears. The feeble couple actually cowers and crouches in an effort to avoid the anger that is vented toward them. It is as if there is an electric current that emanates from the figure of God and that his gesture alone might annihilate them; it is of course damning them to mortality. The gesture, isolated in a void, becomes the focus of the whole scene. Notice how the couple plays the blame game. Their gestures reveal a meek and feeble attempt to

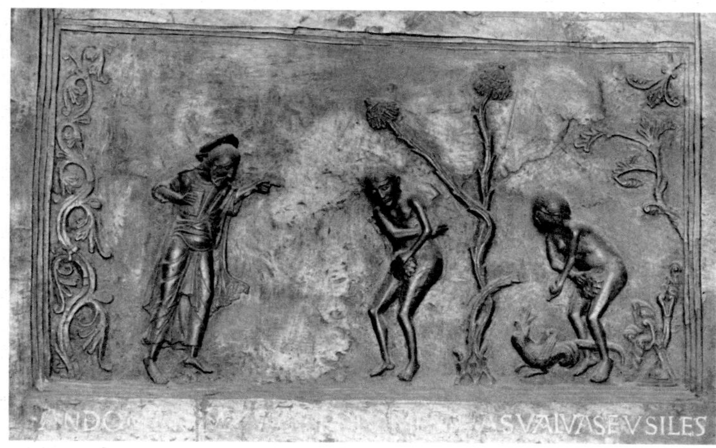


**9-22:** Rebuke of Adam and Eve, Doors of Bishop Bernward, bronze, St. Michael's, Hildesheim, Germany, 1015 CE, 16′6″ height, Dom-Museum, Hildesheim.

deflect blame onto one another. Even the wild gnarly trees seem to point and blame Eve, as she desperately tries to cover herself and point to the evil serpent beneath her.

The emotions are clear and palpable: anger, rage, fear, desperation, guilt, shame, blame, and despair. The emotional impact is certainly heightened by the starkness and flatness of the background.

These images are remarkably similar to a number of illuminations in Carolingian manuscripts, particularly the Grandval Bible (840) a manuscript that either Bernward or his artists might have known.

The doors are a masterpiece not only of Ottonian art, or even medieval bronze casting, but more importantly, of the ability of the artist to communicate with clarity and simplicity the enormity of the Christian message.

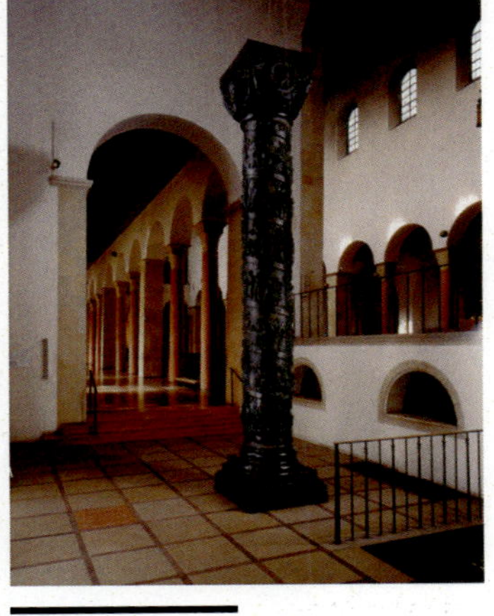

**9-23:** Column of Bernward, bronze, St. Michaels, Hildesheim, Germany, 1015–1022 CE, 12′6″ height, Dom-Museum, Hildesheim.

Bernward also commissioned a large freestanding column with narrative relief scenes depicting Christ's life. The work was commissioned just after the completion of the doors and took seven years to complete. The column was made using the same lost wax technique as the doors but was cast in a single piece (except for the capital and base). It was originally surmounted by a large crucifix. The original capital and crucifix do not survive.

The column is wrapped in a spiral band of narrative reliefs that tell the story of Christ's life in 24 scenes. The scenes begin with his baptism and end with his entry into Jerusalem. Like Trajan's Column in Rome, the narratives are read from bottom to top.

The scenes have the same interest in narrative clarity and the same expressive use of gesture that we saw in the reliefs on the doors. The scenes are however more tightly compacted and the whole surface reads as more densely ornamented.

In all of these works the debt of Ottonian artists to classical and Carolingian sources is evident; however, the works also clearly reflect a boldness and innovative originality that separate Ottonian art from its predecessors.

The Ottonian desire for clarity in design, impactful messaging and strong visual impact is evident in other art forms as well. Perhaps one of the best examples of the power and directness of Ottonian art is found in a large crucifix.

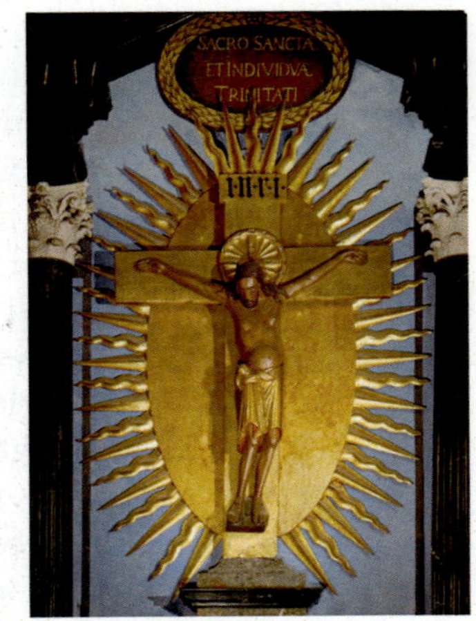


**9-24:** Gero Crucifix, painted and gilded wood, Cologne Cathedral, Germany, c. 970 CE, figure of Christ is 6′ 2″, Cologne Cathedral, Cologne.

This large crucifix was commissioned c. 975 by Archbishop Gero for the Cathedral in Cologne.

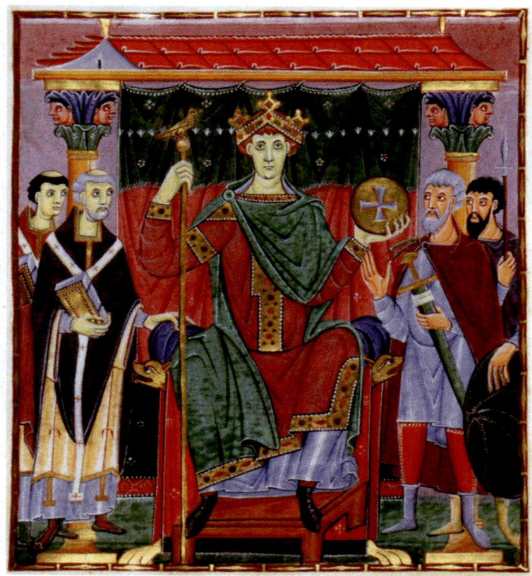

**9-25:** Otto III Enthroned, Gospel Book of Otto III, tempera on vellum, c. 997–1000 CE, 13 × 11", Staatsbibliothek, Munich.

The crucifix, constructed of gilded and painted oak, is generally considered to be the first monumental sculpture created since antiquity. Moreover, it is considered the first monumental image of the crucified Christ in Christian art.

The figure of Christ represents the tradition of the *Christus Patiens* type; an image of Christ dead on the cross.

The *Christus Patiens* image represents the physical death of Christ. Christ is shown hanging on the cross; his slumping pose indicating the weight of his body. His head is forward and bowed to one side and his arms appear to curve downwards, his skin is stretched and taught, and his eyes are closed. Ultimately, the image of the dead Christ is meant to evoke a private, sympathetic devotion among the faithful.

This image of the *Christus Patiens* is significant in that it represents a new concept in the representation of the savior. He is not depicted as an emperor, or a symbolic lamb or a jeweled cross, or even a youthful hero, instead he is depicted as a tortured martyr. Adding to the agony expressed in the work are the streams of blood that drip down Christ's forehead caused by the crown of thorns that he once wore, (now unfortunately lost). The image is intended to depict his humanity above all.

The work, in its powerful directness and monumentality, confronts the viewer with an emotional intensity and drama that is startling.

The last example of Ottonian art is not an image of suffering but one of power.

Otto III, perhaps more than all of the earlier Ottos, wanted to revive the glory of the Roman Empire. He was the son of Otto II and a Byzantine princess named Theophanu, and was very conscious of his descent from both German and Byzantine imperial lines. He moved his capital to Rome but unfortunately died at age 21. He was buried beside Charlemagne at Aachen.

These are facing pages from the Gospel Book made for Otto III about 1000. They show the Emperor, crowned and dressed in imperial robes, enthroned before a cloth of honor draped between two very interesting Corinthian columns that seem to be part of a small classical temple. He holds symbols of universal authority, the scepter and the orb.

He is flanked by representatives of the clergy on his right; they are tonsured and hold books, and barons, holding swords and shields, on his left. Essentially we see him flanked by church and state, symbolic of his secular and sacred power.

On the facing page Otto III is approached by four female personifications labeled "Slavinia," "Germania," "Gallia," and "Roma." The three crowned personifications who carry gifts to the enthroned Otto III are intended to recall the Magi and their gift bearing. The imperial and sacred allusions are not lost as Otto III is temporal ruler, knight, king, and defender of the Christian faith.

The act of bringing gifts or offerings to a lord also reflects the importance of homage in the period. In feudal society it was critical that a vassal demonstrated his loyalty to his lord through the act of homage.

With the death of Otto III the last vestiges of the imperial spirit died with him. The period to follow, the Romanesque, will reject the imperial flavors of classical antiquity and instead embrace a new found religious fervor. This fervor will extend not only to ideas of faith but to the building of tremendous churches, the quest for holy relics, and the recovery and liberation of the holy land.

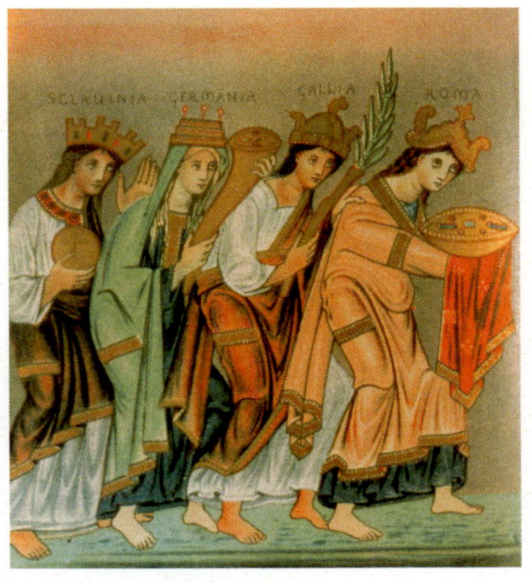

**9-26:** Four personifications of Provinces, Gospel Book of Otto III, tempera on vellum, c. 997–1000, 13″ × 11″, Staatsbibliothek, Munich.

Name ______________________________ Date ______________

# Chapter 9

## Early Medieval Art and Architecture

1. What was found at Sutton Hoo? Describe some of the objects.

2. Which is the most lavishly illuminated Hiberno-Saxon manuscript?

3. Which church plan heavily influenced the palatine chapel at Aachen?

4. What distinguishes Celtic crosses? Where are they found?

5. What is the significance of the date: Christmas Day, 800?

6. What is a Carpet Page? How are they significant?

7. What is the difference between the styles of the Coronation and Ebbo Gospels?

8. Define *colophon* and identify the manuscript that contains one.

9. What is the significance of the design of St. Michaels at Hildeshiem?

10. Which dynastic line succeeded the Carolingians in the mid 10th century?

# ROMANESQUE ART AND ARCHITECTURE

## Chapter 10

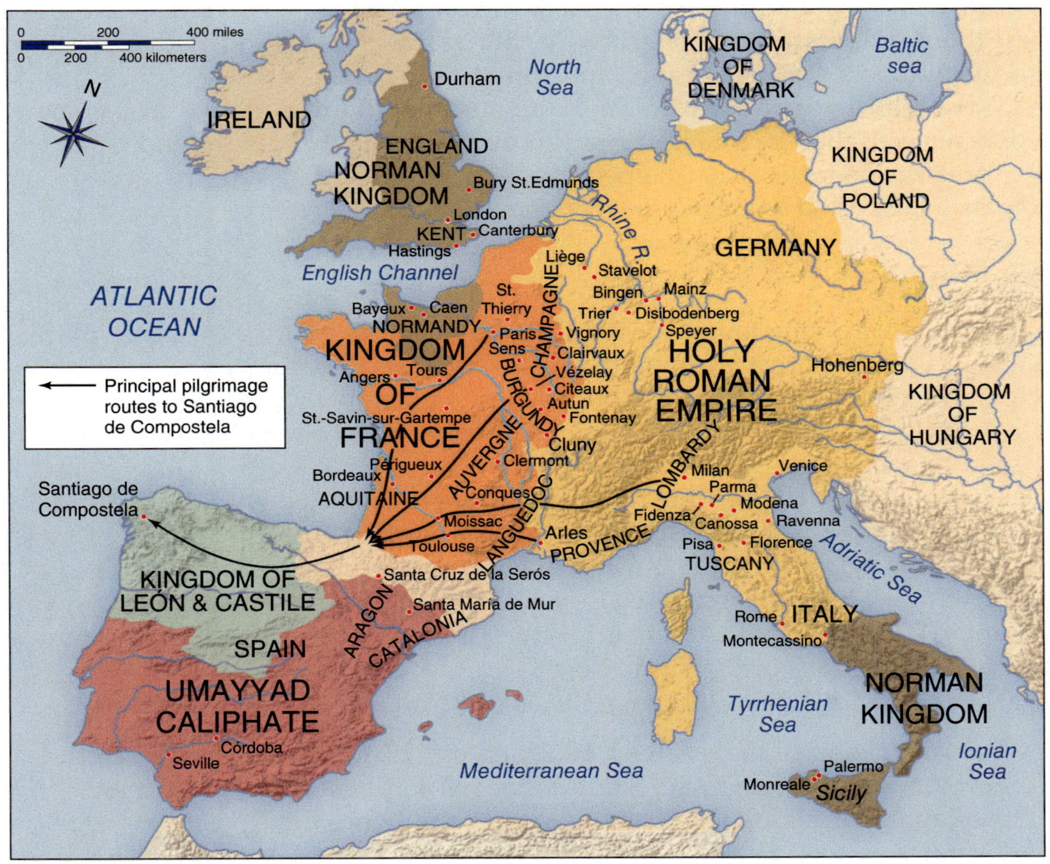


Europe c. 1100.

Romanesque simply means "Roman-like" and was a term first used in the 19th century. The term was applied to 11th and 12th century European architecture, because of its use of "roman-like" rounded arches, barrel, and groin vaults. The term was also used to distinguish buildings that were different from earlier Medieval timber roof structures, as well as from the later Gothic pointed arch constructions.

The Romanesque period, generally dated to c. 1000–1200, also marked a return to monumental stone sculpture, evidenced primarily in the great carved portals of church façades.

A significant feature in Romanesque history was the building, or rebuilding, of thousands of churches and monasteries. These immense building projects attracted pilgrims, many of whom were often looking for relics as well as redemption. It was these thousands of traveling pilgrims that brought with them knowledge, and money, and the numbers that encouraged and supported the rise of cities.

There was a particularly strong religious fervor in this period, in part because people realized that the first millennium had not brought about the end of the world.

Three major factors that helped shape the history, art, and architecture of the Romanesque period were: *pilgrimages*, *crusades*, and *feudalism*.

## Pilgrimages

A pilgrimage is a long journey, especially one made to a shrine or sacred place. The journey is often motivated by faith, or devotion, or to obtain some form of divine help or intervention, or as a form of penance. A person who makes such a journey is called a pilgrim. These journeys were often undertaken despite their physical, mental, and financial tolls.

Christian pilgrimages were first made to sites connected with the life, birth, preaching, and crucifixion of Jesus. Surviving descriptions of Christian pilgrimages to the Holy Land date from the 4th century, when pilgrimage was encouraged by the church fathers. Pilgrimages were also made to Rome and other sites associated with the apostles, saints, and Christian martyrs, as well as to places where there were recorded apparitions of the Virgin Mary.

The major Christian pilgrimage sites in the Romanesque period included:

Jerusalem: Sites of the teaching, trial, and crucifixion of Jesus of Nazareth
Rome: Sites associated with Saints Peter and Paul, martyrs, and Popes
Santiago de Compostela, Spain: Tomb of Saint James the Apostle
Conques, France: Skeleton of 4th century martyr Saint Foy
Vezelay: The relics of St. Mary Magdalene
Cologne, Germany: The relics of the Three Magi

Pilgrims were an important sourse of funding and inspiration for the cities, monasteries, and churches along these routes. The traveling pilgrims influenced churches and monasteries to find and house greater relics (in order to attract more pilgrims) to build more impressive churches (to attract more donations) and to build churches big enough to accomodate the travelling masses (to keep them coming back).

Most scholars agree that pilgrims were the primary economic and conceptual catalyst for art and architecture during the Romanesque period.

## Eastern and Western Christianity

A crucial event for the faithful in 1054 was the Great Schism. The East-West Schism, known also as the Great Schism, was the event that divided Christianity into Western Catholicism and Eastern Orthodoxy. Though it is officially dated to 1054, when Pope Leo IX in Rome and Patriarch Michael I in Constantinople excommunicated each other, the East-West Schism was actually the result of an extended period of estrangement between the two Churches.

The primary causes of the Schism were disputes over papal authority—the Pope claimed he held authority over the four Eastern patriarchs, while the four Eastern patriarchs claimed that the primacy of the Patriarch of Rome was only honorary, and thus he had authority only over Western christians. Another rift was due to the insertion of the *filioque* clause into the Nicene Creed.

In Latin *filioque* means *and the son*. The Nicene Creed states that the Holy Spirit "proceeds from the Father." This creed was first promulgated at the First Council of Nicea in 325 and modified at the First Council of Constantinople in 381. The Nicene Creed is the definitive all-encompassing profession of the Christian faith; and according to the council it is true, correct, and inalterable.

In the Latin-speaking church, however, the phrase *and the son* was added to the Nicene Creed at the Synod of Toledo in Spain in 447, and that is when the problems began.

There were also other catalysts for the Schism, including variance over liturgical practices, unleavened bread for the host, and conflicting claims of jurisdiction. The end result was that the churches split and were ultimately never reunited.

## The Crusades

The Crusades were a series, generally counted as nine, of armed military campaigns, usually sanctioned by the Pope, during the 11th through the 13th centuries. Originally, they were Roman Catholic endeavors to recapture the Holy Land from the Muslims, but some were redirected, such as the Fourth Crusade against Constantinople.

The trigger for the First Crusade in 1095 was the Byzantine Emperor Alexius I's appeal to Pope Urban II for mercenaries to help him resist Muslim advances into the Byzantine Empire. The response was much larger, and less helpful, than Alexius I desired. Instead of troops for defense the Pope called for an invasion force to not merely defend the Byzantine Empire but also to retake Jerusalem; thus the Crusades began.

In Pope Urban's speeches, to find support for his Crusade, he promised rewards both on earth and in heaven; he told those willing to go that there would be a total remission of sins to any who might die in the undertaking.

So the Crusades, by those who undertook them, were seen as a noble and just cause, and those willing to fight for the holy lands and holy sites were literally soldiers for God.

## Feudalism

Feudalism is a socio-political-economic system in which a king (or queen) shared power with the nobility, who in turn required services from the common people in return for allowing them to use the land.

Three primary elements characterize Feudalism: lords, vassals and fiefs. The structure of feudalism is determined by how these three elements work together. A lord was a noble who owned land. A vassal was a person who was granted land by the lord. The land was known as a fief.

In exchange for a fief, the vassal would provide military service to the lord. The lord would provide land and security to his vassal. The obligations and relations between lord and vassal were reciprocal; each had a responsibility to the other.

Pilgrimages, feudalism, crusades, religious fervor, impressive church building, and monumental stone sculpture mark the art and architectural achievements of the Romanesque period.

## The Bayeux Tapestry

The Bayeux Tapestry recounts, in a continuous frieze-like strip, the story of the Norman (French) invasion of England and the Battle of Hastings in 1066.

The Bayeux tapestry is actually not a tapestry but is instead a wool embroidered linen textile. Tapestry designs are woven on a loom as part of the fabric while embroidery designs are sewn with threads.

It is made out of eight separate pieces of linen sewn together and measures roughly 230 feet long and about 20 inches wide. Eight colors were used: the five main colors are blue-green, terracotta, light-green, buff, and grey-blue.

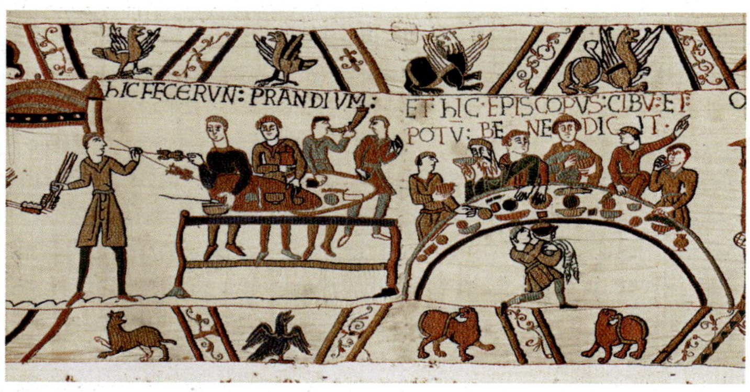


**10-1:** Bayeux Tapestry, detail, 1070–1080, embroidered wool on linen, 1′8″ height, 230′ length, Bayeux Cathedral, France.

The tapestry tells the story, from the Norman point of view, of the circumstances that lead up to the Norman conquest of England and the Battle of Hastings, October 14, 1066. The whole narrative is accompanied above by Latin captions.

Though the tapestry was almost certainly done by women, a man, perhaps a soldier, may have provided details since some of the details are so specific they seem to come from an eyewitness account.

The tapestry contains about 50 different scenes, and one researcher has counted that there are 632 human figures, 202 horses, 55 dogs, 505 other creatures (some clearly mythical beasts), 37 buildings, 41 ships, 49 trees, and nearly 2000 Latin letters.

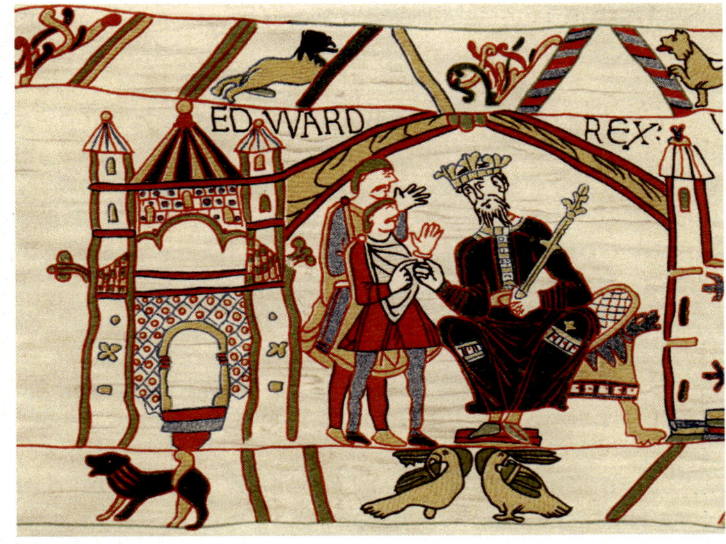


**10-2:** Bayeux Tapestry, Bayeux Cathedral, France, 1070–1080, embroidered wool on linen, 1′8 in high, 230 feet long.

## The Story

The tapestry begins with a panel showing an enthroned image of the English King Edward, who had no heir. King Edward the Confessor (1042–1066) decides to send Harold Godwinson (the Earl of Wessex and the most powerful Earl in England) to visit his cousin William of Normandy.

Harold is sent to tell William that William has been selected by King Edward to be the next king of England. As Harold is in transit across the channel, he is caught in a storm and sent off course and is taken prisoner. William sends two messengers to demand his release, and Harold is freed.

William then invites Harold to come on a campaign with him to relieve a castle under siege. On the way, just outside the famous monastery of Mont St. Michele, two soldiers become mired in quicksand and Harold saves them. The two comrades manage to chase the attackers of the castle away and force them to surrender.

William and Harold bond and celebrate their victory together. At this point Harold pledges an oath of fealty to support William in securing the English throne.

Harold leaves for home and returns to the now sick and dying King Edward. However, the King does not name William as his successor but instead chooses Harold.

This puts Harold in a really bad spot; he already swore his oath of allegiance to William, but King is hard to deny, so he accepts.

King Edward is buried in Westminster Abbey (just consecrated in 1065) in January of 1066, and Harold is crowned the King of England.

Not long after his coronation a unique event occurs that is recorded in the tapestry. The text describes a "hairy star" that streaked across the sky. The star was, as we know now, an appearance of Halley's Comet.

The unusual sighting upsets everyone, including Harold, because almost all seemingly unnatural occurrences in the Middle Ages were interpreted as warnings of impending doom.

On the other side of the channel in Normandy, William hears that he has been betrayed by Harold and vows to amass his armies and invade England.

The Norman invasion force consisted of approximately 7000 men. The invaders reach English soil unopposed. Meanwhile, Harold is involved in a battle with another contender for the throne of England, the Norwegian Harald Hardraada, whom he defeats, but the Norwegians have weakened the English forces.

William, while waiting for the battle to commence, builds fortifications and burns English villages.

The battle final battle took place October 14, 1066, about 65 miles from London. Harold had forced his troops to march all night to get there in three days, which further exhausted his troops.

Both armies were evenly matched but as the day wore on, the English begin to lose strength. Finally William, riding with his knights, moved in and attacked. Harold is struck in the eye by an arrow and dies and the Normans are victorious.

That is the end of the story as it is depicted on the Bayeux Tapestry.

William of Normandy is crowned King of England, Christmas Day, 1066 at Westminster Abbey; after which he is known as William the Conqueror. He ruled England and Normandy until his death in 1087.

The man who may have commissioned the tapestry was Bishop Odo of Bayeux. He was William's the Conqueror's half-brother and his cathedral in Bayeux was consecrated in 1077. It is likely that the tapestry was done to celebrate both William's victory at Hastings and the completion of Odo's cathedral. The length of the linen further suggests it might have intended to serve as decoration in the cathedral.

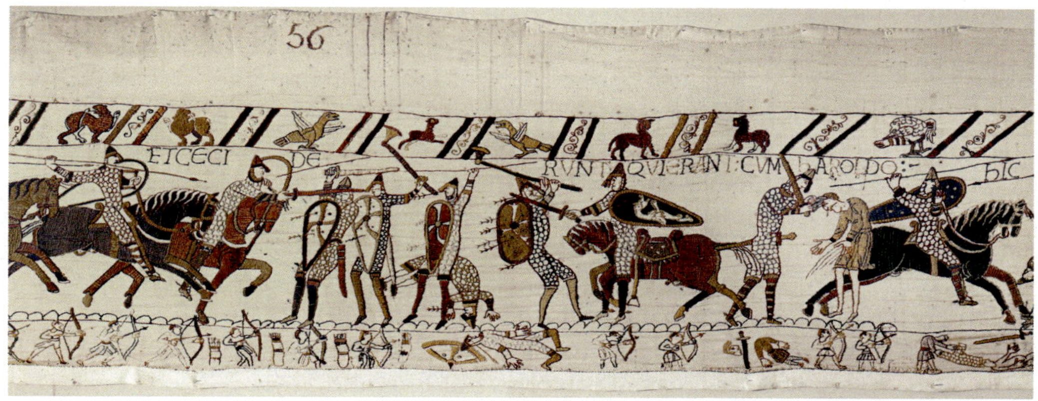


**10-3:** Bayeux Tapestry, detail, 1070–1080, embroidered wool on linen, 1′8″ height, 230′ length, Bayeux Cathedral, France.

The work proves to be not only an exceptional masterpiece of embroidery, and therefore Romanesque art, but also an amazingly detailed and illustrated historical record of a contemporary event.

## St. Etienne

Just after the Battle of Hastings, in 1067, William commissioned the building of an exceptional church dedicated to St. Etienne (St. Stephen). The church was built in the Norman capital city of Caen, France.

While the façade of the building shows influences from both Carolingian and Ottonian architecture, it also shows new and influential elements.

Immediately evident are the three-story elevation and triple portals. Also remarkable are the four huge vertical stone buttresses. These buttresses run the entire height of the façade, dividing it neatly into three vertical sections or bays. These vertical sections then neatly correspond to the interior nave and side aisles. The triple doors, with the largest of the three at the center, provide access to each section.

The towers, added above the two lateral bays, are also neatly divided into three sections, so that each section reveals greater piercing as it progresses upward. (Note that the spires at the very top are later Gothic additions)

The whole façade is neatly worked out into a complex and yet highly organized arrangement of tripartite divisions of mass and space. There are three stories, each divided into three parts, and there are three portals.

The central section of the second and third stories is lighted by three windows, and finally the towers are divided into three stories.

A remarkable feature of the interior is the way that the verticality of the nave is underscored by the use of massive compound piers, that extend the full height of the three-story elevation.

The whole interior is divided and defined by enormous piers which serve to reinforce the solidity and verticality of the space.

There is also a use of pilasters on alternate piers that help to create a subtle rhythmic movement down the nave.

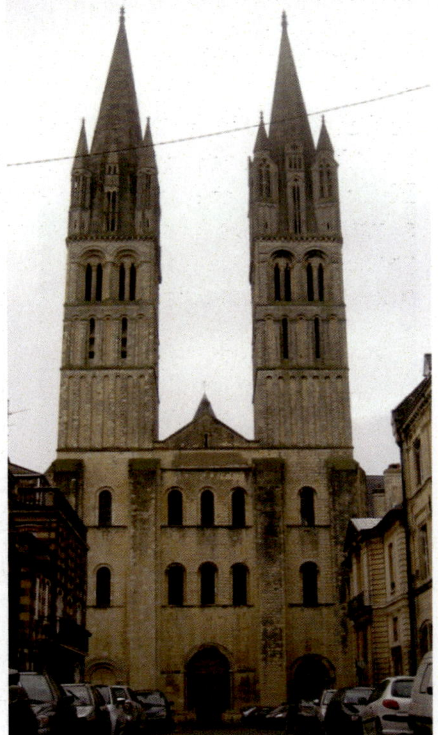

**10-4:** St. Etienne, West façade, begun 1067, Caen, France.

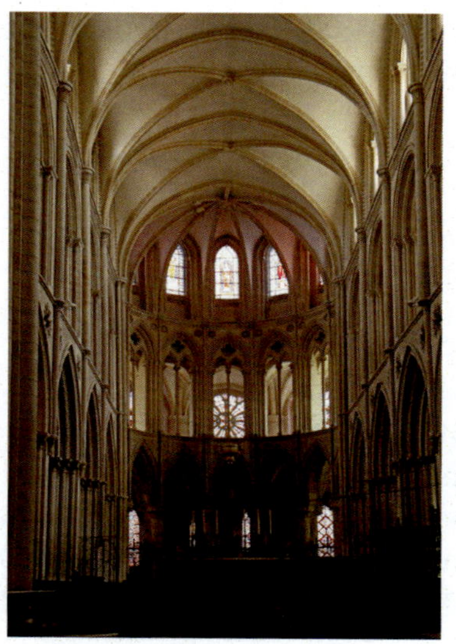

**10-5:** St. Etienne, interior, begun 1067, Caen, France.

To achieve this verticality, it should be noted that the walls had to be incredibly thick to support the weight. Yet, these heavy walls support a clerestory that is large enough to let in a remarkable amount of light; the result is a massive masonry structure that accomplishes a remarkable lightness in terms of actual light and sensation.

An intriguing feature of the interior nave is the floor tomb of William the Conqueror who was buried here in 1087.

His tomb slab reads: *"Here is buried the invincible William the Conqueror, Duke of Normandy and King of England, creator of this church, who died in the year 1087."*

The three-part divisions, on the interior and exterior, and the two towers on the façade at St. Etienne, were very influential and became the standard for almost all later French Gothic churches.

Although the use of stone masonry, three part divisions, and groin vaulting is the norm for many Romanesque churches, and many churches share a number of common traits, it should be remembered that there is a great deal of regional diversity in Romanesque architecture.

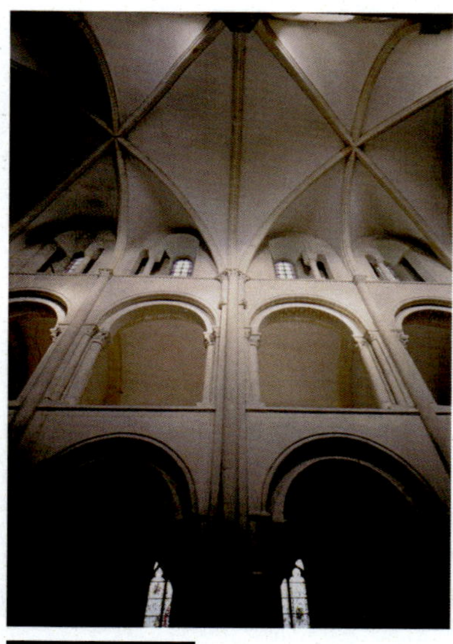

**10-6:** St. Etienne, interior, begun 1067, Caen, France.

## Pilgrimage Road Churches

In 1070 the counts of the city of Toulouse, France began construction on an enormous church in honor of the city's first Bishop, Saint Saturninus, or Saint Sernin.

The need for the church and its impressive size, and the funds to build it, were due in part to the location of the city of Toulouse as an important stop on the route of pilgrims traveling from the North and East, toward Santiago de Compostela in Spain. The massive structure measures roughly 377 feet long, 209 feet wide, and 69 feet tall in the nave.

Saint Sernin is a *pilgrimage road* church; literally a church built on the road of a pilgrimage route.

Due to its location and the masses of people visiting the church, several new design innovations were incorporated into the plan.

First, the expansion and lengthening of the nave, done in order to hold not only the city's residents, but also the numerous traveling pilgrims. Another innovation here is the doubling of the side aisles, so instead of one on either side there are two; this feature helps accomodate crowds and provides an efficient movement of visitors through the church.

The transept arm also includes an aisle that is really an extension of the ambulatory. The apse end of the church, and even the east end of the transept, now include radiating chapels. Radiating chapels are small chapels designed for the display of relics that open directly onto the ambulatory and the transept.

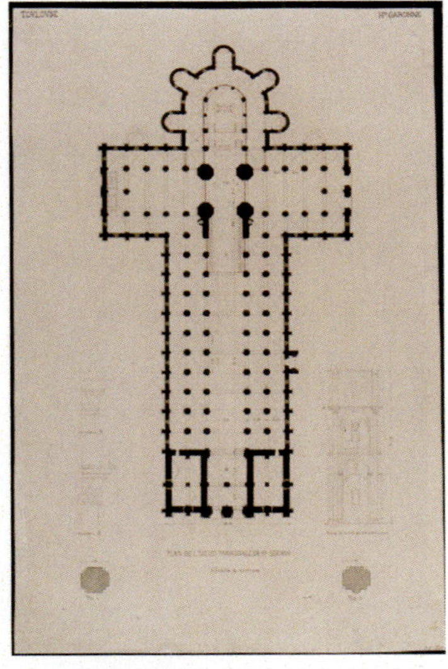

**10-7:** Plan of Saint Sernin, begun c. 1070, Toulouse, France.

Two towers were planned for the west façade that were never completed. The crossing tower is a later Gothic addition.

The entire plan of the church is driven by the sheer numbers of pilgrims and the desire to have them enter and move freely within the church and yet not disturb any liturgical processions or the mass.

The interior is extremely organized and geometrically arranged. Similar to St. Michael's at Hildesheim, the crossing square is used as the basic unit of measure. Each nave bay is one-half the crossing-square and each aisle bay is one-quarter the crossing-square.

St. Sernin also incorporates two types of vaulting: groin vaulting in the aisles and barrel vaulting with transverse arches in the nave. The two-story elevation (nave arcade and tribune) at St. Sernin includes a tribune or gallery. A tribune is a gallery or open arcade that overlooks the nave of a church.

The rational, organized, geometric, large, and vertically emphasized pilgrimage church was highly influential for many other Romanesque and later Gothic churches.

One of the earliest securely attributed and dated large-scale Romanesque sculptural relief panels comes from St. Sernin. An inscription dates the work to 1096 and it is signed by *Bernardus Gelduinus*. The same name appears inscribed on the high altar.

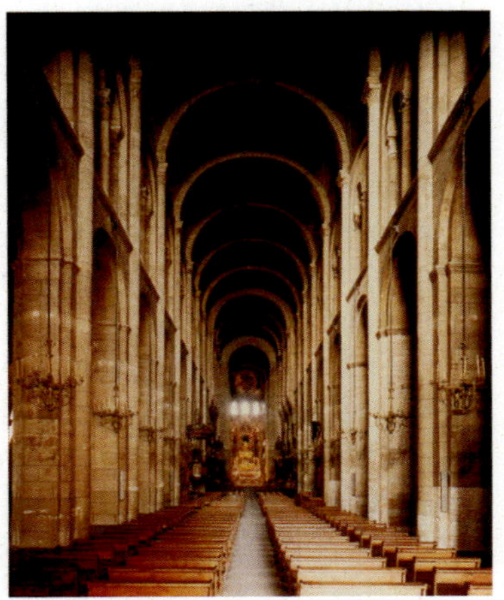

**10-8:** Saint Sernin, interior, central nave, begun c. 1070, Toulouse, France.

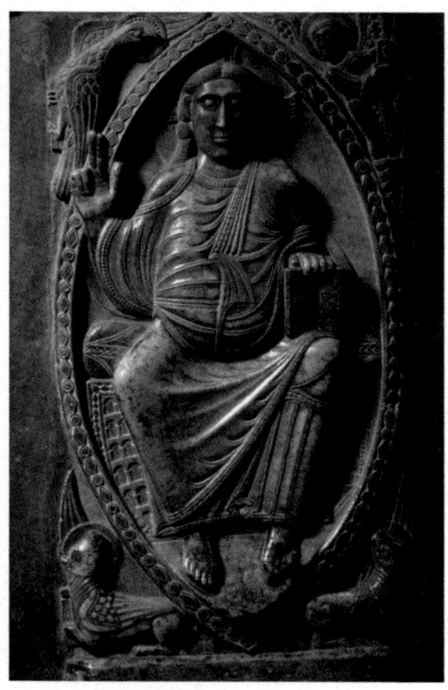

**10-9:** Bernardus Gelduinus, Christ in Majesty, marble relief, ambulatory of St. Sernin, 1096 CE, 4′2″.

This relief of Christ in Majesty was originally part of a group of at least seven marble relief slabs that depicted angels, apostles, and Christ. It is unclear exactly where the original reliefs were located but today they are displayed in the ambulatory.

The relief depicts Christ, seated on a throne, with his right hand raised in blessing and his left hand holding an open book. The book is inscribed with the Latin phrase *Pax Vobis*, peace be with you. The figure is encircled in a great almond-shaped mandorla, from which Christ's blessing hand just slightly overlaps; a hint that we are to read Christ as inside yet capable of extending beyond his mandorla.

The mandorla is surrounded at the four corners by the symbols of the Evangelists; John and Matthew at the top and Luke and Mark at the bottom.

The work is large and represents a shift from small-scale works to works that reflect the size of the new pilgrimage road churches. The relief itself is highly polished and deeply incised, notice how precise and finely cut the lines of Christ's robes and the frame are delineated.

Despite some similarities with earlier works, this relief represents a significant move toward incorporating monumental stone sculpture in the decoration of Christian churches.

## The Revival of Monumental Sculpture

In conjunction with the great wave of church building that occurred during the Romanesque period, there was also a revival of architectural sculpture.

After the fall of the Roman Empire, large-scale stone sculpture had almost totally disappeared.

The new Romanesque churches and their huge facades seemed to insist on equally large stone ornamentation and sculpture. The sculpture, however, was not purely decorative, but rather used to present, in monumental scale, the essential elements of Christian doctrine.

Much of Romanesque sculpture was placed on the entrance façade of the church in order to excite the piety and imagination of the worshippers as they entered.

The typical Romanesque portal, or doorway, included sculptural decoration, though the decoration tended to be found not on the door itself (which was often made of wood) but rather around the door in the archivolts and tympanum. More importantly it is **relief** sculpture, *not* free standing statuary, a kind still associated with pagan idol worship.

The general construction or style of the entrance doorway to the church remained fairly constant.

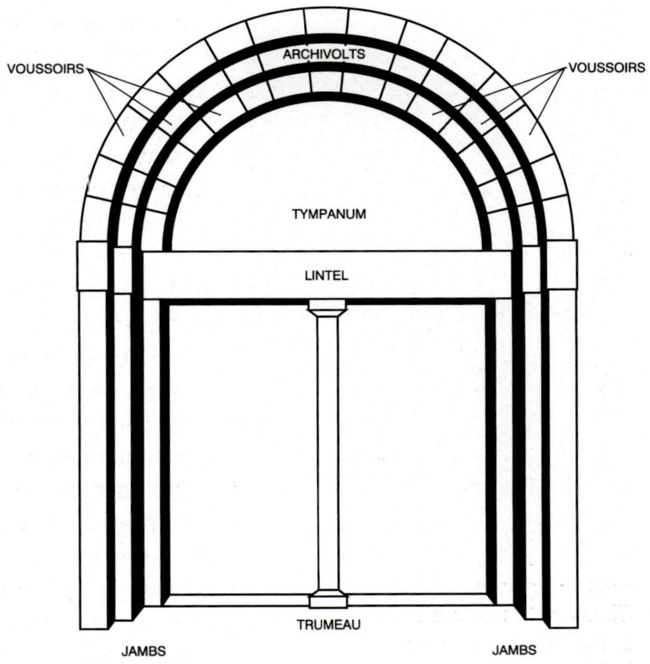


**10-10:** Plan: Romanesque church portal.

## The Major Components of the Romanesque Portal are:

**Voussoirs**: A voussoir is a wedge-shaped block used in the construction of a true arch. The central voussoir, at the apex of the arch, is the keystone; it sets the arch. Together they form the archivolts.

**Archivolts**: Archivolts are the continuous molding or framing around an arch; often found in concentric bands framing the tympanum.

**Tympanum**: The tympanum is a semicircular space or lunette that is located above the door and is bounded by the archivolts and the lintel.

**Lintel:** The lintel is the horizontal beam above the doorway.

**Trumeau:** The trumeau is the pillar or central post in the middle of a doorway that supports the lintel.

**Jambs:** Jambs are the side posts of a doorway.

Three of the best preserved and most dramatic sculptural relief portal programs are found on French Romanesque churches in Southern and Eastern France; they are St. Pierre in Moissac, St. Lazare in Autun and La Madeleine in Vezelay.

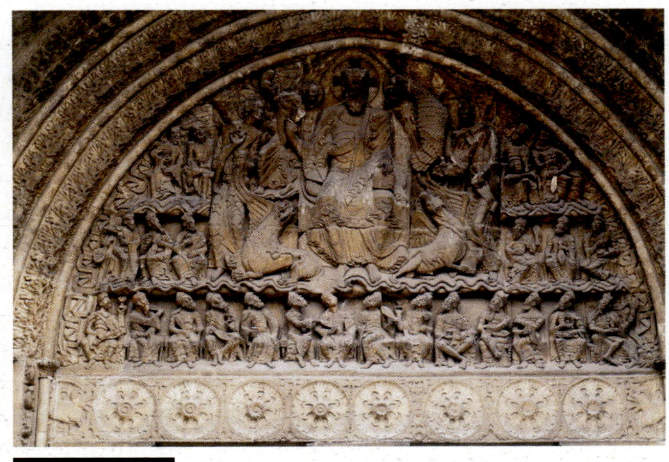

**10-11:** Second Coming of Christ, South Portal, Saint Pierre at Moissac, France, c. 1115–1135.

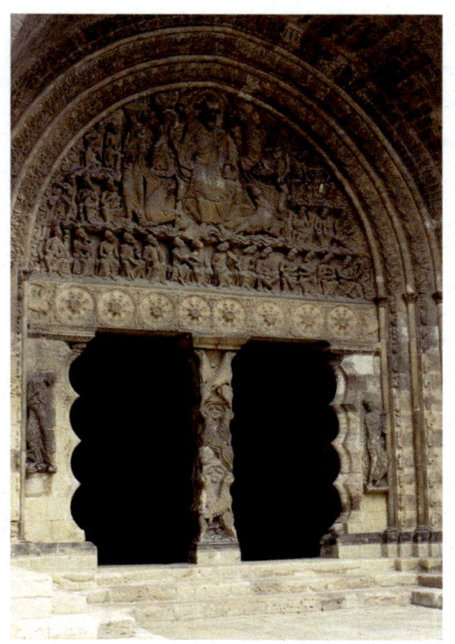

**10-12:** Saint Pierre, South portal, Moissac, France, c. 1115–1135.

The church of St. Pierre at Moissac, a Cluniac monastery, is located on a pilgrimage route road near Toulouse, France. The Cluniac order was a powerful group of Benedictines centered at the abbey of Cluny, one of the largest churches in Western Europe (mostly destroyed in the French Revolution).

St. Pierre is considered one of the most important centers of Romanesque art, and one of the most influential, based in part on the extensive sculptural program on the portals and in the cloister.

The high relief sculpture on the south portal, which faces the town square, is impressive. Not only is the tympanum decorated but also the lintel, trumeau, archivolts, and jambs, creating a kind of elaborate carved portal program.

The subject of the tympanum is a scene described in the Book of Revelations, the last book of the *New Testament*. (Revelations 4:4)

Christ, who is bearded and crowned, sits enthroned at the center, surrounded by two angels who hold scrolls, and the four winged-evangelists symbols holding books.

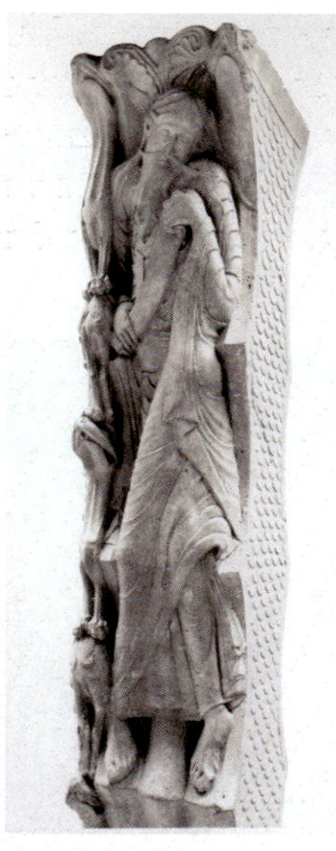

**10-13:** Trumeau, Lions and Old Testament Prophet Jeremiah, marble, Saint Pierre at Moissac, France, c. 1115–1135 6′.

On either side of the tympanum and on the lintel, are the figures of the twenty-four crowned elders, some holding musical instruments and other objects. There are four in the top register, six in the second register, and fourteen along the bottom; all turn their heads to face Christ.

The Book of Revelations nowhere specifically identifies who the twenty-four elders represent. One possible view is that they represent the twelve tribes of Israel plus the twelve apostles.

The choice of subject matter for the tympanum is important as a reminder to the faithful visitor of the end of days and a not-so gentle prompting to consider where and in what state one might find oneself when that event becomes manifest.

On the face of the trumeau are three pairs of criss-crossed roaring lions, stacked one pair above the other. The image is striking and serves not only to create an impressive repetitive pattern on the surface, but to create a pillar of ferocious beasts, to shock visitors who enter the door on either side. Lions can have multiple significances and can signify strength, majesty, fortitude, and watchfulness, or conversely can be interpreted as encapsulated dark forces contained and now subservient to the church.

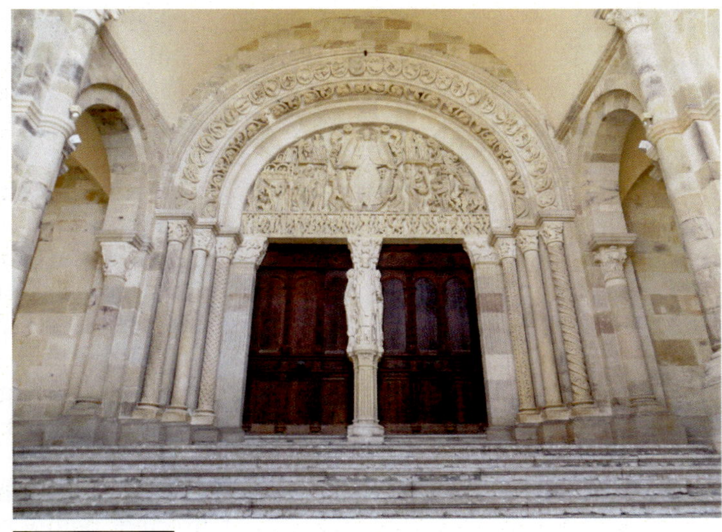

**10-14:** Last Judgment, Gislebertus, Saint Lazare, Autun, France, 1120–1135 CE, marble, 21′ at base.

On either side of the trumeau are representations of *Old Testament* prophets Jeremiah and John the Baptist, though not all scholars agree with those identifications.

Both figures are wildly exaggerated and elongated in order to fill the columnar space. They are also set high up so that they appear to look down on the viewer as he passes.

On the right face is the figure of Jeremiah, who has a long beard and almond-shaped eyes, and holds an unfurled scroll. Like the lions on the front, he stands, almost tip-toed, in a crossed-leg position. His body is extremely elongated in relation to the size of his small head and hands.

Projecting laterally and framing the door, is an exotic scalloped edge frame. This scalloped motif may have been an imported Islamic influence, reflecting the churches position as a pilgrimage road church, and revealing cross-cultural influences. Sculpted relief figures of St. Peter, on the left, and Isaiah, on the right, decorate the flat surface of the scalloped frame. Even the lintel is richly decorated with a repeating pattern of carved rosettes.

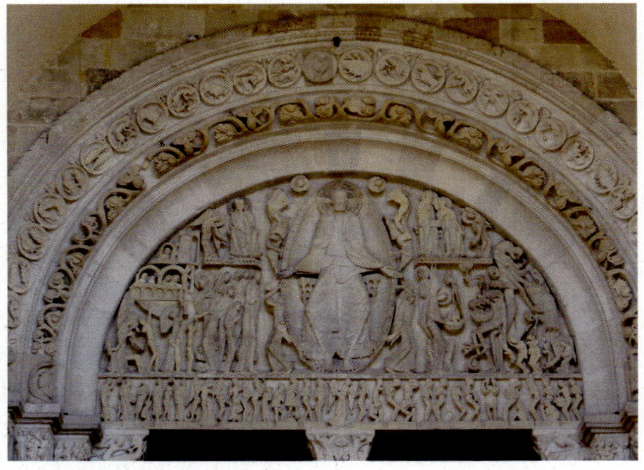

**10-15:** Last Judgment, Tympanum, detail, Gislebertus, 1120–1135, Saint Lazare, Autun, France.

Another important Cluniac church, in the Burgundy region of France, has a similarly impressive carved tympanum, depicting not the arrival of Christ at the second coming, but the Last Judgment.

In 1132 the Cathedral of St. Lazare at Autun, dedicated to a 5th century French Bishop, was consecrated. It reveals an impressive sculptural program like that at Moissac, though here, at St. Lazare, the sculptors name is preserved.

The director of the sculptural program at St. Lazare was a man named Gislebertus, and it is

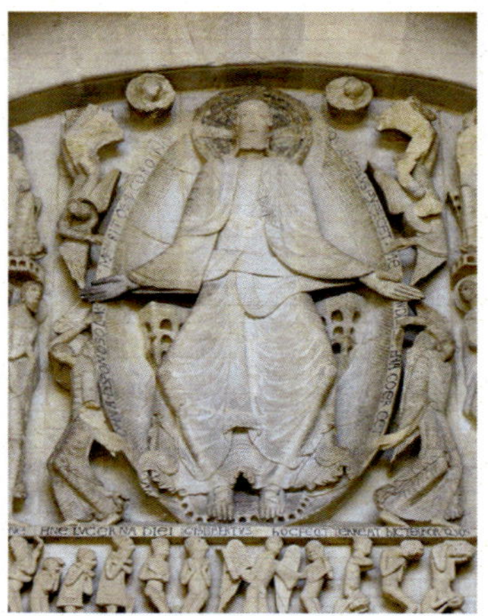

**10-16:** Last Judgment, Tympanum, detail of Christ, Gislebertus, 1120–1135, Saint Lazare, Autun, France.

believed that he either carved or directed the carving of most of the sculptural work done at Autun, between 1120 and 1135. Gislebertus' name is the first sculptor's name ever discovered on any stone work from the Romanesque period.

The tympanum of the central portal of the west façade of Saint Lazare is an expressive and unforgettable image of the Last Judgment signed by the artist.

At the center, larger than any of the other figures, is Christ, encompassed in a mandorla. Attenuated and angular angels support the mandorla on either side. Here, in his role as Judge, Christ separates the saved from the damned; on his right are the saved and on his left are the damned.

On Christ's right, at the top, is an image of the Virgin Mary enthroned. Below her are the elongated figures of the saved, and further to the right is the image of an angel boosting a soul into heaven.

In the center section on Christ's left, are angels weighing souls (psychostasis). An angel and a demon stand on either side of a large scale and physically battle for the souls in the scale. This Christian battle for a soul is called a psychomachia.

The decoration in the lintel depicts a sword-wielding angel who seems to direct the traffic of souls; those sent to the right are saved and those to the left are dammed. A figure who has just been directed to hell looks imploring back at the angel in total despair.

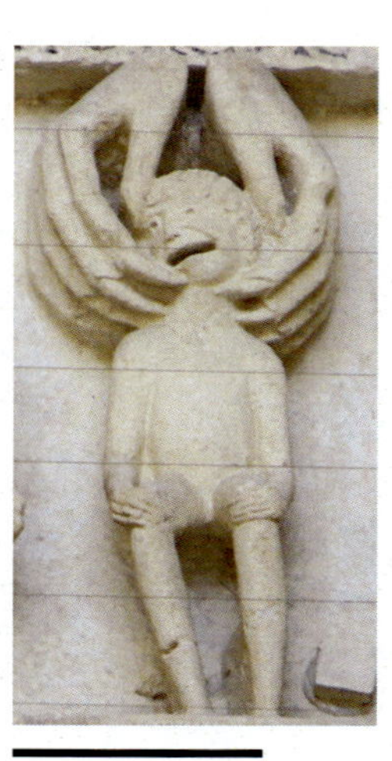

**10-17:** Last Judgment, Tympanum, detail of hands, Gislebertus, 1120–1135, Saint Lazare, Autun, France.

Perhaps the most powerful of all the images on the lintel is a scene of two incorporeal hands clenched around a tiny terrified figure that has been damned.

The images on the portal are meant to frighten worshippers. They are intended to visualize a lasting impression of the terror of hell to which one will be resigned if one does not follow the right path.

Just in case the image is not clear enough, the inscription on the damned side of the lintel reads "May this terror frighten those who are bound by worldly error, for the horror of these images here in this manner truly depict what will be."

Directly beneath the feet of Christ is the name of the sculptor Gislebertus and the words *hoc fecit* (made this). The inclusion of the artist's name is a testament to the growing prestige and pride in accomplishment of Romanesque artists and perhaps a reflection of Gislebertus' personal desire to be remembered.

The tympanum is surrounded above by two deeply-carved archivolts. The larger outer archivolt is decorated with thirty-one medallions representing the Zodiac, seasons, and labors of the months. The inner archivolt is decorated with scrolling foliage.

The trumeau is a 19th century reconstruction of the lost original, which was decorated with the figures of the Virgin Mary, Martha, and Lazarus.

On the interior of the Cathedral, Gislebertus carved over sixty historiated column capitals. Historiated capitals are capitals that have been sculpted to incorporate a narrative scene; much like a historiated initial in manuscript decoration. The capitals are decorated with scenes from the Old and New Testaments, and lives of the saints, including subjects such as the Adoration of the Magi, and the suicide of Judas.

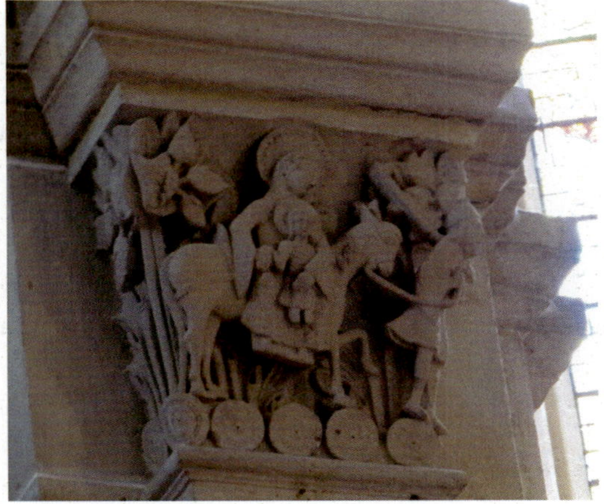

**10-18:** The Flight into Egypt, Nave capital, marble, Gislebertus, Saint Lazare, Autun, France, 1120–1135.

The capital of the Flight into Egypt depicts the Virgin Mary, wearing a large halo and elaborately-sleeved garment, seated side-saddle on the back of a donkey. She holds the Christ child in front of her with one arm protectively in front of him. An aged and bearded Joseph leads the donkey.

Another impressive Cluniac Romanesque church with remarkable sculpture is the basilica of Saint Mary Magdalene ( La Madeleine) in Vezelay, France.

La Madeleine was a pilgrimage church in its own right, holding the relics of St. Mary Magdalene to whom it is dedicated. The church was also situated at the beginning of one of the four major routes through France for pilgrims going to Santiago de Compostela.

The church is of great importance for the Crusades, because it is from this church that in 1146 St. Bernard of Clairvaux preached for the Second Crusade, It is also from this church that in 1190 King Richard I. the Lion-hearted, of England departed for the Third Crusade.

It should not be surprising, then, that the tympanum sculpture of the central portal of the narthex at Vezelay depicts the Pentecost and the Mission of the Apostles. (The description of the event is found in the Acts of the Apostles 2: 1-42.) According to scripture, the Pentecost occurred on the 7th Sunday after

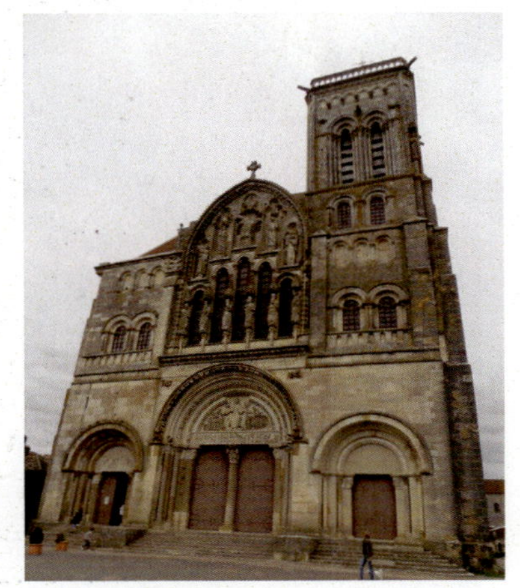

**10-19:** West façade, Saint Marie Madeleine ( La Madeleine), c. 1120–1132, Vezelay, France.

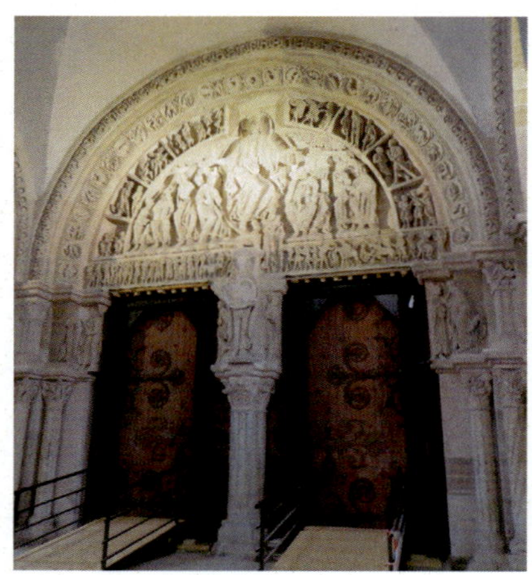

**10-20:** Central Portal, narthex, Saint Marie Madeleine (La Madeleine), c. 1120–1132, Vezelay, France.

Easter (50 days) and is the event at which the Holy Spirit descended to the apostles, the Virgin Mary, and others, and gave them the ability to speak all the languages of the world. This ability to speak all languages was given in part so that Christ's followers could go out and evangelize to the whole world.

The subject resonates profoundly, considering the church's role as a jumping off point for the crusades.

At the center of the tympanum, like at Autun, is a monumental vertical image of Christ, in a mandorla much larger than any other figure. Here the elongated figure of Christ's lower half is arranged into a sort of zig-zag pattern while the upper half remains frontal and looks directly outward.

Rays of light emanate from both of Christ's hands over the heads of the apostles. The apostles sit, holding books, waiting to receive the divine inspiration and knowledge that will take them on their missions to convert the heathen masses.

Those to whom the apostles will spread the word, the heathens, are shown in the lintel and in the eight compartments in the archivolt that encapsulates the central image. The figures depicted are intended to represent the heathens, the deformed or sick, and the faithless.

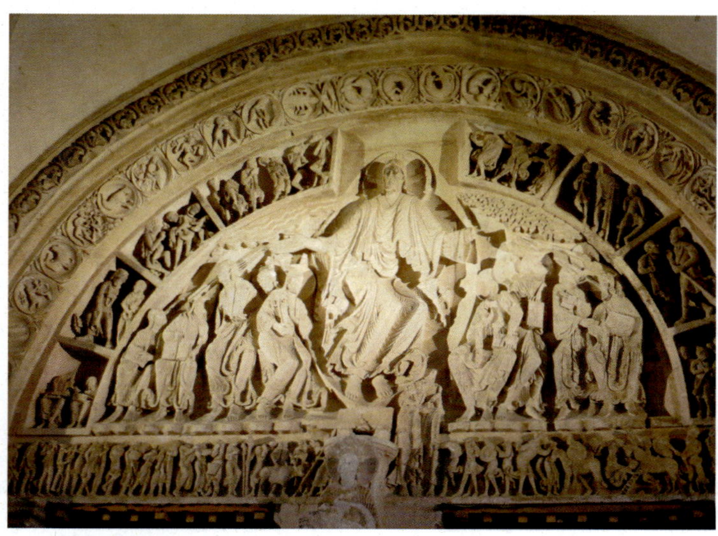

**10-21:** Pentecost and Mission to Apostles, Tympanum, center portal in narthex, La Madeleine, Vezelay, c. 1120–1132.

In the lintel we see an image of the race of pygmies who were so small that they needed ladders to reach the saddles of their horses. On the other side are images of the lame and the blind.

In the compartments above we see images of dog-faced people—creatures with the body of a man and the head of a dog. Also here are images of the pig-snouted peoples, and the peoples whose hair is made of fire. The figures represent those who have clearly been damned or forgotten by God, but through whose mercy will surely be cured or delivered of their hideous afflictions.

As in the other portals, worshippers are reminded that through Christ and the church all will be saved.

The outer most archivolt depicts the signs of the Zodiac, and the labors, and seasons; a program of images intended to represent the passage of time.

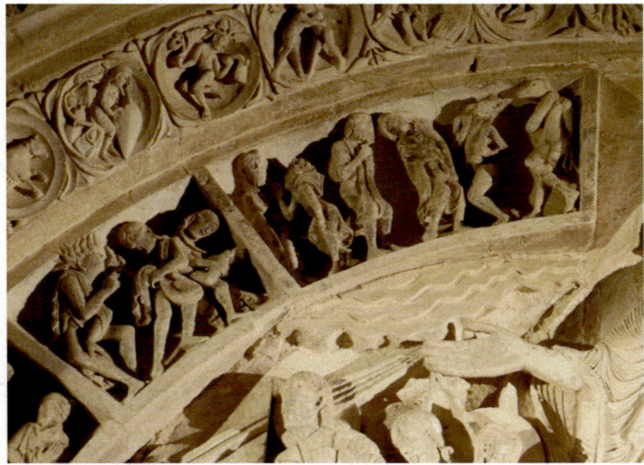

**10-22:** Tympanum compartment, detail, central portal, narthex, Saint Marie Madeleine (La Madeleine), c. 1120–1132, Vezelay, France.

It is important to make the connection here between the subject of the tympanum, and the purpose of the church. It is from this church that men set out in order to do just what the apostles had been charged to do: to convert the heathen masses. The Crusades are here visually equated with a second mission of the apostles, acknowledged and divined by God.

The revival of stone carving, so prominent in the portals and column capitals of Romanesque churches, is one of the hallmarks of the Romanesque period. These sculptures were created for the faithful worshipers, visitors, travelers, and pilgrims who were a mostly illiterate audience. The images served as a visual Bible for the poor, and the images were intended to be clear, dramatic, and easily understood; they were also, as we have seen, cautionary.

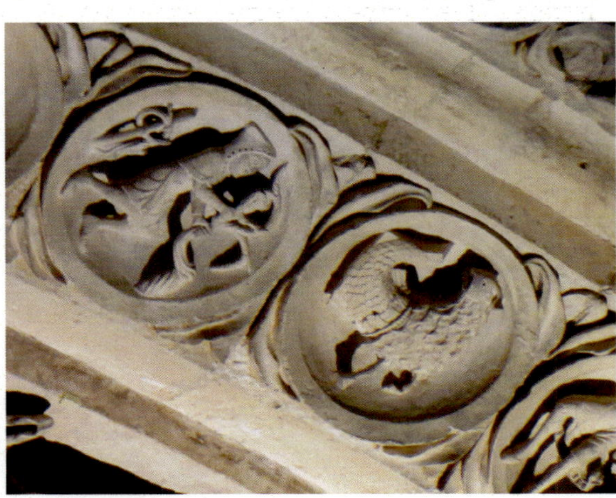

**10-23:** Archivolt, detail, central portal, narthex, Saint Marie Madeleine (La Madeleine), c. 1120–1132, Vezelay, France.

Romanesque stone portals, rather than paintings, frescoes, mosaics, or manuscript illuminations from the period, reached a wider audience and were therefore more impactful. The desire to decorate and elaborate the portals of churches will continue and expand in the Gothic period into full-grown sculptural portal programs.

Name ______________________________ Date ____________

Chapter 10

# Romanesque Art and Architecture

1. What event does the Bayeux tapestry depict?

2. What does the term "Romanesque" refer to?

3. What does the intersection of two barrel vaults create?

4. What is the subject of the west tympanum at the Autun Cathedral?

5. Who was Gelduinus? With what church is he associated?

6. What is the term for a central post separating a doorway at the entrance of a cathedral?

7. What features distinguish "pilgrimage churches" from other church structures?

8. To whom is the church at Vezelay dedicated? Why?

9. What distinguishes Saint Denis from other churches at the time?

10. What architectural convention made the use of large stainedglass windows possible?

# Photo Credits

**Chapter 1**

Prehistoric sites in Western Europe Map: © Kendall Hunt Publishing Company

**1-1:** De Agostini Picture Library/E. Lessing/The Bridgeman Art Library

**1-2:** Erich Lessing/Art Resource, NY

**1-3:** Musee des Antiquites Nationales, St. Germain-en-Laye, France/Giraudon/The Bridgeman Art Library

**1-4:** Album/Art Resource, NY

**1-5:** Caves of Lascaux, Dordogne, France/The Bridgeman Art Library

**1-6:** Caves of Lascaux, Dordogne, France/The Bridgeman Art Library

**1-7:** Ancient Art and Architecture Collection Ltd./The Bridgeman Art Library

**1-8:** © Mauricio Abreu/JAI/Corbis

**1-9:** Image © Vladislav Gajic, 2013. Used under license from Shutterstock, Inc.

**1-10:** Image © Bufo, 2013. Used under license from Shutterstock, Inc.

**Chapter 2**

The ancient Near East Map: © Kendall Hunt Publishing Company

**2-1:** © barbulat/Fotolia

**2-2:** Iraq Museum, Baghdad/Ancient Art and Architecture Collection Ltd./The Bridgeman Art Library

**2-3:** Erich Lessing/Art Resource, NY

**2-4:** Erich Lessing/Art Resource, NY

**2-5:** Image © Kamira, 2013. Used under license from Shutterstock, Inc.

**2-6:** Universal History Archive/UIG/The Bridgeman Art Library

**2-7:** Courtesy of the Penn Museum, image #150283

**2-8:** Courtesy of the Penn Museum, image #B17694.

**2-9:** © The Trustees of the British Museum/Art Resource, NY

**2-10:** De Agostini Picture Library/G. Dagli Orti/The Bridgeman Art Library

**2-11a:** Image © jsp, 2013. Used under license from Shutterstock, Inc.

**2-11b:** Louvre, Paris, France/Giraudon/The Bridgeman Art Library

**2-12:** Louvre Museum. Paris. France./Photo © Tarker/The Bridgeman Art Library

**2-13:** Louvre Museum. Paris. France./Photo © Tarker/The Bridgeman Art Library

**2-14:** Image © khd, 2013. Used under license from Shutterstock, Inc.

**2-15a:** Pergamon Museum./Universal History Archive/UIG/The Bridgeman Art Library

**2-15b:** Image © mtr, 2013. Used under license from Shutterstock, Inc.

**2-16:** Image © arazu, 2013. Used under license from Shutterstock, Inc.
**2-17:** Image © javarman, 2013. Used under license from Shutterstock, Inc.

**Chapter 3**
Ancient Egypt Map: © Kendall Hunt Publishing Company
**3-1:** Egyptian National Museum, Cairo, Egypt/The Bridgeman Art Library
**3-2:** Egyptian National Museum, Cairo, Egypt/The Bridgeman Art Library
**3-3:** Werner Forman Archive/The Bridgeman Art Library
**3-4:** Photos.com
**3-5:** Image © jsp, 2013. Used under license from Shutterstock, Inc.
**3-6:** Image © Nickolay Vinokurov, 2013. Used under license from Shutterstock, Inc.
**3-7:** Image © Lisa S., 2013. Used under license from Shutterstock, Inc.
**3-8:** Image © Antony McAulay, 2013. Used under license from Shutterstock, Inc.
**3-9:** Image © fstockfoto, 2013. Used under license from Shutterstock, Inc.
**3-10:** Egyptian National Museum, Cairo, Egypt/Giraudon/The Bridgeman Art Library
**3-11:** De Agostini Picture Library/The Bridgeman Art Library
**3-12:** Photos.com
**3-13:** Egyptian National Museum, Cairo, Egypt/The Bridgeman Art Library
**3-14:** Album/Art Resource, NY
**3-15:** Image copyright © The Metropolitan Museum of Art. Image Source: Art Resource, NY
**3-16:** Universal History Archive/UIG/The Bridgeman Art Library
**3-17:** Erich Lessing/Art Resource, NY
**3-18:** © The Trustees of the British Museum/Art Resource, NY
**3-19:** Deir El-Bahri, Thebes, Egypt/The Bridgeman Art Library
**3-20:** © Francis G. Mayer/Corbis
**3-21:** Werner Forman Archive/The Bridgeman Art Library
**3-22:** British Museum, London, UK/The Bridgeman Art Library
**3-23:** Werner Forman Archive/The Bridgeman Art Library
**3-24:** Egyptian National Museum, Cairo, Egypt/Ancient Art and Architecture Collection Ltd./The Bridgeman Art Library
**3-25:** Image © tkachuk, 2013. Used under license from Shutterstock, Inc.
**3-26:** © CULTNAT, Dist. RMN-GP/Art Resource, NY
**3-27:** © Vanni Archive/Art Resource, NY
**3-28:** Egyptian National Museum, Cairo, Egypt/Bildarchiv Steffens/The Bridgeman Art Library
**3-29:** Image © bumihills, 2013. Used under license from Shutterstock, Inc.
**3-30:** British Museum, London, UK/The Bridgeman Art Library

**Chapter 4**
Ancient Aegean Map: © Kendall Hunt Publishing Company
**4-1:** Vanni/Art Resource, NY
**4-2:** De Agostini Picture Library/G. Nimatallah/The Bridgeman Art Library

**4-3:** Ancient Art and Architecture Collection Ltd./The Bridgeman Art Library
**4-4:** Knossos, Crete/The Bridgeman Art Library
**4-5:** Courtesy of Margaret Zaho
**4-6:** De Agostini Picture Library/G. Nimatallah/The Bridgeman Art Library
**4-7:** ArchaeologicalMuseumofHeraklion,Crete,Greece/BernardCox/TheBridgeman Art Library
**4-8:** Archaeological Museum of Heraklion, Crete, Greece/Giraudon/The Bridgeman Art Library
**4-9:** Scala/Art Resource, NY
**4-10:** De Agostini Picture Library/G. Dagli Orti/The Bridgeman Art Library
**4-11:** Archaeological Museum of Heraklion, Crete, Greece/Giraudon/The Bridgeman Art Library
**4-12:** Courtesy of Margaret Zaho
**4-13:** Courtesy of Margaret Zaho
**4-14:** Courtesy of Margaret Zaho
**4-15:** Courtesy of Margaret Zaho
**4-16:** Courtesy of Margaret Zaho
**4-17:** Vanni/Art Resource, NY

**Chapter 5**

Ancient Greece and the Mediterranean Map: © Kendall Hunt Publishing Company
**5-1:** Metropolitan Museum of Art. New York. United States./Photo © Tarker/The Bridgeman Art Library
**5-2:** Image copyright © The Metropolitan Museum of Art. Image source: Art Resource, NY
**5-3:** De Agostini Picture Library/G. Nimatallah/The Bridgeman Art Library
**5-4:** Louvre, Paris, France/Giraudon/The Bridgeman Art Library
**5-5:** Image © Vladimir Korostyshevskiy, 2013. Used under license from Shutterstock, Inc.
**5-6:** De Agostini Picture Library/G. Dagli Orti/The Bridgeman Art Library
**5-7:** De Agostini Picture Library/The Bridgeman Art Library
**5-8:** Nimatallah/Art Resource, NY
**5-9:** Courtesy of Eric Robbins
**5-10:** Courtesy of Eric Robbins
**5-11:** Photos.com
**5-12:** Erich Lessing/Art Resource, NY
**5-13:** De Agostini Picture Library/G. Nimatallah/The Bridgeman Art Library
**5-14:** Museo Archeologico, Florence, Italy/Alinari/The Bridgeman Art Library
**5-15:** De Agostini Picture Library/The Bridgeman Art Library
**5-16:** Louvre, Paris, France/Peter Willi/The Bridgeman Art Library
**5-17:** De Agostini Picture Library/The Bridgeman Art Library
**5-18:** Courtesy of Margaret Zaho

**5-19:** Olympia Archaeological Museum. Greece./Photo © Tarker/The Bridgeman Art Library
**5-20:** Archaeological Museum, Olympia, Archaia, Greece/© Paul Maeyaert/The Bridge Art Library
**5-21:** Olympia Archaeological Museum, Greece/Photo © Tarker/The Bridgeman Art Libary
**5-22:** Decoration of the Temple of Zeus in the Sanctuary of Olympia Greece/Photo © Tarker/The Bridgeman Art Library
**5-23:** De Agostini Picture Library/ G. Dagli Orti/The Bridgeman Art Library
**5-24:** Museo Archeologico Nazionale, Reggio de Calabria, Italy/Alinari/The Bridgeman Art Library
**5-25:** Scala/Art Resource, NY
**5-26:** De Agostini Picture Library/G. Nimatallah/The Bridgeman Art Library
**5-27:** Image © abxyz, 2013. Used under the license from Shutterstock, Inc.
**5-28:** Private Collection/De Agostini Picture Library/The Bridgeman Art Library
**5-29:** Courtesy of Margaret Zaho.
**5-30:** Copyright © Museum of Fine Arts, Boston.
**5-31:** Courtesy of Eric Robbins
**5-32:** Album/Art Resource, NY
**5-33:** Scala/Art Resource, NY
**5-34:** De Agostini Picture Library/G. Nimatallah/The Bridgeman Art Library
**5-35:** Werner Forman Archive/The Bridgeman Art Library
**5-36:** Courtesy of Margaret Zaho
**5-37:** Courtesy of Margaret Zaho
**5-38:** Acropolis Museum, Athens, Greece/The Bridgeman Art Library
**5-39:** Courtesy of Margaret Zaho
**5-40:** Courtesy of Margaret Zaho
**5-41:** De Agostini Picture Library/G. Nimatallah/the Bridgeman Art Library
**5-42:** Scala/Art Resource, NY
**5-43:** © Vanni Archive/Art Resource, NY
**5-44:** Vatican Museums and Galleries, Vatican City/Bildarchiv Steffens/Bildarchiv Steffens/Ralph Rainer Steffens/The Bridgeman Art Library
**5-45:** De Agostini Picture Library/A. Dagli Orti/The Bridgeman Art Library
**5-46:** Universal History Archive/UIG/The Bridgeman Art Library
**5-47:** Museo Archeologico Nazionale, Naples, Italy/Alinari/The Bridgeman Art Library
**5-48:** Museo Archeologico Nazionale, Naples, Italy/Alinari/The Bridgeman Art Library
**5-49a:** © v0v/Fotolia
**5-49b:** © v0v/Fotolia
**5-50:** Image © Slimewoo, 2013. Used under license from Shutterstock, Inc.
**5-51:** Louvre, Paris, France/Giraudon/The Bridgeman Art Library

**5-52:** Museo Nazionale Romano, Rome, Italy/Giraudon/The Bridgeman Art Library
**5-53:** Image © Asier Villafranca, 2013. Used under license from Shutterstock, Inc.

**Chapter 6**

The Roman Empire c. 120 CE. Map: © Kendall Hunt Publishing Company
**6-1:** Musei Capitolini, Rome, Italy/The Bridgeman Art Library
**6-2:** The Art Archive at Art Resource, NY
**6-3:** Palazzo Barberini, Rome, Italy/Alinari/The Bridgeman Art Library
**6-4:** Palazzo Torlonia, Rome, Italy/Alinari/The Bridgeman Art Library
**6-5:** The Art Archive at Art Resource, NY
**6-6:** Image © Asier Villafranca, 2013. Used under license from Shutterstock, Inc.
**6-7:** DEA/G. DAGLI ORTI/Getty Images
**6-8:** © wjarek/Fotolia
**6-9:** © wjarek/Fotolia
**6-10:** Image © Philip Lange, 2013. Used under license from Shutterstock, Inc.
**6-11:** Scala/Art Resource, NY
**6-12:** Carlsberg Glyptotek Museum, Copenhagen, Denmark/Photo © Tarker/The Bridgeman Art Library
**6-13a and b:** Courtesy of Margaret Zaho
**6-14:** Courtesy of Margaret Zaho
**6-15:** Courtesy of Margaret Zaho
**6-16:** Courtesy of Margaret Zaho
**6-17:** De Agostini Picture Library/The Bridgeman Art Library
**6-18:** Courtesy of Margaret Zaho
**6-19 a and b:** Courtesy of Margaret Zaho
**6-20:** Galleria Uffizi, Florence, Italy/Alinari/The Bridgeman Art Library
**6-21:** Courtesy of Margaret Zaho
**6-22:** Courtesy of Margaret Zaho
**6-23:** Courtesy of Margaret Zaho
**6-24:** Courtesy of Margaret Zaho
**6-25:** Courtesy of Margaret Zaho
**6-26:** Courtesy of Margaret Zaho
**6-27:** Image © Ammit Jack, 2013. Used under license from Shutterstock, Inc.
**6-28:** De Agostini Picture Library/G. Dagli Orti/The Bridgeman Art Library
**6-29:** bpk, Berlin/(name of museum)/(name of photographer)/Art Resource, NY
**6-30:** Terme Museum, Rome, Italy/The Bridgeman Art Library
**6-31:** Image © sretco milanovici, 2013. Used under license from Shutterstock, Inc.
**6-32:** Courtesy of Margaret Zaho
**6-33:** Courtesy of Margaret Zaho
**6-34:** Courtesy of Margaret Zaho

**Chapter 7**

Expansion of Christianity c. 250 CE. Map: © Kendall Hunt Publishing Company

**7-1:** Catacombs of Priscilla, Rome, Italy/The Bridgeman Art Library
**7-2:** De Agostini Picture Library/G. Dagli Orti/The Bridgeman Art Library
**7-3:** Catacombs of San Callisto, Rome, Italy/Photo © Zev Radovan/The Bridgeman Art Library
**7-4 a and b:** Scala/Art Resource, NY
**7-5:** De Agostini Picture Library/G. Cigolini/The Bridgeman Art Library
**7-6:** De Agostini Picture Library/G. Cigolini/The Bridgeman Art Library
**7-7:** Private Collection/The Bridgeman Art Library
**7-8:** Courtesy of Margaret Zaho
**7-9:** Courtesy of Margaret Zaho
**7-10:** Courtesy of Margaret Zaho
**7-11:** Courtesy of Margaret Zaho
**7-12:** De Agostini Picture Library/A. de Gregorio/The Bridgeman Art Library
**7-13:** iStockphoto/Thinkstock
**7-14:** De Agostini Picture Library/A. Dagli Orti/The Bridgeman Art Library
**7-15:** Album/Art Resource, NY
**7-16:** Eileen Tweedy/The Art Archive at Art Resource, NY
**7-17:** De Agostini Picture Library/The Bridgeman Art Library
**7-18:** British Museum, London, UK/The Bridgeman Art Library

**Chapter 8**

Byzantine Empire c. 565 CE Map: © Kendall Hunt Publishing Company

**8-1:** Courtesy of Margaret Zaho
**8-2:** De Agostini Picture Library/G. Dagli Orti/The Bridgeman Art Library
**8-3:** Image © ruzgar344, 2013. Used under license from Shutterstock, Inc.
**8-4:** Courtesy of Margaret Zaho
**8-5:** Courtesy of Margaret Zaho
**8-6:** Courtesy of Margaret Zaho
**8-7:** Courtesy of Margaret Zaho
**8-8:** Photos.com
**8-9:** Courtesy of Gabriel Ribeiro
**8-10:** Image © InavanHateren, 2013. Used under license from Shutterstock, Inc.
**8-11:** Image © mountainpix, 2013. Used under license from Shutterstock, Inc.
**8-12:** Image © mountainpix, 2013. Used under license from Shutterstock, Inc.
**8-13:** De Agostini Picture Library/A. Dagli Orti/The Bridgeman Art Library
**8-14:** De Agostini Picture Library/A. Dagli Orti/The Bridgeman Art Library
**8-15:** Egypt/© Gerard Degeorge/The Bridgeman Art Museum
**8-16:** Monastery of Saint Catherine, Mount Sinai, Egypt/Ancient Art and Architecture Collection Ltd./The Bridgeman Art Library
**8-17:** De Agostini Picture Library/the Bridgeman Art Library

**Chapter 9**

Western Europe in the Age of Charlemagne, C. 814 c. Map: © Kendall Hunt Publishing Company

**9-1:** Fitzwilliam Museum, University of Cambridge, UK/the Bridgeman Art Library
**9-2:** © The Trustees of the British Museum/Art Resource, NY
**9-3:** Art Resource, NY
**9-4:** © British Library Board/Robana/Art Resource, NY
**9-5:** British Library, London, UK/© British Library Board. All Rights Reserved/The Bridgeman Art Library
**9-6:** British Library, London, UK/© British Library Board. All Rights Reserved/The Bridgeman Art Library
**9-7:** Photos.com
**9-8:** Courtesy of Margaret Zaho
**9-9:** Courtesy of Margaret Zaho
**9-10:** Courtesy of Margaret Zaho
**9-11:** Fitzwilliam Museum, University of Cambridge, UK/the Bridgeman Art Library
**9-12:** Equestrian statue of Charlemagne (742–814) (bronze) (see also 152998), French School, (8th century)/Louvre, Paris, France/Giraudon/The Bridgeman Art Library
**9-13:** Foto Marburg/Art Resource, NY
**9-14:** Erich Lessing/Art Resource, NY
**9-15:** Erich Lessing/Art Resource, NY
**9-16:** Archives Larousse, Paris, France/Giraudon/The Bridgeman Art Library
**9-17:** Aachen Cathedral, Aachen, Germany/Bildarchiv Steffens/The Bridgeman Art Library
**9-18:** De Agostini Picture Library/A. Dagli Orti/The Bridgeman Art Library
**9-19:** Courtesy of Gabriel Ribeiro
**9-20:** Image © Scirocco340, 2013. Used under license from Shutterstock, Inc.
**9-21:** © Vanni Archive/Art Resource, NY
**9-22:** Foto Marburg/Art Resource, NY
**9-23:** Foto Marburg/Art Resource, NY
**9-24:** Erich Lessing/Art Resource, NY
**9-25:** Photos.com
**9-26:** bpk, Berlin/Bayerische Staatsbibliothek, Munich, Germany/Lutz Braun/Art Resource, NY

**Chapter 10**

Europe Map: © Kendall Hunt Publishing Company

**10-1:** Erich Lessing/Art Resource, NY
**10-2:** Photos.com
**10-3:** Erich Lessing/Art Resource, NY
**10-4:** Courtesy of Margaret Zaho
**10-5:** Abbaye aux Hommes (St. Etienne) Caen, France/The Bridgeman Art Library

**10-6:** Abbaye aux Hommes (St. Etienne) Caen, France/Peter Willi/The Bridgeman Art Library
**10-7:** © RMN-Grand Palais/Art Resource, NY
**10-8:** Scala/Art Resource, NY
**10-9:** De Agostini Picture Library/G. Sioen/The Bridgeman Art Library
**10-10:** Courtesy of Gabriel Ribeiro
**10-11:** De Agostini Picture Library/A. Dagli Orti/The Bridgeman Art Library
**10-12:** St. Pierre, Moissac, France/© Elizabeth Disney/The Bridgeman Art Library
**10-13:** St. Pierre, Moissac, France/Giraudon/The Bridgeman Art Library
**10-14:** Courtesy of Margaret Zaho
**10-15:** Courtesy of Margaret Zaho
**10-16:** Courtesy of Margaret Zaho
**10-17:** Courtesy of Margaret Zaho
**10-18:** Courtesy of Margaret Zaho
**10-19:** Courtesy of Margaret Zaho
**10-20:** Courtesy of Margaret Zaho
**10-21:** Courtesy of Margaret Zaho
**10-22:** Courtesy of Margaret Zaho
**10-23:** Courtesy of Margaret Zaho

# Bibliography

Backhouse, Janet. *The Lindisfarne Gospels*. London: Phaidon Press, 1981.

Biers, William. *The Archaeology of Greece: An Introduction*. 2nd ed. New York: Cornell University Press, 1996.

Boardman, John. *The Parthenon and its Sculpture*. Austin: University of Texas Press, 1985.

______. Greek Sculpture: *The Archaic Period*. New York: Thames and Hudson, 1985.

______. Greek Sculpture: *The Classical Period*. New York: Thames and Hudson, 1987.

Brendel, Otto J. *Prolegomena to the Study of Roman Art*. New Haven: Yale University Press, 1979.

Carpenter, Thomas H. *Art and Myth in Ancient Greece*. New York: Thames & Hudson, 1991.

Chilvers, Ian and Harold Osbourne,eds. *The Oxford Dictionary of Art*. 3rd ed. New York: Oxford University Press, 2004.

Chippendale, Christopher. *Stonehenge Complete*. New York: Thames & Hudson, 1994.

Coldstream, Nicola. *Medieval Architecture*. New York: Oxford University Press, 2002.

Collon, Dominique. *First Impressions: Cylinder Seals in the Ancient Near East*. 2nd ed. London, British Museum, 1993.

D'Ambra, Eve. *Roman Art*. New York: Cambridge University Press, 1998.

Dodwell, Charles R. *The Pictorial Arts of the West, 800–1200*. New Haven: Yale University Press, 1993.

Elsner, Jaś. *Imperial Rome and Christian Triumph*. New York: Oxford University Press, 1998.

Frazier, Nancy. *The Penguin Concise Dictionary of Art History*. New York: Penguin, 2000.

Garnsey, Peter and Richard Saller. *The Roman Empire: Economy, Society, and Culture*. Berkeley: University of California Press, 1987.

Grabar, André. *Christian Iconography*. Princeton: Princeton University Press, 1980.

Grape, Wolfgang. *The Bayeux Tapestry: Monument to a Norman Triumph*. New York: Prestel, 1994.

Hall, James. *Illustrated Dictionary of Subjects and Symbols in Eastern and Western Art*. New York: Icon Editions, 1994.

Henderson, George. *From Durrow to Kells: The Insular Gospel Books, 650–800*. London: Thames and Hudson, 1987.

Henig, Martin, ed. *A Handbook of Roman Art*. Ithaca: Cornell University Press, 1983.

Higgins, Reynold. *Minoan and Mycenean Art*. Rev.ed. New York: Thames & Hudson, 1997.

Hurwit, Jeffrey M. *The Acropolis in the Age of Pericles*. New York: Cambridge University Press, 2004

Jensen, Robin Margaret. *Understanding Early Christian Art*. New York: Routledge, 2000.

Kitzinger, Ernst. *Byzanine Art in the Making*. Cambridge: Harvard University Press, 1980.

Kleiner, Fred S. *A History of Roman Art*. Belmont: Wadsworth, 2007.

______. *Gardner's Art through the Ages: The Western Perspective*. Boston: Wadsworth, 2010.

Kovacs, Maureen Gallery. Trans. *The Epic of Gilgamesh*. Stanford: Stanford University Press, 1985.

Ling, Roger. *Ancient Mosaics*. Princeton, N.J.:Princeton University Press, 1998.

______. *Roman Painting*. New York: Cambridge University Press, 1991.

Lowden, John. *Early Christian and Byzantine Art*. London: Phaidon, 1997.

Loyn, H.R. ed. *The Middle Ages: A Concise Encyclopedia*. London: Thames & Hudson, 1989.

Lucie-Smith, Edward. *The Thames and Hudson Dictionary of Art Terms*. 2nd ed. New York: Thames and Hudson, 2004.

Luttikhuizen Henry and Dorothy Verkerk. *Snyder's Medieval Art*. Upper Saddle River: Prentice Hall, 2006.

MacCormack, Sabine. *Art and Ceremony in Late Antiquity*. Berkeley: University of California Press, 1981.

Mathews, Thomas P. *The Clash of the Gods: A Reinterpretation of Early Christian Art*. Rev. ed. Princeton: Princeton University Press, 1999.

Murray, Peter, and Linda Murray. *A Dictionary of Art and Artists*. 7th ed. New York: Penguin, 1998.

Mütherich, Florentine and Joachim Gaehde. *Carolingian Painting*. New York: Braziller, 1976.

Nordenfalk, Carl. *Early Medieval Book Illumination*. New York: Rizzoli, 1988.

Osborne, Robin. *Archaic and Classical Greek Art*. New York: Oxford University Press, 1998.

Pollitt, J.J. *Art and Experience in Classical Greece*. New York: Cambridge University Press, 1972.

______. *The Art of Ancient Greece: Sources and Documents*. New York: Cambridge University Press, 1990.

______. *The Art of Rome c.753 B.C.–A.D. 337: Sources and Documents*. New York: Cambridge University Press, 1983.

Quenot, Michel. *The Icon: Window on the Kingdom*. Crestwood: St. Vladimir's Seminary Press, 1991.

Reid, Jane D. *The Oxford Guide to Classical Mythology in the Arts 1300–1990s*. 2 vols. New York: Oxford University Press, 1993.

Richter, Gisela, M. *A Handbook of Greek Art*. 9th Edition. New York: Da Capo Press, 1987.

Ridgway, Brunilde S. *Roman Copies of Greek Sculpture: The Problem of the Originals*. Ann Arbor: University of Michigan Press, 1984.

Robins, Gay. *The Art of Ancient Egypt*. Cambridge: Harcard University Press, 1997.

Romer, John. *Valley of the Kings: Exploring the Tombs of the Pharaohs*. New York: Holt, 1994.

Scarre, Chris. *The Penguin Historical Atlas of Ancient Rome*. New York: Penguin, 1995.

Schapiro, Meyer. *The Sculpture of Moissac*. New York: Thames and Hudson, 1985.

Sear, Frank. *Roman Architecture*. Rev. ed. Ithaca: Cornell University Press, 1989.

Sekules, Veronica. *Medieval Art*. New York: Oxford University Press, 2001.

Spivey, Nigel. *Greek Art*. London: Phaidon, 1997.

Stokstad, Marilyn. *Medieval Art*. Boulder: Westview Press, 2004

______. *Art History A View of the West*. Upper Saddle River, 2008.

Stalley, Roger. *Early Medieval Architecture*: New York: Oxford University Press, 1999.

Sutton, Ian. *Western Architecture: From Ancient Greece to the Present*. New York: Thames & Hudson, 1999.

Weitzmann, Kurt. *Late Antique and Early Christian Book Illumination*. New York: Braziller, 1977.

______. *The Icon*. New York: Dorset, 1987.

White, Randall. *Prehistoric Art: The Symbolic Journey of Humankind*. New York: Abrams, 2003.

Woodford, Susan. *Images of Myths in Classical Antiquity*. New York: Cambridge University Press, 2003.

Zanker, Paul. *The Power of Images in the Age of Augustus*. Ann Arbor: University of Michigan Press, 1988.

# Index